THE DRINK- AND DRUG-DRIVE OFFENCES: A HANDBOOK FOR PRACTITIONERS

THIRD EDITION

THE DRINK- AND DRUG-DRIVE OFFENCES: A HANDBOOK FOR PRACTITIONERS

THIRD EDITION

P. M. Callow

WS &H

Wildy, Simmonds & Hill Publishing

ISBN: 978-0-85490-302-3

British Library Cataloguing in Publication Data

A catalogue record for this book is available from the British Library

First edition 2011
Second edition 2018

This edition published in 2024 by

Wildy, Simmonds & Hill Publishing
Wildy & Sons Ltd
Lincoln's Inn Archway
Carey Street
London WC2A 2JD
www.wildy.com

Typeset by Heather Jones, North Petherton, Somerset.
Printed in Great Britain by CPI Group (UK) Ltd, Croydon CR0 4YY.

Contents

Table of Cases

References are to page numbers

Table of Statutes

References are to page numbers

Table of Statutory Instruments, Codes of Practice, etc

References are to page numbers

Table of Conventions

References are to page numbers

Preface

The statutory provisions creating the drink- and drug-drive offences, and regulating the procedure for investigating suspected offences, are contained in Road Traffic Act 1988, ss 3A to 11. The Road Traffic Offenders Act 1988 contains further provisions concerning the use of specimens of breath, blood or urine in proceedings for these offences. These provisions, and their statutory predecessors, have undoubtedly contributed to greater road safety. Fatalities where at least one driver was over the drink-drive limit fell steadily over the years to 2010, plateauing at about 240 per year. Estimates for 2021, however, show a reversal of the trend, to 260.

Since the second edition of this book was published in 2018, the offences under s 5A – driving, attempting to drive or being in charge with a concentration of a specified controlled drug above the limit – have come into their own. These offences were introduced in 2015, and, while there is so far little reported case law specifically on their application and interpretation, they now account for almost as many convictions as the equivalent excess alcohol offences. Overall, though, the number of convictions for the drink- and drug-driving offences taken together has continued to fall since peaking in 2010. No doubt pressure on resources and the COVID-19 pandemic have contributed to this decline. Nevertheless, the conviction rate continues to be extremely high, at approximately 95 per cent.

The consequences of conviction for a drink- or drug-drive offence go beyond the immediate penalty of a fine, a community penalty or imprisonment. They include disqualification from driving, which may lead to loss of employment and, in due course, to greatly increased insurance premiums. These factors no doubt account for the readiness of some defendants to look for 'loopholes' by which to avoid conviction. For many years, the statistical likelihood of conviction did not deter some motorists and their advisers from devising highly imaginative challenges to the legislative regime. A relatively small number of statutory provisions gave rise, over the years, to a disproportionately large volume of case law. The result is a body of law of deceptive complexity.

More recently, however, the challenges have tended to be of a somewhat different character. Although the provisions creating the excess specified drug offences (including s 3A(1)(ba) – causing death by careless driving while having an excess of a specified controlled drug) came into force in 2015, it was not until July 2023 that the Sentencing Council introduced sentencing guidelines for these offences. Leading up to that, there had been a series of sentencing appeals concerning the extent to which the guidelines for the drink-drive offences could be invoked when dealing with drug-driving. The new guidelines should resolve these issues.

Another line of cases concerns challenges to decisions on adjournments – often featuring lack of diligence in preparation for trial and/or failure by the court below properly to scrutinise the application for adjournment. The appellate courts have remained constant in insisting on 'rigorous scrutiny' of requests for adjournments and have robustly applied the Criminal Procedure Rules aimed at avoiding delay.

In this edition, the commentary on the difficult cases of *DPP v Carless* [2005] EWHC 3234 (Admin) and *R v Coe (Christopher Steven)* [2009] EWCA Crim 1452 has been revised to emphasise that neither case sets a precedent for the admission in evidence of the analysis of blood specimens taken outside the regime of the 1988 Act. And the case law on the circumstances in which judicial review is an appropriate method of challenge has been drawn together.

The purpose of this book is to bring together the statutory provisions and the case law on the drink- and drug-drive offences in an accessible, practical way, elucidating issues which are often surprisingly difficult. It is intended for all practitioners concerned with this area of law, whether police, prosecution or defence, and adopts a neutral standpoint between their various interests. It is up to date to January 2024.

The author is grateful to Francis Meylan, Chair of the MGDD Form Editing Group, and Dr Paul Williams, formerly Head of Forensic Support at Lion Laboratories, and now a forensic science consultant, both of whom very kindly reviewed this work in draft and contributed extensively. Thanks too to Roger Agombar MBE, who assisted on earlier editions. The benefits of their long experience in this area of law, and their vast accumulated wisdom, are greatly appreciated. The author will be glad to hear from readers who have any comments or suggestions concerning this work.

PMC
January 2024

Chapter 1

Introduction

1.1 THE BACKGROUND

Early legislation featured, in various forms, an offence of driving when unfit to do so through drink or drugs. It was defined by reference to the impairment of driving ability, regardless of the quantity of alcohol or drugs which may have been in the defendant's body. In 1967, a prescribed limit for alcohol was introduced. It was, and still is, in England and Wales, 80 milligrammes of alcohol in 100 millilitres of blood. The offences of unfitness through drink or drugs remained, but it became an offence simply to be over the limit, regardless of ability to drive. At the same time, the 'breathalyser' was introduced as a method of preliminary screening to provide an indication of whether or not a driver might be over the limit. Following a positive breathalyser test, alcohol concentration was measured by laboratory analysis of a specimen of blood or urine. New offences of refusing (now failing) to take a breath test or to supply a specimen were also created.

The Transport Act 1981 contained provisions reflecting the fact that technology had advanced to the point where alcohol in the body could be measured accurately by analysing breath, using an instrument which could be installed at a police station. Preliminary (or 'roadside') testing continued. Persons whose roadside tests were positive were arrested and required to provide breath specimens for analysis, although there remained certain circumstances in which blood or urine specimens, rather than breath specimens, could be required. The results of analysing the specimen provided the evidential base for any prosecution. This continues to be the usual procedure, now under the Road Traffic Act 1988.

More recently, offences of driving, attempting to drive or being in charge with a concentration of a specified controlled drug above a specified limit were introduced. Testing for these is, for the time being, by means of blood analysis only.

1.2 THE OFFENCES

1.2.1 Causing death

Road Traffic Act 1988, s 3A creates the offence of causing death by driving without due care and attention or without reasonable consideration for other road users ('careless driving'), when the driver:

- is unfit through drink or drugs;
- has excess alcohol in the breath, blood or urine;
- has an excess of a specified controlled drug in the blood or urine; or
- has failed without reasonable excuse to provide a specimen for analysis, or to allow the analysis of a specimen taken while the driver was incapable of consenting to its being taken.

The offence is one of five offences of causing death under the Road Traffic Act 1988. The remaining four are not considered in this work, but are:

- causing death by dangerous driving (s 1);
- causing death by careless or inconsiderate driving (s 2B);
- causing death by driving while unlicensed or uninsured (s 3ZB); and
- causing death by driving while disqualified (s 3ZC).

Section 3A is considered in Chapter 6.

1.2.2 Driving, attempting to drive or in charge when unfit

Section 4 provides for the offences of driving, attempting to drive or being in charge when unfit through drink or drugs. Unfitness to drive means that the ability to drive properly is impaired. A person may be deemed not to have been in charge if there was no likelihood of driving while remaining unfit. The section is headed 'Driving, or being in charge, when under influence of drink or drugs', and the expression 'under the influence' is sometimes used as an alternative to the word 'unfit'. The offences under s 4 are discussed in Chapter 7.

1.2.3 Driving, attempting to drive or in charge with excess alcohol

Section 5 concerns driving, attempting to drive, or being in charge with excess alcohol. It is a defence to an allegation of being in charge to show that there was no likelihood of driving while over the limit. See Chapter 8.

There is clearly some overlap between unfitness to drive through drink, and being over the prescribed limit. A person may be both unfit and over the limit. Another may be unfit to drive but not over the limit. Less likely is that a person may be over the limit but still appear able to drive unimpaired.

As explained in para 1.1, the offences of unfitness predate those of excess alcohol. While the majority of prosecutions are now for the excess alcohol offences under s 5, the s 4 offences remain important, for example, as the basis for proceeding against a person who was impaired but failed to provide a specimen.

1.2.4 Driving, attempting to drive or in charge with excess of a specified drug

Section 5A provides for the offences of driving, attempting to drive, or being in charge with a concentration, in blood or urine, of a specified controlled drug above the specified limit for that drug. This section was brought into force on 2 March 2015, in response to concerns about the incidence of driving while under the influence of drugs. While there remains scope for further developing the methods of detecting drugs in the body, to date, limits have been set for drugs in the blood only. The number of convictions for the drug-driving offences has steadily increased since 2015. In 2021, there were just short of 28,000 convictions for drug-driving, compared with almost 34,000 for drink-driving. There is a defence in relation to drugs prescribed for medicinal purposes. See Chapter 8.

1.3 THE INVESTIGATION

The procedure for investigating a suspected drink- or drug-drive offence is set out in ss 6 to 8. It usually comprises a preliminary screening test at the roadside, to establish whether or not a suspect is likely to be over the limit. If the test is positive, the suspect is arrested and taken to a police station where further specimens are taken and subjected to more rigorous testing. It is the result of this analysis which forms the basis of any prosecution.

1.3.1 Preliminary tests

Section 6(1) to (5) sets out the circumstances in which a constable may require a person to co-operate with a preliminary test. They are where the constable reasonably suspects the commission of an offence under s 4, s 5 or s 5A, or another moving traffic offence. The power also arises when there has been an accident. Section 6(6) renders it an offence, without reasonable excuse, to fail to co-operate with a preliminary test. There is, therefore, no power randomly to administer breath tests (with a limited exception in Northern Ireland – see para 2.2), although there is no such restriction on stopping vehicles.

Sections 6A, 6B and 6C define three types of preliminary test, and provide for the administration of the tests:

- a preliminary breath alcohol test, using an approved device;
- a preliminary impairment test in which a constable approved for the purpose observes the subject performing certain divided attention tasks (such as standing on one leg while counting aloud), and observes the person's physical state, in accordance with a code of practice;
- a preliminary drug test of a specimen of saliva or sweat, using an approved device.

Section 6D(1) allows a constable to arrest a person who fails a preliminary test. A constable may also arrest a person who fails to co-operate with a preliminary test if the constable reasonably suspects that the person has alcohol or a drug in the body. A patient at a hospital may not be arrested under s 6D.

Section 6E provides a power of entry where there has been an accident and the constable reasonably suspects that a person – presumably, including the suspect – has been injured. The constable may enter, using reasonable force if necessary, to require a person to co-operate in a preliminary test, or to arrest a person under s 6D. There is no express power to enter a suspect's private property in other circumstances.

Sections 6 to 6E are discussed in Chapter 2.

1.3.2 Specimens for analysis

Section 7 sets out the procedure for providing specimens for analysis, usually at a police station, following arrest.

Section 7(1) empowers a constable who is in the course of investigating a suspected offence under s 3A, s 4 or s 5 to require two breath specimens for immediate analysis, or a blood or urine specimen to be analysed later at a laboratory. In relation to the s 5A offences, the power is to require a blood or urine specimen (s 7(1A)).

Breath specimens are analysed using what is referred to in the legislation as an 'approved device', now also known as an 'evidential breath analysis instrument'. In anticipation of the type approval of portable evidential breath analysis instruments, the section also contains provisions facilitating evidential breath analysis elsewhere than at a police station.

Sometimes it is not feasible to analyse breath specimens – the device may be out of order, or the suspect may be in hospital. In these cases, a specimen of blood or urine may be required instead. The procedure at a hospital is governed by s 9 (see below). The circumstances in which a specimen of blood or urine, rather than breath, may be required at a police station are restricted to those where:

- the constable has reasonable cause to believe that there are medical reasons why breath cannot be provided or should not be required;
- the approved device is not available or is not reliable, or for any other reason it is not practicable to use it;
- breath specimens have been analysed but the officer has reasonable cause to believe that a reliable indication of the alcohol concentration has not been produced.

Whether the alternative specimen is to be one of blood or urine is a matter for the constable (s 7(4)). Blood specimens are taken by a medical practitioner or a health care professional, but if the practitioner advises that there are medical reasons for not taking blood, the constable may then require a urine specimen (s 7(4A)). In that case, a first specimen of urine is discarded and a second specimen must be produced within an hour of the initial requirement (s 7(5)).

Section 7(5A) provides power to arrest a person who fails to provide a breath specimen when so required, if the officer reasonably suspects the person has alcohol in his or her body.

Section 7(6) makes it an offence to fail, without reasonable excuse, to provide a specimen, but the constable must, when requiring a specimen, warn the person that failure to provide it may lead to prosecution (s 7(7)). The expression 'reasonable excuse' is not defined and has given rise to a substantial body of case law.

The procedure for requiring specimens under s 7 is discussed in Chapters 3 and 4, while the offence of failing to provide is dealt with in Chapter 10.

Section 7A contains provisions authorising taking a blood specimen without consent from a person who is incapable of consenting – usually someone who is unconscious. The power arises where the person has been involved in an accident, and there would otherwise be power to require a blood specimen. The specimen may not be laboratory tested without the consent of the person from whom it was taken, although failure without reasonable excuse to give such consent is an offence. Section 7A is considered in detail in Chapter 5.

Challenges to the procedures followed in individual cases have been legion, and the resulting case law is discussed throughout this work.

1.3.3 The lower reading

Section 8 gives potential defendants an advantage in that, of the two breath specimens analysed, that which yields the higher reading is to be disregarded, and the specimen which produces the lower reading is used in any proceedings. See Chapter 3.

1.3.4 The statutory option

For many years, where the lower breath reading was 50 microgrammes or below (the limit is 35 microgrammes), the suspect could elect to provide a blood or urine specimen to replace the breath specimen. Originally a precautionary measure in these so-called 'borderline' cases, the option was eventually repealed, other than in the Channel Islands, reflecting greater confidence in the accuracy of the evidential breath analysis devices. Some of the case law originating in these 'option' cases nevertheless remains relevant, and is mentioned throughout the text.

1.3.5 Hospital patients

Section 9 confers protection on hospital patients, requiring consultation with the medical practitioner in charge of the case before a patient is required to co-operate in a preliminary test or provide a specimen. The constable may not proceed if the doctor objects on the ground that to do so would be prejudicial to the proper care and treatment of the patient. Section 9 is reviewed in Chapter 5.

1.3.6 Detention following investigation

Section 10 authorises persons who have been investigated to be detained at the police station until no longer unfit or over the limit. The power is not available, however, where it ought reasonably to be apparent that there is no likelihood of driving or attempting to drive while unfit or over the limit. A constable must consult a medical practitioner on questions concerning the impairment through drugs of any detainee, and must act on the advice given. See Chapter 3.

1.4 DEFINITIONS

Section 11 contains definitions. The prescribed limit for the purpose of the excess alcohol offences is:

> (a) 35 microgrammes of alcohol in 100 millilitres of breath,
> (b) 80 milligrammes of alcohol in 100 millilitres of blood, or
> (c) 107 milligrammes of alcohol in 100 millilitres of urine,
>
> or such other proportion as may be prescribed.

Despite many calls for the lowering of the limit, the above limits have never been amended in so far as they relate to England and Wales. The limit in Scotland has, however, been reduced to 50 milligrammes of alcohol in 100 millilitres of blood, and in Northern Ireland legislation has been passed which, when in force, will reduce the limit there, with even lower limits for certain classes of driver. The limits clearly contemplate that drinking before driving is permitted, up to a certain point. That point is expressed in terms of the amount of alcohol found in the body, not in terms of amounts consumed. It is common knowledge that the effects of alcohol depend on factors such as its strength, the amount drunk and the time over which it is drunk, while body weight, gender, diet and any food consumed are also relevant. These issues make it more difficult for an ordinary person to know whether or not, having taken alcohol, he or she is likely to be under or over the limit. For as long as it is permitted to drink before driving, this question of interpreting the limit is of real practical significance. Further, even if the limit were zero, most individuals would not know when, after drinking, their bodies would be free of alcohol.

It is the policy of the Crown Prosecution Service, based on guidelines in Home Office Circular 46/1983, not to prosecute for drink-driving if the breath alcohol is below 40 microgrammes of alcohol in 100 millilitres of breath, even though the limit is 35. This allows for the tolerance built into the calibration range of the analysis devices (see para 3.4.3), and for any disadvantage resulting to individuals from breath analysis rather than blood analysis.

The specified drugs, for the purposes of s 5A, and the limits in blood applying to each, are listed in the Drug Driving (Specified Limits) (England and Wales) Regulations 2014 (SI 2014/2868), as amended by the Drug Driving (Specified Limits) (England and Wales) (Amendment) Regulations 2015 (SI 2015/911). Seventeen drugs are specified, each having a different limit. They include drugs generally associated with illegal use, as well as drugs having legitimate therapeutic uses. See Chapter 8.

Section 11(3) contains provisions on what constitutes co-operation with a preliminary test, and on what constitutes providing a specimen of breath for analysis, and is discussed in Chapters 4 and 10. Section 11(4) deals with the provision of blood specimens, stipulating that the subject must consent, and identifying those authorised to take such specimens. See Chapter 4.

1.5 USE OF SPECIMENS IN PROCEEDINGS

Road Traffic Offenders Act 1988, s 15(2) requires that the result of analysing a specimen is to be taken into account in any prosecution that follows. It is to be assumed that the level of alcohol or a drug at the time of the alleged offence was no lower than in the specimen. This is commonly known as the 'statutory assumption'. It applies even though the alcohol or drug concentration may have been rising (because the alcohol or drug was still being absorbed) or falling (because the alcohol or drug was being eliminated) between the time of the alleged offence and the time the specimen was provided. To ensure that the analysis reflects as accurately as possible the concentration at the time of the alleged offence, specimens are taken without delay. The procedure may not be held up, even for the suspect to take legal advice.

The statutory assumption may be displaced by what is sometimes called the 'hip flask' or 'post-incident consumption' defence, where the defendant establishes having consumed alcohol, or the drug in question, after the alleged offence, and that it was that alcohol or drug which caused the defendant to be unfit or over the limit (s 15(3) and (3A)).

Section 15(4) provides for a blood specimen to be disregarded if it was not taken with the defendant's consent and by the appropriate professional person. A blood specimen taken from a person incapable of consenting is to be disregarded unless the person gave permission for it to be analysed.

Section 15(5) and (5A) sets out the procedure for dividing a blood specimen into two parts and, upon request, giving one part to the suspect for independent analysis if the suspect so chooses.

The provisions of s 15 are discussed in Chapters 4 and 8.

1.6 TRIAL

The offence in Road Traffic Act 1988, s 3A of causing death by careless driving when under the influence of drink or drugs is triable on indictment only. All the remaining offences dealt with in this work are triable summarily only.

1.7 PENALTIES

The penalties for the drink- and drug-drive offences are set out in Road Traffic Offenders Act 1988, sch 2. Unsurprisingly, the offence of causing death, under Road Traffic Act 1988, s 3A, carries the most severe penalty. The offences of driving or attempting to drive when unfit, with excess alcohol or with an excess of a specified drug attract more severe maximum penalties than the offences of being in charge in such a condition. The maximum penalty for failing to supply evidential specimens is the same as that for the offence which was being investigated, and so again is higher where the police are investigating driving or attempting to drive, rather than being in charge. Failing to co-operate with a preliminary test attracts a lower penalty.

The sentencing court must consider disqualifying the offender from driving. Disqualification is obligatory for the offence under s 3A, and for the driving or attempting to drive offences, but is a matter for the discretion of the court in an 'in charge' case. For failing to provide specimens, disqualification again depends on the offence which was being investigated, and is obligatory in the driving or attempting to drive cases, and discretionary in the 'in charge' cases.

Road Traffic Offenders Act 1988, s 34 provides that where disqualification is obligatory, the minimum period of disqualification is usually 12 months, unless for special reasons the court thinks fit to disqualify for a shorter period, or not at all. In certain circumstances the minimum period of disqualification is greater than 12 months. The expression 'special reasons' is not defined in the legislation, and has given rise to an abundance of case law, which is reviewed in Chapter 13.

Road Traffic Offenders Act 1988, ss 34A, 34B and 34C contain provisions allowing courts to order that a disqualification for 12 months or longer may be reduced if the offender satisfactorily completes an approved course. Conversely, the period of disqualification is extended where an immediate custodial sentence is imposed, or where the person being sentenced is already serving a custodial sentence, so that the disqualification is served while the offender is at liberty: ss 35A and 35B.

Guidelines issued by the Sentencing Council provide further information on the likely penalty for a particular offence.

Penalties and sentencing are considered in Chapter 12.

1.8 THE MG DD FORMS

The National Police Chiefs' Council and the Crown Prosecution Service have jointly prepared a series of forms for use by police officers investigating drink- and drug-drive offences. They are completed to provide a contemporaneous record of an investigation, and include notes and reminders to ensure that the procedure is carried out fully and correctly. The forms are modified from time to time to reflect developments in the law. The principal form is form MG DD/A: *Drink/Drugs: Station Procedure*. There are supplementary forms for use where a blood or urine specimen is being required (MG DD/B), for the procedure at a hospital (MG DD/C), and others. The forms can be viewed and downloaded at www.gov.uk/government/publications/manual-of-guidance-drink-and-drug-driving-mgdd. The fact that these forms total so many pages reflects the complexity of the procedures and the number of issues which can arise during an investigation.

The forms have no special status in law. Forms MG DD/A and B were described by Turner J, in *DPP v Smith* [2000] RTR 341 at 349, as no more than a plain man's guide to the procedures, to ensure that those implementing them do not omit a relevant step. The frequency and ingenuity of challenge by reference to the contents and use of the forms suggests, however, that, in practice, they may not be quite as straightforward as the judgment in *Smith* implies. See also *DPP v Chajed* [2013] EWHC 188 (Admin), [2013] 2 Cr App R 6 (para 11.12), where the Administrative Court remarked that form MG DD/A has no statutory force. There is no obligation on the officer to complete a form: *Cawley v DPP* [2001] EWHC 83 (Admin) (see para 10.8). The fact that the form is not fully completed does not of itself defeat a prosecution: *Kang v DPP* [2016] EWHC 3014 (Admin) (see para 3.5.2) and *Afolayan v CPS* [2012] EWHC 1322 (Admin) (see para 3.5.1). See also the cases mentioned in para 3.5.1, where guidance in the form was not followed.

1.9 THE CROWN PROSECUTION SERVICE

The advice given to crown prosecutors on many aspects of the drink- and drug-drive legislation is available at www.cps.gov.uk/legal-guidance/road-traffic-drink-and-drug-driving.

1.10 RAILWAYS, TRAMWAYS, SHIPPING AND AVIATION

The Transport and Works Act 1992 contains provisions applying to those working on railways, tramways and other guided transport systems used by the public. It creates offences of being unfit to work through drink or drugs, and of being over the limit while at work, and provides for an investigatory and evidentiary regime broadly similar to that applying to road traffic. The Railways and Transport Safety Act 2003 contains comparable provisions in relation to shipping and aviation, and operators of these modes of transport are subject to lower alcohol limits than those applying to road traffic. These enactments are not considered in this work.

Chapter 2

Preliminary Tests

2.1 INTRODUCTION

Preliminary testing for alcohol, impairment or drugs is governed by Road Traffic Act 1988, ss 6, 6A, 6B and 6C. Sections 6D and 6E confer powers of arrest and of entry. Section 6 was substituted, and ss 6A to 6E inserted, by the Railways and Transport Safety Act 2003, with effect from 30 March 2004. Those amendments were made to allow for preliminary testing for impairment and for drugs, as well as for alcohol. Further amendments, in force from 2 March 2015, were made by the Crime and Courts Act 2013, to allow for preliminary testing in relation to the offences of excess specified drugs under Road Traffic Act 1988, s 5A, then being introduced. The provisions give police officers powers to administer preliminary tests to provide an indication whether a person is likely to have excess alcohol, to be unfit to drive through drink or drugs, or to have an excess of a specified drug. Preliminary testing is in the nature of screening, to eliminate those who are almost certainly not offending. There is no requirement for preliminary testing before evidential analysis by way of breath, blood or urine specimens.

Section 6 provides that if any of s 6(2) to (5) applies, a constable may require a person to co-operate with any one or more preliminary tests. The preconditions in s 6(2) to (4) are that the officer reasonably suspects that the person:

- is driving, attempting to drive or is in charge of a motor vehicle on a road or other public place and has alcohol or a drug in the body, or is under the influence of a drug;
- has been driving, attempting to drive or in charge of a motor vehicle on a road or other public place, while having alcohol or a drug in the body or while unfit to drive because of a drug, and is still in that condition;
- is or has been driving, attempting to drive or in charge of a motor vehicle on a road or other public place and has committed a traffic offence while the vehicle was in motion. Traffic offences are defined in s 6(8)(b).

Section 6(5) applies if an accident occurs owing to the presence of a motor vehicle on a road or other public place and a constable reasonably believes that the person to be tested was driving, attempting to drive or in charge of the vehicle at the time of the accident.

It is an offence to fail without reasonable excuse to co-operate with a preliminary test (s 6(6)); see Chapter 10.

Preliminary tests may take one of three forms:

- a preliminary breath test under s 6A;
- a preliminary impairment test under s 6B;
- a preliminary drug test under s 6C.

Before 2004, the only type of preliminary testing was breath testing, often referred to as a roadside breath test. It gave rise to much case law, which, it is submitted, applies to all three types of preliminary test so far as relevant.

2.2 STOPPING OF VEHICLES

Although there is no power randomly to administer preliminary tests (with an exception in Northern Ireland – see below), the police have wide discretion to stop vehicles. Road Traffic Act 1988, s 163 is headed 'Power of police to stop vehicles'. While it does not expressly confer power to stop, it provides that a driver must stop if required to do so by a uniformed police officer. The Divisional Court has held that officers had power at common law to stop vehicles as part of a 'random crime check', even though the statutory provision (now in s 163) did not entitle them to do so. Having then smelled alcohol on a driver's breath, they were entitled to require a breath test: *Steel v Goacher* [1983] RTR 98.

In Northern Ireland, however, random breath testing is permitted at a checkpoint authorised by an officer of at least the rank of inspector. Such a breath test may be required of anyone stopped at the checkpoint while driving or in charge.

In *Chief Constable of Gwent v Dash* [1986] RTR 41, officers had been randomly stopping cars to find whether the drivers had been drinking. They stopped the defendant and smelled alcohol on his breath, which led to the breath testing procedure and prosecution. The Divisional Court held that the requirement that the officer should have reasonable cause to suspect that a person has alcohol in his body applies to the breath testing, not to the stopping of the vehicle. Bad faith apart, there is no restriction on stopping motorists and then requiring a breath test if the officer then and there genuinely suspects that the motorist has been drinking.

The Divisional Court confirmed the position in *DPP v Minton* [2002] EWHC 805 (Admin), saying that the law:

> prohibits police officers from requiring breath tests at random, but does not prohibit the random stopping of cars provided that that stopping is in the execution of a police officer's duty and is not as a result of some oppression, caprice or malpractice. (at [6])

See also the Scottish case of *Stewart v Crowe* 1999 SLT 899, to the same effect, in which the High Court of Justiciary (Appeal) ruled on a police campaign in the weeks before Christmas. Police were stopping vehicles, explaining the campaign and asking drivers to take breath tests. If they declined, they were allowed to drive on, unless officers smelled alcohol. The court ruled that this was not oppressive. It was general, not random, and so did not amount to the unfair use of power against particular citizens. Furthermore, drivers were being asked, not required, to give breath samples.

Where a vehicle has been lawfully stopped, the driver must keep it at a standstill for a reasonable period to allow the officer to complete any lawful enquiries: *Lodwick v Saunders* [1985] 1 WLR 382 (DC), a case in which the officers suspected the vehicle was stolen.

2.3 TRESPASS AND BAD FAITH

The case of *Morris v Beardmore* [1981] AC 446 had established that a requirement to provide breath was not lawful where the officer making the requirement was trespassing in the suspect's home. Following an accident, police had gone to the home of a motorist, where the motorist's son let them in. The motorist did not wish to speak to the officers and sent them a message, via his son, that they were trespassers and that he wished them to leave. The officers went upstairs to a bedroom, where they asked the suspect for a sample of breath. He refused and was arrested for failing to provide the sample. The House of Lords held that Parliament must be presumed not to have intended to authorise tortious conduct. To constitute a valid requirement, the officer must be acting lawfully towards the person required to undergo a breath test at the moment the requirement is made. An officer is not acting lawfully if committing the tort of trespass. The requirement and the arrest were unlawful.

In *Snook v Mannion* [1982] RTR 321, police followed a motorist until he parked in the driveway of his house. The officers walked onto the driveway and asked the motorist to take a breath test. He refused, saying 'fuck off'. He was arrested and taken to the police station. The Divisional Court held that, in the absence of a locked gate or notice to the contrary, police officers, like all citizens, had an implied licence to proceed from the gate to a front or back door of a dwelling if they had, or reasonably thought they had, legitimate business with the occupier. Such an implied licence could be withdrawn by an express withdrawal of consent. It was for the justices to decide whether the licence had been terminated in all the circumstances. They decided that the words used were no more than vulgar abuse and did not operate to terminate the licence. Likewise, in *Gilham v Breidenbach* [1982] RTR 328, the Divisional Court upheld a decision of justices to treat similarly vulgar language as coarse abuse rather than as a request to leave, and no question of revocation of the implied licence arose.

Since *Morris v Beardmore* [1981] AC 446, the Transport Act 1981 was passed, substituting revised provisions in the legislation then in force (the Road Traffic Act 1972). The new provisions gave officers a power of entry (by force if need be) to require a person to provide a specimen where there had been an accident involving injury to another person, or to arrest a person who has failed to provide a specimen when required to do so. The power of entry did not, however, extend to other situations where officers wished to administer a preliminary breath test. There then followed the case of *R v Fox; Fox v Chief Constable of Gwent* [1986] AC 281, in which the facts were comparable with those in *Morris v Beardmore*. A driver had left the scene of an accident. Officers went to his home, which they entered without his permission. He refused to provide a breath specimen and was arrested – unlawfully, since the police were trespassers. At the police station he provided breath specimens and was charged with driving with excess alcohol, and convicted. The House of Lords found that, under the substituted provisions, a lawful arrest was no longer a prerequisite for breath testing, and there was no general principle that there could be no conviction for an excess alcohol offence if the evidence by which it was sought to prove the offence had been obtained unlawfully. In general, relevant evidence was admissible even though obtained illegally, though there might be a discretion to exclude it if it had been obtained oppressively or by means of a trick. The fact that the defendant had been unlawfully arrested before giving the specimen of breath was therefore irrelevant in considering whether he was guilty of the offence of driving with excess alcohol.

In *Matto v Wolverhampton Crown Court* [1987] RTR 337, police pursued a motorist because he was speeding. When they caught up with him he had turned into private property. The officers asked for a breath sample. The motorist replied, 'this is private property; you can't do this'. The officers understood that their implied licence to be on the property had therefore been terminated and that, in proceeding, they were in excess of their powers. An officer said, 'we know what we're doing; if I wrongfully arrest you, you can sue me, OK?' The driver then provided a sample which was positive. He was arrested and in due course convicted of driving with excess alcohol. The Crown Court dismissed his appeal on the ground that, although the officers were knowingly acting in excess of their powers and therefore *mala fides*, the screening sample had been given voluntarily. The Divisional Court allowed the motorist's further appeal. The Crown Court had adopted the wrong approach. The finding that the officers had acted *mala fides* was inconsistent with the finding that the breath sample had been given voluntarily. It was open to the Crown Court to have concluded that the officers' oppressive behaviour at the house was still affecting the fairness of what happened at the police station and refuse to admit the evidence of the breath analysis under Police and Criminal Evidence Act 1984 (PACE), s 78. That section authorises a court to refuse to admit prosecution evidence if it appears to the court that, in all the circumstances, admitting it would have such an adverse effect on the fairness of the proceedings that the court ought not to admit it (see para 11.9).

In *Ogden v DPP* [1992] COD 314, police had pursued a speeding motorist to the drive of his house, where the motorist said he had not been drinking. The officers followed him into his house, having neither been invited in nor asked to stay outside. One of the officers arrested the driver for failing to provide a breath sample. Subsequent breath analysis showed he was over the limit. He was acquitted of failing to provide the sample, since he had never been required to do so. He was, however, convicted of driving with excess alcohol. The justices found no bad faith by the police, and exercised their discretion under s 78 to admit the evidence of the breath analysis. The Divisional Court found that even though there had been no *mala fides*, it was still possible for the evidence to be excluded pursuant to s 78. But the justices had considered the discretion properly and exercised it in a way to which they were entitled. The conviction for driving with excess alcohol was upheld.

By contrast, in *Sharpe v DPP* [1993] RTR 392, officers had seen a driver driving on the wrong side of the road and causing an oncoming vehicle to brake hard. They followed him home and onto his driveway where an officer smelled alcohol on him and heard that his speech was slurred. The defendant made clear to the police that they were unwelcome and were trespassers. He was then led or dragged back to the road where he failed a breath test. He was arrested and breath analysis showed excess alcohol. At his trial for driving with excess alcohol, he argued that since the officers had been acting illegally, the court should consider exercising its discretion under s 78 to exclude the evidence of the breath analysis. He also sought witness summonses in respect of two neighbours who could give evidence of the officers' alleged oppressive behaviour on the driveway. The justices admitted the breath analysis and declined to issue the witness summonses. The Divisional Court found that they had not exercised their discretion at all. What they did amounted to saying that they would not have excluded the evidence of the breath analysis no matter how bad the behaviour of the police and regardless of what the witnesses might have said. The motorist's appeal succeeded.

In *DPP v Macphail*, unreported, 8 July 1997, following conflicting evidence, justices found that two roadside breath tests had been administered within a short time of each other. The first was negative, the second positive. Both were conducted before 20 minutes had elapsed since the motorist's last drink (see para 2.5.9). They found that the officer had acted in bad faith, but that if they were wrong on that, they would exclude the evidence of the breath analysis at the police station under s 78. The Divisional Court upheld the decision of the justices, but emphasised that it is not necessary to find *mala fides* before exercising the discretion to exclude evidence under s 78.

The overall position therefore seems to be that, apart from the power now in Road Traffic Act 1988, s 6E (following an accident; see below), there is no express power for an officer to enter a suspect's private property. A suspect may require an officer who has done so to leave. Arrest for failing thereafter to co-operate in a preliminary test would be unlawful and could not ground a prosecution for failing to co-operate. But it would not affect the validity of evidential testing (see Chapters 3 and 4) unless PACE, s 78 is in play. In that event, the courts are, generally, tolerant of genuine error by police officers, but intolerant of bad faith, although evidence may be excluded under s 78 even in the absence of bad faith.

2.4 THE PREREQUISITES

2.4.1 Constable in uniform

When administering a preliminary test, the constable must be in uniform (Road Traffic Act 1988, s 6(7)). But where the test is being administered under s 6(5) following an accident, there is no requirement that the officer must be in uniform.

An officer wearing uniform except for the helmet is 'in uniform' for these purposes: *Wallwork v Giles* [1970] RTR 117 (QBD). In *Taylor v Baldwin* [1976] RTR 265, a motorist was stopped by a police officer who had a raincoat on over his uniform and was not wearing a hat. The officer formed the suspicion that the motorist had been drinking, went back to his car and took off the raincoat before returning to administer a breath test. The Divisional Court held that the officer had been in uniform at the material time, that is, when he required the breath test. There was no requirement to be in uniform at the time of forming the suspicion.

There is a presumption that an officer who administers a test is in uniform: *Gage v Jones* [1983] RTR 508, where the defendant collided with a vehicle driven by an off-duty police officer, but did not stop. The off-duty officer sought assistance from a police sergeant on duty in the street. The sergeant drove to the defendant's house and asked for a sample of breath. The defendant refused and was arrested. Before the justices, there was no evidence that the sergeant had been in uniform, and he was not cross-examined on the point. The Divisional Court held that there was a presumption that a police officer was in uniform if he was on duty in the streets and if a member of the public was able to recognise him as a police officer.

2.4.2 Reasonable suspicion

Road Traffic Act 1988, s 6, as in force before 30 March 2004, required the officer, before requiring a breath test, to have 'reasonable cause to *suspect*' driving, attempting to drive or being in charge; or, in the case of an accident, 'reasonable cause to *believe*' that a person had been driving, attempting to drive or in charge. The provisions now in force require that the officer, respectively, 'reasonably suspects' or 'reasonably believes'. In the absence of anything to suggest otherwise, there seems to be little to distinguish 'reasonable cause to suspect' from 'reasonably suspects', or 'reasonable cause to believe' from 'reasonably believes'. There is, however, a distinction between reasonable suspicion, and the more stringent test of reasonable belief applying in accident cases (see para 2.4.3).

A question of fact

Whether or not an officer has reasonable grounds to suspect or, now, 'reasonably suspects', that a motorist has alcohol in the body is a question of fact. Individually or taken together, performing a U-turn, using the wrong indicator on a roundabout, and speeding, did not give such grounds: *Williams v Jones* [1972] RTR 4 (QBD). In these circumstances, however, an officer may be entitled to require the driver to undertake a preliminary test under what is now s 6(4)(b), on the basis of a reasonable suspicion that a traffic offence has been committed.

The fact that an officer requires a sample does not of itself establish the necessary suspicion: *Siddiqui v Swain* [1979] RTR 454 (DC).

In *DPP v Godwin* [1991] RTR 303, police had been carrying out routine traffic stops. They stopped the defendant and asked him if he had been drinking. He said he had not. He refused to provide a breath sample and was arrested for that. At the police station, evidential breath analysis showed he was over the limit and he was charged with driving with excess alcohol. The justices found that the officer had had no reasonable cause to suspect the defendant had alcohol in his body before requesting the breath test. They considered PACE, s 78 (see para 11.9), excluded the evidence of the breath analysis, and dismissed the charge. The Divisional Court upheld that decision. The substantial breach of the protection afforded by the relevant section – that the officer must have reasonable cause to suspect – had been denied to the defendant, with the result that the prosecutor had obtained evidence he would not otherwise have had and which prejudiced the defendant. There was no need to find bad faith on the part of the police to exercise the discretion under s 78.

On the other hand, in *DPP v Kay* [1999] RTR 109 (DC), the arresting officer's account of the defendant's appearance, of his speech being slurred and his breath smelling of alcohol, and of what the defendant said to him at the roadside, all of which had been unchallenged, gave ample cause to suspect that the defendant had alcohol in his body.

See also para 2.6, on the code of practice for administering preliminary impairment tests, and what is said there concerning the requisite suspicion.

Time at which the suspicion arises

The suspicion need not arise while the person is actually driving. Nor need there be any nexus between the police arriving and the suspicion arising. In *Blake v Pope* [1986] 1 WLR 1152, other motorists forced the defendant to stop, took his car keys and restrained him. When police arrived, an officer saw that the defendant was unsteady on his feet and smelled of alcohol. The officer required a breath sample. The requirement was upheld by the Divisional Court. The court rejected the defendant's arguments that the officer's suspicion about his condition had to arise while he was driving, and that, since he had ceased driving some 10 minutes before the police arrived on the scene, the nexus between the driving and the arrival of the police was severed.

In *DPP v McGladrigan* [1991] RTR 297, the defendant was stopped by police and admitted he had consumed alcohol. The Divisional Court found that the admission gave the officer reasonable cause to suspect that the defendant had alcohol in his body, entitling the officer to require a breath test. The question of reasonable cause to suspect was not to be restricted to while the car was being driven. See also *Chief Constable of Gwent v Dash* [1986] RTR 41 (see para 2.2), to the effect that the suspicion need not arise before stopping the vehicle.

Based on information from another

The officer's reasonable suspicion that a person has alcohol in his body may derive from what he is told by another officer: *Erskine v Hollin* [1971] RTR 199.

Relevant information may properly be given by a member of the public, but the reasonable suspicion must be founded on facts relating to the driving in question. In *Monaghan v Corbett* (1983) 147 JP 545, neighbours told police they had seen the defendant and his wife drive away that day, and that they usually went to a pub. An officer, who had smelled alcohol on the defendant the day before, waited until the defendant returned home and required a breath test. The Divisional Court found there was not enough to amount to a reasonable suspicion in respect of a journey the day after alcohol had been smelled, and quashed the conviction for driving with excess alcohol.

A 'tip-off' also featured in *DPP v Wilson* [1991] RTR 284. An officer received an anonymous telephone call telling him of a place where the police would come upon a drink driver. The officer passed the information to another officer, who went to the place in question and identified the car which had been mentioned. He waited for it to move off, and after it had travelled about 200 yards, he stopped it, even though there had been no moving traffic offence. He smelled alcohol, and set in motion the breath testing procedure. On the prosecutor's appeal against the acquittal of the motorist for driving with excess alcohol, the Divisional Court found ample authority that the police may act on information given, even anonymously, by a third party. The fact that the officer smelled alcohol on the defendant's breath was enough to justify the conclusion that there was reasonable cause for suspicion, and that the suspicion arose in connection with the defendant's driving. There was no malpractice, and the justices should not have excluded the evidence of the breath-alcohol analysis under PACE, s 78.

In the Scottish case of *Thomson v Ritchie* 2000 SLT 734, an anonymous caller telephoned a police station saying that a particular car was being driven by a driver who had been drinking, and gave an address. The information was passed to officers by a civilian clerk. Some four minutes later, officers began observing the car. The defendant and another got into it, and the defendant drove it away. The officers stopped the car and required the defendant to take a roadside breath test. The court rejected an argument that there was insufficient evidence to show the officers had reasonable cause to suspect an offence so as to entitle them to require a specimen. The driver appealed against conviction for driving with excess alcohol. The High Court of Justiciary found that the telephone call was sufficient to give rise to reasonable cause to suspect driving with excess alcohol. There was no need for anything else, such as the smell of alcohol, or erratic driving. There had been no material break in continuity between the telephone call giving rise to the suspicion and the stopping of the defendant.

2.4.3 Following an accident

Road Traffic Act 1988, s 6(5) allows for preliminary testing where an accident occurs owing to the presence of a motor vehicle on a road or other public place, and the officer reasonably believes that the person in question was driving, attempting to drive, or in charge of the vehicle at the time of the accident.

Meaning of 'accident'

It is a prerequisite that an accident – often also referred to as a 'road traffic collision' – has in fact occurred; it is not sufficient that the officer thinks or believes there has been an accident. There is no statutory definition of 'accident'. Where the steering pulled to the left and the car hit a kerb and a gatepost, the driver was injured and his car damaged, that was held to amount to an accident in *R v Pico* [1971] RTR 500 (CA). In *R v Morris* [1972] 1 WLR 228, the Court of Appeal found that an accident is an unintended occurrence which has an adverse physical effect. In that case, the unintended occurrence was that the bumpers of two cars, one of which was pushing the other, became interlocked. The court emphasised that the word 'accident' was to have its ordinary meaning.

That approach was endorsed in *Chief Constable of the West Midlands v Billingham* [1979] 1 WLR 747, where the Queen's Bench Division held that an accident could include the outcome of a chain of events which included a deliberate act. The test was whether the ordinary man in the street would say that there had been an accident owing to the presence of a motor vehicle on the road. In that case, the accident consisted of releasing the brakes of a car so that the car rolled down the hill, hit a telegraph pole and carried on down an embankment.

In *Chief Constable of Staffordshire v Lees* [1981] RTR 506, the defendant deliberately drove through locked gates. The Divisional Court held that an accident could be said to occur when arising through a deliberate and intended act, as long as any ordinary person would say that there had been an accident. Any ordinary person would say that there had been an accident on the facts of the case.

Owing to the presence of a vehicle

The accident must have occurred 'owing to the presence of a motor vehicle' on a road or other public place. These words were reviewed in *Quelch v Phipps* [1955] 2 QB 107, a case on the duty to report an accident. The Divisional Court found that there must be some direct connection between the motor vehicle and the happening of the accident. A bus had been crossing a junction, and a passenger, despite warnings by the conductor, stepped off the platform and fell forward on to the road, injuring himself. The court found that the accident had occurred owing to the presence of the motor vehicle on the road.

For the meanings of 'motor vehicle' and 'road or other public place', see Chapter 8.

Reasonable belief

Under s 6(5), the officer must reasonably *believe* that the person in question was driving, attempting to drive, or in charge of the vehicle at the time. This is a more stringent test than that of reasonable suspicion under the other limbs of s 6. The distinction was referred to in *Baker v Oxford* [1980] RTR 315. Police found a vehicle, which had been involved in an accident, abandoned not far from the scene. An officer used the police computer to find out who owned the vehicle, and apprehended the owner and another person running away. Both refused to provide specimens or to say who had been driving. The owner was prosecuted for failing to supply a specimen, and argued that the officer had not had reasonable cause to believe that he had been driving. The justices found that using the computer to identify the owner and finding the owner near the accident were sufficient grounds to form the belief that the defendant was driving. The Divisional Court upheld that decision. The justices had appreciated the difference between 'suspect' and 'believe'. There was evidence that the officer had reasonable grounds to believe that the defendant was the owner or keeper of the car, which was *prima facie* evidence that he had been driving.

In *Johnson v Whitehouse* [1984] RTR 38, a witness to an accident had seen a person alight from a car, lock it and walk away. A police officer arrived on the scene 10 minutes later, found blood on the front seat of the car and documents bearing the defendant's name. He went to the address and saw the defendant enter the garden and fall over in a drunken state. He was bleeding and had in his possession keys which fitted the car. The officer required a breath test, saying he had reasonable cause to *suspect* he had been driving and involved in an accident. The Divisional Court found that the distinction between suspicion and belief is important, but that the facts were sufficient to have given the officer a reasonable cause to believe the defendant had been driving, and that the use of the word 'suspect' was no more than 'an inaccurate use of language'.

See also the cases mentioned in paras 4.3.1 and 4.4.3, on reasonable cause to believe for the purposes of Road Traffic Act 1988, s 7, allowing an officer to require a blood or urine specimen in place of breath specimens.

2.4.4 Summary of prerequisites

In summary, the prerequisites for requiring a preliminary test seem to be:

- random stopping of vehicles is permitted, but random breath testing is not (there is a limited exception in Northern Ireland – see para 2.2);

- unless there has been an accident, there is no express power for an officer to enter private property, and an officer who does so may be required to leave. If the officer does not leave and the suspect refuses to co-operate, arrest for failing to co-operate in a preliminary test would be unlawful and could not ground a prosecution for failing so to co-operate. But such irregularity would not necessarily invalidate later evidential testing;
- except where there has been an accident, the constable requiring the test must be in uniform;
- the officer must have a reasonable suspicion of driving, attempting to drive or being in charge under s 6(2), (3) or (4) (alcohol, drugs or moving traffic offence); or a reasonable belief in an accident case under s 6(5);
- in a s 6(5) 'accident' case, an accident must have actually occurred, the word 'accident' having its ordinary meaning.

2.5 PRELIMINARY BREATH TEST

Section 6A(1) defines a preliminary breath test as:

> a procedure whereby the person to whom the test is administered provides a specimen of breath to be used for the purpose of obtaining, by means of a device of a type approved by the Secretary of State, an indication whether the proportion of alcohol in the person's breath or blood is likely to exceed the prescribed limit.

2.5.1 Purpose

In *Breckon v DPP* [2007] EWHC 2013 (Admin), [2008] RTR 8, the Divisional Court emphasised the statutory definition, to the effect that the purpose of the preliminary test is to obtain an indication of whether the proportion of alcohol was likely to exceed the prescribed limit, not to determine whether the limit has in fact been exceeded. See also *Snelson v Thompson* [1985] RTR 220 (DC) (see para 3.4.6).

2.5.2 Words used to make the requirement

No particular form of words need be used to require a breath sample. In *R v O'Boyle* [1973] RTR 445, it was sufficient to say, 'I intend to give you a breath test'. It is enough that the language used can fairly be said to amount to a requirement. The word 'require' need not be said.

2.5.3 Place for administering

A preliminary breath test must be administered at or near the place where the requirement for it was imposed (Road Traffic Act 1988, s 6A(2)). A breath test required following an accident may instead, if the constable thinks it expedient, be administered at a police station specified by the constable (s 6A(3)). In *Arnold v Chief Constable of Kingston-upon-Hull* [1969] 1 WLR 1499, the Divisional Court ruled that the expression 'there or nearby', in an earlier version of the provisions on breath testing, is a matter of fact and degree in each case.

2.5.4 Approved devices

A number of devices have been type-approved for preliminary breath testing. The relevant approval orders can be found at www.gov.uk/government/publications/breath-testing-devices-transport-safety. A court may take judicial notice of the approval of a breath testing device: *Bentley v Northumbria Police* [1984] RTR 276 (DC). The devices used for preliminary breath screening have traditionally been considered less accurate than the evidential breath analysis devices used following arrest (see, e.g. *Lafferty v DPP*, unreported, 27 April 1994 – para 3.4.7), although this may be less so in respect of those most recently developed (see para 2.5.6).

2.5.5 Repeating the requirement or the procedure

If the suspect fails to provide a breath sample when first required to do so, there is nothing to prevent the officer making a second requirement: *Revel v Jordan, Hillis v Nicholson* [1983] RTR 497 (QBD), where the only reason for repeating the requirement was fairness to the defendants.

Where the screening device apparently malfunctioned, and the officer then used another device which operated satisfactorily, the subsequent procedure was not invalidated: *Sparrow v Bradley* [1985] RTR 122 (DC). See also *Price v Davies* [1979] RTR 204.

In *DPP v Kennedy* [2003] EWHC 2583 (Admin), (2004) 168 JP 185 (DC), a suspect made several attempts to provide breath for a roadside breath test. The officer did not change the mouthpiece on the screening device between attempts. The Divisional Court found that this did not invalidate the test, and that the arrest following the test was lawful.

2.5.6 Advanced devices and breath-alcohol readings

The more recently approved breath testing devices go further than simply screening for whether or not a person is likely to be above or below the limit, but analyse the breath provided. Some such devices display the breath alcohol concentration, while all of them store a limited number of records of the results. Such a device was used in *DPP v Karamouzis* [2006] EWHC 2634 (Admin) to carry out a preliminary breath test, and showed excess alcohol. The Divisional Court held that it was nevertheless a preliminary breath test rather than an evidential analysis.

In *Murphy v DPP* [2006] EWHC 1753 (Admin), it was argued that Road Traffic Offenders Act 1988, s 15(2) (evidence of the proportion of alcohol in a specimen of breath to be taken into account – see Chapter 8) requires the prosecution to obtain and produce in evidence the result of any analysis by a preliminary testing device. The Divisional Court held that such a result would be admissible in evidence if it had been retrieved and placed before the court, but that there is no duty on the prosecution to obtain the result from the device.

In *Smith v DPP* [2007] EWHC 100 (Admin), [2007] 4 All ER 1135, it was again contended that, pursuant to s 15(2), the prosecution was obliged to adduce in evidence the result in figures of the roadside breath test. The Divisional Court rejected that submission. The specimens of breath used to establish whether or not a defendant has committed an offence are those required under Road Traffic Act 1988, s 7 (see Chapters 3 and 4). Road Traffic Offenders Act 1988, s 15(2) applies only to those evidential specimens. Nevertheless, the court considered it good practice, where it can easily be done, for the reading from the roadside breath sample to be disclosed to the defence. It is likely to support the prosecution case, but it may provide a basis for challenging the accuracy of the analysis of the evidential specimens. See also *Rose v DPP* [2010] EWHC 462 (Admin).

In *Breckon v DPP* [2007] EWHC 2013 (Admin), [2008] RTR 8, the Divisional Court followed *Smith v DPP* to the effect that there is no duty on a prosecutor to disclose a breath alcohol reading taken at the preliminary testing stage, but pointed out that to disclose such a reading would often be to the serious disadvantage of the defendant, given that it would usually be higher than the later readings.

In *Kang v DPP* [2016] EWHC 3014 (Admin) (see para 3.5.2), it was held that a roadside reading was admissible as one piece of evidence, among others, to support the reliability of the police station procedure. See also *DPP v Hill* [1991] RTR 351 and *Lafferty v DPP*, unreported, 27 April 1994 (para 3.4.7) to the same effect.

2.5.7 Sufficiency of specimen

The amount of breath provided must be sufficient to enable the test to be carried out, and it must be provided in such a way as to enable the object of the test to be satisfactorily achieved (Road Traffic Act 1988, s 11(3)). If it is not, the subject may be guilty of failing without reasonable excuse to co-operate in the preliminary test; see Chapter 10.

2.5.8 No preliminary test administered

It may be arguable that, as long as police act *bona fide*, it does not matter that they omit to administer a preliminary breath test. As noted above, there is no statutory requirement for preliminary testing before evidential analysis of breath, blood or urine specimens. In *Anderton v Royle* [1985] RTR 91, a motorist was stopped by police officers, one of whom smelled alcohol on his breath, suspected that he had alcohol in his body, and asked him to accompany them to the police station to provide a breath test there. They did not ask for a breath sample at the roadside. At the police station, evidential breath analysis showed excess alcohol and the motorist was convicted of driving with excess alcohol. It is not apparent from the judgment why no preliminary breath test was carried out, but the Divisional Court upheld the conviction, on the ground that it was not necessary to prove a valid arrest.

See also *R (CPS) v Wolverhampton Magistrates' Court* [2009] EWHC 3467 (Admin) (para 2.8), where a conviction for driving with excess alcohol was upheld in the absence of a preliminary test, the defendant having been arrested on suspicion of driving while unfit. In *Kohler v DPP* [2010] EWHC 2886 (Admin), the Administrative Court again acknowledged that it is not a prerequisite to the admissibility of specimens that there has been a preliminary breath test.

2.5.9 Manufacturer's instructions

In *DPP v Carey* [1970] AC 1072, the House of Lords held that while the device must be assembled in accordance with the manufacturer's instructions, otherwise it is not an approved device, there is no requirement at law that the manufacturer's instructions for use are followed. The manufacturers advised that at least 20 minutes should elapse between consuming alcohol and using the device, and that smoking immediately before using it should not be allowed. The House of Lords ruled that while officers should endeavour to use the devices correctly and in accordance with those instructions, there is no duty to ask when the suspect last drank or smoked.

Where there was no reason to suppose that failure to comply with the manufacturer's instructions in a particular respect would render the test favourable to the Crown, or could prejudice the defendant, the test was valid: *Attorney-General's Reference No 1 of 1978* (1978) 67 Cr App R 387 (CA).

Where there was no evidence that the officer had not complied with the manufacturer's instructions for a roadside breath test, and no evidence that if those instructions had not been followed the results would have favoured the prosecutor, there was no basis for an appeal against conviction for driving with excess alcohol: *Blake v Bickmore* [1982] RTR 167 (DC).

In *Woon v Maskell* [1985] RTR 289, the officer pressed the 'read' button on the breath testing device and it gave a positive result. He did not keep the button depressed for the full 40 seconds as advised in the manufacturer's instructions. The Divisional Court found that this did not compromise the procedure which followed and upheld the motorist's conviction for driving with excess alcohol.

In *DPP v Kay* [1999] RTR 109, the Divisional Court confirmed that *DPP v Carey* [1970] AC 1072 remained good law, finding that where the officer was unaware of the requirement to wait 20 minutes, and administered the test only five minutes since the driver's last drink, the test was nevertheless valid.

In *Grant v DPP* [2003] EWHC 130 (Admin), (2003) 167 JP 459, a motorist had been followed by police for about four miles. When they stopped him, he said he had had a drink within the preceding five minutes, he knew his rights, and that the officers had to wait 20 minutes before administering a roadside breath test. He refused to provide a breath sample and was convicted, *inter alia*, of failing without reasonable excuse to provide a specimen for a breath test. The Divisional Court rejected the contention that the officer should have waited 20 minutes. The court below had found the police officers to be reliable and honest witnesses, and was entitled to conclude that the motorist had not been truthful in saying he had had a drink within the preceding five minutes.

2.6 PRELIMINARY IMPAIRMENT TEST

Road Traffic Act 1988, s 6B contains provisions on testing for impairment with a view to ascertaining whether a person is unfit to drive. Section 6B(1) defines a preliminary impairment test as a procedure in which the constable administering the test observes the subject performing specified tasks, and makes such other observations of the person's physical state as the constable thinks expedient.

The test may be carried out at or near the place where the requirement for it is imposed, or, if the constable thinks expedient, at a police station (s 6B(4)). It may be carried out only by a constable approved for the purpose by the chief officer of the constable's police force (s 6B(6)).

Section 6B(2) authorises the Secretary of State to issue (and revise) a code of practice concerning:

- the tasks to be administered and observations to be made under s 6B(1);
- the manner of administering a preliminary impairment test; and
- the inferences that may be drawn from observations made in the course of such a test.

In issuing or revising the code, the Secretary of State must aim to ensure that the test is designed to indicate whether a person is unfit to drive, and, if so, whether or not the unfitness is likely to be due to drink or drugs (s 6B(3)). The code of practice may include provisions concerning the approval of officers to administer tests, and the kind of training or qualification which should be required (s 6B(7)).

A constable must have regard to the code of practice (s 6B(5)).

The most recent code of practice issued by the Secretary of State for Transport pursuant to these provisions is dated April 2017, and is available at https://assets.publishing.service.gov.uk/media/5a81c768ed915d74e340002f/Fit_Code_of_Practice_1st_April_2017.pdf. It sets out the training and qualifications required before a constable may be approved for these purposes. It emphasises that a preliminary impairment test is not a prerequisite of arrest or an essential element in a prosecution.

Paragraph 15.5 emphasises that, before requiring a preliminary impairment test, there must be a suspicion that the subject is impaired to drive. Such suspicion may arise from the manner of driving, and/or from signs of drug use observed by witnesses.

Paragraphs 7 to 11 describe the procedures to be carried out:

- observation of the eyes and estimation of the size of the pupils using a gauge;
- the 'modified Romberg balance test', a test of the ability to balance and to estimate the passage of time;
- the 'walk and turn' test to check for balance and the ability to follow instructions while walking heel-to-toe along a defined line;

- the ‘one leg stand’ to test for balance while counting out loud;
- the ‘finger to nose’ test of depth perception and, again, balance.

The code includes notes on ensuring the safety of the subject and on the significance of disability, injury or illness. It enumerates the matters which the constable should record in respect of the subject’s performance, pointing out that while there is no scoring system such as would indicate that a subject has passed or failed, the intention is that the constable should be able to form an overall opinion whether the person is impaired for driving by drink or drugs. In coming to that opinion the constable should take account not only of the outcome of the exercises, but also of what the constable knows about the subject’s driving and demeanour, and anything garnered from general conversation or observation. The constable should then be able to decide whether there is sufficient evidence to arrest.

Form MG DD/F is used to create a contemporaneous record of the conduct of a preliminary impairment test.

2.7 PRELIMINARY DRUG TEST

Road Traffic Act 1988, s 6C(1) defines a preliminary drug test as a procedure in which a specimen of sweat or saliva is obtained and used to provide, by means of a device of a type approved by the Secretary of State, an indication whether the person has a drug in the body; if so, whether the drug is a specified controlled drug, and, if it is, whether the proportion of it in the blood or urine is likely to exceed the specified limit.

At the time of writing (January 2024), there has been no case law on what constitutes ‘reasonable suspicion’ of a drug-drive offence as a prerequisite to administering a preliminary drug test. The manner of driving, the person’s appearance or behaviour, and what the person says, may all be relevant.

The test may be administered at or near the place where the requirement for the test is imposed, or, if the constable thinks it expedient, at a police station (s 6C(2)). The devices which have been approved are listed at www.gov.uk/government/publications/approved-drug-testing-devices. At the time of writing (January 2024), two devices have been approved – the Dräger Drug Test 5000 and the more commonly used Securetec DrugWipe 3S S303G. Both are for use either at the roadside or at a police station. They test for cannabis and cocaine, using a specimen of saliva.

Section 6C(2) allows for up to three preliminary drug tests to be administered, but does not specify the circumstances in which a second or third test may be appropriate. As screening devices for specified drugs other than cannabis and cocaine are developed, it may well be that some will test for certain specified substances only, while others test for other substances. In such circumstances, a second (or third) test may be appropriate to screen for a drug not detectable by the first test (or first and second tests).

2.8 POWER OF ARREST

Road Traffic Act 1988, s 6D(1) allows a constable to arrest without warrant a person if, as a result of a preliminary breath or drug test, the constable reasonably suspects that the person has excess alcohol in the breath or blood, or has an excess of a specified drug in the blood or urine. There is also a power to arrest without warrant a person who fails to co-operate with a preliminary test in pursuance of a requirement under s 6, if the constable reasonably suspects that the person has alcohol or a drug in the body, or is under the influence of a drug (s 6D(2)). Section 6D(3) provides that a person may not be arrested under s 6D while at a hospital as a patient. For the position of patients in hospital, see Chapter 5.

Two subsections, 6D(1A) and 6D(2A), were introduced with effect from 1 July 2005, in contemplation of the type approval of portable evidential breath analysis instruments for use elsewhere than at a police station – usually at the roadside or at a hospital. A person arrested under s 6D may, instead of being taken to a police station, be detained at or near the place where the preliminary breath test was or would have been administered, with a view to requiring evidential specimens at that place by means of a portable device (s 6D(2A)). Further, the power of arrest under s 6D(1) is available where the person has provided evidential specimens under s 7 (see Chapters 3 and 4), if the constable who required those specimens has reasonable cause to believe that the portable device used to analyse them has not produced a reliable indication of the proportion of alcohol in the person's breath (s 6D(1A)). At the time of writing (January 2024), no portable evidential analysis devices have been approved. Given the length of time that has elapsed since the introduction of these subsections, and the practical difficulties of implementing evidential breath analysis other than at a police station, it seems unlikely that subsections 6D(1A) and 6D(2A) will come into operation for some time.

Section 10 further provides a power to detain at a police station a person who has been required to provide a specimen of any kind, if the officer has reasonable grounds to believe that, if driving or attempting to drive, the person would commit an offence under s 4 (unfit), s 5 (with excess alcohol) or s 5A (with excess of a specified drug). The power does not arise if it ought reasonably to appear to the officer that there is no likelihood that the person would drive or attempt to drive while impaired, or while having excess alcohol or an excess of a specified drug. In contemplation of the introduction of portable evidential breath analysis devices (see above), there is a similar power to arrest and take to a police station a person who has provided a positive evidential breath specimen at the roadside.

PACE, s 24 contains a general power of arrest without warrant, subject to the preconditions set out in the section. The judgment in *R (CPS) v Wolverhampton Magistrates' Court* [2009] EWHC 3467 (Admin) suggests, however, that the general power should not be invoked to avoid the specific precondition to the exercise of the power of arrest in s 6D. While there is no specific power of arrest if a preliminary test has not been carried out, the *Wolverhampton Magistrates' Court* case confirms that there is power to arrest upon reasonable suspicion of driving when unfit.

The fact that a roadside breath test is negative does not preclude arrest on suspicion of driving while impaired: *DPP v Robertson* [2002] EWHC 542 (Admin), [2002] RTR 22, where a driver passed a roadside breath test, but in the ensuing conversation police believed he slurred his speech. They arrested him, and breath analysis showed excess alcohol. The Queen's Bench Division upheld the arrest and ruled the evidence of the breath analysis admissible.

2.9 POWER OF ENTRY

Road Traffic Act 1988, s 6E gives constables a power of entry where there has been an accident. A constable may enter any place (using reasonable force if necessary) for the purpose of requiring a person to undergo a preliminary test, or arresting a person under s 6D (above). This power is available only following an accident where the constable reasonably suspects that the accident involved injury to any person. 'Any person' presumably includes the suspect.

In *Lunt v DPP* [1993] Crim LR 534, the defendant was seen alighting from a vehicle which had been involved in an accident. Police officers went to his address, where he refused to open the door. The officers, relying on what is now s 6E, identified themselves and said that if they were not allowed in, they would force entry, but did not say why they wanted to enter. The defendant refused to open the door, and the officers forced entry and arrested the defendant for driving when unfit through drink. He was charged with obstructing a police officer in the execution of his duty, contrary to Police Act 1964, s 51(3). The Divisional Court found that the defendant was not entitled to keep the officers out. They had a statutory right to enter which was not affected by their failure to give reasons. The occupier had no right to be told of the precise legal authority under which the officers were acting.

In *Harper v DPP* [2001] EWHC 1071 (Admin), police had followed a trail being left by a damaged car to the defendant's house where they saw the car, parked. There was a smell of alcohol in the car and the air bag was inflated. They suspected the driver might have been drinking, and knocked on the door of the house. A person was seen to duck out of sight and the lights went off. No one answered the door and the officers said they would use force. They then entered by force, calling to the occupants to identify themselves. The Divisional Court found that in the circumstances there had been a need to use force. The court rejected a suggestion that the officers should have gone to see if the back door was open.

2.10 TIME FOR CAUTION

In *Ridehalgh v DPP* [2005] EWHC 1100 (Admin), [2005] RTR 26, the defendant, himself a police officer, went to a police station on police business. A sergeant smelled alcohol on him. An inspector asked if he had been drinking, and if he had driven to the police station. He said he had been drinking the night before, and had driven to the police station that morning. The inspector required a breath test, which was positive. The accused was then arrested and cautioned. On a charge of driving with excess alcohol, he argued that the questions were an interview and he should therefore have been cautioned, as required by the PACE Code of Practice, Code C. The Divisional Court ruled that it was not until the officers had reasonable grounds to suspect that an offence had been committed that the caution was necessary. When the questions were put, they did not know whether or not the defendant had been driving, or how much he had drunk. All they knew was that there was a smell of alcohol. The justices were right to find that no caution was necessary before putting the questions.

Nor was it an interview for the purposes of PACE when police saw a person driving out of a pub car park, stopped him and asked if he had been drinking, and he answered that he had had three pints. The Divisional Court held that that was sufficient to entitle the officer to require a roadside breath test, but it was not until the test showed a positive result that the officer had grounds to suspect an offence so that a caution should be administered: *Sneyd v DPP* [2006] EWHC 560 (Admin), [2007] RTR 6.

See also the cases discussed in para 8.2.3, and *DPP v Billington* [1988] 1 WLR 535 (para 10.7.3).

Chapter 3

Evidential Breath Specimens

3.1 INTRODUCTION

Road Traffic Act 1988, s 7 confers on investigating officers powers to require specimens of breath, blood or urine, with a view to their being analysed to ascertain the level of alcohol in a suspect's body. It is the result of this analysis which forms the basis of any ensuing prosecution. There are restrictions on the places at which specimens may be required. The circumstances in which a constable may require a blood or urine specimen, rather than breath specimens, are specified. Blood and urine specimens are considered in Chapter 4.

It is an offence without reasonable excuse to fail to provide a specimen, and a suspect is to be warned of this when being required to provide specimens. The penalties for failing to provide are, generally, no less severe than for the principal offences.

The interplay between the unavoidability of providing specimens, and the counterbalancing safeguards for suspects, has led to what the press has, sometimes misleadingly, portrayed as the exploitation of loopholes, allowing the undeserving to escape conviction. While there have certainly been some unmeritorious acquittals, the safeguards remain an important element of the regime, and have been unequivocally supported in the courts.

3.2 THE POWER TO REQUIRE SPECIMENS

Section 7(1) provides for the power to require specimens:

> In the course of an investigation into whether a person has committed an offence under section 3A, 4 or 5 of this Act a constable may, subject to the following provisions of this section and section 9 of this Act, require him—

(a) to provide two specimens of breath for analysis by means of a device of a type approved by the Secretary of State, or
(b) to provide a specimen of blood or urine for a laboratory test.

Section 7(1A) concerns the power to require blood or urine specimens where an excess of a specified drug is suspected, and is considered in Chapter 4.

3.2.1 Arrest not a precondition

It has been noted that lawful arrest is not a precondition for requiring a preliminary breath test. Nor is it a precondition for requiring specimens of breath, blood or urine: *R v Fox, Fox v Chief Constable of Gwent* [1986] AC 281 (see para 2.3); *Gull v Scarborough* [1987] RTR 261 (DC); *Hartland v Alden* [1987] RTR 253 (DC). Nor need it be shown that the suspect was lawfully detained at the police station; there is no difference between detention and arrest: *DPP v Porter*, unreported, 15 February 2000 (QBD).

3.2.2 Procedure not an interview

The procedure under s 7 is not an interview for the purposes of the PACE Codes of Practice: *DPP v Rous and D (A Minor)* [1992] RTR 246 (DC), and the current (2017) edition of Code C, para 11.1A. The provisions of Code C concerning interviews (on the procedure, records and special provisions in relation to juveniles, the mentally disordered and vulnerable persons) do not therefore apply. In *Rous and D (A Minor)*, where both defendants were charged with driving with excess alcohol, it was held that the contemporaneous record of the procedure need not be given to the defendant to read or sign. Nor was there any need for an appropriate adult to be present with a juvenile who was undergoing the investigative procedure.

See also the cases on the time for caution (para 2.10); admissions of driving (para 8.2.3); delay in providing specimens pending legal advice (para 10.7.3); and the discretion to admit or exclude evidence under PACE, s 78 (para 11.9).

3.2.3 'In the course of an investigation'

It is a prerequisite for requiring an evidential specimen that the constable is in the course of an investigation into whether a person has committed an offence under s 3A (causing death by careless driving when under the influence of drink or drugs – see Chapter 6), s 4 (driving or in charge when under the influence of drink or drugs – see Chapter 7), s 5 (driving or in charge with excess alcohol –

see Chapter 8) or s 5A (driving or in charge with an excess of a specified drug – see Chapter 8).

In *Graham v Albert* [1985] RTR 352, there had been an accident. The driver of one of the vehicles involved got out of her car. An officer smelled alcohol on her breath and required a roadside breath specimen. The driver refused and was arrested for failing to take the test and on suspicion of having driven with excess alcohol. At the police station, she was required to provide specimens for analysis and refused. At the hearing, she argued that the officers had been investigating an accident, not a possible offence. On the prosecutor's appeal against acquittal, the Divisional Court had no hesitation in finding that the station officer was investigating an allegation by the arresting officer that the defendant had committed an offence of driving with excess alcohol. The requirement for specimens was lawful and her refusal constituted the offence of failing without reasonable excuse to provide specimens.

In *Pearson v Commissioner of Police of the Metropolis* [1988] RTR 276, police arrested three people on suspicion of theft and interference with a motor vehicle. At the police station, officers suspected that they had all been drinking and that one of them had been driving. All three were required to provide specimens of breath for analysis. All refused and all were convicted of failing to provide. On appeal by one of the three, the Divisional Court dismissed an argument that breath specimens may be required only when the driver has been identified, finding that in the circumstances the officer in question was in the course of an investigation into whether the person of whom the requirement was made had committed an offence.

As long as the officer is *bona fide* investigating whether or not an offence has been committed, a requirement for specimens is lawful even if it later transpires that no offence was in fact committed. In *Hawes v DPP* [1993] RTR 116, a motorist was charged with driving in a public place while unfit, contrary to s 4(1), and with failing without reasonable excuse to provide two specimens of breath for analysis, contrary to s 7(6). In fact the place where he had been driving was not a public place and the s 4(1) charge was dismissed, but the justices convicted him of failing to provide. The Divisional Court found that the question was whether or not there was a *bona fide* investigation into whether the suspect had committed an offence under s 4 or s 5. In the absence of any challenge to the good faith of the police officers, they were concerned to discover whether the defendant had been guilty of an offence under s 4 and with nothing else. The requirement for a breath test was lawful and the appeal against conviction for failing to provide it was dismissed.

In *DPP v Earnshaw*, CO/1425/98, 11 June 1988 (DC), the accused had been standing, unsteadily, by a car while another person was in the driving seat. The accused told a police officer that he was the owner, and that they were 'putting the car round the back', then tried to make off. It was held that, on the facts, police were in the course of an investigation for the purposes of s 7(1) and were entitled to require a specimen.

The place at which a suspect's vehicle is when a requirement for specimens is made is immaterial. All that is necessary is that an investigation is in progress: *DPP v Webb* [1988] RTR 374 (DC) (see para 9.2).

The Divisional Court has confirmed that, under s 7, there is no requirement that the officer should have reasonable cause for suspicion; it is enough that the officer is in the course of an investigation: *R v South Norfolk Justices ex parte Keymer*, unreported, 12 October 1994 (DC).

3.3 THE PLACE AT WHICH SPECIMENS MAY BE REQUIRED

Road Traffic Act 1988, s 7 contains provisions governing the place at which breath specimens for analysis are to be provided:

> (2) A constable may make a requirement under this section to provide specimens of breath only if—
>
> (a) the requirement is made at a police station or a hospital,
> (b) the requirement is imposed in circumstances where section 6(5) of this Act applies, or
> (c) the constable is in uniform.
>
> (2C) Where a constable has imposed a requirement on the person concerned to co-operate with a relevant breath test at any place, he is entitled to remain at or near that place in order to impose on him there a requirement under this section.
> (2CA) For the purposes of subsection (2C) 'a relevant breath test' is a procedure involving the provision by the person concerned of a specimen of breath to be used for the purpose of obtaining an indication whether the proportion of alcohol in his breath or blood is likely to exceed the prescribed limit.
> (2D) If a requirement under subsection (1)(a) above has been made at a place other than at a police station, such a requirement may subsequently be made at a police station if (but only if)—

(a) a device or a reliable device of the type mentioned in subsection (1)(a) above was not available at that place or it was for any other reason not practicable to use such a device there, or

(b) the constable who made the previous requirement has reasonable cause to believe that the device used there has not produced a reliable indication of the proportion of alcohol in the breath of the person concerned.

Section 7(2) was amended by the Serious Organised Crime and Police Act 2005 in anticipation of the type approval of portable evidential breath analysis instruments for use at the roadside and in hospitals rather than at the police station. At the time of writing (January 2024), no such instruments have been approved, and the type approvals of the evidential breath analysis instruments currently in use (see para 3.4.1) have been modified to limit their approval to use at police stations. For the time being, therefore, the only place at which evidential breath specimens may be taken is a police station. Section 7 was further amended, from 10 April 2015, by the Deregulation Act 2015, to remove any suggestion that a preliminary breath test is necessary before requiring an evidential breath specimen at the roadside.

3.4 THE BREATH ANALYSIS DEVICE

3.4.1 Type approval

Road Traffic Act 1988, s 7(1)(a) confers the right to require breath specimens for analysis 'by means of a device of a type approved by the Secretary of State'. There are currently three approved devices: the Camic Datamaster, the Intoximeter EC/IR and the Lion Intoxilyzer 6000UK; see *The Breath Analysis Devices Approval 2017* (Home Office, 5 December 2017).

A court may take judicial notice of the approval of a breath testing device: *Bentley v Northumbria Police* [1984] RTR 276 (DC). Although the *Bentley* case related to a roadside breath testing device, there seems to be no reason why it should not apply equally to the evidential devices.

In *Hayward v Eames; Kirkpatrick v Harrigan* [1985] RTR 12, motorists sought to challenge the status of the Lion Intoximeter 3000 – one of the devices then in use. The Divisional Court found that the device was approved and that the relevant approval order provided easy proof of that. It was not necessary for the Act to confer a specific power of approval on the Secretary of State. The fact that the device had been approved before the coming into force of the section authorising police to require specimens for analysis had no bearing on the question. An approval order does not constitute expert evidence: *Murphy v DPP* [2006] EWHC 1753 (Admin).

The fact that the approval order contained an error in the name of the company which manufactured the device did not invalidate the approval: *Chief Constable of Northumbria v Browne* [1986] RTR 113 (DC).

The case of *DPP v McKeown, DPP v Jones* [1997] 1 WLR 295 (HL) established that where the printout from the device showed the wrong time, the device was nevertheless an approved device, there being no requirement that an approved device should have an accurate clock.

In *DPP v Memery* [2002] EWHC 1720 (Admin), [2003] RTR 18, the Divisional Court found that the Crown Court was not permitted to rule on the validity of an approval order. The reasons were that the point at issue in the case was the admissibility of the reading; that Parliament could not have intended every defendant to have the right to challenge the approval of the device; and that in any event the approval in question was not *Wednesbury* irrational. See *Brown v Gallacher* 2002 SLT 756 for the same conclusion by the High Court of Justiciary in Scotland.

The approval status of a particular device may be challenged only on the basis that modifications made to it take the device out of the description in the schedule to the approval order, such that it is no longer an approved device: *Richardson v DPP* [2003] EWHC 359 (Admin). In *Kemsley v DPP* [2004] EWHC 278 (Admin), (2005) 169 JP 148, the court below had accepted expert evidence that the device in question had been modified to such an extent that it was no longer an approved device. The Divisional Court ruled that that decision was fatal to the admissibility of the evidence produced by the device. The court was, however, careful to confine its decision to the particular facts, emphasising that it did not extend to breath alcohol cases in general.

In *Breckon v DPP* [2007] EWHC 2013 (Admin), [2008] RTR 8, the Divisional Court held that the device used was an approved device. The test was whether, after modification or alteration, the device remained one to which the description in the approval order still properly applied. Subject to that, sensible modifications may be made without having to seek a new approval.

The Divisional Court again stressed that type approval is concerned with description in *Coxon v Manchester City Magistrates' Court* [2010] EWHC 712 (Admin). The issue is whether a device meets the description set out in the schedule to the type approval order, and this is a separate issue from reliability or quality. A computer running LIBIS software (which took the investigating officer through the procedure) was connected to the breath analysis device. The motorist's expert evidence did not show that the device was thereby so significantly altered as to take it out of its description, and the device remained within its type approval.

The evidence adduced to challenge the device must relate to the device in question, not to devices of that type in general, or to a device of that type situated elsewhere: *Fearnley v DPP* [2005] EWHC 1393 (Admin), (2005) 169 JP 450.

Defence counsel is entitled to cross-examine a prosecution witness with a view to discovering whether modifications to the device could take it outside the approval order: *Young v Flint* [1987] RTR 300 (DC).

Once it is conceded that the requirement under s 7(1)(a) to provide breath specimens is lawful, then there can be no ground for arguing that the device was not of an approved type, since s 7(1)(a) refers to analysis by means of an approved device: *Wright v DPP* [2005] EWHC 1211 (Admin).

3.4.2 The presumption of reliability

The case law on the reliability of breath analysis devices arises in two contexts: first, reliability for the purpose of proving the proportion of alcohol in a defendant's breath, discussed here. The second issue – of unreliability for the purposes of Road Traffic Act 1988, s 7(3)(b), authorising an investigating officer to require a blood or urine specimen as an alternative to breath specimens – is dealt with in Chapter 4 (see para 4.4).

The courts have been consistent in their reluctance to go behind an approval order. In *DPP v Brown; DPP v Teixeira* [2001] EWHC 931 (Admin), [2002] RTR 23, the Divisional Court made clear that, once a device is approved by the Secretary of State, it is presumed to be reliable. It is not for justices to determine whether a device should have been approved, although they are required to examine carefully whether the presumption that a device is reliable has been rebutted by the evidence before them. On the evidence in these cases, the presumption had not been rebutted. In *Rose v DPP* [2010] EWHC 462 (Admin), [2010] RTR 25, the Administrative Court rejected an argument that *DPP v Brown; DPP v Teixeira* did not survive the case of *Zafar v DPP* [2004] EWHC 2468 (Admin), [2005] RTR 18 (see para 4.5.1).

In *Grant v DPP* [2003] EWHC 130 (Admin), (2003) 167 JP 459, the Divisional Court again refused to entertain a challenge to *DPP v Brown; DPP v Teixeira* on the point concerning type approval. In *Skinner v DPP* [2004] EWHC 2914 (Admin), [2005] RTR 17, it further held that, in the absence of evidence to the contrary, it could be assumed that the device in question in the case, being an approved device, was operating with the correct type-approved software and was operating correctly. The court reiterated that a device does not cease to be approved by modification unless the alteration is such that the description of the device in the schedule to the approval order no longer applies to it. The assumption that, in the absence of evidence to the contrary, an approved device is operating correctly, and with the correct type-approved software, was again applied in *Murphy v DPP* [2006] EWHC 1753 (Admin).

In *Richardson v DPP* [2003] EWHC 359 (Admin), the Administrative Court emphatically stated that an approved device is assumed to be effective and sufficiently accurate for the purposes of s 5(1)(a) and that is the end of the matter. Although type approval can be challenged by judicial review, the question whether approval is apt or inapt is not for a criminal court.

Once again, in *Robertson (Eric) v DPP* [2004] EWHC 517 (Admin), software changes and the fact that the breath analysis device could not detect mouth alcohol did not take it outside the scope of the approval order.

3.4.3 Calibration

The approved devices perform a self-calibration check before and after analysing each of the two breath specimens in a cycle. Such checks are to be taken as satisfactory as long as they are within the range 32.0 to 37.9 microgrammes per 100 millilitres. The results of the calibration checks appear on the printout. Readings from the two specimens are acceptable if separated by no more than 15 per cent of the lower reading, or by 5 microgrammes per 100 millilitres, whichever is the greater, up to a maximum of 200 or 220 microgrammes, depending on the instrument in question. Form MG DD/A (see para 1.8) contains a table of breath differences, to facilitate identifying cases which fall outside the range where the two breath specimens are taken in more than one instrument cycle.

In the absence of any evidence to the contrary, evidence of calibration is conclusive evidence that the device is operating reliably: *DPP v Schon*, unreported, 27 June 1997 (DC).

The importance attached to correct calibration was illustrated in *R v Kingston upon Thames Justices ex parte Khanna* [1986] RTR 364. The printout, which showed excess alcohol, also showed that one of the calibration checks was outside the limits of tolerance, but this was not noticed at the time. On the day of the hearing, a police officer told the defendant's solicitor that the device had been working correctly. On the solicitor's advice, the defendant pleaded guilty to driving with excess alcohol. The printout was not before the court and the prosecutor did not mention the calibration checks. The calibration error later came to light. The Divisional Court found that an order of *certiorari* was available to quash the conviction, in view of the gross irregularity in the proceedings, which were initiated on no evidence. See also *Waite v Smith* [1986] Crim LR 405 (see para 4.4.2), where the fact that the calibration was outside the range was a sufficient basis for the investigating officer to find the device unreliable and require a blood or urine specimen instead.

The fact that the investigating officer did not know the calibration limits was not, of itself, to be taken to mean that she was not properly trained or that the device was not working properly: *Haggis v DPP* [2003] EWHC 2481 (Admin), [2004] 2 All ER 382 (DC).

In *Mercer v DPP* [2003] EWHC 225 (Admin), [2004] RTR 8, the device detected an interfering substance when analysing the second breath specimen. It terminated the cycle without re-calibrating, as it was designed to do. The investigating officer commenced a fresh cycle and the defendant was convicted on the basis of the lower of the first readings from the two cycles. The Divisional Court found that the reading relating to the first specimen was reliable because the instrument had self-calibrated successfully just before that specimen was given. Having detected an interfering substance, it re-calibrated itself at the beginning of its next cycle. The device had been functioning correctly throughout. It did not matter that it had not re-calibrated when it terminated the first cycle.

Proof of calibration

To secure a conviction based on breath specimens, it must be shown that the calibration checks were carried out satisfactorily. That may be by producing the printout, or by oral evidence of what appeared on the display of the device: *Mayon v DPP* [1988] RTR 281, where the device, in both of two separate cycles, analysed the first specimen, then, when the second specimen was provided, registered 'abort'. The Divisional Court held that, in the absence of evidence of calibration, there was nothing to show that the analyses were accurate, and the motorist's conviction was overturned. See also *Greenaway v DPP* [1994] RTR 17, where the officer gave unchallenged oral evidence that all the readings showed the device was working properly. The Divisional Court found that, although perhaps in shorthand, that was sufficient to establish reliability. See also *Sneyd v DPP* [2006] EWHC 560 (Admin), [2007] RTR 6.

Where, on the other hand, the printout was not produced because it had not been served, and there was no oral evidence of calibration, justices could not convict on the basis of oral evidence of the breath-alcohol reading: *Owen v Chesters* [1985] RTR 191 (DC).

To establish calibration by reference to the printout, the printout must be properly adduced in evidence, as it was in *R v Pydar JJ ex parte Foster* (1996) 160 JP 87 (DC), where the officer who had administered the procedure gave evidence and formally produced the documentary record, but was not questioned about the calibration or functioning of the device. At the close of the prosecution case, the defendant submitted there was no case to answer. The justices then examined the document, found it to contain the necessary details, and rejected the submission. On appeal against conviction, it was argued that the justices did not have the document before them, or examine it, until after the prosecution had closed its case. The Divisional Court ruled that once an exhibit is produced, the court has jurisdiction over it, and can examine it whenever it pleases. On the facts, it simply was not necessary to do so until the defence made the submission of no case. See also *Greenaway v DPP* [1994] RTR 17 (above), where again the printout was not handed to the justices until after the prosecution had closed its case. Compare *Hasler v DPP* [1989] RTR 148 (see para 11.3.1), where the printout was not produced in evidence.

Where the printout was before the court, and no point was taken as to calibration, the matter could not later be raised: *Derham v DPP*, unreported, 19 May 1998 (DC). In *Gibson v DPP* [2001] EWHC 131 (Admin), the Divisional Court held that where the printout was before the court, the court had evidence of calibration and was entitled to conclude that the device was working correctly.

Where the printout showed calibration checks of 32 to 37, but the officer, presumably in error, said that, to be correct, the readings should be 33 to 36, it was not irrational for the justices to find the device reliable: *Melia v DPP*, CO/1492/98, 5 June 1998 (DC).

In *Dunwoodie v DPP*, CO/0442/98, 23 March 1998, the Divisional Court accepted as proof of calibration the investigating officer's evidence that he was fully trained in the procedure, holding that it was then open to the court properly to infer that he had gone through the necessary steps, including checking that the calibration was correct. The court did, however, point out that it would have been preferable if the officer had been specifically asked about calibration.

The requirement to prove calibration of the breath analysis device does not arise where the defendant is charged with failing to provide breath specimens for analysis: *DPP v Deveney*, unreported, 28 June 1994 (DC); nor where the prosecution is based on a blood specimen: *Prince v DPP* [1996] Crim LR 343 (DC) and *Branagan v DPP* [2000] RTR 235 (DC).

It is not necessary to show that the device purged itself before analysing a specimen: *DPP v Parkin* [1989] Crim LR 379 (DC).

3.4.4 The date and time

A number of early cases featured challenges based on the fact that the printout showed the wrong date and/or time. Thus, where the printout recited the date as 14 October 1984, erroneously showing that day to have been a Saturday rather than a Sunday, the error would go to the weight of the evidence in the printout, but did not undermine its admissibility. The ambiguity could be remedied by oral evidence: *Fawcett v Gasparics* [1986] RTR 375 (DC). But for the purposes of s 7(3)(b), allowing an investigating officer to require a blood or urine specimen if the breath analysis device is unreliable, see *Slender v Boothby* [1986] RTR 385. In that case, the device did not take account of leap years and showed the date as 1 March instead of 29 February. It was held that the officer was entitled to find the device unreliable and require a blood specimen.

Where the printout plainly showed that times were recorded by reference to Greenwich Mean Time, even though British Summer Time was in operation, the printout was nevertheless reliable: *Parker v DPP* [1993] RTR 283. Where, again, the device recorded the time in Greenwich Mean Time, and the officer handwrote the time in British Summer Time onto the printout retained by the police, the alteration was unwise, but the admissibility of the printout was not affected: *Beck v Scammell* [1986] RTR 162 (DC).

The unreported case of *DPP v Bateson*, 3 June 1998, featured discrepancies between the times at which calibrations took place and specimens were provided, as recorded by the investigating officer, and as shown on the printout. The Divisional Court followed *DPP v McKeown, DPP v Jones* [1997] 1 WLR 295 (HL) to the effect that it did not matter whether or not the breath analysis device was accurately recording the time, or whether its clock had been accurately set. There was nothing to suggest any data corruption.

3.4.5 The printout

The fact that the device does not produce a printout does not render the device unreliable: *Morgan v Lee* [1985] RTR 409, a case concerning Road Traffic Act 1988, s 7(3)(b) and the power to require an alternative specimen if the breath analysis device is unreliable.

The fact that the printout is not signed by the investigating officer does not render it inadmissible in evidence: *Garner v DPP* (1990) 90 Cr App R 178 (QBD) (see para 11.3.1).

Where the original printout was lost and the officer used the device to produce a further printout, the latter was admissible as an original document: *DPP v Hutchings* [1991] RTR 380 (DC).

In *Burditt v Roberts* [1986] RTR 391, the Divisional Court held that keying errors by the operator, appearing on the printout, did not render the device unreliable. The errors were that the word 'station' appeared as 'sation' and the suspect's name, which was Roger P Burditt, appeared as 'ROGERPBUIURDITTTT'. Mr Burditt's conviction for driving with excess alcohol in breath was upheld.

In *DPP v Barber* (1999) 163 JP 457, the printout again showed excess alcohol, but was printed in such a way that the first two characters of each line were missing. The records of the calibration, the purges and the breath analyses were, however, complete. The defendant submitted that the device was not reliable. The magistrate agreed, and refused to allow the prosecutor to adduce evidence from an engineer who had later examined the device and repaired the printer. The prosecutor appealed against the dismissal of the case. The Divisional Court held that the case should not have been dismissed when it was; the magistrate should have allowed the engineer to give evidence of the reliability of the device.

3.4.6 Relationship between evidential and later screening tests

A challenge based on comparing the readings from an evidential test with the results of a later screening test failed in *Snelson v Thompson* [1985] RTR 220 (DC). (For the practice of holding a person until below the limit, see para 4.16.) The appellant questioned analyses timed at 1.31 and 1.36, which showed excess alcohol, on the basis of a negative screening test taken just over an hour later. The Divisional Court pointed out that the screening device is designed to give a general indication only, while the evidential device is designed to give a precise reading. The justices were entitled to conclude that they could rely on the readings from that device. By comparison, in *O'Sullivan v DPP* [2005] EWHC 564 (Admin) (see para 4.5.1), the reading from a later screening test, which was consistent with the breath analysis, was interpreted as supporting the breath analysis.

See also *Parish v DPP* [2000] RTR 143 (para 4.15.4).

3.4.7 Challenging the reliability of the device

In *Cracknell v Willis* [1988] AC 450 (HL), the justices had refused to allow the motorist to adduce evidence of the amount he had drunk to challenge the reading from the breath analysis device. The House of Lords found that the wording of the statutory assumption (in what is now Road Traffic Offenders Act 1988, s 15(2); see para 8.9) gave no support for the view that Parliament intended any challenge to the reliability of a device to be limited to a particular type of evidence. The assumption is not that the device is working correctly, but that the proportion of alcohol at the time of the offence was not less than in the specimen. In the case of a blood specimen, justices might have to choose between differing analyses by the prosecution and by the defence. In the case of a breath specimen, the device is presumed reliable, but if the presumption is challenged by relevant evidence the magistrates must be satisfied that it has provided a reading upon which they can rely before making the assumption. The House expressed the hope that the good sense of magistrates and the growing acceptance of the reliability of the breath analysis devices would mean there would be few such challenges.

In the event, there have been a great many challenges.

In the unreported case of *R v Ealing Justices ex parte Wheeler*, 12 May 1986 (DC), it was held that the justices were entitled to find that the breath analysis device was working correctly despite evidence of data corruption within the two months spanning the date in question. They were satisfied that it was working correctly on the evening in question and the evidence of data corruption at other times did not lead them to alter that view.

A decision by justices to accept the defendant's claim that he had drunk only half a pint of lager, and to find that the breath analysis device must have been unreliable, was overturned in *DPP v Hill* [1991] RTR 351. Although the justices accepted that the defendant's vision was glazed at the time, they dismissed the charge of driving with excess alcohol. The Divisional Court said that if the defendant were to be believed, the surprising consequences would be that the roadside device was faulty, the breath analysis device was faulty, and there would have had to be some other explanation for the defendant's glazed vision.

In *Lafferty v DPP*, unreported, 27 April 1994, the defendant, charged with driving with excess alcohol, asserted that he had not drunk enough to take him over the limit. He adduced expert evidence that if he had drunk only as much as he claimed, he would have been below the limit. The Divisional Court held that it is open to the prosecution to rebut such an assertion by any relevant evidence. The result of the roadside breath test was admissible for this purpose, even though its accuracy was not as great as that of an evidential breath analysis device.

A motorist charged with failing to provide breath specimens for analysis sought to argue that the device was defective. The record, completed by the sergeant conducting the procedure, showed that she supplied a first breath specimen at 12.19 am, but that the machine shut down at 12.20. At 12.34 the sergeant offered the motorist a chance to provide another specimen. She declined. The sergeant gave evidence that he was not aware that the breath analysis device was supposed to allow three minutes for the two specimens to be given. He thought it was usual for it to allow about two minutes. He believed the machine had been working correctly. He was not challenged about his record of timings. The motorist adduced expert evidence to the effect that the Home Office specified that an approved breath analysis device should allow three minutes for the two specimens to be given; and that if the machine in question had aborted after one minute, there must have been something wrong with it. The prosecutor adduced expert evidence from an experienced engineer employed by the manufacturers of the machine, that he saw no indication on the printouts of any malfunctioning; he had never known a machine allow anything other than the prescribed three minutes. The Administrative Court acknowledged that the court below had found that there was no mechanical defect, and, in so doing, to some extent rejected the officer's timings as set out in the record. But it was never put to the sergeant that his timings were wrong. The court below was entitled to find that there was no defect in the device. The evidence of the engineer was *prima facie* admissible, and there was no reason, in the circumstances of the case, why it should not be admitted. See *Hingley-Smith v DPP* [1997] EWHC 952 (Admin).

In *DPP v Spurrier* [2000] RTR 60, breath analysis showed that the motorist was just over four times the limit, although she displayed no signs of erratic driving, was not unsteady on her feet, nor were her eyes glazed. But for the smell of alcohol, there were no observable signs that she had consumed alcohol. The justices accepted that she had been drinking the day before her arrest, but not for a little over 12 hours immediately before she was arrested. They concluded that the amount she had consumed was not compatible with the high reading; nor were her observable behaviour and condition compatible with that high reading. They found the breath analysis device unreliable and acquitted her. The prosecutor appealed, arguing that the justices could not properly conclude that the device was unreliable without medical or scientific evidence. The Divisional Court found that, on the basis of the evidence which was accepted, the inference drawn was not one to which no reasonable bench properly directing themselves could come, although other magistrates may well not have come to the same conclusion.

The judgment in *Spurrier* includes a list of points which a fact-finding tribunal might consider in approaching evidence in cases such as this. They include:

- A discrepancy between the amount said to have been consumed and the reading can point to the unreliability of the machine or the unreliability of the defendant's evidence. It is essential for justices to consider the reliability of the defendant's evidence having regard to the presumption that the device is reliable.

- Where the defendant claims to have had a minimal amount to drink, but the reading is very high, and there is little or no other evidence on the point, the discrepancy would be based solely on the defendant's claimed consumption. Rebutting the presumption that the device is reliable in such circumstances is most likely to be very difficult.
- Where there are no observable signs of alcohol, save on the breath, justices should have in mind, as a matter of general knowledge, that certain people can develop a tolerance for a high level of alcohol without being observably under its influence.
- Where arguments of low consumption, or of consumption long ago, are advanced, it is to be expected that the result of the breath analysis would be a great surprise to the person under arrest. The absence of any evidence of surprise is a factor for justices to consider.

In his concurring judgment in *Spurrier*, Simon Brown LJ said he was inclined to think that the case 'bumps up against the borderline' at which it becomes perverse for justices, without expert evidence, to infer that the device was unreliable.

In *Williams (John Robert) v DPP* [2001] EWHC 932 (Admin), the justices adopted the robust view advocated in *Spurrier* and rejected the motorist's argument that he had not drunk enough to be over the limit. He adduced expert evidence that if he had consumed the amount he claimed, then his breath alcohol level at the time he provided the specimens would have been zero. The Divisional Court noted the justices' findings that his eyes were glazed, his breath smelled strongly of alcohol, the roadside breath test was positive, and the breath analysis device gave a reading of 60. In making those findings, they must have rejected the evidence of the appellant, and were entitled, on the evidence, to find as a fact that the defendant had consumed sufficient alcohol to exceed the prescribed limit.

In *Ashton v DPP* [1998] RTR 45 at 50, Balcombe LJ said, *obiter*, that if it was sought to exclude evidence from an approved device, then it would be appropriate to do so under PACE, s 78 (see para 11.9). The case concerned the fact that the device made an allowance if it detected acetone in the breath specimen. At the time it was thought that the presence of acetone could interfere with the reading, although that is no longer the prevailing scientific view.

Over the years, more and more far-fetched arguments have been devised to challenge positive breath analyses. In *R (Hassani) v West London Magistrates' Court* [2017] EWHC 1270 (Admin), the Divisional Court remarked that:

> time wasting, extension of hearings and taking hopeless points in the hope of wearing down an opponent or the court are neither proper nor legitimate ways in which to conduct a case.

In *CPS v Cipriani*, unreported, 24 June 2016 (www.judiciary.gov.uk/wp-content/uploads/2016/09/cps-v-cipriani-judgment.pdf), a decision of the Westminster Magistrates' Court, Senior District Judge Howard Riddle urged that it is in the 'interests of all that summary trials concentrate on the real contested issues and do not descend into a game of smoke and mirrors'.

As to the time at which a challenge must be raised, see *Santos v Stratford Magistrates' Court* [2012] EWHC 752 (Admin) and *DPP v Chajed* [2013] EWHC 188 (Admin), [2013] 2 Cr App R 6 (para 11.12).

Burden of proof

If the reliability of the device is challenged, the burden of proving reliability is on the prosecution. In *O'Sullivan (Sarah) v DPP*, unreported, 27 March 2000 (QBD), the device appeared to be operating correctly and at 1 am produced readings of 57 and 56. Between 2.30 and 2.45 am, a further specimen analysed by the same device produced a reading of 23. The motorist argued that the court could not be sure that the device was reliable in view of the difference between the readings, which indicated a rate of fall in alcohol level equivalent to 43 milligrammes in blood per hour. She adduced evidence that, when tested some months later, her own blood alcohol level fell at the rate of 24 milligrammes per hour. Both defence and prosecution called expert evidence concerning the incidence, in the population as a whole, of an elimination rate of 43, and that it was confined to heavy drinkers. Her appeal against conviction for driving with excess alcohol succeeded because, the Queen's Bench Division held, the court below had applied the wrong burden of proof. It was not for the appellant to prove that the machine was unreliable; the prosecution must prove affirmatively that it was reliable. Nor was it for the appellant to prove that the difference in readings was impossible; it was for the respondent to prove that the difference in readings gave rise to no reasonable doubt about the reliability of the results. Lastly, it was not for the motorist to prove that she was not a heavy drinker.

More recently, in *Ali v DPP* [2020] EWHC 2864 (Admin), [2020] 4 WLR 146, breath analysis produced a lower reading of 46 microgrammes of alcohol in 100 millilitres of breath. The driver claimed (among other matters) that he had drunk only a single glass of wine and adduced evidence that the device should therefore have returned a reading of zero. The deputy district judge found that the presumption of reliability had not been rebutted on the balance of probability and that the device had been working correctly. On appeal, the Administrative Court found that the deputy district judge had erred in finding that the defendant had to establish unreliability on the balance of probability. It is sufficient to bring relevant evidence that the reading was not reliable. The burden of proof then passes to the prosecution to establish, to the criminal standard, that it was reliable. This issue was not, however, relevant here, as the court below had gone on to find, to the criminal standard, that the reading was reliable. That finding was based on evidence that the appellant had smelt of alcohol; his eyes were glazed; he failed two roadside breath tests; and the officer who administered the evidential breath analysis was an experienced officer, had no concerns about the functioning of the device, saw no error messages and was satisfied as to calibration.

Disclosure of documents and witness summonses

Disclosure of documents relating to particular breath analysis devices has been the subject of a number of appeals. A flurry of cases followed the introduction of evidential breath analysis, in which it was sought to challenge the new devices by seeking disclosure of documentation such as logs and service records. In *R v Coventry Magistrates' Court ex parte Perks* [1985] RTR 74, a motorist was charged with driving with excess alcohol in breath. He successfully applied to magistrates for witness summonses, under Magistrates' Courts Act 1980, s 97(1), against police officers, requiring production of the log relating to the device which had been used, covering a period of one month. His intention was to examine the log before entering a plea. Section 97(1) authorises the issue of such a summons where a justice is satisfied that a person is likely to be able to give material evidence, or produce any document or thing likely to be material evidence, at a summary trial, and it is in the interests of justice to issue a summons to secure the person's attendance. The police sought an order of *certiorari* to quash the witness summonses. The Divisional Court ruled that the basis of the power in s 97(1) is that the evidence or document must be material. The record of the device over a period of a month could not be material to the hearing of a charge related to a particular incident on a particular date. It would have no probative value so far as the charge was concerned. Its only potential use would be as a basis for cross-examining the prosecution about the reliability of the device at the time in question. The summonses were 'a fishing expedition' and were quashed.

The cases of *R v Skegness Magistrates' Court ex parte Cardy; R v Manchester Crown Court ex parte Williams* [1985] RTR 49 followed a few months later. In both, the motorist sought to challenge the reliability of the breath analysis device by way of witness summonses to produce technical documents relating to a specific device, and to breath analysis devices in general. The Divisional Court again emphasised that the crucial question is whether the documents are likely to be material evidence. On the facts of both cases, they were not. The unreported cases of *R v Teesside Justices ex parte Payne*, 21 December 1984 (DC), *R v Kingston-upon-Hull Justices ex parte Walton*, 17 May 1985 (DC) and *R v Pirehill North Justices ex parte Stoddard*, 24 July 1985, are all to the same effect, as was

R v Tower Bridge Magistrates' Courts ex parte DPP [1989] RTR 118 (DC), in which Watkins LJ referred to the 'most impudent efforts' made by defendants to try to show that the device was defective.

But in a different set of circumstances, justices were wrong not to issue a witness summons. A motorist was defending a charge of driving with excess alcohol. He challenged the accuracy of the breath analysis device, and argued that it was not an approved device. The prosecution adduced a statement concerning approval procedures, written by an employee of the Forensic Science Service. He was willing to give evidence and could probably attend before the expected end of the trial, but, because he was a civil servant, he could not do so unless a witness summons was issued. The justices, however, refused the defendant's application for a witness summons on the basis that it was made late. The Divisional Court found that the justices were wrong to refuse the witness summons; it was not opposed and the witness was willing to attend. See *Fearnley v DPP* [2005] EWHC 1393 (Admin), (2005) 169 JP 450.

The issue of disclosure of documents relating to particular devices arose again in the context of Criminal Procedure and Investigations Act 1996, s 8. Section 8 applies when a defendant has given a defence statement under the Act, and the prosecutor has complied, or purported to comply, or failed to comply, with the resulting duty of disclosure. If the defendant has reasonable cause to believe that there is prosecution material which should have been disclosed but was not, the defendant may apply to the court for an order that the prosecutor disclose the material.

In *Rothon v DPP* [2006] EWHC 3330 (Admin), a motorist charged with driving with excess alcohol called as a witness an expert in breath analysis devices. To advise on the reliability of the device, the witness wished to see certain records concerning it, which were in the possession of the prosecution. The defendant sought disclosure of those documents under s 8. The prosecutor called its own expert, who gave evidence that he had seen the records, and that there was nothing in them to suggest the machine was outside its type approval or unreliable. Disclosure was refused and the defendant was convicted. The Administrative Court ruled that up to the point where the prosecution called its expert, the refusal of disclosure was justified. But having heard that witness, the suggestion was that the justices might not otherwise have been satisfied as to the proper working of the machine. They should have ruled on the application for disclosure one way or the other before hearing that witness. But in the unusual situation of having heard him, natural justice, the right to a fair trial (under the European Convention on Human Rights, art 6) and common sense indicated that they should have acceded to an application for disclosure of the material.

In *DPP v Wood; DPP v McGillicuddy* [2006] EWHC 32 (Admin), motorists had been charged with driving with excess alcohol. In both cases, the court ordered the manufacturer of the device to disclose documents. The company disclosed some, but declined to disclose the remainder, on the grounds of commercial confidentiality. In both cases the proceedings were then stayed as an abuse of process. The prosecutor appealed. The Divisional Court ruled that disclosure of the material ordered, even if otherwise justified, should have been refused on the grounds that the defence statement did not raise any issue to which reliability or type approval was relevant. The material sought to be disclosed must have some potential for bearing on the issue in respect of which it is raised. In considering disclosure applications based on a claim of unreliability, the court should take into account the safeguards built into the Act: the taking of two specimens, the intervening clearances of the device, the use in evidence of the lower reading, the scope for providing specimens of blood or urine, and the fact that there is leeway above the breath limit before prosecution takes place. These matters are relevant to whether the alleged unreliability could possibly advance the stated defence.

On the question whether the material sought was 'prosecution material' for the purposes of the Criminal Procedure and Investigations Act 1996, the only basis upon which that could be contended would be that the prosecutor was, or included, the manufacturer of the device. That was an impossible contention. The prosecutor was the Crown Prosecution Service and the manufacturer was a third party. The correct procedure would have been to seek a witness summons under Magistrates' Courts Act 1980, s 97.

By comparison, in *Watling v Chief Constable of Suffolk Constabulary and G4S Health Services (UK) Ltd* [2019] EWHC 2342 (QB), [2020] RTR 23 (see para 4.6), G4S Health Services provided medical services to the police. For the purposes of Human Rights Act 1998, s 6 (acts of public authorities), it was found to be a 'hybrid' authority, exercising both private and public functions.

In the joined cases of *R (Cunliffe) v West London Magistrates' Court, v Ealing Magistrates' Court, v Hastings Magistrates' Court* [2006] EWHC 2081 (Admin), defendants raised arguments that the breath analysis devices used had lost their type approval because of modifications, and that the amount of alcohol consumed was insufficient to produce readings over the legal limit. Witness summonses under Magistrates' Courts Act 1980, s 97(1), as amended by Serious Organised Crime and Police Act 2005, s 169(2), were sought and granted. They required the manufacturer of the devices to produce technical documents relating to the devices in question. The Divisional Court ruled that the test to be applied under s 97(1) is, first, whether the person is likely to be able to give material evidence or the document is likely to be material evidence. Second, it must be in the interests of justice to issue the summons, as required by s 97(1)(b). Both limbs must be satisfied before any summons is issued. Further, the court ruled, the information sought was not disclosable under Criminal Procedure and Investigations Act 1996, s 8. The test in s 8 is in broader terms than that under s 97 of the 1980 Act. Therefore, if the documents in question do not fall to be disclosed as a matter of law under s 8, they do not satisfy the admissibility provisions of s 97. On the facts, the documents sought were not material evidence and witness summonses should not have been issued.

R (DPP, Blakeley) v Manchester and Salford Magistrates' Court; R (DPP, Whyte) v Manchester and Salford Magistrates' Court [2017] EWHC 3719 (Admin), [2019] 1 WLR 2617 again featured defence applications for disclosure of numerous documents relating to the breath analysis devices used, and followed a pattern of disclosure requests of this kind which were being routinely made. The Divisional Court reiterated that, before disclosure can be ordered, there must be a proper evidential basis for concluding that the material sought is reasonably capable of undermining the prosecution or of assisting the defence. It is not enough for the defence to say that the amount drunk would not put the defendant over the limit and therefore the device must be unreliable. To provide a basis for disclosure of material, the defence must address two critical features:

> The first requirement is the basis for contending how the device might produce a printout which, on its face, demonstrated that it was operating in proper fashion, but which could generate a very significantly false positive reading, where, on the defence case, the true reading would have been well below the prosecution limit. The second requirement is to identify how the material ... sought could assist to demonstrate how that might have happened. Those are the two issues which arise and which the expert evidence in support of disclosure should address.

See also *R (DPP) v The Crown Court at Caernarfon and Davies* [2019] EWHC 767 (Admin), where the principles in *DPP v Manchester and Salford* were applied in the context of a speeding offence and a speed measurement device.

In *R (DPP, Bhusal) v Walsall Magistrates' Court; R (DPP, Thaiss) v Lincoln Magistrates' Court* [2019] EWHC 3317 (Admin), [2020] RTR 14, the DPP sought judicial review of decisions, in both cases, to order disclosure in drink-drive cases. In the *Walsall* case, disclosure of logs and historical test data relating to the Intoxilyser used was ordered on the basis that the gas calibration certificate for the device had expired some two months before the date of the breath analysis in question. In the *Lincoln* case, disclosure of logs, memory downloads, calibration certificates and pre-release breath tests was ordered on the basis that the alcohol reading was close to the limit and the prosecution had not properly responded to the application for disclosure under Criminal Procedure and Investigations Act 1996, s 8. The DPP argued that in both cases the material sought was not relevant because it could not reasonably be considered capable of undermining the prosecution case or assisting the defence case. The DPP also argued that in the *Lincoln* case, the defence had delayed seeking to have its application for disclosure heard such that it was unreasonable to grant it.

The Divisional Court reviewed the requirements to be met when seeking disclosure, as set out *Cracknell v Willis* and *Manchester and Salford*. It found that it had jurisdiction to deal with the orders for disclosure as the issues raised were of wide application, not dependent on the final result, and there was no other way effectively to challenge them. In the *Walsall* case, no evidence at all had been served in support of the application for disclosure. The judge was right to adjourn the trial for the attendance of experts on the relevance to the accuracy of the Intoxyliser readings of the fact that the gas calibration certificate had expired, but there was no justification for ordering wide disclosure in the absence of evidence establishing its relevance. In the *Lincoln* case, the evidence in support of the application for disclosure fell far short of demonstrating the relevance of the material sought; it was a series of generalised and, for the most part, unexplained assertions. The delay in pursuing the application for disclosure was a further reason for refusing it.

Both disclosure orders were quashed. The court went on to draw attention to Criminal Procedure Rules, Part 19 on expert evidence, and, in particular, r 19.4 on the contents of an expert report, and criticised in strong terms the expert reports in the present cases for failures to comply.

3.5 THE PROCEDURE FOR REQUIRING SPECIMENS

3.5.1 Guidance in the MG DD forms

Where the investigating officer does not follow the guidance in the *pro forma* MG DD/A, the requirement to provide breath specimens for analysis is not necessarily invalid. In *DPP v Coulter* [2005] EWHC 1533 (Admin), a suspect had been arrested and, in the course of the procedure at the police station, the officer asked if he had eaten anything. He replied, 'I might have had a Tic Tac'. The advice in form MG DD/A was to wait 20 minutes before testing a suspect who has eaten anything. The Divisional Court found that there is nothing in the Road Traffic Act 1988 to render a requirement for breath specimens unlawful if the officer does not follow the guidance in the *pro forma*, although there may be circumstances in which such failure would affect the reliability of the specimen. In the present case, the suspect had in any event refused to provide breath specimens and the argument concerning the failure to wait 20 minutes was of no relevance.

In *Scheiner v DPP* [2006] EWHC 1516 (Admin), a motorist had been convicted of driving with excess alcohol in the breath. On appeal, he argued that the procedure was invalid since the investigating officer had given evidence that he had probably had his mobile phone with him and that, if so, it would have been switched on. The judgment recites that the manufacturer's instructions for using the device include the words, 'As a precaution all radio sets and mobile telephones in the room where the evidential breath testing instrument is in use should be switched off'. These words appeared in the *pro forma* MG DD/A (note to para A16 of version 4.3, January 2004), and it is suggested that the judgment should have referred to the form rather than to the manufacturer's instructions. In any event, since there was no evidence that the operation of the device might have been affected by the presence of a mobile phone which was switched on, the Divisional Court had little difficulty in dismissing the argument and upholding the conviction.

In *Ivic v DPP* [2006] EWHC 1570 (Admin), it was conceded that a police radio was left on during the breath testing procedure at the police station. The district judge rejected an application to exclude the evidence of the breath analysis on this basis, and the Divisional Court upheld that decision. *DPP v Carey* [1970] AC 1072 (see para 2.5.9) was cited. In addition, there was unchallenged expert evidence that the accuracy or reliability of the breath analysis device would not be affected by a police radio which was on.

In *Afolayan v CPS* [2012] EWHC 1322 (Admin), the form had not been completed in relation to certain aspects of the procedure for taking a blood specimen. The magistrates were nevertheless satisfied, on the evidence of the officers concerned and of the analyst of the specimen, that the procedure had been properly carried out, and the motorist's appeal against conviction was dismissed.

See also the cases on the significance of the manufacturer's instructions for use of the devices, in para 2.5.9.

3.5.2 Repeat requirements and multiple specimens

There is nothing in the legislation to prevent the officer repeating the requirement for breath specimens if the motorist fails to provide them in response to the first requirement: *Owen v Morgan* [1986] RTR 151 (DC), where the motorist failed to provide breath specimens for analysis at the first attempt, but did so when asked again 15 minutes later.

Where more than two evidential breath specimens are provided, the third and any subsequent specimens are not to be taken into account. See *Howard v Hallett* [1984] RTR 353 (para 3.6), and *Chief Constable of Avon & Somerset v Creech*

[1986] RTR 87, in which it was also decided that the two specimens need not be provided in the same cycle. The first specimen produced a reading of 95, but the motorist failed to produce a second specimen before the device ran out of time. The procedure was begun afresh and two satisfactory specimens were produced. The magistrates dismissed the information on the ground that the two specimens should have been provided during the same operating cycle. The Divisional Court found that there was no evidence, and no reason to infer, that the accuracy of the first operation in the operating cycle of the device was in any way compromised by the omission of a second. The prosecutor was entitled to put in evidence the results of the first two tests.

Where the motorist supplied two breath specimens, but they were not analysed because the device was not ready, it was lawful to require further breath specimens: *Morrison v DPP*, unreported, 12 October 1994 (DC).

Nor is there anything to prevent an officer repeating a requirement for breath specimens even after moving on to require a blood specimen. In the unreported case of *Durdan v Chief Officer, Metropolitan Police*, 28 July 1994, the motorist was at the police station and complained of stomach pains and ulcers. He was twice asked to provide breath specimens but did not reply. The officer conducting the procedure took the view that there was reasonable cause to believe that for medical reasons a specimen of breath could not be provided or should not be required (see para 4.8.2), and so asked for a specimen of blood. Again the motorist did not reply. The officer called the forensic medical examiner, who confirmed that the motorist was suffering from spasmodic stomach pains, but that he could provide a specimen of breath between spasms. The doctor was not asked whether the motorist was fit to provide blood. The officer again asked for a specimen of breath and the motorist said he could not. The motorist was charged with failing without reasonable excuse to provide specimens of breath. The Divisional Court found that there is nothing in s 7 to preclude asking for a further specimen of breath, even after the officer has moved on to requiring a sample of blood.

In *Jubb v DPP* [2002] EWHC 2317 (Admin), [2003] RTR 19, where the officer believed that the device may not have produced a reliable indication (s 7(3)(bb) – see para 4.5), the Administrative Court confirmed that it was lawful for the officer to invite further breath specimens, but not to require them. Where further breath specimens are requested in such circumstances, it is not appropriate or necessary to make the requirement for specimens again, or to repeat the warning of the consequences of failure to provide: *Edmond v DPP* [2006] EWHC 463 (Admin), [2006] RTR 18 (see para 10.9).

In *Stewart (John Kimball) v DPP* [2003] EWHC 1323 (Admin), [2003] RTR 35, the officer again believed that the device had not produced a reliable indication and gave the suspect the choice of providing further breath specimens, or a blood or urine specimen. The Divisional Court held that the officer was not obliged to go on to require blood or urine. Nor was he precluded from offering a further breath test. Since the first two specimens had not enabled the objective of the analysis to be satisfactorily achieved, effectively no specimens had been provided and there was nothing to stop the officer making a further requirement for breath, although he was not obliged to do so.

In *Kang v DPP* [2016] EWHC 3014 (Admin), a roadside test showed 157 microgrammes of alcohol in 100 millilitres of breath. At the police station, the breath analysis procedure was begun. The calibration check was satisfactory, but, before the first breath specimen was provided, the device produced the message 'ambient fail' and aborted the procedure. The procedure was begun again, the error message did not recur, and the lower reading was 143. The officer did not require blood or urine instead of breath, nor offer the suspect the opportunity to provide an alternative specimen. The magistrates found that the error message had occurred because the suspect held the breath tube too close to his mouth before providing the first specimen, and that the reading of 143 was reliable. The defendant was convicted of being in charge with excess alcohol. On appeal, the Administrative Court held that the officer was entitled to require further breath specimens when the procedure aborted, as no breath specimens had been provided. There was no requirement on the officer to require a blood or urine specimen instead of proceeding as he did. Arguments based on non-completion of part of the MG DD/A form, and on non-compliance with advice given in the form, also failed; see para 3.5.1.

See also *Blake v Bickmore* [1982] RTR 167 (DC) (para 2.5.9) and *Sparrow v Bradley* [1985] RTR 122 (DC) (para 2.5.5), which concern roadside screening tests, and *Denny v DPP* [1990] RTR 417 (para 4.4.7), where the device was unreliable and the suspect was taken to another police station where there was a functioning device.

3.5.3 The statutory warning

Road Traffic Act 1988, s 7(7) provides that, when requiring specimens under s 7, the officer must give a warning that failure to provide will render the person liable to prosecution. See para 10.9.

3.6 LOWER BREATH READING TO BE USED

Road Traffic Act 1988, s 8 is headed 'Breath specimen showing higher alcohol level to be disregarded'. Section 8(1) is to the effect that, subject to s 8(2), of two specimens of breath provided pursuant to s 7, that with the lower proportion of alcohol is to be used and the other disregarded. The indication from the cases is that 'used' means adduced in evidence.

In *R v Brentford Magistrates' Court ex parte Clarke* [1987] RTR 205, the printout showed 75 in respect of both breath specimens. Expert evidence was adduced that the device could read to one decimal point, but that the printout showed only a whole number, omitting any digits after the decimal point. The Queen's Bench Division roundly rejected an argument that neither reading could be admitted in evidence because a lower reading was not available. It was abundantly clear that the purpose of the provision was to give an accused person the benefit of the lower reading if they differ.

Where, in error, three specimens were provided, it was the lower of the first two which was to be used. In *Howard v Hallett* [1984] RTR 353, a motorist gave a first specimen of breath, but, in error, the officer operating the machine failed to ask for a second specimen within the required time. The procedure was begun afresh and two further specimens taken. The last two readings were put before the justices; the first was not, although it was the lowest of the three. The Divisional Court found that the officer had no power to require more than two specimens. The first two readings should have been in evidence, and the defendant could have been convicted only on the basis of the first of those two, which was the lower. See also *Chief Constable of Avon & Somerset v Creech* [1986] RTR 87 (para 3.5.2), to the effect that it does not matter that the two specimens are taken in two different cycles of the device.

Conversely, a defendant cannot be convicted of an excess alcohol offence on the basis of a single specimen: *Cracknell v Willis* [1988] AC 450 (HL).

3.7 CONCLUSION OF THE BREATH ANALYSIS PROCEDURE

By way of summary of the above requirements, at the end of the breath analysis procedure, the position should be that:

- two satisfactory breath specimens have been analysed, leading to release, or charge;
- the officer has reasonable cause to believe that, for medical reasons, breath cannot be provided or should not be required, in which case a specimen of blood or urine may be required instead (see para 4.3);
- the officer has reasonable cause to believe that a device or a reliable device is not available, or for any other reason it is not practicable to use such a device, when, again, a specimen of blood or urine may be required (see para 4.4);

- specimens have been analysed but the officer has reasonable cause to believe that the device has not produced a reliable indication of the alcohol level. An alternative specimen may then be required (see para 4.5); or
- there is evidence of failure to provide, with no reasonable excuse, leading to a charge of failing without reasonable excuse to provide specimens (see Chapter 10).

Road Traffic Act 1988, s 7(5A) provides a power to arrest a person who fails to provide a breath specimen when required to do so under s 7 if the officer reasonably suspects the person to have alcohol in the body. See para 4.16 for the power to detain a person following the completion of the investigation.

Chapter 4

Blood and Urine Specimens

4.1 INTRODUCTION

Road Traffic Act 1988, s 7(1) (see para 3.2) provides the power to require evidential specimens of breath, or of blood or urine, in relation to investigations into the offences of causing death by careless driving when under the influence of drink or drugs (s 3A); driving, attempting to drive or in charge when unfit through drink or drugs (s 4); or driving, attempting to drive or in charge with excess alcohol (s 5). Section 7(1A) authorises officers to require blood or urine specimens when investigating possible offences of excess drugs under s 5A. The officer requiring a specimen must be 'in the course of an investigation' (see para 3.2.3).

Considerations of speed, simplicity and cost all favour ascertaining body alcohol by analysing breath specimens, but there are circumstances in which this is not possible. Section 7(3) stipulates the conditions under which a specimen of blood or urine may be required instead of breath:

> A requirement under this section to provide a specimen of blood or urine can only be made at a police station or at a hospital; and it cannot be made at a police station unless—
>
> (a) the constable making the requirement has reasonable cause to believe that for medical reasons a specimen of breath cannot be provided or should not be required, or
>
> (b) [specimens of breath have not been provided elsewhere and] at the time the requirement is made a device or a reliable device of the type mentioned in subsection (1)(a) above is not available at the police station or it is then for any other reason not practicable to use such a device there, or
>
> (bb) a device of the type mentioned in subsection (1)(a) above has been used [(at the police station or elsewhere)] but the constable who required the specimens of breath has reasonable cause to believe that the device has not

> produced a reliable indication of the proportion of alcohol in the breath of the person concerned.

The presence of drugs is proved by analysing a specimen of blood or urine rather than breath, and s 7(3) goes on to provide powers to require blood or urine specimens in suspected drugs cases, where:

> (bc) as a result of the administration of a preliminary drug test, the constable making the requirement has reasonable cause to believe that the person required to provide a specimen of blood or urine has a drug in his body, or
>
> (c) the suspected offence is one under section 3A, 4 or 5A of this Act and the constable making the requirement has been advised by a medical practitioner or a registered health care professional that the condition of the person required to provide the specimen might be due to some drug.

A requirement under s 7(3) may be made:

> notwithstanding that the person required to provide the specimen has already provided or been required to provide two specimens of breath.

The words in s 7(3)(b) and (bb) which appear in square brackets above were added with effect from 1 July 2005, by the Serious Organised Crime and Police Act 2005, in contemplation of the type approval of portable evidential breath analysis devices. As already noted, no such devices have, at the time of writing (January 2024), been approved.

The above provisions are considered in turn in this chapter.

4.2 THE PLACE AT WHICH SPECIMENS MAY BE REQUIRED

While a requirement for breath specimens for analysis may, at least for the time being, be made only at a police station, a requirement for a blood or urine specimen may be made at a police station or at a hospital. Road Traffic Act 1988, s 9, on protection for hospital patients (see Chapter 5), applies where the person from whom a specimen is required is a patient.

Although the requirement must be made at a police station or hospital, the specimen itself need not necessarily be taken there. The case of *Russell v Devine* [2003] UKHL 24, [2003] 1 WLR 1187 was decided by the House of Lords on appeal from the Court of Appeal (Criminal Division) (Northern Ireland). It concerned the Road Traffic (Northern Ireland) Order 1995 (SI 1995/2994), the relevant provisions of which are in the same terms as in s 7. A motorist had been required, at a police station, to provide a blood specimen, and consented. The officer contacted a doctor. It transpired that the doctor was the only doctor on duty at a nearby health centre, and the doctor asked the officer to bring the motorist to the health centre. He did so. At the health centre, the officer repeated the requirement for the blood specimen, and a specimen was taken. The House of Lords found that the Court of Appeal had been right to hold that, after the requirement for the blood specimen had been made in the police station, the specimen could be taken elsewhere by a medical practitioner. The requirement made at the police station had not been superseded by the requirement made at the health centre some 15 minutes later.

See also *Denny v DPP* [1990] RTR 417 (para 4.4.7).

4.3 MEDICAL REASONS WHY BREATH CANNOT BE PROVIDED OR SHOULD NOT BE REQUIRED

The first circumstance in which an officer may require a blood or urine specimen in place of a breath specimen is where the officer has reasonable cause to believe that for medical reasons a specimen of breath cannot be provided or should not be required.

4.3.1 Reasonable cause to believe

In *Horrocks v Binns* [1986] RTR 202, the motorist failed to provide breath specimens for analysis, saying he had difficulty because of a cut on his head. The officer did not believe the cut affected the motorist's ability to provide breath specimens, but concluded that it was not practicable to require them and asked instead for a specimen of blood. The motorist refused, but was acquitted of failing without reasonable excuse to provide a blood specimen. On the prosecutor's appeal, the Divisional Court found that the precondition for requiring a blood or urine specimen, in what is now Road Traffic Act 1988, s 7(3)(a), was not met because the officer himself did not think that the defendant had any medical reason which prevented him from providing a specimen of breath. Furthermore, a reliable device was available and it was practicable to use it.

In *White & Gaskell v Proudlock* [1988] RTR 163, at the police station, a motorist was unable to provide breath specimens. The officer formed the view that he might have a medical condition and required a specimen of blood, which the motorist refused to provide. The question for the Divisional Court was whether the officer had had reasonable cause to require the blood specimen. It found that the officer need only have reasonable cause to believe; he need not in fact believe. There may be cases where the officer does not know whether or not to believe that a suspect has a medical condition, but that does not undermine the power to make the requirement.

In *Dempsey v Catton* [1986] RTR 194, when required to provide evidential breath specimens, the suspect said that he had a 'phobia about machines'. The officer required a blood specimen instead, which the suspect refused to provide. On the question of the validity of the requirement for blood, the Divisional Court held that the officer was not required to determine whether the phobia asserted was recognised by medical science. All he could do as a layman was determine whether or not it is capable of being such a condition. If so, the officer has grounds to require a blood specimen. The decision is that of the officer. He need not call a doctor or seek a medical opinion.

The test is objective. In *Davis (Paul) v DPP* [1988] RTR 156, the motorist failed to provide breath specimens, saying he had asthma and a heavy cold. The constable was of the opinion that the motorist could have provided breath specimens but had not made a determined effort. He nevertheless went on to require a blood specimen instead and the motorist was convicted of driving with excess alcohol in blood. Again there was an appeal on the question whether the requirement for a blood specimen was valid. The Divisional Court held that what is or is not a reasonable cause to believe is to be objectively determined; it is immaterial whether the constable actually believes, is dubious, sceptical, or, as here, disbelieving. The motorist's appeal against conviction was dismissed.

In *Davies (Gordon) v DPP* [1989] RTR 391, the motorist refused to supply breath specimens, saying he was taking a drug, which a psychiatrist had told him would influence the alcoholic content of his blood. The officer accepted this as a medical reason why breath specimens could not be provided or should not be required and went on to require a blood specimen. The motorist again declined, saying he had haemophilic tendencies, so the officer required a urine specimen. This time the motorist said there was no medical reason why he could not do so, but that he was taking various vitamins which would influence the result, and again refused. The Divisional Court upheld the officer's decisions to proceed to requiring a blood specimen, then a urine specimen, confirming that in both cases he had reasonable cause to do so.

4.3.2 Medical reasons

Medical reasons why breath specimens cannot be provided or should not be required are not necessarily the same as medical reasons why a blood specimen cannot or should not be taken (see para 4.8.2, and *Steadman v DPP* [2002] EWHC 810 (Admin), [2003] RTR 2 (DC), below). Nor are they necessarily the same as those which would give a defendant a reasonable excuse for failing to provide specimens (see para 10.6.2).

In *Webb v DPP* [1992] RTR 299, the motorist made three attempts to blow into the breath analysis device but failed to provide specimens. She said she did not suffer from any medical condition and was blowing as hard as she could. The officer conducting the procedure saw that she was shaken, upset, apparently distressed and of slight build. He concluded that for medical reasons breath specimens could not be provided and went on to require a blood specimen instead. The question for the Divisional Court was whether the facts could amount to medical reasons. The court emphasised that the test is objective; scepticism is immaterial; and the officer was a layman in medical matters. The facts were capable of amounting to a medical condition within s 7(3).

In *Young (Paula) v DPP* [1992] RTR 328 (DC), it was held that intoxication can amount to a reason why breath cannot be provided or should not be required, although it cannot amount to a reasonable excuse for failing to provide breath specimens (see para 10.7.4).

In *Steadman v DPP* [2002] EWHC 810 (Admin), [2003] RTR 2 (DC), a motorist had with him at the police station a single tablet. He was not asked what it was or what it was for, but he was asked whether he suffered from any illness or injury, and whether he had any medical problems. He said he took sleeping tablets. He was convicted of driving with excess alcohol on the basis of breath specimens. On appeal, he argued that if the officer had considered whether there was reasonable cause to believe that for medical reasons he could not or should not provide specimens of breath, he may have concluded that there was such reasonable cause, and that the breath analysis should not therefore be allowed in evidence. The Divisional Court rejected that. The mere fact that the appellant was taking sleeping pills, and had a tablet on him which he was not asked about, could not have given the police sergeant reasonable cause to believe that the appellant should not be required to provide specimens of breath. Section 7(4) (medical practitioner being of the opinion that there are medical reasons why a specimen of blood cannot or should not be taken – see para 4.8.2) has no bearing on a requirement for breath specimens under s 7(3)(a). There is no requirement under s 7(3)(a) for the officer to seek a medical opinion. Indeed, since it is for the officer to make the decision, seeking a medical opinion might undermine the case.

In *Bodhaniya v CPS* [2013] EWHC 1743 (Admin), (2014) 178 JP 1, the officer was found to have had reasonable cause to believe that for medical reasons breath specimens could not be provided or should not be required. The motorist had been involved in a major motorway accident. At the police station, he provided one specimen of breath but, despite five attempts, did not provide a second specimen.

The investigating officer decided instead to require a blood specimen, which was taken and in due course revealed excess alcohol. On the motorist's appeal against conviction for driving with excess alcohol, the Administrative Court upheld the district judge's finding that it was reasonable to infer that the officer had decided that the appellant had not been able to provide the specimen because of the shock of the road traffic accident, and that in law this could amount to a medical reason to require a blood specimen under s 7(3).

The officer may revert to requiring breath specimens even after moving on to require a blood specimen: see *Durdan v Chief Officer, Metropolitan Police*, unreported, 28 July 1994 (para 3.5.2), where the officer thought there was reasonable cause to believe that for medical reasons breath specimens could not be provided or should not be required, and asked for a blood specimen. But when a doctor was called, the doctor said the suspect could provide breath specimens between spasms of stomach pain, and the officer again asked for breath specimens.

4.4 DEVICE UNRELIABLE, UNAVAILABLE OR IMPRACTICABLE TO USE

4.4.1 At the time of the requirement

The breath analysis device must be unreliable, unavailable or impracticable to use 'at the time the requirement is made', to entitle the officer to require an alternative specimen under Road Traffic Act 1988, s 7(3)(b). It is sufficient that the device proves unreliable while in use in the investigation in question. In *Cotter v Kamil* [1984] RTR 371, the defendant provided two specimens of breath, but the device then indicated that it had reached a temperature at which analysis was unsatisfactory. The officer decided the device was unreliable and required a blood specimen, which the suspect refused to supply. The Divisional Court upheld the requirement for a blood specimen, finding that the time referred to is the time the requirement for the blood or urine is made, not the time at which breath specimens are required.

In *Oxford v Baxendale* [1987] RTR 247, the motorist had provided breath specimens which showed excess alcohol. He was detained, and, some one and a half hours later, the officer realised that the printout revealed a calibration irregularity. The officer therefore required a specimen of blood instead, which the motorist refused to supply. The Divisional Court found that the justices had erred in assuming that they would need further evidence of the unreliability of the device at the time the blood specimen was required; it was open to them to have found that the device remained unreliable.

4.4.2 The meaning of 'unreliable'

A number of cases illustrate the meaning of 'unreliable'. These decisions are to be distinguished from those in which the reliability of the device has been challenged as a way of impugning the resulting breath analysis (see para 3.4.7). The courts have been far readier to find unreliability in the s 7(3)(b) cases.

In *Slender v Boothby* [1986] RTR 385, the breath analysis device did not take account of leap years and the printout showed the second sample to have been taken on 1 March instead of 29 February. The Divisional Court found that the officer was justified in finding that the device was unreliable and going on to require a blood specimen.

Where a calibration check automatically performed by the device was outside the manufacturer's specified range, the officer was entitled to consider the device unreliable and to require a blood specimen: *Waite v Smith* [1986] Crim LR 405, where the final calibration check showed the operating temperature of the device was '38° C high', against the maximum permissible temperature of 37.9° C specified by the manufacturer.

On the other hand, in *Morgan v Lee* [1985] RTR 409, the device had operated correctly but had failed to produce a printout because the paper was tangled. The officer made a record of the result from the display panel on the machine, but concluded that the device was unreliable and required a blood specimen. The suspect refused to supply the specimen. The Divisional Court found that the officer had not had grounds to require a blood specimen. The fact that the printout was not produced did not render the device as a whole unreliable. The officer could have given oral evidence of the matters which would have been on the printout. The motorist had not acted unlawfully in refusing to provide the blood specimen.

By contrast, where the officer knew in advance that there was a printer malfunction, and on the basis that the device was unreliable, required a blood specimen without commencing the breath analysis procedure, the officer's belief that the device was malfunctioning was reasonable and the requirement for a blood specimen was valid: *Haghigat-Khou v Chambers* [1988] RTR 95 (DC), distinguishing *Morgan v Lee.*

Where an 'ambient fail' message appeared and the procedure aborted, but the procedure was then re-started, the error message did not recur, and the breath analysis proceeded normally, there was no requirement on the officer to require a blood or urine specimen. The court was correct to find the breath reading reliable and to convict: *Kang v DPP* [2016] EWHC 3014 (Admin) (see para 3.5.2).

4.4.3 Reasonable belief

The court must address the reasonableness of the officer's belief that the device is unreliable. In *Thompson v Thynne* [1986] RTR 293, the two breath readings were 145 and 117. Because of the wide discrepancy, the officer took the view that the device was not reliable and required a blood specimen. The motorist appealed against conviction for driving with excess alcohol in blood. The Divisional Court found that the words 'a reliable device' meant a device which the officer reasonably believes is reliable. On the facts, the officer's belief that the device was unreliable was reasonable, and the requirement for a blood specimen was lawful.

Where breath analysis readings were 189 and 191 (more than five times the limit), but the suspect showed no signs of intoxication, the officer thought that the breath analysis device might not be reliable, and required a blood specimen instead. The blood analysis result broadly equated with the breath readings. On the motorist's appeal against conviction on the basis of the blood specimen, the Divisional Court confirmed that the test is subjective. What had to be considered was whether or not the officer reasonably believed the device was not reliable. Since the justices had not made a finding on that point, the appeal had to be allowed. See *DPP v Dixon* [1993] RTR 22.

In *Evans v DPP*, *The Times*, 30 May 1996, the device was in working order and calibrated correctly, but the readings were disparate. The officer concluded that the motorist was not blowing correctly and that the results were unreliable. He required an alternative specimen. A urine specimen was provided and the motorist was convicted of driving with excess alcohol in urine. The Crown Court found that the urine specimen had been required unlawfully, given that the device was in proper working order, but nevertheless upheld the conviction of the motorist on the basis of the breath analysis. On further appeal, the Divisional Court found that the only evidence was that from the breath specimens, and that was not sufficient to prove excess alcohol in urine.

In two unreported decisions, the stated cases indicated that the justices had made clear findings that the officers in question had reasonably believed the breath analysis devices to be malfunctioning. As there was nothing before the Divisional Court to counter those findings, the court would not go behind the stated facts to re-examine the question of reasonableness. See *Wootton v DPP*, unreported, 16 June 1992 and *Rathbone v DPP*, unreported, 20 January 1995.

In *Hague v DPP* [1997] RTR 146, the officer mistakenly but honestly believed that the device had not been properly calibrated, and required a blood specimen, which the motorist refused to supply. It later became clear that the breath analysis device was correctly calibrated and was reliable. The Divisional Court found that the breath sample remained admissible in evidence unless and until it was replaced by an admissible sample of blood or urine. The breath specimens were obtained lawfully and in accordance with the statutory procedure by what was found at the trial to be a properly calibrated device. See also *Sykes v DPP* [1988] RTR 129 (para 4.7).

The investigating officer's decision was again upheld in *Kneale v DPP*, unreported, 15 May 2000, where the officer relied on an inspector's written note that if the clock on the breath analysis device was more than one minute wrong, an alternative specimen should be required. The officer knew that the manufacturer's handbook suggested a tolerance of four minutes, but she was also aware that defendants were being acquitted if breath was analysed on machines with clocks which were more than one minute wrong. A blood specimen was taken and the defendant was convicted on the basis of the blood analysis. The Divisional Court said that it did not assist to interpret s 7(3)(b) as imposing a subjective or objective test. The test is that the officer must have a belief based upon reasonable cause or grounds that the machine in unreliable. It is possible reasonably to hold such a belief even if it is not so. She was entitled to heed the advice of the senior officer, whether that advice was right or wrong.

In *Kelsey v DPP* [2008] EWHC 127 (Admin), the Administrative Court rejected an argument that the introduction into s 7(3) of the new provisions in s 7(3)(bb) and (3)(bc) meant that s 7(3)(b) had to be read as imposing an objective test, so that the prosecution had to show that the device had in fact been unreliable or unavailable. The test remains subjective, and where the custody sergeant told the investigating officer that the device was not available because it had a technical fault, the test in s 7(3)(b) was met and the defendant's conviction, on the basis of a blood specimen, was upheld.

4.4.4 Reason to be given to suspect

The officer must tell the suspect the reason he is requiring the blood or urine specimen, and the suspect must understand that a blood specimen will be taken by a doctor, not by the officer: *DPP v Jackson; Stanley v DPP* [1999] 1 AC 406 (HL) (see para 4.13). Where the reason for requiring a blood or urine specimen is that the breath analysis device is not available, it is sufficient that the officer says it is not available; there is no need to elaborate further: *Clayton v DPP*, unreported, 19 October 1998 (DC). Where it was the custody sergeant rather than the investigating officer who told the suspect that the device was not working properly, the suspect suffered no prejudice and the requirement was satisfied: *Bobin v DPP* [1999] RTR 375 (DC).

4.4.5 The meaning of 'not practicable'

Where, at the time the blood specimen was required, there was no officer at the police station who was trained to operate the breath analysis device, it was not practicable to use the device: *Chief Constable of Avon & Somerset v Kelliher* [1987] RTR 305 (DC). Where the suspect was told that the device was not working, that amounted to being told that it was not practicable to use it and the suspect was sufficiently informed of the reason why breath specimens could not be used: *Rawal (Sushil) v DPP*, unreported, 21 March 2000 (DC).

4.4.6 Evidence

The prosecutor must put before the court evidence of the problem with the breath analysis device which justified requiring a blood specimen instead. In *Dye v Manns* [1987] RTR 90, a suspect at the police station was told that no approved breath testing device was available and that a blood specimen was therefore required. There was no evidence before the court that a device had been unavailable. The Divisional Court found that the police must prove the non-availability of a device. The officer's statement did not amount to such evidence in the absence of any response from the suspect that he accepted it or at least did not contradict it. The requirement for a blood specimen was therefore unlawful.

In *Stokes v Sayers* [1988] RTR 89, the Divisional Court stressed that, to justify requiring a blood specimen, it must be shown that the officer believed the breath analysis device was unreliable and that there was evidence upon which the officer could have formed that view. The officer had seen on the visual display of the device the words, '34 low abort'. He concluded that the device was unreliable and required a blood specimen. There was no evidence before the court of the visual display or of the officer's belief that the machine was unreliable. The justices found that the prosecution had failed to establish that the device was unreliable. The Divisional Court concluded that a reasonable bench could have reached that decision and that the blood analysis was therefore inadmissible.

Where a stipendiary magistrate relied on knowledge derived from another case, that only one breath analysis device was installed in the police station in question, the Divisional Court found that to be wrong in principle. On the facts of the case, however, the evidence given by the officer was sufficient to confirm that no other device was available, and the requirement for a blood specimen on the basis that the breath analysis device was not working was therefore valid: *Jarvis v DPP* [1996] RTR 192.

4.4.7 Alternative device

If the breath analysis device proves unreliable, the investigating officer may, rather than go on to require a blood specimen, instead make a further requirement to provide breath specimens into a different device elsewhere. In *Denny v DPP* [1990] RTR 417, the breath analysis device stopped functioning properly after the two specimens had been given. The suspect was taken to another police station where a reliable device was available. Further breath specimens were provided and the defendant was convicted on the basis of the lower reading from those specimens. The Divisional Court found that there was nothing in the statutory provisions to confine the officer to requiring a blood or urine specimen when the breath analysis device has proved unreliable, and upheld the decision to make a repeat requirement for breath specimens.

But the officer is under no obligation to take such a course. In *Chief Constable of Kent v Berry* [1986] RTR 321, the breath analysis device was unreliable, having failed to purge after the first breath specimen, and the suspect was therefore required to provide a blood specimen. He was taken to another police station where a doctor was available to take the blood. The Divisional Court found that the requirement for the blood specimen had been properly made at the first police station. It was not necessary to repeat it at the second station, or to inquire into the possibility of using the breath analysis device installed there.

4.5 DEVICE NOT HAVING PRODUCED A RELIABLE INDICATION

The final situation in which a blood or urine specimen may be required in place of a breath specimen is set out in Road Traffic Act 1988, s 7(3)(bb). It provides for circumstances in which, although the device is operating correctly, there is nevertheless some reason to believe that the breath specimen(s) is or are unsatisfactory with the result that no analysis is made, or that the alcohol concentration indicated may not be reliable. The fact that this provision is invoked does not imply unreliability of the device, only that there may be something amiss with the specimens. The provision also reflects the fact that the present generation of devices is able to detect and signal certain unsatisfactory matters, including:

- an unacceptably wide difference between the two breath readings. See para 3.4.3 for the acceptable range. Such a difference may be detected and indicated by the device itself, or, if the two specimens are taken from two machine cycles, by reference to a table of differences contained in the form MG DD/A;

- the presence of any 'interfering substance', which would again be detected by the device. Such substances include petrol, acetaldehyde and acetone;
- a reading which is 'out of range' (see para 3.4.3);
- the presence of mouth alcohol;
- no reading given.

Where the investigating officer has reasonable cause to believe that the device has not produced a reliable indication of the proportion of alcohol in the subject's breath, whether on the basis of one of the matters listed above or, presumably, on any other basis, the officer may either offer the suspect the opportunity to provide further breath specimens or go on to require a blood or urine specimen under s 7(3)(bb).

In *Jubb v DPP* [2002] EWHC 2317 (Admin), [2003] RTR 19, the officer believed that the device might not have produced a reliable indication. The readings were 52 and 63. The officer offered the motorist the opportunity to repeat the breath analysis procedure, stressing that he was not obliged to do so. In the event he declined, and was required to provide a blood specimen under s 7(3)(bb). The Administrative Court confirmed that it was lawful for the officer to *invite* further breath specimens, but not to require them. It was also lawful to require a blood specimen.

In *Stewart (John Kimball) v DPP* [2003] EWHC 1323 (Admin), [2003] RTR 35, two breath specimens had been analysed and the device generated the message 'breath difference'. The investigating officer gave the suspect the choice of providing further breath specimens, or a blood or urine specimen. The suspect opted to give further breath specimens, and was in due course convicted on the basis of those specimens. The Divisional Court held that s 7(3)(bb) does not oblige the officer to require blood or urine; nor does it preclude offering a further breath test. Since the first two specimens had not enabled the objective of the analysis to be satisfactorily achieved, as required by s 11(3)(b) (see para 10.5.2), effectively no specimens had been provided and there was nothing to stop the officer making a further requirement for breath, although he was not obliged to do so.

In *DPP v Smith (Robert James)* [2000] RTR 341, the Divisional Court upheld the officer's decision that a device had not produced a reliable indication. The two breath readings were 43 and 33. The officer referred to the table of breath difference ranges in the *pro formas* MG DD/A and B, and concluded that the difference was such that there was cause to believe the device had not produced a reliable indication. As advised in the *pro forma*, he went on to require a blood specimen under s 7(3)(bb). The justices found that the decision to require blood was not based on a reasonable cause or belief, but on automatic adherence to the advice in the form, and found no case to answer. On the prosecutor's appeal, the Divisional Court found that, although the device had self-calibrated correctly and was therefore reliable, where there was a disparity between the two readings as great as in this case (30.3 per cent), any reasonable person would be minded to conclude that the indication was unreliable. The status of the form MG DD/A was not in issue.

In *Taylor v DPP* [2009] EWHC 2824 (Admin), the breath analysis readings were 63 and 52, and the device recorded 'breath difference'. The officer administering the procedure thought this was because the motorist had blown too hard and too fast when giving the second specimen. Following the guidance on the MG DD/A form, he decided that, although the device appeared reliable, it may not have produced a reliable indication of the proportion of alcohol. He therefore required a specimen of blood under s 7(3)(bb). The Divisional Court held that the officer's view of why a wide breath difference may have occurred, namely that the appellant had been blowing too hard or too fast, would not of itself constitute reasonable grounds for doubting the veracity of the test results. But the discrepancy between the two breath readings – some 20 per cent over three or four minutes – coupled with the fact that the printout referred to breath difference, entitled the justices to conclude that there was reasonable cause for the officer to determine that the blood test should be taken.

See also *Hussain v DPP* [2008] EWHC 901 (Admin), [2008] RTR 30 (para 10.5.2) and *Kang v DPP* [2016] EWHC 3014 (Admin) (para 3.5.2) where the device registered 'ambient fail'.

4.5.1 Mouth alcohol

The question of mouth alcohol has given rise to a series of cases. The evidential breath analysis devices are designed to measure the alcohol content of 'deep lung air' – the air delivered in a plateau at the end of exhalation. It is a condition of type approval that they do so. This air, having been in close contact with the arterial blood vessels, provides the most accurate indication of the amount of alcohol in the body. Mouth alcohol, usually produced by regurgitation of the stomach contents to the mouth ('eructation', 'reflux' or 'burping'), is to be avoided as it may have the effect of producing a falsely high reading, which would almost always be unfair to a suspect. The effect is, however, short-lived, and it seems that for each of two breath specimens to be affected the subject would have to regurgitate twice – once before each specimen is given.

Not long after the introduction of the new generation of approved devices, it appeared that one of them – the Intoximeter EC/IR – does not in fact always detect mouth alcohol. This question was before the Divisional Court in *DPP v Brown; DPP v Teixeira* [2001] EWHC 931 (Admin), [2002] RTR 23. Magistrates had accepted expert evidence that the Intoximeter EC/IR devices used in the two cases did not always detect mouth alcohol. They found that the devices, and therefore the readings, were unreliable, and acquitted both motorists of driving with excess alcohol. The Divisional Court ruled that, although defendants are entitled to challenge the usual assumption that the device is reliable (*Cracknell v Willis* [1988] AC 450 (HL); see para 3.4.7), no issue of mouth alcohol had arisen on the facts of either case. There was therefore no evidence to challenge the presumption of reliability. The conclusions of the magistrates were overturned.

Brown and Teixeira led to the addition of two questions to the standard procedure. They were to be asked by officers using the Intoximeter EC/IR only, and these two questions gave rise to the argument in *McNeil v DPP* [2008] EWHC 1254 (Admin), [2008] RTR 27. In *McNeil*, before the suspect provided specimens of breath into an Intoximeter EC/IR, the investigating officer, referring to form MG DD/A, asked the first of the two questions – whether or not the suspect had brought up anything from his stomach. The reply was 'no'. The suspect provided two specimens, giving readings of 58 and 59. He was then asked the second question – whether he had burped since the earlier question had been asked. He replied that he had. The officer therefore required a specimen of blood under s 7(3)(bb), as advised in form MG DD/A. The motorist was convicted on the basis of the blood analysis. He appealed, arguing that the blood specimen had been taken unlawfully because the officer did not have reasonable cause to believe the device had not produced a reliable indication. Extraordinarily, the appeal succeeded. The Divisional Court found that the fact that the specimen of breath was or may have been affected by eructation did not give the officer grounds to believe the breath specimens were unreliable, and so the officer was not entitled to require a blood specimen. The conviction was set aside.

The surprising decision in *McNeil* came about as a result of a series of cases which began with *Zafar v DPP* [2004] EWHC 2468 (Admin), [2005] RTR 18. Magistrates had convicted Zafar of driving with excess alcohol, on the basis of breath specimens analysed by an Intoximeter EC/IR, both showing he was well over the limit. On appeal, the Crown Court accepted that he suffered from heartburn causing occasional reflux of the stomach contents to the mouth, and that he had felt discomfort in the stomach during the course of the evening in question and just before blowing into the device. The appellant adduced expert evidence that the device in question was inadequate at detecting mouth alcohol, and argued that it was therefore for the prosecution to prove that the breath analysis was based on deep lung air, not mouth alcohol. The Crown Court rejected that contention and dismissed the appeal. On further appeal, the Divisional Court again upheld the conviction. The question for the court was whether the meaning of 'breath' in Road Traffic Act 1988, s 5 and Road Traffic Offenders Act 1988, s 15(2) was to be confined to deep lung air, or whether it included all of that which was exhaled. The court – perhaps because it was reluctant to allow an unmeritorious appeal – concluded that there was nothing in either Act to suggest that 'breath' should have a special meaning or that the dictionary definition should not apply. As the dictionary definition of 'breath' was not confined to deep lung air, the motorist's appeal failed.

Some four months after its decision in *Zafar*, the Divisional Court gave judgment in *O'Sullivan v DPP* [2005] EWHC 564 (Admin). This was another case concerning mouth alcohol and the Intoximeter EC/IR, although, surprisingly, *Zafar* was not mentioned in the judgment. In *O'Sullivan*, breath specimens analysed by an Intoximeter EC/IR produced readings of 71 and 73. Two and a half hours later, a screening device showed the motorist's breath alcohol to be 53.9. He was convicted of driving with excess alcohol. He appealed, arguing that the Intoximeter EC/IR was unreliable in detecting mouth alcohol and that the breath analysis could have been tainted by mouth alcohol if regurgitation had taken place. He said he had suffered from indigestion, heartburn and a chesty cough for some years but had not sought medical help; he could not remember regurgitating on the night he had provided specimens. The Crown Court upheld the conviction. It found that his positive roadside test indicated that the appellant was over the limit. The closeness of the two Intoximeter readings meant that reflux would have to have taken place to virtually the same degree at regular intervals to produce such close readings. The defendant had not stated in evidence that he had experienced indigestion, heartburn or the like. The final screening test was consistent with the breath analysis readings. The Crown Court concluded that the specimens of breath had not been affected by mouth alcohol or alcohol vapour. The Divisional Court dismissed the motorist's further appeal, finding that the Crown Court had had ample evidence upon which to base its conclusion.

The next relevant case was *Woolfe v DPP* [2006] EWHC 1497 (Admin), [2007] RTR 16, in which *Zafar* was followed. Two specimens were analysed by an Intoximeter EC/IR and the suspect's breath alcohol was shown to be almost twice the limit. The justices found that the defendant suffered from a 'medical condition of regurgitation of the stomach content into the oesophagus with inadequate clearance by the oesophagus'. Since the effect of reflux lasts for a matter of seconds only, they found that repeated reflux could account for the reasonably consistent readings. Following *Zafar*, they found no difference between deep lung breath and breath contaminated by alcoholic mouth contents, and convicted. The Divisional Court confirmed that 'breath' included breath that has been infused with alcohol from the stomach by way of oesophageal reflux, giving a reading that does not reflect the blood alcohol level. (See also *Ng v DPP* [2007] EWHC 36 (Admin), [2007] RTR 35, para 13.3.)

The later cases of *DPP v Darwen* [2007] EWHC 337 (Admin) and *Rweikiza v DPP* [2008] EWHC 386 (Admin) are also relevant to the question of mouth alcohol and breath specimens. These cases differed from those outlined above in two respects. First, the defendants were charged, not with driving with excess alcohol, but with failing without reasonable excuse to provide specimens of breath for analysis. Second, in these cases the court took into account Road Traffic Act 1988, s 11(3), on the sufficiency of specimens (see para 10.5.2). The background to the two decisions is the earlier case of *DPP v Heywood* [1998] 1 RTR 1. In *Heywood*, the driver had blown into a roadside device with insufficient force to make it operate correctly, such that any reading would have been reliable if positive, but unreliable if negative. She was charged with failing without reasonable excuse to provide a specimen for a breath test. The Divisional Court considered s 11(3) and found that the motorist had failed to provide a specimen in that she had given breath in such a quantity or in such a way that it could not be established reliably whether or not it was positive. The objective of s 11(3) was to obtain a reliable reading one way or the other, and her conviction was upheld.

The decision in *Heywood* was applied to evidential breath specimens for analysis in *Darwen*. The suspect Darwen provided a number of partial specimens, and in each case the device recorded that the specimen was incomplete, but nevertheless provided an analysis. The device used was a Lion Intoxilyzer 6000, the only device capable of analysing incomplete specimens. Justices found that the respondent had provided specimens, albeit that they registered as incomplete because the breath supplied did not constitute deep lung air. It is not clear whether or not they relied on *Zafar* in reaching this conclusion, although there is some suggestion in the judgment that perhaps they did. In any event, they dismissed the charge. The prosecutor appealed, on the question whether the justices were correct to find that the specimens were sufficient to satisfy s 11(3). Counsel for the motorist argued that since, following *Zafar*, 'breath' had its ordinary dictionary definition, then the respondent in *Darwen* had provided breath. The Divisional Court, however, relied on *Heywood*, and decided that the respondent had not provided a specimen in accordance with s 11(3). In *Rweikiza v DPP*, on similar facts, the Divisional Court rejected an argument that *Darwen* had been wrongly decided, again finding that the requirements of s 11(3) had not been met, and that the meaning of 'breath' as defined in *Zafar* had no effect on the meaning of 'specimen' in s 11(3).

The effect of these cases was that an officer could not rely on s 7(3)(bb) to require a blood specimen instead of a breath specimen where the suspect answered 'yes' to either of the two questions introduced into the procedure. The unsatisfactory outcome, in theory at least, seemed to be that a person could be convicted on the basis of mouth alcohol alone. These undesirable consequences appear to have arisen from the Divisional Court's unusual decision in *Zafar* to interpret the statutory language without reference to the intention of Parliament and without reference to the breath testing regime as a whole, and from the fact that in *McNeil v DPP* much of the existing case law on s 7(3) was not before the court and was not therefore taken into account.

Form MG DD/A now contains only a single question about the regurgitation of stomach contents. It advises officers to ask the suspect whether, in the preceding 20 minutes, he or she has brought up anything from the stomach. The question is to be asked before requiring breath specimens, and applies regardless of which of the approved devices is in use. Officers are advised to wait 20 minutes before taking specimens in the event of a positive reply to the question. This certainly simplifies the procedure, and appears to have laid to rest arguments concerning contamination of specimens by stomach contents.

4.6 SPECIMENS FOR DRUG TESTING

A specimen of blood or urine for testing for drugs may be taken at a police station only where the suspect has failed a preliminary drug test, or the investigating officer has been advised by an appropriate professional that the condition of the person in question might be due to some drug. Failure to co-operate with a preliminary drug test does not give rise to a right to require a blood or urine specimen. Where a suspect has failed to co-operate with a preliminary test at the roadside, an investigating officer might, at the police station, offer a second chance to do so. If the second offer is taken up, it might save having to call out a medical professional. It would not, though, exonerate the suspect from liability to prosecution for the initial failure to co-operate: see para 3.5.2 and *Hingley-Smith v DPP* [1997] EWHC 952 (Admin) (para 3.4.7).

The statutory powers are contained in s 7(3)(bc) and (c). Section 7(3)(bc) provides that a blood or urine specimen may not be required at a police station unless a preliminary drug test has been administered and, as a result, the officer has reasonable cause to believe that the person has a drug in his or her body. Section 7(3)(c) authorises the investigating officer to require a blood or urine specimen where a medical practitioner or health care professional has advised that the condition of the person in question might be due to some drug. Section 7(3)(c) applies where the suspected offence is one of causing death by careless driving when under the influence of drink or drugs (s 3A); driving or in charge when unfit through drink or drugs (s 4); or driving or in charge with a specified drug above the specified limit (s 5A), but not to suspected excess alcohol cases under s 5.

The officer may make a requirement under s 7(3)(bc) or (c) even if breath specimens have already been provided or required, for example, where breath specimens have proved negative but the person nevertheless appears unfit to drive.

Under s 7(3)(c), the officer's authority to require the blood or urine specimen depends upon there having been a clear oral statement from the doctor (or, now, registered health care professional) that the suspect's condition may be due to some drug. In *Cole v DPP* [1988] RTR 224, a motorist had provided breath specimens which yielded readings of zero. Because of his appearance, the officer thought the motorist might be under the influence of a drug, and called a doctor. The doctor formed the view that the motorist's condition might be due to a drug, or epilepsy, but did not communicate this to the officer. The officer required a blood specimen; the motorist refused, and was convicted of failing without reasonable excuse to provide it. On appeal, the Divisional Court held that there must be a clear oral statement by the doctor to the police officer of his opinion. That had not been done. The requirement for a blood specimen was therefore unlawful and the motorist's appeal succeeded.

On the facts in *Bell v DPP*, unreported, 30 July 1997, the test had been met. Officers stopped a motorist who had been driving erratically. They found white powder on him, which he admitted was amphetamine. He was arrested and at the police station a doctor was called, and examined the motorist. The *pro forma* which the investigating sergeant used to record the procedure contained observations by the doctor, and the words 'impairment through drugs after medical advice' were recorded as the reason for requiring a blood specimen. A blood specimen was taken and the motorist was prosecuted for driving while unfit. The doctor did not give evidence before the justices, nor was any statement by him served on the defence. The defendant argued that the doctor had not advised the sergeant that his condition might be due to some drug, and that the blood specimen had therefore been taken unlawfully. The justices rejected that and convicted him. On appeal, the Divisional Court found that the unchallenged evidence of the sergeant and the contents of the form entitled the justices to infer that the sergeant had been clearly told by the doctor that the defendant's condition might be due to drugs. The appeal was dismissed.

In *Angel v Chief Constable of South Yorkshire* [2010] EWHC 883 (Admin), the Administrative Court said that the purpose of the requirement for medical advice is to protect a suspect from the invasive requirement of a blood test where there is a clear medical explanation for the suspect's condition which excludes the influence of drugs. The condition referred to in s 7(3)(c) is the person's condition at the time of driving. The doctor is entitled to take into account all relevant information relating to the person's earlier condition. The person's condition at the police station may alone be sufficient to enable the doctor to give the necessary advice, but the doctor is not limited to the findings from the police station examination. The issue to be addressed by the medical practitioner is the suspect's condition at the time of the alleged offence, rather than at the time of the medical examination.

In *Twigg v R* [2019] EWCA Crim 1553, [2019] 1 WLR 6533, the appellant driver had left the scene of an accident. He was arrested at home. The arresting officer smelt cannabis and asked the driver if he had smoked anything; he replied, 'not recently'. In interview, he again lied to police, saying that he had not smoked cannabis for months. He told the health care professional that he had not taken any drugs. The health care professional reported that there were no alcohol or drug issues and took the specimen, which showed an excess of delta-9-tetrahydrocannabinol (THC) (cannabis). The appellant was tried for causing death by careless driving while over the limit for a specified drug. At trial, he admitted he was a cannabis user at the relevant time. The trial judge concluded that, although there had been a breach of procedure in taking the blood sample, in all the circumstances, admission of that evidence would not have such an adverse impact on the fairness of the trial that it would be unfair under PACE, s 78 (see para 11.9) to allow the prosecution to adduce it. The driver appealed against conviction, on the ground that the police were not lawfully allowed to require the specimen because the health care professional had not advised that the appellant's condition might be due to some drug. The healthcare professional said she took the specimen because the police had asked for it, but that if the appellant had answered honestly about his drug use, she would have reviewed her opinion about whether he was affected by cannabis.

The Court of Appeal affirmed the general principle that there is no automatic rule requiring the exclusion of evidence because of the manner in which it was obtained. The trial judge was entitled to exercise the judgment she did under s 78 and refuse to exclude the evidence of the blood sample, because the appellant had lied to the health care professional about whether or not he had been taking drugs; if he had not lied, the health care professional's opinion as to whether his condition might have been due to drugs would have altered.

In *Watling v Chief Constable of Suffolk Constabulary and G4S Health Service (UK) Ltd* [2019] EWHC 2342 (QB), [2020] RTR 23, police stopped a vehicle which was being driven erratically. The driver was unable to produce speech or answer questions; there was phlegm around his mouth; his body and arm were shaking; there was no smell of alcohol; the officer had to help him switch off the car engine. A roadside breath test was negative. The driver was arrested for driving while under the influence of drugs. In fact, he had had a stroke, but it was not until a doctor was called to the police station some time later that this was discovered and the suspect was taken to hospital. The claimant sought declarations and damages under the Human Rights Act 1998, alleging that the police and G4S (the company contracted to provide forensic and medical services to detainees) had violated European Convention on Human Rights, arts 3 (prohibition on torture or inhuman or degrading treatment or punishment) and/or 8 (the right to respect for private and family life), in that, had he been dealt with more quickly, the medical outcome would have been better.

The Queen's Bench Division dismissed the claim, finding that the signs of stroke were not the classic ones. They were subtle and would not necessarily be observable by anyone other than a doctor. There were no grounds on which the officers should reasonably have known that the claimant was someone other than a suspected drug-driver. The officers conscientiously kept the claimant under review while he was in custody in an open-minded fashion; they reasonably concluded this was a section 4 case, not a medical emergency. Neither defendant knew or ought to have known otherwise.

The Faculty of Forensic and Legal Medicine has published a *pro forma* to assist forensic physicians in deciding whether a person has a condition which might be due to drink or drugs. It can be viewed at https://fflm.ac.uk/wp-content/uploads/2019/08/Section4_RTAform_Jun19.pdf.

4.7 RELATIONSHIP BETWEEN BLOOD AND BREATH SPECIMENS

There have been situations in which a police officer has required a blood specimen, but then for some reason decided to go back and instead rely on the original breath specimens, or failure to provide them. As noted above (see para 3.5.2), there is nothing to prevent an officer repeating a requirement for breath specimens even after moving on to require a blood specimen: *Durdan v Chief Officer, Metropolitan Police*, unreported, 28 July 1994. But breath analysis may be relied on to found a conviction only if no alternative specimen has in fact been provided. In *Badkin v DPP* [1988] RTR 401, the breath analysis device had failed to produce a printout. The officer decided it might be unreliable and required a blood specimen. A blood specimen was taken and analysed, but the result was not served on the defendant. At the trial, two officers gave evidence of the breath analysis. It also transpired that the clock in the device had been wrong by some five minutes. The defendant was convicted on the basis of the breath analysis. On appeal, the Divisional Court held that if the officer decides that the breath analysis device is not reliable and requires a specimen of blood which is then provided and analysed, any prosecution can thereafter be based only on the analysis of blood and not on that of breath. In any event, in view of the unreliability of the device, the appeal had to be allowed. See also *McLellan v DPP* [1993] RTR 401 (DC), in which *Badkin* was applied.

In *Sykes v DPP* [1988] RTR 129, the motorist provided a first breath specimen which produced a reading of 93, and deliberately failed to provide a second. The officer then, in error, required a specimen of blood, which the motorist refused to supply. The Divisional Court held that the wrongful requirement for blood did not render inadmissible the evidence of the failure to supply breath specimens. His conviction for failing without reasonable excuse to provide breath for analysis was upheld. See also *Hague v DPP* [1997] RTR 146 (para 4.4.3) and *DPP v Boden* [1988] RTR 188 (para 10.6.2). In *Boden*, the defendant had failed to provide first breath specimens, then blood specimens. The Divisional Court found that the prosecutor was entitled to proceed on the basis of the refusal to provide breath.

The Divisional Court has recognised that in some circumstances, evidence of breath analysis may be admissible even if the prosecution is based on another type of specimen. In *Slasor v DPP* [1999] RTR 432, the breath analysis device failed its final calibration test. The motorist was therefore required to provide a specimen of blood, which was duly taken. While transferring the blood from the syringe to the two bottles, it was seen that one of the bottles was cracked. Using a different syringe, the doctor transferred the blood from the damaged bottle to another. The motorist was charged with driving with excess alcohol in the blood. He contended that the blood specimen may have been contaminated. The prosecutor argued that evidence of the breath test should be admitted to show its compatibility with the blood analysis. The Divisional Court held that if there is some relevant and clearly identified purpose for which it is to be adduced, and subject to the exercise of the court's discretion, evidence of breath test results may properly be admissible where the prosecution is based on the analysis of a blood specimen. The prosecution had to prove that the blood analysis was reliable. If the breath results were broadly equivalent to the blood result, then the former might support the reliability of the latter, but expert evidence of the significance of the relationship would be necessary. On the facts, it was unclear whether any such expert evidence had been given, but in any event, the justices were correct to find that the blood analysis result was reliable, even without reference to the breath analysis.

4.8 CHOICE OF SPECIMEN: BLOOD OR URINE

Road Traffic Act 1988, s 7(4), which applies regardless of the offence under investigation, confers on the investigating officer the decision whether the specimen is to be of blood or urine, and who is to take the specimen:

> If the provision of a specimen other than a specimen of breath may be required in pursuance of this section the question whether it is to be a specimen of blood or a specimen of urine [and, in the case of a specimen of blood, the question who is to be asked to take it shall be decided (subject to subsection (4A)) by the constable making the requirement].

Section 7(4A) provides that a constable may not require a blood specimen under s 7(4) if:

(a) the medical practitioner who is asked to take the specimen is of the opinion that, for medical reasons, it cannot or should not be taken; or
(b) the registered health care professional who is asked to take it is of that opinion and there is no contrary opinion from a medical practitioner.

Where (a) or (b) above applies, the constable may require a specimen of urine instead.

The words in square brackets were substituted, and s 7(4A) added, by the Police Reform Act 2002 with effect from 1 April 2003. They introduced the alternative that blood or urine specimens may be taken by a 'registered health care professional', rather than by a medical practitioner. A 'registered health care professional' is a registered nurse, or a registered member of a health care profession designated for the purposes in an order made by the Secretary of State (Road Traffic Act 1988, s 11(2)). Paramedics were so designated by the Registered Health Care Profession (Designation No 2) Order 2003 (SI 2003/ 2462). The provision now appearing in s 7(4A)(a) (blood specimen not to be taken if the medical practitioner is of the opinion that, for medical reasons, it should not be taken) was, before these amendments, contained in s 4.

4.8.1 The choice

Section 7(4) does not require the officer to invite the suspect to express a preference for giving blood or urine: *DPP v Warren* [1993] AC 319. In *Joseph v DPP* [2003] EWHC 3078 (Admin), [2004] RTR 21 (see para 4.8.2), the Divisional Court said that the officer has the 'broadest of discretions' to determine what sort of specimen should be required. In practice, blood is preferred to urine because the taking of the specimen is cleaner and more dignified.

At the time of writing (January 2024), the limits for specified controlled drugs are set as concentrations in blood only, not urine (see para 8.8). A prosecution under s 5A must therefore be based on blood analysis. In practice, however, if there is evidence of impairment, officers would go on to require urine if that were the only specimen obtainable, on the basis that prosecution for unfitness through drugs (see Chapter 7) might be possible.

The House of Lords, in *DPP v Warren* [1993] AC 319, confirmed that s 7(4) is to be construed in the same way whether the requirement for a blood or urine specimen is being made because it is impossible or inappropriate to rely on specimens of breath for one of the reasons in s 7(3), or whether the suspect opted to provide an alternative specimen under s 8(2) because the breath reading is no more than 50. As noted in para 1.3.4, the 'statutory option' in s 8(2) has now been repealed, but, on the basis of *Warren*, it is submitted that case law on s 7(4) arising out of 'option' cases remains good law in relation to blood or urine specimens required under s 7(3) in place of breath specimens. The provisions of s 7(3) to (7) specifically apply to drug-drive cases by virtue of s 7(1A) (see para 4.1).

In *Wyllie v CPS* [1988] Crim LR 753, a case where no breath analysis device was available, the Divisional Court held that the purpose of s 7(4) is to allocate to the investigating officer, rather than to the suspect, the decision whether blood or urine should be required. The subsection does not restrict the officer to requiring only one or the other specimen, so that where the suspect failed to provide a blood specimen, the officer was entitled to require a urine specimen instead. See also *DPP v Taylor* (1997) *The Independent*, 28 July (DC) and *Barnes v Chief Constable of Durham* [1997] 2 Cr App R 505 (para 11.8). In *Hayes v DPP* [1994] RTR 163, a statutory option case, the court acknowledged that the officer, having decided that the specimen was to be a blood specimen, but then being unable to find a doctor to take the specimen, was free to change his mind and require a urine specimen instead.

Where the procedure for requiring a blood specimen was not correctly followed, but it was not then possible to obtain a blood specimen and a urine specimen was required instead, the analysis of the urine specimen was admissible in evidence: *DPP v Garrett* [1995] RTR 302. There, the breath analysis device was not working and the officer required a blood specimen, but there was no record that the officer asked whether there was any reason why blood could not be given (see below). A doctor was called, but, for medical reasons, was unable to take a blood specimen. The officer then required a urine specimen, which showed excess alcohol. The Divisional Court held that the officer was entitled to change his mind about the type of specimen required, and that the right continues up to the time a specimen is actually obtained. Compare the cases of *May v DPP* [2005] EWHC 1280 (Admin) (see para 8.6.1) and *Sykes v DPP* [1988] RTR 129 (see para 4.7).

4.8.2 Medical reasons why blood cannot or should not be taken

As noted above, 'medical reasons' for the purposes of s 7(4A) are not the same as medical reasons why breath specimens cannot be provided or should not be required (see para 4.3.2). Further, the requirement in s 7(4A) that medical reasons be determined by a medical practitioner is in contrast with the position under s 7(3)(a), where the decision is that of the officer alone. See also *Butler (Michael Joseph) v DPP* [2001] RTR 28 and *Townson v DPP* [2006] EWHC 2007 (Admin) (para 5.2.3). Nor are medical reasons under s 7(4A) necessarily the same as medical reasons in the context of a reasonable excuse for failing to provide specimens (see para 10.6.2).

For the officer's duty to ask whether there are any medical reasons why a blood specimen cannot or should not be taken, see *DPP v Jackson; Stanley v DPP* [1999] 1 AC 406 (para 4.13).

Where there are medical reasons why a blood specimen cannot or should not be taken, a urine specimen may be required instead.

In *Johnson v West Yorkshire Metropolitan Police* [1986] RTR 167, a statutory option case, the Divisional Court decided that a repugnance of needles is capable of amounting to a medical reason why blood could not or should not be taken. When the suspect raised such a fear, it was for a medical practitioner, not the officer, to decide whether or not it was a valid medical reason for not providing a blood specimen. In similar circumstances, where a medical practitioner advised the officer, by telephone, that a fear of needles does not amount to a medical reason for not supplying a blood specimen, it was not for the court to question the correctness or otherwise of the medical opinion and the officer was entitled to require a blood specimen: *Andrews v DPP* [1992] RTR 1 (DC). In another 'fear of needles' case, the fear was capable of being a medical reason, and the officer was not entitled, on the basis of that alone, to insist on a blood specimen: *R v Epping Justices ex parte Quy* [1998] RTR 158.

When, in response to the question whether there was any reason why a specimen of blood could not or should not be taken, the suspect replied, 'I do take tablets', that could have amounted to a medical reason, and the officer should have considered it. Where he did not consider it but went straight on to ask for a blood specimen, the Divisional Court overturned the appellant's conviction on the basis of that blood specimen: *Wade v DPP* [1996] RTR 177.

In *DPP v Wythe* [1996] RTR 137, when asked whether there was any medical reason why a blood specimen could not or should not be taken, the defendant said he was a diabetic and needed two injections a day. He did not want other people to use needles on him. The officer, observing that the defendant had pierced ears and tattoos, proceeded to require a blood specimen, and the defendant replied, 'if you take it out of my finger, yes; if it is going to come out of my arm, no'. The officer asked a medical practitioner whether there was a medical reason why blood could not or should not be required. There was no evidence of the outcome, and the defendant was charged with failing without reasonable excuse to provide a blood specimen for analysis. The Divisional Court found that the defendant had raised a medical condition which, although not particularly convincing, should have caused the officer to delay requesting the blood specimen until a medical practitioner had expressed an opinion. In the circumstances, the requirement to provide a blood specimen was unlawful.

The officer need not tell the suspect that his only right to object to giving blood and to give urine instead would be for medical reasons, which would be determined by a medical practitioner. It was sufficient that the officer asked whether there were any medical reasons why the suspect should not provide a blood specimen: *DPP v Joiner* [1997] RTR 387.

Where a medical officer was of the view that an arrested person was probably under the influence of some drug, and the investigating officer then required a blood specimen, the suspect answering, 'you are not going to examine me', that did not amount to a medical reason why a blood specimen could or should not be given: *DPP v Gibbons* [2001] EWHC 385 (Admin), 165 JP 812.

Where the suspect said there was no medical reason why a blood specimen could not or should not be taken, but had with him tablets and a spray, the officer was not obliged to seek medical advice: *Kinsella v DPP* [2002] EWHC 545 (Admin).

In *Jubb v DPP* [2002] EWHC 2317 (Admin), [2003] RTR 19, the defendant said at the police station that he occasionally suffered from asthma for which he had medication, but when asked whether there was any medical reason why a blood specimen should not be taken, he said there was none. The Administrative Court held that the requirement to provide a blood specimen was lawful.

Joseph v DPP [2003] EWHC 3078 (Admin), [2004] RTR 21 was an old statutory option case. Here, before deciding whether the specimen was to be of blood or urine, the suspect, a Rastafarian, said he could not give blood for religious reasons. The officer understood that a blood specimen was to be required unless there were medical reasons why not, and did not consider the alternative of a urine specimen. The defendant was convicted on the basis of the breath specimens. The Divisional Court found that s 7(4) does not require that a blood specimen be taken unless there are medical reasons why that should not be done, but confers on the officer a wide discretion to decide which sort of specimen should be required. In the rare circumstances of this case, the court found that the officer should have considered the religious reason proffered before making his decision. The appeal against conviction succeeded. It is submitted that the officer's discretion survives the repeal of the statutory option.

If a suspect simply refuses to provide a blood specimen, the officer is under no duty to investigate the reason, or to call a doctor to advise whether there may be a medical reason why a blood specimen could or should not be taken: *Grix v Chief Constable of Kent* [1987] RTR 193 (DC).

The principles which emerge from this line of case law are that, where a blood or urine specimen is to be required instead of a breath specimen:

- the investigating officer has the decision whether the specimen is to be of blood or urine;
- if the suspect refuses to provide a blood specimen, or if it proves impossible to obtain such a specimen, the officer may require a urine specimen. The case law does not confirm that an officer who has required a urine specimen may then require a blood specimen instead;
- medical reasons for not providing a blood or urine specimen are to be decided by the medical practitioner, or health care professional if not contradicted by a medical practitioner;
- a fear or repugnance of needles may be capable of being a medical reason for not providing a blood specimen and should not be dismissed without consideration by a medical professional.

4.9 TIME FOR PROVIDING URINE SPECIMEN

Road Traffic Act 1988, s 7(5) is to the effect that a specimen of urine is to be provided within one hour of its being required, and 'after the provision of a previous specimen of urine'. Thus, it is the second of two specimens, provided within an hour of the requirement, which forms the basis of any prosecution; the first is discarded. The first specimen need not be of any particular quantity: *R v Radcliffe* [1977] RTR 99 (CA).

In *Prosser v Dickeson* [1982] RTR 96, the suspect had begun to urinate and was told by the officer to stop. The officer emptied and washed the receptacle and told the suspect, who had not put his penis away, to continue urinating. The entire operation took no more than two minutes. The Divisional Court upheld the justices' finding that the procedure amounted to a single operation, momentarily discontinued, and there had been only one specimen, not two. By contrast, in *Over v Musker* [1985] RTR 84 (DC), although there was only a short lapse of time – one minute – between giving the two specimens, the court found that two specimens were nevertheless provided. The distinction was that in *Over v Musker*, the defendant provided the first specimen. A sergeant told him to say when he was ready to provide the second specimen. The defendant dressed and resumed his seat. He then, albeit only a short time later, said he was ready to provide the second specimen. Even so, this appears not to meet the purpose of the procedure, which is to void the bladder of urine which may have been there for some time, and then wait until a specimen of freshly secreted urine can be taken. See also the cases described in para 10.5.8.

Ryder v CPS [2011] EWHC 4003 (Admin), (2012) 176 JP 558 concerned the provision of a urine specimen from a motorist who had been involved in a road traffic accident and was in hospital with a catheter in place. The catheter had two chambers; the first collected urine in a continuous flow and drained it into a second, larger chamber. When the procedure for taking the evidential specimen began, the first chamber was drained to the lower chamber and allowed to refill. One minute later, the first chamber was drained again and when it had filled once more, the officer took a specimen from the first chamber. The specimen was analysed and showed excess alcohol. The motorist appealed against conviction, arguing that a person provides a specimen only by excreting it; and that, since urine was flowing continuously, there had not been separate specimens. The Administrative Court rejected both arguments, finding that the statute does not require the suspect to urinate, but that the specimen be provided; and that, once the first chamber was emptied, urine which then flowed into it was not the same sample as that which had been drained away, but a separate specimen.

4.10 FAILING WITHOUT REASONABLE EXCUSE TO PROVIDE

Road Traffic Act 1988, s 7(6) makes it an offence to fail without reasonable excuse to provide a specimen when required to do so under s 7. This is considered in detail in Chapter 10.

4.11 THE STATUTORY WARNING

Road Traffic Act 1988, s 7(7) stipulates that, when requiring a specimen under s 7, a constable must warn the suspect that failure to provide it may lead to prosecution. In *DPP v Jackson; Stanley v DPP* [1999] 1 AC 406, the House of Lords found that failure to give the warning must lead to the acquittal of the accused. The case law on the warning is considered in Chapter 10 (see para 10.9).

4.12 CONSENT TO THE TAKING OF A BLOOD SPECIMEN

Road Traffic Act 1988, s 11(4) stipulates that a person provides a specimen of blood if, and only if:

- the person consents to the taking of such a specimen. Road Traffic Offenders Act 1988, s 15(4) provides for a blood specimen to be disregarded if it was not taken with consent; and
- the specimen is taken by a medical practitioner or a registered health care professional.

In *R v Palfrey, R v Sadler* [1970] 1 WLR 416, it was argued that consent to taking blood specimens had not been proved, although it was not said that the specimens had been taken against the will of the suspects. The Court of Appeal ruled that if a defendant believed a specimen had been taken without true consent, it would be for the defendant to raise the issue and show that there is at least some substance to the assertion. The court would then have a discretion whether or not to exclude the analysis of the specimen.

In *Hier v Read* [1978] RTR 114, the suspect agreed to provide a blood specimen but then asked to read the consent form before signing it. The Divisional Court found that this was not a conditional agreement amounting to refusal. The question was whether or not he had agreed to provide the specimen, not whether or not he had agreed to sign the form.

For many years the practice was to call the medical practitioner to the police station and ask the suspect for consent in the presence of the medical practitioner. The MG DD/B form, however, now provides for the officer to ask the suspect to consent before the medical practitioner (or, now, health care professional) is summoned to the police station. No doubt this is to avoid the trouble and expense of calling the professional person to the police station only then for the suspect to decline to give the specimen. The Divisional Court considered the consequences of this change in *Persaud v DPP* [2010] EWHC 52 (Admin). The court, following the Scottish case of *Friel v Dickson* [1992] RTR 366, said, *obiter*, that consent given in the presence of the investigating officer alone does not obviate the need for consent to be given in the presence of the medical practitioner or health care professional who would actually take the specimen. See also *Rawlins v Brown* [1987] RTR 238. The current version of the MG DD/B form also now includes (para B7) provision for consent to be sought again in the presence of the person who is to take the specimen.

As to certificates of consent, see para 11.3.2.

4.13 THE PROCEDURE FOR MAKING THE REQUIREMENT

The House of Lords has twice reviewed the procedure to be adopted by the investigating officer when requiring specimens of blood or urine. In *DPP v Warren* [1993] AC 319, a motorist had been arrested. At the police station, the breath analysis device was not working properly and the officer administering the procedure therefore required a specimen of blood or urine under Road Traffic Act 1988, s 7(3)(b). He used the following words:

> The approved evidential breath testing device cannot be used on this occasion because the calibration check has proved unsatisfactory. Accordingly, I require you to provide an alternative specimen, which will be submitted for laboratory analysis. The specimen may be of blood or urine but it is for me to decide which. If you

> provide a specimen you will be offered part of it in a suitable container. If you fail to provide a specimen you may be liable to prosecution. Are there any reasons why a specimen of blood cannot or should not be taken by a doctor? … Will you provide a specimen of blood?

A blood specimen was taken and the motorist was charged with driving with excess alcohol. The magistrate found no case to answer because the wording used did not allow the motorist to make representations as to which type of specimen he would prefer to supply, as then required under *DPP v Byrne (Paul)* [1991] RTR 119 (DC). On the prosecutor's successful appeal to the House of Lords, it was held that the formula to be used to make the requirement is 'no more and no less than the formula used in the instant case or words to the like effect', but there is no need to invite the driver to express a preference for giving blood or urine. The case of *DPP v Byrne* was overruled.

In the cases which followed, courts were inconsistent in their responses to failure to meet the requirements in *DPP v Warren* [1993] AC 319. Sometimes failure to observe a requirement was held to lead automatically to an acquittal; sometimes it was found not necessarily to be a bar to conviction. The issue was again before the House of Lords in *DPP v Jackson; Stanley v DPP* [1999] 1 AC 406, in which it was held that, with three exceptions, the requirements in *Warren* are not mandatory in the sense that non-compliance should lead to acquittal. The first two exceptions are that, when the requirement is made under s 7(3), the warning of the risk of prosecution for failure to provide, and the statement of reason why breath specimens cannot be taken or used, must both be given; if either is omitted, the prosecution fails. The third exception relates to the former 'statutory option' (see para 1.3.4) and is no longer of relevance. In respect of s 7(3), the House of Lords went on to find that a suspect should be aware of the role of the doctor, but that it does not matter whether it is the officer who makes him aware. As long as the suspect realises that the specimen will be taken by a doctor (or, now, by a registered health care professional), not by the officer, the charge should not be dismissed because the officer failed to tell the suspect that the specimen would be taken by a doctor. Officers should still use the formula in *DPP v Warren*, but in relation to reasons why a blood specimen could or should not be taken, the House of Lords found nothing in the legislation and no considerations of fairness requiring the officer to ask the suspect about non-medical reasons. The suspect should therefore be asked whether there are any *medical* reasons why a blood specimen could or should not be taken.

In *Jackson*, a motorist had been charged with failing without reasonable excuse to provide a specimen of blood for analysis. Police had arrested him on suspicion of driving while unfit through drink or drugs. At the police station, he was examined by a doctor, whose opinion was that his symptoms were consistent with having taken drugs. The sergeant conducting the procedure then requested a sample of blood or urine, warning of the consequences of refusal. The motorist refused. He was warned for a second time and asked if he had any representations whether the sample should be of blood or urine, and again refused. The sergeant asked if there was any reason why a specimen could not be taken, adding that his only right to object to giving blood and to give urine instead would be for a medical reason to be determined by a doctor. The motorist replied, 'I don't like needles but I'm not giving anything anyway'. The House of Lords upheld the Divisional Court's rejection of the defendant's argument that the statement, 'I don't like needles' raised a potential medical reason for not providing a specimen of blood. Whether or not it did so was a question of fact, and, on the facts, the officer was not obliged to investigate further. There is no need for a police officer to ask whether there are non-medical reasons for a blood specimen not being given. The defendant had made clear that he was not going to give a specimen of blood or urine, and had suffered no prejudice.

In *Chand v DPP; DPP v Chand*, unreported, 19 October 1998 (DC), the motorist was charged with, *inter alia*, failing to provide a specimen of blood. The breath analysis device was unavailable because of a defect. The officer told the motorist that he required him to provide a specimen of blood or urine for a laboratory test; the motorist would have an opportunity to make representations as to which it would be, but that he, the officer, would make the final decision; and that refusal would render the motorist liable to prosecution. The motorist agreed to provide a specimen, and the officer asked if he had any representations why it should not be blood. The motorist refused to supply a blood specimen, and there was no further conversation. The Divisional Court upheld the justices' finding that the officer did not inform the respondent that he had decided that the specimen would be one of blood, and that he had not therefore required a specimen of blood. The prosecutor's appeal against acquittal was dismissed.

The requirements established by the case law are reflected in the standard form MG DD/B used by investigating officers, which suggests that officers use the following wording:

> As:
>
> - a reliable breath testing device is not available for use or it is not practicable to use a breath testing device; or
> - I have reasonable cause to believe that for medical reasons a specimen of breath cannot be provided or should not be required; or
> - I have reasonable cause to believe that the device used has not produced a reliable indication of the proportion of alcohol in your breath;
>
> I will require you to provide me with a specimen of blood or urine which, in the case of blood, will be taken by a doctor or health care professional. It is for me to decide which it will be unless a doctor or health care professional is of the opinion

> that for medical reasons a specimen of blood cannot or should not be taken, in which case it will be of urine. You may inform the doctor or health care professional of medical reasons why a specimen of blood cannot be taken by them, but the matter will be for the doctor or health care professional to determine. … I warn you that failure to provide a specimen will render you liable to prosecution. Before I decide whether the specimen shall be of blood or urine, are there any medical or other reasons why a specimen of blood cannot or should not be taken by a doctor or health care professional?

See also *Roberts v DPP* [2008] EWHC 643 (Admin) and *Morris v DPP* [2008] EWHC 2788 (Admin), (2009) 173 JP 41 (para 11.7).

4.14 TAKING AND DIVIDING THE SPECIMEN

Road Traffic Offenders Act 1988, s 15(5) and (5A) reads as follows:

> (5) Where, at the time a specimen of blood or urine was provided by the accused, he asked to be provided with such a specimen, evidence of the proportion of alcohol or any drug found in the specimen is not admissible on behalf of the prosecution unless—
>
> (a) the specimen in which the alcohol or drug was found is one of two parts into which the specimen provided by the accused was divided at the time it was provided, and
> (b) the other part was supplied to the accused.
>
> (5A) Where a specimen of blood was taken from the accused under section 7A of the Road Traffic Act 1988, evidence of the proportion of alcohol or any drug found in the specimen is not admissible on behalf of the prosecution unless—
>
> (a) the specimen in which the alcohol or drug was found is one of two parts into which the specimen taken from the accused was divided at the time it was taken; and
> (b) any request to be supplied with the other part which was made by the accused at the time when he gave his permission for a laboratory test of the specimen was complied with.

The clear purpose of these provisions is to allow a defendant to have part of the specimen independently analysed, for comparison with the analysis conducted for the prosecutor. But where the police, in error, notified a person who had supplied a blood specimen that no further action would be taken, and he then threw away his part of the specimen without having it analysed, his conviction was upheld. He had taken no steps to have his part of the specimen analysed. Nor had he indicated any wish to challenge the prosecution's analysis: *Mokhra v DPP*, unreported, 10 December 1996 (DC).

In *Byrne (Simon David) v DPP* [2003] EWHC 397 (Admin), the trial court was shown a video recording of a conversation between the custody sergeant and the defendant. As he handed the defendant his part of the sample, the sergeant was heard to say that if the defendant had his specimen analysed, it would probably come back three times over the limit, it would be expensive, and that no one had done so before. On an argument that this discouraged him from sending his part of the specimen for analysis, the Administrative Court noted that the trial court had found as a fact that the appellant was given written instructions with his sample, and ruled that he was not discouraged at all from sending his sample away for analysis. There was no question of unfairness, although the court emphasised that it is extremely undesirable for police officers to give advice of the kind given in this case, even if what is said is true.

4.14.1 Request by suspect a prerequisite

It is for the suspect to initiate the division of the specimen, except where the specimen is taken from a person who is incapable of consenting (see Chapter 5). There is no requirement that the right to do so be explained, although Form MG DD/B includes the wording, to be read to the suspect when a blood or urine specimen is required, 'you will be supplied with part of the specimen if you so require'. Under earlier versions of the legislation, by contrast, the investigating officer was obliged to offer part of the specimen to the suspect. The present position may be a balancing exercise between the suspect who provides breath specimens and clearly cannot take away part for comparative analysis, and the suspect who provides a blood or urine specimen who has long had the right to a part. In practice, those who supply blood or urine are still offered part of the specimen, and this is covered in the MG DD forms. The notes there also suggest that it is usual practice to divide the specimen, regardless of whether or not the suspect has asked for part, or has been offered a part and declined it.

In *Campbell v DPP* [2003] EWHC 559 (Admin), the Administrative Court made plain that cases decided in relation to Road Traffic Act 1962, s 2(5) no longer applied. That provision required the officer to offer a part of a blood or urine specimen to the suspect, or, if it was not practicable to divide a blood specimen, to supply another specimen which the suspect might consent to provide. The court did, however, remark that there might be circumstances in which a defendant might challenge the admissibility of an analysis on the basis of having suffered prejudice by being unaware of the right to request a specimen.

But in *Jones v CPS* [2003] EWHC 1729 (Admin), (2003) 167 JP 481, the Divisional Court found no irregularity if part of the specimen is not offered. The specimen was divided and the suspect was asked which part she wanted; she pointed to one of the specimens but did not take hold of it. Both parts were sealed and placed in the refrigerator. Shortly afterwards, the suspect was released; she did not ask for the specimen. The Divisional Court held that pointing to one of the specimens did not amount to a request for it:

> There must be a request by the accused to be provided with a specimen. The scheme of the Act is clearly that this triggers the process of dividing the specimen. It may be that the specimen, as here, was divided without a request, but without a request, the provisions of section 15(5) do not engage.

The Court of Appeal of Northern Ireland reached the same conclusion in *McClenaghan v McKenna* [2001] NI 327, on the basis of a provision couched in the same terms.

In the case of a person incapable of consenting to the taking of the specimen, Road Traffic Offenders Act 1988, s 15(5A) envisages the division of the specimen when it is taken, so that a part is available should the accused later request it.

4.14.2 No choice as to part

Road Traffic Offenders Act 1988, s 15(5) contemplates that a person may ask 'to be provided with such a specimen'. This is the wording despite the fact that what is to be supplied is part of a single specimen.

The suspect has no choice as to which part is supplied. In *Lidington v DPP* [2006] EWHC 1984 (Admin), the suspect was unconscious and a blood specimen was taken under Road Traffic Act 1988, s 7A (see Chapter 5). When the suspect recovered consciousness, the officer told her a specimen had been taken. The suspect did not ask for part of the specimen, but the officer gave her one of the phials, without offering her a choice between the two. She was in due course convicted on the basis of an analysis of the blood, and appealed. The Divisional Court roundly rejected the argument that there was a choice about which part the suspect is to have.

4.14.3 Envelopes and labelling

In *Perry v McGovern* [1986] RTR 240, the defendant had elected to take part of the blood specimen for independent analysis. The part given to her was not put into an envelope, sealed and signed in the conventional way, and the officer, in error, told her that because of this, her part of the specimen could not be submitted for analysis as the correct procedure had not been followed. She therefore did not seek to have it analysed. She was convicted by justices, but the Divisional Court overturned her conviction on the basis that she had been misled, albeit in good faith.

In *DPP v Snook* [1993] Crim LR 883, it was held that the procedure for dividing a blood specimen was correctly followed where the phial containing the defendant's part was not placed in an envelope. He was given an envelope separately. He contacted an analyst the next day, who told him that analysis would be of little value because the specimen had not been sealed in an envelope. As a result, he decided not to go ahead with the analysis. On the prosecutor's appeal against acquittal, the Divisional Court emphasised that what is known as the 'brown envelope procedure' is not a statutory requirement; what the analyst had said was nothing to do with the prosecution or the police. The statutory requirements had been met.

The fact that a blood specimen was wrongly labelled did not mean that it had not been supplied: *Butler v DPP* [1990] RTR 377 (DC), where the doctor inadvertently labelled the specimen with the name of the officer conducting the procedure rather than with the name of the suspect. The analyst to whom the defendant submitted the specimen declined to analyse it upon discovering the error, but gave no further explanation. The Divisional Court nevertheless found that the wrong labelling did not mean the specimen had not been supplied for the purpose of the legislation.

A challenge under European Convention on Human Rights, art 6 featured in *DPP v Higgins* [2001] EWHC 871 (Admin). The custody sergeant inadvertently labelled the specimen with the name of another prisoner. The laboratory to which the defendant sent his part for analysis declined to proceed because the specimen bore the name of someone other than the person requesting the analysis. The defendant took no further steps to have the specimen analysed. The prosecutor appealed against the justices' decision to stay proceedings as an abuse of process. The Divisional Court found the case on all fours with *Butler v DPP* [1990] RTR 377 (DC). There was no evidence that the error had prevented the respondent from obtaining an independent analysis. He could have explained the error, or contacted another analyst, but did not. There was no evidence that the error prevented a fair trial or made the trial in any way unfair.

4.14.4 Taking the specimen

Police forces have kits containing the necessary equipment for taking and dividing specimens of blood and urine. The containers are pre-packed with preservative to prevent bacterial activity which could raise or lower the alcohol content, while packs for blood specimens also contain anti-coagulant. Each kit carries a unique bar-coded serial number, which is printed onto the tamper-evident bags; labels with the same barcode are provided for attaching to the specimen vials. Form MG DD/B contains notes on the handling of the specimens. These include instructions that the containers are to be shaken for at least

30 seconds until the preservative dissolves, and advice on labelling and sealing in tamper-evident bags. As noted above (see para 4.14.2), a suspect who wishes to take a part of the specimen is not entitled to choose which part to take, although in practice it is customary to offer a choice (except where the subject is not capable of consenting to the taking of the specimen; see Chapter 5). The suspect's part is placed in a tamper-evident bag and sealed. The suspect is given a list of analysts and advised on storage of the specimen. If the suspect declines to accept part of the specimen, depending on local practice, both parts may be sent to the laboratory together, or the suspect's part may be retained by the police in secure refrigerated exhibit storage. Normally, only one part is analysed, but there seems nothing to prevent the laboratory from analysing the second part if, for example, the first part proved insufficient.

Where the specimen is to be analysed for excess drugs, it should be refrigerated or chilled as soon as possible and should remain chilled in transit to the laboratory. The officer should also send to the laboratory a completed Form MG DD/E, setting out the offence(s) (s 5, excess alcohol; s 5A, excess drugs or s 4, impairment) in respect of which analysis is required. The notes to the form emphasise that, because of the large number of drugs affecting behaviour or driving performance, their lower concentration in body fluids and the limited volume of a specimen, as much information as possible should be provided to the laboratory concerning symptoms, behaviour and other circumstances of the case. At the time of writing (January 2024), four laboratories are accredited in respect of all the drugs listed in s 5A, but not all of them undertake analysis on behalf of potential defendants.

The officer should also obtain from the medical professional who took the specimen a certificate (form HO/RT5) of having taken the specimen with the consent of the suspect (see para 4.12).

Once a suspect has provided a blood specimen, there is no obligation to supply a further specimen. In *Beck v Watson* [1980] RTR 90, the defendant was properly required to provide a blood specimen, and the doctor took a specimen which was sufficient and suitable for analysis. But the doctor then spilled part of the specimen, and what remained was insufficient for analysis. The prosecution was not permitted to rely on a second blood specimen which was then requested and given.

In *Dear v DPP* [1988] RTR 148, the doctor took two attempts to obtain a sufficient blood specimen. The police retained part of the second specimen, while the part given to the suspect was a mixture from the first and second specimens. The Divisional Court took the view that, since the legislation refers to a specimen taken on a single occasion, the procedure had been incorrect and the evidence from the blood analysis conducted on behalf of the prosecutor was inadmissible.

Where, albeit unknowingly, swabs containing alcohol, which could result in artificially high alcohol readings in the specimens, had been used before taking blood specimens, an order of *certiorari* was available to overturn the convictions: *R v Bolton Magistrates' Court ex parte Scally and Others* [1991] 1 QB 537.

A conviction may be based on a third or even later urine specimen. In *Nugent v Ridley* [1987] RTR 412 (DC), the defendant refused to provide a breath specimen, saying he had a bad cold. He then refused to supply a blood specimen, saying he was afraid of needles. A doctor was called, who was satisfied that he did have a phobia about needles but persuaded him to produce a urine specimen. The first urine specimen was discarded. The officer began the procedure for requiring urine specimens and two further specimens were provided. The latter of those two was sent for analysis and showed excess alcohol. The motorist argued that the statute permitted only two urine specimens and that the analysis of a third was not therefore admissible. The Divisional Court found nothing to prevent the specimen on which the prosecution is based being the third or even a later specimen, as long as it was provided after the provision of a previous specimen, and within an hour of the request, in accordance with what is now s 7(5). The case law relating to the taking of breath specimens (see *Howard v Hallett* [1984] RTR 353 (para 3.6)) does not apply to urine specimens.

See also the cases discussed in para 10.5.8.

4.14.5 The provenance of the specimen

In a number of cases, defendants have sought to challenge the provenance of the specimen analysed for the prosecution.

In *Bentley v Northumbria Police* [1984] RTR 276, an analyst gave oral evidence that he had analysed blood from a phial marked 'Bentley', which had been accompanied by a form showing a sample number allocated by the laboratory, and that the alcohol level was 247.6. No certificate of analysis was adduced in evidence. The Divisional Court found that the justices knew only that a sample of blood had been taken from the defendant on the day of the alleged offence, and that a sample of blood bearing the name 'Bentley' was analysed, but there was no evidential link between the sample taken and the sample analysed. There could have been a number of reasons why the sample analysed may not have been the one taken from the defendant, none of which was fanciful. Mr Bentley's appeal against conviction succeeded.

In *Stevens v DPP*, unreported, 9 December 1992, the defendant submitted that it was not proved that the blood analysed was his. There had been no evidence of the writing on the label, so that the label was hearsay. The Divisional Court found that the details on the label coincided with the findings of fact by the Crown Court, which had the label before it. The defendant had not challenged the label. Nor had he questioned the officer whether or not he had written on the label. There was therefore ample material before the Crown Court to entitle it to conclude that the sample of blood analysed was, indeed, that of the appellant.

Where there was no evidence of how a specimen was transported from the police station to the laboratory, that was not of itself sufficient to cast doubt on the provenance of the specimen. In *Tremlett v Fawcett*, *The Times*, 9 October 1984 (QBD), a motorist provided a urine specimen, which was divided and sealed in the usual way. One part was given to him and the other was placed in the refrigerator at the police station. A labelled specimen was received at the Home Office Forensic Science Laboratory a few days later. It showed 271 milligrammes of alcohol in 100 millilitres of urine. At the hearing, the motorist submitted that there was no case to answer because the prosecution had failed to prove that the specimen had been properly taken from the refrigerator at the police station and delivered to the laboratory. That submission was rejected and he was convicted. On appeal, the Queen's Bench Division found that there was ample evidence upon which the justices could be satisfied that the sample analysed was the appellant's. It would be 'coincidence upon coincidence upon coincidence' that the sealed container should be labelled with the details which corresponded precisely with those given by the officers. They included the name (correctly recorded) of the appellant, the police force, the division, the station, the date, the time and the officer in the case.

In *Gregson v DPP* [1993] Crim LR 884, the defendant argued that there was insufficient evidence to show that the specimen analysed was the specimen taken from him. The sergeant had labelled two containers with the motorist's name, the police force, division and station, the time, and the name of the officer in the case. The doctor also signed the labels. One container was put in a bag for transmission to the laboratory and the sergeant gave evidence that he had labelled the bag with the initials 'JVR'. The officer who later sent the specimen for analysis gave evidence that the bag was marked 'JVR 1'. The Divisional Court found that this amounted to overwhelming evidence that the specimen analysed was that taken from the defendant.

The mere fact that, for an unknown reason, the analyst had deleted the defendant's forenames from the form which accompanied the specimen to the laboratory did not disentitle the justices from finding that the specimen which had been analysed was that taken from the defendant: *McGinty v DPP*, unreported, 18 March 1996 (DC).

Inconsistencies in the documentation likewise did not defeat the prosecution in *Rawal v DPP*, unreported, 21 March 2000. In that case, the officer had marked the specimen with his initials, but the police courier who took the specimen to the laboratory for analysis noted that it was marked with the defendant's name and the initials of the doctor who took the specimen. Further, the label referred to a police station other than the station to which the defendant had been taken. The Divisional Court noted that the specimen taken to the laboratory was labelled with the name of the defendant, as was the specimen analysed. The label also showed the correct date and time, the police force, and the name of the arresting officer.

In *Mills v DPP* [2003] EWHC 1451 (Admin), on the other hand, there was sufficient doubt about the provenance of the specimen that the Divisional Court overturned the appellant's conviction. The officer conducting the procedure said he had labelled the specimen, but did not say he had put it into the refrigerator from which the driver took it for delivery to the laboratory. The officer said he had marked the specimen 'ERP 2100', but the driver said the specimen he took to the laboratory was marked 'CJ/210/01'. The label on the specimen which was analysed 10 days later included further details. It was not known who had added these details, but they included that the specimen had been taken at Chorley, although the suspect had been at Skelmersdale police station.

The fact that there was no proof of service of the certificate of the analyst of a blood specimen meant that there was no evidence concerning the labelling of the specimen at the police station, and therefore nothing to identify the specimen as having been supplied by the defendant: *Whyte v DPP* [2003] EWHC 358 (Admin) (see para 11.3.3).

In *Byrne v DPP* [2003] EWHC 397 (Admin), the defendant, among other matters, argued that there was no proper evidence that the blood analysed was his. There had been no evidence of the labelling of the specimen. The Administrative Court, however, upheld the district judge's finding that the blood analysed was that of the appellant on the basis that the appellant's name and a reference code, comprising three letters and 10 digits, appeared above a barcode on the *pro forma* MG DD/B referred to in the case stated, on a sticker attached to the doctor's certificate, and on a label on the glass phial received by the analyst. The code could be treated as a unique code.

Again, in *Khatibi v DPP* [2004] EWHC 83 (Admin), (2004) 168 JP 361, the defendant submitted, *inter alia*, that there was no evidence of how the specimen had been labelled and therefore no inference could be drawn that the blood analysed was hers. On appeal against conviction, the Divisional Court noted that the label gave details of the exact time at which the sample was taken, 00.15 on 13 November 2001, which was consistent with the doctor's evidence that he took it between 12.10 and 12.20 am on that date. The name of the arresting officer was also correctly stated, as was the name of the doctor who took the sample and where he took it. An assistant to the analyst gave evidence confirming that a sample so labelled had been received at the laboratory on 15 November 2001. The justices were entitled to find that the blood analysed was the defendant's.

In *Rainsbury v DPP* [2007] EWHC 1138 (Admin), a nurse had taken a blood specimen. He shook the vials for about 15 seconds, spoke to the defendant, then shook them again, ensuring that the preservative crystals were dissolved. The defendant adduced expert evidence that the vials should have been shaken for 30 seconds to ensure adequate mixing of the blood with the preservative, although there was no authoritative stipulation to that effect. The Administrative Court ruled that a fact-finding tribunal is fully entitled to differ from an expert if there is a rational basis for doing so. The district judge had evidence that the relevant consideration was whether the vials were adequately shaken. The nurse gave evidence that they were, and there was no evidence to the contrary. The defendant also argued that the fact that the alcohol concentration revealed by the blood analysis was almost the same as that shown by the breath analysis an hour earlier, rather than having fallen, suggested contamination of the blood. The Administrative Court dismissed this point, ruling that if the breath analysis had been admitted in evidence, it would have enabled the Crown to argue that the blood alcohol level would still have been over the limit even after a fall of the order postulated by the expert witness.

In *Taylor v DPP* [2009] EWHC 2824 (Admin), a blood specimen was taken at Leamington Spa police station. The vial was marked with the motorist's name and a serial number, and put in the fridge. The person who took the specimen from the fridge later that same day and sent it for analysis recorded the serial number, but made an error in one of the digits. The blood specimen showed excess alcohol and the motorist was convicted. He appealed, arguing, *inter alia*, that there was no admissible evidence that the blood analysed was his. The Divisional Court took into account that the sample bore the appellant's name, that it was taken from Leamington Spa Police Station, and that the sample that was sent was taken from the fridge at most some eight hours after a sample had been taken from the defendant, and both bore the name Martin Taylor. In such a short period it was highly unlikely that there would be a confusion resulting from there being two samples with exactly the same name. Although the serial numbers were not identical, they were very similar – the kind of everyday error of transcription that arises when individuals are putting down strings of numbers. Had the serial number been markedly different, the outcome might have been different. See also *Rainsbury v DPP* (above), where a minor difference in the serial numbers appearing on the specimen bag and on the certificate of analysis was dismissed as a mere typographical error.

4.14.6 At the time it is provided

A lapse of two minutes between taking the specimen and dividing it meets the requirement to divide the specimen 'at the time it is provided': *DPP v Elstob* [1992] RTR 45 (DC), although the two operations must be closely linked in time and performed as part of the same event.

4.14.7 Supplied to the accused

The suspect must be given his part within a reasonable time, preferably before leaving the police station, but not necessarily so. If it is supplied later, it is a question of fact whether it was supplied within a reasonable time, and the court should consider all the circumstances, including the reason for the delay and any inconvenience or injustice caused to the defendant: *R v Sharp* [1968] 2 QB 564 (CA), where, on the facts, supply at 10.00 am the following day was held to be reasonable.

In *Johnson (Antony Harold) v DPP*, unreported, 13 October 1994, part of the specimen was handed to the suspect, then taken by an officer and put into the refrigerator to prevent deterioration. When the suspect left the police station, he took his possessions, but not the blood specimen. Neither he nor his solicitor later sought to recover the specimen. The Divisional Court found that the specimen had been supplied to him, and upheld his conviction.

Placing a blood specimen in the defendant's handbag, which was with her personal belongings on a hospital trolley, constitutes 'supply' for the purposes of s 15(5)(b): *Jones v DPP* [2004] EWHC 3165 (Admin), [2005] RTR 15.

Where a blood specimen was taken, and the accused's part was supplied to his friend because the accused was in the accident and emergency department at hospital and unable to take possession of it himself, the specimen was supplied for the purposes of s 15(5). See *O'Connell v DPP* [2006] EWHC 1419 (Admin), where the court said that the word 'supply' is capable of a number of interpretations, depending on the facts of the case and the purpose for which the word is used in the statute.

In *Blyth v CPS (Essex)* [2022] EWHC 2558 (Admin), [2023] RTR 11, a blood specimen was taken and divided. The subject requested part, and that part was placed with his property at the police station, and thereafter kept with his property while he remained in custody on other matters. It was not refrigerated in the prison. The subject did nothing to ensure its integrity. Nor did he show any intention of having it analysed. On appeal against conviction for drug-driving, the

Divisional Court dismissed his argument that his part had not been supplied in accordance with s 15(5). Supply does not connote a physical exchange of the sample between police officer and accused, but the effective transfer of control over it. The sample was available and accessible to the appellant's direction and control. Nor, on the facts, were there any grounds to exclude from evidence the prosecution analysis of its part of the specimen under PACE, s 78 (see para 11.9).

4.15 THE ANALYSIS

4.15.1 Alcohol: the 6 milligrammes allowance

It is a standard practice of analysts of blood specimens to allow a margin in favour of the suspect, of 6 per cent, or 6 milligrammes, whichever is lower. This has been recognised in the case law. In *Walker v Hodgins* [1984] RTR 34 (DC), the analysis conducted for the prosecution showed excess alcohol both before and after deducting the 6 milligrammes allowance, but the analysis for the defendant showed 83 milligrammes before deducting the allowance, leaving 77 milligrammes. Both analysts had proceeded in good faith and their methods were unimpeachable. The prosecution's evidence included that the analysis was inherently unreliable to a very small extent, and that 6 milligrammes was therefore deducted. The justices applied the same deduction to the defendant's analysis, bringing it below the limit, and acquitted him. The Divisional Court upheld the justices' findings.

An argument that the court should 'round down' a blood analysis as well as applying the 6 milligrammes allowance failed in *Oswald v DPP* [1989] RTR 360. Analysis for the prosecution produced four results ranging between 86.7 and 89.6 milligrammes, and averaging 88.2. The defendant's part of the specimen had been separately analysed, yielding six results, ranging from 85.4 to 87.1, averaging 86.2. The defendant argued that this average of 86.2 should be reduced by the usual 6 milligrammes then rounded down to 80, raising a reasonable doubt whether the motorist had been over the limit. The justices rejected the argument and convicted. The Divisional Court found that deducting the 6 milligrammes was not necessarily appropriate where a range of results was produced; it might or might not be appropriate to make the deduction from the average. In any event, the justices had found as a fact on the evidence that the defendant had in excess of 80 milligrammes of alcohol in 100 millilitres of blood, and that finding was unassailable. The court was not required to round down the figure.

On the other hand, justices were wrong to apply the allowance only to the lowest of four results, averaging 87.6. By doing so, the result came to below 80, and the justices dismissed the charge. The prosecutor's appeal was successful. See *DPP v Welsh (Eric Thomas)* (1997) 161 JP 57 (DC).

In *DPP v Perkins*, unreported, 5 April 1995 (DC), justices were found to have been wrong to decide that the 6 milligrammes allowance might not be enough. The prosecution evidence was that four tests had produced a rounded-down average of 87 milligrammes, leaving 81 after deducting the 6 milligrammes allowance. The forensic scientist gave evidence that he thought the possibility of the result being more than 6 milligrammes out was so remote that it could be discounted. The motorist did not adduce any argument. The justices dismissed the charge on the apparently unsupported basis that the allowance might have been insufficient. The Divisional Court allowed the prosecutor's appeal.

4.15.2 Analysis for specified drugs

While preliminary screening for drugs is available in relation to only two of the specified drugs (see para 2.7), a blood specimen can be analysed for the full range. Typically, the specimen is tested in series for all 17 drugs. As in the case of alcohol, allowances for variations in analysis are built into the process for testing blood specimens for specified controlled drugs. The methodology is designed to provide 99.7 per cent certainty. The Forensic Science Regulator's Code of Practice (March 2023, www.gov.uk/government/publications/statutory-code-of-practice-for-forensic-science-activities/forensic-science-regulator-code-of-practice-accessible), in force from 2 October 2023, contains provisions (para 107) relating to the analysis and reporting of forensic specimens for the purposes of Road Traffic Act 1988, s 5A. It recognises that, although the legislation allows for the taking and analysis of both blood and urine specimens in relation to the s 5A offence, the limits are set as maxima in blood, not urine. For this reason, the code deals with blood specimens only. It proceeds on the basis that (as in the case of the s 5 offence – see para 4.15.4) the prosecution does not have to prove a particular concentration of a drug, only that the concentration is above the specified limit. It sets out a standard approach to accounting for uncertainty of measurement, and includes, for each of the specified drugs, a common reporting threshold. Only results exceeding the common reporting threshold are to be reported as above the legal limit. The code applies to analysts instructed both by prosecution and by defence.

If the analysis shows an excess of a specified controlled drug, a charge under s 5A usually ensues; if not, and there is sufficient evidence of impairment, a charge under s 4 (unfitness to drive through drink or drugs – see Chapter 7) would be appropriate. The Crown Prosecution Service suggests that, where more than one drug is found, the decision whether to pursue one or more charges depends on the circumstances. High readings may lead to more than one charge, especially if the consequences of driving were serious. On the other hand, there may be cases where the court might impose a nominal penalty for a second offence, such that a guilty plea to a single charge would satisfy the prosecution. Charging each drug offence separately allows for the possibility that the suspect may have taken one of the drugs on medical advice and so have a legal defence (see para 8.13) in relation to that drug. It also avoids argument that a charge which includes two or more drugs, with their different limits, might be bad for duplicity. See www.cps.gov.uk/legal-guidance/road-traffic-drink-and-drug-driving. Further, since the presence of more than one specified drug is an aggravating factor for sentencing purposes (see para 12.1.4), it may be argued that it is in the public interest to charge each drug found.

4.15.3 Preservatives

The question of the presence, or adequacy, of preservative in the specimen has been raised in a number of cases. In *Gregory v DPP* [2002] EWHC 385 (Admin), the police surgeon gave evidence that she had taken a specimen of approximately 4 millilitres, which she divided into two phials, each containing about 2 millilitres. A toxicologist called by the defendant gave evidence that if the phial is not filled to its capacity of 6 millilitres, the amount of preservative in the phial is such that the result may be distorted when headspace gas chromatography is used to analyse the specimen. The analyst for the prosecution gave evidence of how she had analysed the specimen, but did not comment on the toxicologist's evidence. The justices convicted the defendant on the basis of the prosecution's analysis. The Divisional Court found that the defence witness had given evidence which was not merely theoretical, but was based on certain uncontroversial facts. The court below should not have rejected that evidence without a rational basis for so doing.

In *Dhaliwal v DPP* [2006] EWHC 1149 (Admin), the prosecution's analyst gave evidence about the procedure in the laboratory and about the defendant's specimen. In response to a question put during cross-examination, she consulted her file and said that her assistant had checked that the specimen contained a preservative. The motorist appealed against conviction, arguing that it was necessary to prove that preservative had been added, and that what the analyst had said was hearsay and inadmissible. The Administrative Court found that, given how the question had arisen, and since the defence had not raised any issue of the absence of preservative, the prosecution did not have to prove that it had been added. The real question was whether the court was satisfied that the appellant had excess alcohol in his blood and that the analysis was reliable. On the facts, the court below was entitled to be so satisfied.

In *Carter v DPP* [2006] EWHC 3328 (Admin), [2007] RTR 22, the Divisional Court affirmed that a court is entitled to presume that the procedures for preparing blood testing kits, including the addition of preservative, have been carried out, unless there is something to suggest otherwise.

4.15.4 Challenging the analysis

Since the purpose of allowing a suspect a part of a specimen is to permit comparative analysis, it is unsurprising that there have been challenges to the prosecution's analysis. Where there are two conflicting analyses, the court may accept one and reject the other. In *Froggatt v Allcock* [1975] RTR 372, the prosecution's analysis of a blood specimen showed 230 milligrammes of alcohol in 100 millilitres of blood. The defendant's analysis showed 93. The latter specimen, however, was slightly clotted when it arrived at the laboratory and was of low volume. The capsule was properly sealed but the bag containing it was unsealed. The Queen's Bench Division upheld the justices' finding, following a proper evaluation of the evidence, that the prosecution's analysis was the correct one.

It is sufficient for the prosecution to prove, on the basis of a laboratory analysis, that the defendant's alcohol level was above the prescribed limit. It is not necessary to establish an exact reading: *R v Coomaraswamy* [1976] RTR 21 (CA), where the prosecutor's and the motorist's analyses of a urine specimen showed, respectively, not less than 251, and 156 milligrammes of alcohol in 100 millilitres of urine. A possible cause of the wide discrepancy was that the samples were small and alcohol had evaporated from them. See also *Thomas v Henderson* [1983] RTR 293 (DC) and *Gordon v Thorpe* [1986] RTR 358 (DC). The principle of *de minimis* does not apply: *McGarry v Chief Constable of Bedfordshire* [1983] RTR 172 (DC).

The prosecution's analysis of a specimen may be challenged only by analysis of the part supplied to the defendant. See *R v Rutter* [1977] RTR 105 (CA), where the defendant had thrown away his part without having it analysed, and was not allowed to adduce expert evidence based on hypothetical calculations.

In *Collins v Lucking* [1983] RTR 312, a urine specimen was analysed for the prosecutor and showed excess alcohol. It also revealed the presence of micro-organisms capable of creating alcohol. The analyst stated that it was unlikely that the organisms had significantly contributed to the result, unless the defendant was diabetic. The Divisional Court held that this was insufficient to justify conviction. The analyst had not discounted what might be reasonable possibilities, with the result that the justices could not be sure that the offence had been committed.

In *Lomas v Bowler* [1984] Crim LR 178 (DC), the prosecution's two analyses of a urine specimen showed 191.1 and 190.2 milligrammes of alcohol in 100 millilitres of urine. The defendant claimed to have drunk only two pints of beer. An analyst instructed by him found 80 and 82 milligrammes in 100 millilitres, and gave evidence that he found no sign that the specimen had been tampered with. The justices found that the defendant's manner of driving was consistent with his having had too much to drink. They were not satisfied that the specimen analysed for the defendant was the correct specimen because the result was inconsistent with what he said he had drunk. The Divisional Court confirmed that the justices were entitled to rely on the prosecution's analysis.

The outcome was the same in *Sophocleous v Ringer* [1988] RTR 52, where the prosecution's analyst, in cross-examination, agreed it would have been possible for the alcohol level in the specimen to increase after it had been taken if it contained certain antibodies, but she knew of no recorded instance of such an occurrence. The Divisional Court upheld the justices' decision to accept the analyst's evidence that the specimen contained excess alcohol.

Where the prosecution's analyst used a more modern method of analysis than the defendant's analyst, the justices were entitled to find the former more accurate than the latter and to prefer it: *Stephenson v Clift* [1988] RTR 171, where the Divisional Court emphasised that the question is one of fact for the justices.

Where justices were satisfied on the evidence that the specimen analysed for the defendant had been adulterated by the addition of blood containing no alcohol, producing a reading below 80 milligrammes, they were justified in preferring the prosecution's analysis showing he had been over the limit. They were also correct in not taking into account, as part of the evidence of the alcohol level in the blood, evidence about the breath analysis, that evidence having been adduced to establish the propriety of offering the (now repealed) option of providing a blood specimen. See *Yhnell v DPP* [1989] RTR 250 (DC).

In *Parish v DPP* [2000] RTR 143, a motorist provided a blood specimen. Twelve minutes later, an Alcolmeter screening device showed that he was not over the limit, and he was released. Analysis of the blood specimen, however, showed not less than 100 milligrammes of alcohol in 100 millilitres of blood, and he was charged with driving with excess alcohol. The defence provided the prosecution with, *inter alia*, an expert report to the effect that it was impossible for anyone to have a rate of alcohol metabolism compatible with the difference between the blood analysis and the breath test. At the time of the hearing the prosecution had been in possession of the latter report for over six months, but it was not until the hearing itself that it disclosed its own expert report, disputing the defendant's expert witness. The court refused to allow the defendant an adjournment to consider the prosecution's report, ruled that the result of the pre-release test could not impugn the analysis, and convicted him. The Divisional Court found that it is for the justices to consider all the evidence and decide whether or not the defence has cast doubt on the accuracy and reliability of the prosecution evidence. The evidence which the appellant sought to call was admissible and the justices could and should have considered it before deciding whether the prosecution had proved its case. It was an error of law to refuse the adjournment to enable that evidence to be called. See also *O'Sullivan v DPP* [2005] EWHC 564 (Admin) and *Snelson v Thompson* [1985] RTR 220 (DC) (para 3.4.6).

Where the defendant's part of a blood specimen was not properly stored before being supplied to her, and so could not later be analysed, the defendant's conviction for causing death by careless driving while unfit through drink or drugs was overturned. In *R v Boyd* [2002] EWCA Crim 2836, [2004] RTR 2, following a fatal accident, a blood specimen was taken from the driver, who was in hospital. Analysis for the prosecution gave a positive screening for free morphine and opiate drugs. The defence disputed the finding but could not conduct a comparative analysis because, in error, the specimen had not been refrigerated and had become unfit for testing. A chartered biologist for the defence gave evidence that a second test might have yielded results more favourable to the defendant. The Court of Appeal (Criminal Division) allowed the defendant's appeal against conviction, finding that the result of the prosecution's analysis was open to challenge. An alternative analysis might have established that there was no drug materially affecting the defendant when she drove. The prosecution had deprived the defendant of establishing a defence which might have been available.

4.15.5 The Randox cases

Early in 2017, it emerged that certain data relating to the quality control of the drug testing process within Randox Testing Services – one of the companies contracted to analyse blood specimens for the purposes of the Road Traffic Act 1988 – had been manipulated, rendering the results unreliable. The UK Accreditation Service (UKAS) suspended Randox's accreditation for drug testing, and a programme of re-testing the relevant specimens was put in place. Press reports at the time suggested that as many as 10,000 cases may have been affected, while the court in *R v Wilson, Walmsley, York and Senior* [2019] EWCA Crim 2410 (below) recited that the number of samples affected by the problem has been estimated at exceeding 8,000.

In *R v Bravender* [2018] EWCA Crim 723, forensic testing by Randox had shown a level of THC of 2.5 microgrammes per litre of blood (the limit being 2), and 186 microgrammes benzoylecgonine (BZE) per litre of blood (the limit being 15). Re-testing by a different company showed 59 microgrammes BZE; the remaining blood sample was insufficient to test for THC. On appeal against sentence, the Court of Appeal proceeded on the basis of the second set of results, disregarding the possibility that there could be instability in BZE after long-term storage (15 months in this case).

In *R v Ward* [2018] EWCA Crim 872, the appellant had been convicted of a number of offences, including causing death by careless driving when unfit through drugs. His blood specimen had been analysed by Randox Testing Services. On his appeal against conviction, the Crown no longer relied on the Randox analysis. The blood sample had been re-tested by another company, and showed a level of GHB/GBL of 97 microgrammes per millilitre, compared with the 96 microgrammes reported by Randox. The Court of Appeal found that the failure of a forensic science laboratory was a matter of deep concern, potentially going to the integrity of the criminal justice system, but that the safety of a conviction is fact-specific. In the present case, there was overwhelming evidence to establish the careless driving, which pointed strongly to the appellant's unfitness being attributable to drugs. The evidence came from other drivers, the officers who attended the scene, medical practitioners who interacted with the appellant and to whom the appellant disclosed his use of drugs, and expert evidence on the general effects of those drugs on ability to drive. The report from the second expert, which was undisputed, put that conclusion beyond doubt. The appeal was dismissed.

R v Senior [2018] EWCA Crim 837 was an appeal against conviction for driving with an excess of cannabis over the specified limit. Randox conducted two tests. The first did not detect any of the s 5A drugs. Apparently, there had been a problem with the testing equipment. A second test found a level of THC above the limit. The charge was based on that second test. In the light of the problems at Randox, the appellant's blood specimen was tested again by another company which found THC, but at a level below the specified limit. The Court of Appeal emphasised that each case involving testing by Randox turns on its own facts. In the present case, there was no reliable evidence to indicate the level of cannabis at the time the appellant was stopped by police. The conviction was therefore unsafe and was quashed.

R v Wilson, Walmsley, York and Senior [2019] EWCA Crim 2410 concerned a number of convictions, including convictions for drug-driving based on blood analyses carried out by Randox. The drug-drive offences had all been sent to the Crown Court for trial, along with other charges, under Crime and Disorder Act 1988, s 51. The defendants in question pleaded guilty to the drug-driving offences following convictions for other offences dealt with on indictment. The Court of Appeal found that the convictions in question all fell within the requirements established in *Scally* (see para 4.14.4); the prosecution conceded that the three Randox cases were analogous to fraud in that the evidence, as now known, would not make out the offences charged; the fault lay with the prosecution; the accused were denied a proper opportunity to decide how to plead, indeed were denied a complete defence; there was no real dispute as to the facts; and there was certainty of acquittal. After reviewing the authorities, the Court of Appeal, however, did not have jurisdiction to hear appeals against summary convictions in these circumstances; nor would appeal by way of case stated be appropriate because the convictions were neither wrong in law nor in excess of jurisdiction. But, reconstituting itself as a Divisional Court, the Court of Appeal (Criminal Division) granted permission to apply for judicial review, abridged the procedures and quashed the drug-driving convictions. In one of the cases, the Court of Appeal (Criminal Division) had already quashed the conviction for drug-driving without considering the question of jurisdiction; that decision would stand.

4.16 DETENTION FOLLOWING THE PROCEDURE

Road Traffic Act 1988, s 10 contains provisions allowing a person who has been investigated for a drink- or drug-drive offence to be detained at the police station if there is a risk that an offence, or a further offence, would be committed if the person were to be released immediately. A person may be detained at the police station after providing breath, blood or urine if the officer has reasonable grounds to believe that, if released, and if driving, the person would be unfit to do so or over the limit for alcohol or a specified drug. The power is not available where it ought reasonably to appear to the officer that there is no likelihood that the person will drive or attempt to drive while impaired or with excess alcohol or excess of a specified drug, for example, where the person is being driven away from the police station by someone else. If there is any question whether the person's ability to drive might be impaired through drugs, the officer must consult a medical practitioner (not a registered health care professional) and must act on the advice of the medical practitioner.

In anticipation of evidential breath analysis away from the police station, s 10 also provides a power to arrest a person who has provided a breath specimen elsewhere, with a view to detaining the person at a police station. The power of arrest is subject to the same terms as the power to detain.

Chapter 5

Incapacity to Consent and Hospital Patients

5.1 PERSONS INCAPABLE OF CONSENTING

Section 7A was inserted into the Road Traffic Act 1988 by the Police Reform Act 2002 and came into force on 1 October 2002. It was believed that, in the absence of a specimen, some drivers were escaping prosecution, or being prosecuted for less serious offences than if a specimen was available. Section 7A therefore contains provisions which authorise taking a blood specimen from a person who is incapable of consenting, usually because the person is unconscious. In the absence of the new provision, taking a blood specimen without consent might amount to an assault and breach medical ethics.

The power arises where the person has been involved in an accident and police are investigating any of the drink- or drug-drive offences. The person must be someone from whom an officer could otherwise require a blood specimen, and the incapacity must be one which appears to the officer to be attributable to medical reasons. The specimen is not to be taken by a medical practitioner having responsibility for the clinical care of the person, and is to be taken by a police medical practitioner if one is available. It is lawful for a medical practitioner to take a specimen pursuant to the section, although there is no obligation to do so. The specimen may not be laboratory tested without the consent of the person from whom it was taken. Failure without reasonable excuse to give such consent is an offence.

The section is as follows:

> (1) A constable may make a request to a medical or health care practitioner for him to take a specimen of blood from a person ('the person concerned') irrespective of whether that person consents if—
>
> (a) that person is a person from whom the constable would (in the absence of any incapacity of that person and of any objection under section 9)

be entitled under section 7 to require the provision of a specimen of blood for a laboratory test;

(b) it appears to that constable that that person has been involved in an accident that constitutes or is comprised in the matter that is under investigation or the circumstances of that matter;

(c) it appears to that constable that that person is or may be incapable (whether or not he has purported to do so) of giving a valid consent to the taking of a specimen of blood; and

(d) it appears to that constable that that person's incapacity is attributable to medical reasons.

(2) A request under this section—

(a) shall not be made to a medical or health care practitioner who for the time being has any responsibility (apart from the request) for the clinical care of the person concerned; and

(b) shall not be made to a practitioner other than a police medical or health care practitioner unless—

(i) it is not reasonably practicable for the request to be made to a police medical or health care practitioner; or

(ii) it is not reasonably practicable for such a practitioner (assuming him to be willing to do so) to take the specimen.

(3) It shall be lawful for a medical or health care practitioner to whom a request is made under this section, if he thinks fit—

(a) to take a specimen of blood from the person concerned irrespective of whether that person consents; and

(b) to provide the sample [*sic*] to a constable.

(4) If a specimen is taken in pursuance of a request under this section, the specimen shall not be subjected to a laboratory test unless the person from whom it was taken—

(a) has been informed that it was taken; and

(b) has been required by a constable to give his permission for a laboratory test of the specimen; and

(c) has given his permission.

(5) A constable must, on requiring a person to give his permission for the purposes of this section for a laboratory test of a specimen, warn that person that a failure to give the permission may render him liable to prosecution.

(6) A person who, without reasonable excuse, fails to give his permission for a laboratory test of a specimen of blood taken from him under this section is guilty of an offence.

(7) In this section—

'medical or health care practitioner means a medical practitioner or a registered health care professional;

'police medical or health care practitioner' means a medical practitioner, or a registered health care professional, who is engaged under any agreement to provide medical or health care services for purposes connected with the activities of a police force.

The references to health care practitioners were inserted into the section by the Deregulation Act 2015 and came into force on 10 April 2015.

It is for the police officer, not the medical or health care practitioner, to assess capacity by reference to medical reasons, although there is no definition of 'medical reasons'. According to the explanatory notes to the Act, the requirement that the specimen be taken by a medical practitioner other than one having clinical care of the person is to avoid undue pressure and possible conflicts of interests. The preference for a police practitioner also reflects the separation of the investigative and clinical functions to avoid conflict.

The Faculty of Forensic & Legal Medicine has issued guidance for practitioners on taking blood specimens from incapacitated drivers (available at https://fflm.ac.uk/resources/publications/taking-blood-specimens-from-incapacitated-drivers/). The guidance emphasises that it is for the police officer to decide whether or not the legal preconditions for asking that a blood specimen be taken are met. It points out that the person asked to take the specimen should be satisfied that the subject lacks capacity to consent but that taking a specimen is nevertheless lawful. The guidance emphasises that the officer cannot *require* the practitioner to take the specimen, merely request the practitioner to do so, suggesting that a practitioner should decline to take a specimen if:

- there are medical reasons why it should not be taken or to do so would be detrimental to the patient's care and treatment;
- the patient refuses or resists, since it is not ethically acceptable for health care practitioners to use force or restraint; whether such patients would be treated as competent and convicted for failing to provide a specimen would be a matter for a court to decide at a later date;
- the person is expected to recover capacity within a short period of time, for example if he or she is temporarily paralysed for the purpose of a clinical investigation. The practitioner taking the specimen should seek to ascertain from the treating doctor whether this is likely to be the case.

The guidance emphasises that the role of the treating doctor is confined to objecting to the taking of a specimen if it would be prejudicial to the proper care and treatment of the patient, as where it would introduce unacceptable delay to treatment.

Under s 7A(4), the specimen is not to be laboratory tested unless the subject, having regained capacity, consents. Again according to the explanatory notes to the Police Reform Act 2002, this is to avoid placing the subject at a disadvantage compared with a person who refuses to provide a specimen.

For the purposes of Road Traffic Offenders Act 1988, s 15 (see para 8.9) on the use of specimens in proceedings for an offence under Road Traffic Act 1988, ss 4, 5 or 5A, amendments made to s 15 have the effect that specimens taken under s 7A are treated in the same way as those taken with prior consent.

5.2 HOSPITAL PATIENTS

Road Traffic Act 1988, s 9 contains special provisions relating to hospital patients, the effect of which is to give priority to care and treatment rather than to the investigative procedure. A patient at hospital is not to be required to undergo a preliminary test or provide a specimen unless the medical practitioner in immediate charge of the patient's case has been notified and does not object. The medical practitioner may object where the requirement, the provision of the specimen, or the giving of the warning of the consequences of failing to provide, would be prejudicial to the proper care and treatment of the patient. Where a requirement is made, the preliminary test, or the provision of the specimen, takes place at the hospital. Where a blood specimen is to be taken, a doctor or health care professional contracted to the police usually attends to take the specimen. The terms of the section are as follows:

> (1) While a person is at a hospital as a patient he shall not be required to co-operate with a preliminary test or to provide a specimen under section 7 of this Act unless the medical practitioner in immediate charge of his case has been notified of the proposal to make the requirement; and—
>
> (a) if the requirement is then made, it shall be for co-operation with a test administered, or for the provision of a specimen, at the hospital, but
> (b) if the medical practitioner objects on the ground specified in subsection (2) below, the requirement shall not be made.
>
> (1A) While a person is at a hospital as a patient, no specimen of blood shall be taken from him under section 7A of this Act and he shall not be required to give his permission for a laboratory test of a specimen taken under that section unless the medical practitioner in immediate charge of his case—

> (a) has been notified of the proposal to take the specimen or to make the requirement; and
> (b) has not objected on the ground specified in subsection (2).
>
> (2) The ground on which the medical practitioner may object is—
>
> (a) in a case falling within subsection (1), that the requirement or the provision of the specimen or (if one is required) the warning required by section 7(7) of this Act would be prejudicial to the proper care and treatment of the patient; and
> (b) in a case falling within subsection (1A), that the taking of the specimen, the requirement or the warning required by section 7A(5) of this Act would be so prejudicial.

The reference in s 9(1) to requiring a specimen under s 7 was substituted with effect from 1 July 2005, by the Serious Organised Crime and Police Act 2005. Before then, the subsection referred only to preliminary tests and to specimens for laboratory testing. The section now contemplates evidential breath testing at, among other places, a hospital, in readiness for the type approval of portable evidential breath testing instruments (see para 1.3.2).

5.2.1 Protection from arrest

A person who is a patient at a hospital is protected from arrest by virtue of Road Traffic Act 1988, ss 6D(3) and 10(2A). Section 6D(3) prohibits the arrest of a person who has failed, or refused to take, a preliminary breath test if the person is a patient at a hospital. Section 10(2A) further provides that a person who is at a hospital as a patient is not to be arrested and taken from the hospital to a police station under s 10 (on the detention of persons to prevent driving while unfit or with excess alcohol – see para 4.16) if it would be prejudicial to the person's proper care and treatment as a patient.

Where a person was arrested while at hospital as a patient, however, that did not invalidate the subsequent procedures. In *DPP v Wilson* [2009] EWHC 1988 (Admin), [2009] RTR 29, a motorist had been involved in a road traffic accident and was taken to hospital. With the consent of the doctor in charge, a breath specimen was taken and was positive. An officer, unaware that s 6D(3) prohibits the arrest of a person being treated at hospital, then arrested and cautioned the motorist. A blood specimen was taken. The motorist was later discharged from hospital and the officer took him to the police station. Analysis of the blood specimen revealed 133 milligrammes of alcohol in 100 millilitres of blood, and the motorist was charged with driving with excess alcohol. The justices found the specimen had been taken unlawfully and dismissed the charge. On the prosecutor's appeal, the Divisional Court found that the fact that an arrest is prohibited does not invalidate the subsequent procedures provided they are carried out in accordance with the other statutory requirements.

In *Kohler v DPP* [2010] EWHC 2886 (Admin), the defendant was a patient at a hospital, but there was no doctor on duty and she was not under the charge of a medical practitioner. She was awaiting an ambulance to take her to another hospital. The officer required her to take a preliminary breath test. It was positive and the officer arrested her, in breach of s 6D(3), and took her to the police station, where breath analysis showed excess alcohol. There was no question of bad faith on the part of the officer. The Administrative Court applied *R v Fox; Fox v Chief Constable of Gwent* [1986] AC 281 (see para 2.3). It found that the fact that the evidence of excess alcohol had been unlawfully obtained did not render it inadmissible, and upheld the conviction.

5.2.2 Patient at a hospital

One of the first questions arising is whether a person falls into the category of a patient at a hospital. 'Hospital' is defined in Road Traffic Act 1988, s 11 as an institution which provides medical or surgical treatment for in-patients and out-patients.

Hollingsworth v Howard [1974] RTR 58 (QBD) concerned Road Traffic Act 1972, s 8(2), which provided similar protection for hospital patients. It was decided in that case that a driver being conveyed to hospital in an ambulance is not 'at a hospital as a patient'. A police officer had therefore properly requested a breath specimen in the ambulance.

Attorney-General's Reference (No 1 of 1976) [1977] 1 WLR 646 (CA) also concerned s 8(2) of the 1972 Act. The court there held that the words 'at a hospital' were not to be construed in a limited way and could refer to anywhere within the hospital precincts. 'A patient' is someone who is at the hospital for the purpose of being treated, and ceases to be a patient as soon as the treatment contemplated for that visit is over. Where a patient was about to leave the hospital, but was advised by a doctor to sit down for half an hour before leaving the premises, that would be part of the treatment, but a person ceases to be a patient when he leaves to go home. Whether or not a person was 'at a hospital' and whether or not he was there 'as a patient' were mixed questions of law and fact.

In the Scottish case *Watt v Macneill* 1980 1 SLT 178, the High Court of Justiciary concluded that it was a question of fact and circumstance whether a person had ceased to be a patient. It was not possible or desirable to attempt to define exhaustively the circumstances which would lead to a conclusion one way or the other.

In *Askew v DPP* [1988] RTR 303, a motorist had been involved in a road traffic accident and was taken to hospital. Police officers went to the hospital. A nurse told the motorist that the doctor had discharged him and he dressed. The officers then asked him to step outside the hospital building. He did so and the officers began the breath testing procedure. The Divisional Court ruled that whether or not a person is a patient is a question of fact. On the facts in this case, the motorist was no longer a patient when he was asked for a breath sample. The relevant considerations include whether the person has had treatment, whether the treatment has come to an end, whether the doctor in charge or a nurse has told the police the treatment is at an end, and whether the person has begun preparing to leave. That the person has not actually left the precincts of the hospital is not necessarily conclusive.

In *Webber v DPP* [1998] RTR 111, a driver had been involved in an accident and was taken to hospital, where she was required to provide breath for a screening test, but refused. She was then required to provide a blood specimen. She agreed, but was discharged before providing it. She was arrested for failing to provide a specimen for a screening test, and, at the police station, she provided a blood specimen. She was convicted of driving with excess alcohol on the basis of the blood specimen. On appeal, she argued that, on being discharged from hospital she was also discharged from the obligation to comply with the requirement for a blood specimen. The procedure under Road Traffic Act 1988, s 7 should have been started afresh. The Divisional Court dismissed this argument, finding that the police had, by requiring a breath specimen for a screening test, set in train a procedure which was not varied or discharged by the fact that the defendant was discharged from hospital.

5.2.3 Procedure at hospital

Where a blood specimen is required at a hospital, the usual requirement to say why a breath specimen is not being required (see para 4.13), is irrelevant. In *R v Burton upon Trent Justices ex parte Woolley* [1995] RTR 139, a driver had been taken to hospital, where an officer, with the consent of the doctor in charge, required a breath specimen. The motorist refused because of his injuries, and the officer then asked for a specimen of blood or urine, asking whether there were any matters the driver wished taken into account in deciding which. The driver said he knew of none. A blood specimen was taken and analysed, and the driver pleaded guilty to driving with excess alcohol. The Crown Prosecution Service then contacted the driver to say there had been an error in the procedure in that the officer had not asked whether there was any medical reason why a blood specimen could not be taken. The driver sought an order of *certiorari* to quash the conviction. The Divisional Court found that when requiring a specimen at a hospital, there is no requirement to say why a breath specimen cannot be taken. Further, the inquiry about medical reasons is otiose. Neither the Road Traffic Act 1988 nor the case of *DPP v Warren* [1993] AC 319 (see para 4.13) suggests that either is necessary. It is enough to ask whether there is any reason why the specimen of blood should not be taken, to give the motorist the opportunity to proffer anything which might amount to a reasonable excuse for not providing the specimen.

In *Jones (Vivian Mary) v DPP* [2004] EWHC 3165 (Admin), [2005] RTR 15 (DC), it was again held that it was not necessary for an officer, when requiring blood specimens at a hospital, to explain why breath specimens were not being required.

At the time of both these decisions, there was no power to require evidential breath specimens at a hospital. The section has, however, since been amended to accommodate evidential breath analysis at hospitals (see para 5.2), and the ruling that there is no need to say why breath specimens cannot be taken may need to be revisited in due course. The MG DD/C form already provides for the investigating officer to explain why evidential breath specimens cannot be taken.

Otherwise, the usual requirements in s 7 (see Chapter 4) appear to apply where the specimen is required at a hospital. The fact that a blood specimen for analysis for drugs may be required at a hospital without a prior positive preliminary drug test or a professional opinion that the subject's condition may be due to some drug (see para 4.6) means that the procedure for requiring a blood specimen in a hospital is simpler than at a police station.

In *Butler (Michael Joseph) v DPP* [2001] RTR 28, a motorist at a police station was asked whether there was any medical reason why breath specimens could not be provided or should not be required, and he said 'immune system breakdown'. The motorist complained of chest pains and was taken to hospital. There, a police sergeant asked the doctor in charge if a specimen of blood or urine could be taken, but did not relay what had been said about 'immune system breakdown'. Blood was taken and the motorist was convicted of driving with excess alcohol. He appealed. The Divisional Court held that s 7 applies to specimens required both at a hospital and at a police station, while s 9 imposes additional requirements in hospital cases. Under s 9, the medical practitioner has to be notified of the proposal to require the patient to provide a specimen, affording the medical practitioner the opportunity to object. Before deciding, pursuant to s 7(4), whether the specimen should be of blood or urine, the officer has to consult a medical practitioner if he is aware of a potential medical reason affecting that decision. In the unusual circumstances of this case, the officer was required to inform the doctor that the defendant had said that he suffered from 'immune system breakdown'. Since he had not done so, the blood specimen was not admissible and the conviction was quashed.

The court came to a similar conclusion in *Townson v DPP* [2006] EWHC 2007 (Admin). A motorist was at hospital and the doctor in charge of his case assured a police sergeant that there was no medical objection to a breath test or to supplying blood, or to the warnings. The motorist refused to supply a specimen of breath, saying he was 'hurting too much'. He then refused to supply a blood specimen, citing difficulty in finding a vein during recent tests and that he was in pain. He also said he was a diabetic and had high blood pressure. The motorist was convicted of failing to provide a specimen of blood and appealed. The Divisional Court held that the sergeant was not entitled to conclude that the reasons advanced were incapable of being medical reasons such that a medical opinion was unnecessary. Section 7(4A) envisaged it is for a medical practitioner alone to decide whether a specimen should be taken, having regard to the reasons advanced by the suspect. While such reasons might sometimes be self-evidently incapable of forming a medical reason, in the present case, once diabetes and high blood pressure were mentioned, the officer, not having been in possession of this information at the time he first spoke to the doctor, should have sought the opinion of a medical practitioner. The conviction was quashed.

Whitfield v DPP [2006] EWHC 1414 (Admin) was another case where a blood specimen was taken at a hospital. A police sergeant explained the procedure, following the *pro forma* MG DD/C, and a doctor took the specimen. A question arose whether the sergeant had properly warned the defendant of the consequences of failing to provide a specimen. The Divisional Court found that the justices were entitled to use their knowledge of the procedure set out in the booklet, if necessary after refreshing their memories from it, to find that the officer had followed the procedure and had given the warning. The booklet had been disclosed to the defence and they could have cross-examined the sergeant concerning it.

In *R v Bryan* [2008] EWCA Crim 1568, [2009] RTR 4 (CA (Crim)), a motorist had been charged with, *inter alia*, causing death by careless driving while over the limit, contrary to s 3A(1)(b). His vehicle had overturned, killing one of the passengers. The motorist was taken to hospital where a blood specimen was taken by a police surgeon. It showed excess alcohol. At his trial, the motorist challenged the procedure, saying that he had not been warned of the consequences of failing to provide a blood specimen, as required by s 7(7). The hospital doctor gave evidence that he could not remember being asked, on this or any other occasion, whether a person was fit to provide specimens. On the basis of that, the defence argued that if the officer had not obtained the doctor's consent, it was likely that he had also omitted to warn the motorist. The judge directed the jury that the prosecution did not have to prove that the hospital doctor's consent was obtained before a specimen of blood was taken; while it was good practice to do so, if it was not done, it was more likely that there had been no warning. The defendant was convicted and appealed, arguing that the judge misdirected the jury concerning the role of the medical practitioner. The Court of Appeal held that the judge's observation to the jury was erroneous in two respects. First, the requirement is mandatory and not mere good practice. Second, what is required is not the treating doctor's consent, but that he should have been notified of the proposal to take blood and not have objected. It was, however, implicit in the jury's verdict that they accepted the investigating officer's evidence and were satisfied that he had given the warning. In these circumstances, the judge's errors were immaterial. The appeal was dismissed.

See also *R v Coe (Christopher Steven)* [2009] EWCA Crim 1452 (para 6.7).

5.2.4 Medical practitioner in immediate charge

Cherpion v DPP [2013] EWHC 615 (Admin) featured an argument about whether or not a particular medical practitioner was the doctor in charge for the purposes of Road Traffic Act 1988, s 9(1). A motorist had been involved in a road traffic accident. A PC Shaw attended, and remained with the motorist until he arrived at hospital, where PC Shaw handed him over to a Dr Kropelnicki, whom he described as 'the doctor in charge of Mr Cherpion's welfare'. Dr Kropelnicki agreed that a blood test could be taken by a police forensic examiner. PC Shaw identified Dr Kropelnicki as the person responsible for the motorist's welfare to a second officer, who conducted the drink-drive procedure and, on the *pro forma*, noted that Dr Kropelnicki was the doctor in charge. The forensic medical examiner took the specimen, confirming that the police had obtained consent, although she could not remember from which doctor. The motorist agreed that Dr Kropelnicki took care of an injury to his leg and sent him for an X-ray. The magistrates found that Dr Kropelnicki was the doctor in immediate charge of the appellant. On appeal, the Divisional Court held that the magistrates were entitled to look at the evidence as a whole and draw common-sense conclusions from it; given their findings of fact, they were entitled to conclude she was the doctor in charge.

Chapter 6

Causing Death

6.1 INTRODUCTION

Road Traffic Act 1988, s 3A provides for the offence of causing death by careless driving when under the influence of drunk or drugs:

> (1) If a person causes the death of another person by driving a mechanically propelled vehicle on a road or other public place without due care and attention, or without reasonable consideration for other persons using the road or place, and—
>
> (a) he is, at the time when he is driving, unfit to drive through drink or drugs, or
> (b) he has consumed so much alcohol that the proportion of it in his breath, blood or urine at that time exceeds the prescribed limit, or
> (ba) he has in his body a specified controlled drug and the proportion of it in his blood or urine at that time exceeds the specified limit for that drug, or
> (c) he is, within 18 hours after that time, required to provide a specimen in pursuance of section 7 of this Act, but without reasonable excuse fails to provide it, or
> (d) he is required by a constable to give his permission for a laboratory test of a specimen of blood taken from him under section 7A of this Act, but without reasonable excuse fails to do so,
>
> he is guilty of an offence.
>
> (2) For the purposes of this section a person shall be taken to be unfit to drive at any time when his ability to drive properly is impaired.
>
> (3) Subsection (1)(b), (ba), (c) and (d) above shall not apply in relation to a person driving a mechanically propelled vehicle other than a motor vehicle.

Section 3A was introduced into the Road Traffic Act 1988 with effect from 1 July 1992, by the Road Traffic Act 1991. Section 3A(1)(ba) was added with the introduction of the new excess drugs offence in s 5A, and came into force on

2 March 2015. Section 3A(1)(d) was added by the Road Safety Act 2006 and came into force on 24 September 2007. The s 3A offence comprises elements of other offences under the Road Traffic Act 1988 and it is assumed that the case law in relation to those elements applies. For the other offences of causing death by driving, see para 1.2.1. While the definitions of those offences do not include drink or drugs, the presence of drink or drugs is relevant to sentencing.

There may be some reluctance to charge the s 3A offence. For example, in *R v Clark* [2003] EWCA Crim 991, [2003] 2 Cr App R 23, a driver who was under the influence of alcohol knocked over and killed a cyclist. There were no witnesses, and the driver drove away. He reported the accident the next morning, when he was no longer under the influence of alcohol. He said he thought he had hit a badger, and admitted he had drunk seven or eight pints the night before. He was charged with doing an act tending to pervert the course of public justice. He appealed against conviction. The Court of Appeal found that there had to be some positive act to constitute the offence charged; simply not stopping after an accident and driving home to avoid being breath tested was not enough. The court did not accept that a driver who is over the limit must hand himself in to avoid prosecution for perverting the course of justice, but went on to point out that, on the evidence of what the appellant had drunk, it would have been possible to charge him under s 3A(1)(a). While there might have been some doubt whether the Crown could prove carelessness and/or unfitness to drive, with the benefit of hindsight, those matters should perhaps have been left for the jury to decide.

For the meanings of 'mechanically propelled vehicle', 'road or other public place' and 'motor vehicle', see paras 8.4.1, 8.5 and 8.6, and 8.4, respectively. The offence under s 3A arises where the vehicle in question is a motor vehicle, except in a case of being unfit through drink or drugs under s 3A(1)(a), when it can be committed when driving the wider category of mechanically propelled vehicle. This reflects the position under ss 4, 5 and 5A.

6.2 CAUSING DEATH

The first constituent of the offence is that the defendant caused the death of another by driving. The question of causation was considered in *R v Hennigan* [1971] 3 All ER 133, a case of causing death by dangerous driving. The Court of Appeal (Criminal Division) found that the driving must be *a* cause of death, and something more than *de minimis* – a real cause rather than a minimal cause, although it need not necessarily be a substantial cause.

In *R v Shepherd, R v Wernet, Attorney General's Reference Nos 14 and 24 of 1993* [1994] 1 WLR 530 (CA), however, Taylor LCJ said that Parliament's intention in introducing the offence in Road Traffic Act 1988, s 3A – to strengthen the criminal law, specifically targeting those who cause death while driving with excess alcohol – does not require proof of a causal connection between the drink and the death.

In *R v Hodnitt* [2003] EWCA Crim 441, police attended the scene of an accident where they found a motor cycle jammed between a telegraph pole and bushes, the rider astride the cycle and his passenger on the ground nearby. The passenger died soon afterwards, while the rider suffered retrograde amnesia and could not remember what had happened. A blood specimen was taken some three and a half hours after the officers attended the scene. Back-calculation showed that, on the assumption that no drink had been taken within an hour preceding the accident, the blood alcohol level at the time of the accident would have been between 117 and 147 milligrammes in 100 millilitres of blood. The motor cyclist was convicted of causing death by careless driving while over the limit. On appeal against conviction, the Court of Appeal (Criminal Division) found that it was necessary for the prosecution to prove two limbs of the offence – the driving and the excess alcohol. It was not to be assumed that the motor cycle had left the road as a consequence of careless driving; the prosecution could not rule out the real possibility that some other agency may have been involved in the accident. In addition, there was a period of about one hour immediately before the accident during which the motor cyclist's actions were unaccounted for; the prosecution could not remove from consideration the possibility that drink had been taken in that hour, rendering the back-calculation unreliable. This was 'one of those rare cases where the court is left with lurking doubt'. The conviction was quashed.

Following the introduction of the offences of causing death by driving when unlicensed, uninsured or disqualified (ss 3ZB and 3ZC; see para 1.2.1), a number of cases came before the courts concerning the interpretation of the words 'causes death by driving' in these contexts. In *R v Hughes* [2013] UKSC 56, the Supreme Court applied the test in *R v Hennigan* [1971] 3 All ER 133 to a case of causing death by driving while uninsured and while unlicensed. The appellant driver had been convicted, even though his driving had been faultless; the deceased had been under the influence of heroin, over-tired, and had veered into the appellant's vehicle. The appellant was knowingly uninsured and had only a provisional driving licence. The Supreme Court found that, to give effect to the expression 'causes death by driving' there must be something properly to be criticised in the driving of the defendant, which contributed in some more than minimal way to the death. The appellant's appeal against conviction was allowed.

The Supreme Court has ruled to the same effect in the context of Theft Act 1968, s 12A (aggravated vehicle taking), that there must be at least some act or omission in the control of the car, which involves some element of fault, whether or not amounting to careless/inconsiderate driving, which contributes in some more than minimal way to death: *R v Taylor* [2016] UKSC 5, [2016] 1 WLR 500.

Whether or not the tests in *R v Hughes* and *R v Taylor* would apply to the s 3A offence has not yet come before the courts. It may well be that the very fact that a driver meets any of the conditions in s 3A(1)(a) to (d) is a sufficient indicator of fault. Indeed, in *Hughes*, the Supreme Court suggested (among other examples) that driving slightly over a speed limit, such that the driver could not stop before striking an oncoming drunken driver's car, would be sufficient to put his driving at fault and to amount to a cause of death.

See also *R v Norman* [2023] EWCA Crim 1112, confirming that the offence under s 3A(1)(ba) is an offence of strict liability; it is not necessary for the prosecution to show that it was the effect of the drugs which caused the offender to drive carelessly so as to cause death.

6.3 DRIVING WITHOUT DUE CARE AND ATTENTION

The second constituent of the offence is that the defendant was driving carelessly or without reasonable consideration for others. Driving without due care and attention is a separate offence from driving without reasonable consideration for other persons using the road: *R v Surrey Justices ex parte Witherick* [1932] KB 450 (KBD).

A person drives without due care and attention if (and only if) the manner of driving falls below what would be expected of a competent and careful driver (Road Traffic Act 1988, s 3ZA(2)). The circumstances of which a driver could be expected to be aware, as well as those shown to have been within the driver's knowledge, are to be taken into account (s 3ZA(3)).

Section 3ZA came into force on 24 September 2007. The competent and careful driver featuring in the current statutory definition replaces the reasonable, competent and prudent driver who had emerged from the earlier case law. The change seems not to have brought about any real difference and much of the early case law remains relevant.

Section 3ZA(2A) was added with effect from 26 October 2022, by the Police, Crime, Sentencing and Courts Act 2022, introducing a different standard for trained police drivers. It applies to designated persons, driving for police purposes, who have undertaken prescribed training. Such a person drives without due care and attention if (and only if) the way the person drives falls below what would be expected of a competent and careful constable who has undertaken the same prescribed training. This provision gives trained officers a degree of protection in that their driving, if challenged, is judged by the standards of their peers, rather than those of the ordinary careful, competent driver. The Road Traffic Act 1988 (Police Driving: Prescribed Training) Regulations 2022 (SI 2022/1112) set out the training courses which qualify for these purposes, and make provision for refresher training.

All drivers must exercise due care and attention. The standard is objective, impersonal and universal, and (apart from the exception in relation to trained police drivers, above) is not related to the proficiency or experience of the individual: *McCrone v Riding* [1938] 1 All ER 157 (KBD). In *R v Bannister* [2009] EWCA Crim 1571, [2010] RTR 4, the Court of Appeal held that a driver's special skill or lack of special skill was not to be taken into account when considering whether the driver had driven dangerously. Although the offence charged in *Bannister* was one of dangerous driving, the same test by reference to the competent and careful driver test applies (Road Traffic Act 1988, s 2A(1)(a)). The appellant Bannister was a grade 2 advanced police driver who might now invoke s 3ZA(2A), but the court's insistence on the objective standard remains in place.

In *Simpson v Peat* [1952] 2 QB 24, the Queen's Bench Division found that the question turned on whether the defendant exercised the degree of care and attention which a reasonable and prudent driver would exercise in the circumstances. The offence can be committed even if no accident occurs. Conversely, the fact that an accident occurs does not mean that a particular person drove carelessly. The reason for falling below the standard is irrelevant.

Whether the failure to meet the standard of the reasonable and prudent driver arises from a deliberate act or from an error of judgment is immaterial: *Taylor v Rogers* (1960) 124 JP 217 (DC).

Falling asleep at the wheel amounts to careless driving: *Henderson v Jones* (1955) 119 JP 304.

A breach of *The Highway Code* does not of itself mean that the driver was driving carelessly, although the Code may be taken into account in determining the issue: *Jarvis v Fuller* [1974] RTR 160 (DC).

In an emergency, the test is what was reasonable in the circumstances, not a standard of perfection which might be contemplated in hindsight. In *R v Bristol Crown Court, Jones v Chief Constable of Avon and Somerset Constabulary* [1986] RTR 259, a lorry driver whose lights failed while he was driving at speed on a motorway immediately pulled onto the hard shoulder, where he collided with a car he had not been able to see. The Queen's Bench Division held that this did not amount to careless driving.

The facts may speak for themselves. In *Wright v Wenlock* [1971] RTR 228, the Queen's Bench Division ruled that although the principle *res ipsa loquitur* does not apply in criminal cases, a rule to similar effect may apply where the defendant offers no explanation. The defendant failed to negotiate a bend and came off the road, colliding with a telegraph pole. He could not explain what had happened, but did not say there was anything wrong with the vehicle. The court found that the only proper inference was that he had been driving carelessly. See also *Watts v Carter* [1971] RTR 232 and *Rabjohns v Burgar* [1971] RTR 234, to the same effect.

In *R v Millington* [1996] RTR 80 (CA), a driver was convicted of causing death by careless driving while over the limit. He admitted driving with excess alcohol, but denied driving without due care and attention, saying he had not been affected by what he had drunk – six vodkas and two pints of beer. His breath alcohol reading was 64. On his appeal, the Court of Appeal held that the court was entitled to look at all the circumstances. Evidence of the amount drunk is admissible if it tends to show that it would adversely affect a driver, or that the driver was in fact adversely affected. The jury was capable of assessing for itself, as a matter of common sense and general experience, the likely effects of having consumed so much alcohol. Expert evidence was not required. Being over the limit does not necessarily mean that the driver was driving carelessly. The question is one of fact and degree.

The Court of Appeal (Criminal Division) approved *Millington* in *R v Irvine* [2002] EWCA Crim 827, and applied the same principle in a case where the defendant was unfit to drive through the drug ecstasy, allowing into evidence the evidence of two experts concerning the effects of the drug.

In *Jones v CPS and Croydon Crown Court* [2019] EWHC 2826 (Admin), [2020] 1 WLR 99, the question on appeal was whether the offence of careless driving can be established solely by reference to the physical condition of the driver. The appellant had been attacked, sustaining head injuries. He fell and lost consciousness. Shortly afterwards, he drove away, while his head wounds were still bleeding. There was an accident and the appellant was convicted of driving without due care and attention. The Administrative Court held that the test for careless or inconsiderate driving is the same as that for dangerous driving, except that for dangerous driving the driver must fall 'far below', rather than simply 'below' what would be expected of a competent and careful driver. The court followed *R v Webster* [2006] EWCA Crim 415, [2006] Cr App R 6, which concerned whether a driver could be guilty of dangerous driving when the reason for the danger was the state of the driver rather the manner of driving, concluding that it is not sufficient merely to rely on the condition of the driver to prove the offence of careless driving or of causing death by careless driving. The condition of the driver is relevant and admissible, but it does not determine whether the way in which the defendant drove was careless.

6.4 DRIVING INCONSIDERATELY

Road Traffic Act 1988, s 3ZA(4) provides that a person is driving without reasonable consideration for others only if others are inconvenienced by the driving. In *Dilks v Bowman-Shaw* [1981] RTR 4, a motorist on a two-lane motorway overtook on the left. A charge of driving without reasonable consideration was dismissed, the justices finding that the element of danger did not fall for consideration. Two other drivers said they had not been inconvenienced and police evidence confirmed that. On the prosecutor's appeal, the Divisional Court found that potential danger might, in a proper case, be considered as one of the circumstances, but the justices had adopted the right approach. The decision was not, however, to be taken as authority for passing on the left.

6.5 OTHER PERSONS

'Other persons using the road' include the passengers of the person said to have driven carelessly: *Pawley v Wharldall* [1966] 1 QB 373, where a bus driver drove without reasonable consideration for his passengers.

6.6 UNFIT OR WITH EXCESS ALCOHOL OR DRUGS

For the interpretation of the provisions in Road Traffic Act 1988, s 3A(1)(a), (b) and (ba), relating to unfitness to drive or excess alcohol or drugs, see Chapters 7 and 8.

6.7 FAILURE TO PROVIDE SPECIMENS

On failing to provide specimens, or failing to allow a specimen to be laboratory tested (in Road Traffic Act 1988, s 3A(1)(c) and (d)), see Chapter 10.

Section 3A(1)(c) applies where a driver has caused the death of another by careless or inconsiderate driving and has then failed, without reasonable excuse, to provide evidential specimens when required to do so under s 7. In *R v Coe (Christopher Steven)* [2009] EWCA Crim 1452, a motor cyclist was convicted under this provision. He had hit and killed a pedestrian who was crossing a dual carriageway at a pelican crossing. The motor cyclist was injured and was taken to hospital. Blood specimens were taken for medical purposes. The doctor in charge of the case told police that there was no reason why the motor cyclist could not give specimens. The police required the motor cyclist to provide breath specimens but he did not reply, and did not react when the mouthpiece of the device was placed against his lips. The doctor said that the motor cyclist might have been 'in and out of consciousness', so the officer decided to proceed under s 7A (specimens of blood from persons incapable of consenting) and called for a police surgeon. When the police surgeon arrived, the motor cyclist opened his eyes and refused to provide a specimen, despite being warned that it would be an offence to refuse without a reasonable excuse. The police later obtained an order for production of a blood specimen taken by the hospital, which showed 210 milligrammes of alcohol in 100 millilitres of blood. The blood analysis was admitted in evidence. The motor cyclist appealed against conviction under s 3A(1)(c).

The Court of Appeal ruled that, since the offence charged was contrary to s 3A(1)(c), the prosecution had to prove only that the defendant was driving without due care and attention (it not being disputed that the impact caused the victim's death) and that the appellant had no reasonable excuse for failing to provide specimens of breath and blood. The prosecution did not have to prove that the appellant had taken drink or how much drink he had taken, as would have been the case if the charge had been contrary to s 3A(1)(a) or (b). There was ample evidence of both matters independently of the blood sample analysis. If the evidence of the analysis of the blood sample had been admitted in error, it would not have affected the safety of the conviction.

The appeal was dismissed, but the Court of Appeal went on to express the view that the evidence of the analysis was rightly admitted. This was because it was relevant to whether the appellant was driving without due care and attention, and relevant to the reasons for refusing to supply specimens. Further, Road Traffic Offenders Act 1988, s 15 (evidence of the proportion of alcohol or any drug in a specimen to be taken into account – see Chapter 8) had no bearing on the admissibility of the blood analysis. This was because, although s 15(1) limits the application of the entire section to proceedings for offences under ss 3A, 4 and 5 (and now, presumably, s 5A), the court said, Parliament must have intended it to apply to s 3A(1)(a) and (b) only (driving unfit or with excess alcohol), and not to the matters in s 3A(1)(c) and (d) – failing to provide or failing to consent to analysis.

See also para 8.9.3 concerning the admissibility in evidence of the blood specimen in *Coe*.

Chapter 7

Unfitness to Drive

7.1 INTRODUCTION

Road Traffic Act 1988, s 4 is headed 'Driving, or being in charge when under influence of drink or drugs'. It provides:

> (1) A person who, when driving or attempting to drive a mechanically propelled vehicle on a road or other public place, is unfit to drive through drink or drugs is guilty of an offence.
> (2) Without prejudice to subsection (1) above, a person who, when in charge of a mechanically propelled vehicle which is on a road or other public place, is unfit to drive through drink or drugs is guilty of an offence.
> (3) For the purposes of subsection (2) above, a person shall be deemed not to have been in charge of a mechanically propelled vehicle if he proves that at the material time the circumstances were such that there was no likelihood of his driving it so long as he remained unfit to drive through drink or drugs.
> (4) The court may, in determining whether there was such a likelihood as is mentioned in subsection (3) above, disregard any injury to him and any damage to the vehicle.
> (5) For the purposes of this section, a person shall be taken to be unfit to drive if his ability to drive properly is for the time being impaired.

Unfitness to drive is also referred to in s 3A(1), on causing death by careless driving while under the influence of drink or drugs; see Chapter 6.

An offence of driving, attempting to drive or being in charge when unfit through drink or drugs featured in the Road Traffic Act 1930, pre-dating the fixed blood alcohol limit, and any form of breath testing. While most prosecutions are now based on being over the limit for alcohol or drugs, the offences of unfitness through drink or drugs have not been repealed. Prosecutions for these offences are now relatively rare, but s 4 remains significant, not least because it provides for the prosecution of those whose driving skills are impaired by drugs other than the controlled drugs specified for the purposes of s 5A (see Chapter 8). It also allows for the prosecution of those who are unfit to drive, whether through drink or drugs, but not over the relevant limit.

Section 4 does not create separate offences in respect of drink and drugs. It is the state of incapacity, whether caused by drink or drugs, which constitutes this element of the offence. A conviction for being in charge while under the influence of drink or a drug was not bad for uncertainty: *Thomson v Knights* [1947] KB 336 (decided under the Road Traffic Act 1930). Compare s 5(1) – driving or in charge with excess alcohol – which creates six different offences (see para 8.1); and s 7(6) – failing to provide – which creates a single offence (see para 10.2.2).

For the meanings of 'driving', 'attempting to drive', 'mechanically propelled vehicle', 'road or other public place' and 'in charge', see Chapter 8.

To secure a conviction, it must be proved both that the defendant was unfit to drive, and that the unfitness was caused by drink or drugs: *R v Hawkes* (1931) 22 Cr App R 172.

7.2 THE MEANING OF 'UNFIT TO DRIVE'

Road Traffic Act 1988, ss 3A(2) and 4(5) provide that a person is unfit to drive if his ability to drive properly is impaired. The terms 'unfitness' and 'impairment' appear to be interchangeable. Both are imprecise and the cases turn on their own facts:

> Fitness to drive may depend upon all sorts of circumstances. The amount of alcohol which will make one man unfit to drive does not necessarily make another man unfit. (Lawton LJ in *R v Richards* [1975] 1 WLR 131, CA)

In *R v Lanfear* [1968] 2 QB 77 (CA), the driving when unfit consisted of driving down a well-lit road on a fine night with a clear view of 100 yards, and running into the back of a parked car with a parking light. The defendant drove with the brake on. When he got out of his car, he was swaying, his eyes were glazed and his speech was slurred.

In *R v Hunt* [1980] RTR 29, the Court of Appeal held that where a driver, for no apparent reason, collided with a stationary van which should have been plainly visible to him, it could be inferred that the driver's ability to drive properly was impaired.

See also *Leetham v DPP* [1999] RTR 29 and *Willicott v DPP* [2001] EWHC 415 (Admin), (2002) 166 JP 385 (below).

Approved police officers may, subject to certain conditions, conduct preliminary impairment tests under Road Traffic Act 1988, s 6B, as described in Chapter 2. The Secretary of State's code of practice concerning such tests says that they are designed to indicate whether a person is unfit to drive and, if so, whether the unfitness is likely to be due to drink or drugs. They are not conclusive, but should enable the officer to form an overall opinion whether or not the subject is impaired, taking into account his driving, his demeanour, what is said and observed, as well as performance in the tests.

7.3 EVIDENCE OF UNFITNESS

It is for the court to determine whether or not a defendant was unfit. A witness may give a general impression as to whether a driver had taken drink, but must describe the facts relied upon. Merely being a driver does not make a witness an expert witness who can express an opinion as to unfitness: *R v Davies* [1962] 1 WLR 1111.

The evidence of a medical practitioner, whether or not a police surgeon, who examines a suspect at the request of the police, is to be regarded as that of an independent expert with the sole desire to assist the court, unless the practitioner himself indicates otherwise: *R v Nowell* [1948] 1 All ER 794 (CCA); *R v Lanfear* [1968] 2 QB 77 (CA).

A medical practitioner is entitled to give evidence of the amount which must have been consumed to reach the level shown by the analysis of a specimen. The rate at which alcohol is destroyed in the body is a matter within the ordinary knowledge of a general medical practitioner, and such a witness was allowed to refresh his memory from a publication by the British Medical Association giving current knowledge on the point. The fact that the practitioner is not an expert on such matters goes to the weight of the evidence, not its admissibility: *R v Somers* [1963] 1 WLR 1306 (CCA).

On the facts in *Leetham v DPP* [1999] RTR 29, justices were entitled to find unfitness to drive through drugs without evidence from the medical practitioner who took a blood specimen from the defendant, or other expert medical evidence. The defendant had been driving too fast and badly. He admitted he had smoked cannabis and that he was in possession of cannabis. His eyes were red and glazed, his speech was slurred and his answers to questions slow. A blood sample confirmed the presence of a cannabis compound. The scientist who analysed the blood gave evidence of the effects of cannabis and that it might adversely affect driving. The Divisional Court found that the evidence taken as a whole was sufficient for a finding of guilt. This included evidence of the manner of driving, the admission of having consumed cannabis, the presence of cannabis in the blood specimen, the effects of that drug, and the evidence of the police officers of the condition of the defendant.

In *Hurst v DPP* [1998] EWHC 486 (Admin), the Divisional Court upheld the justices' finding of unfitness to drive. Their decision was based on police evidence that, immediately after an accident, the defendant's breath smelled reasonably strongly of alcohol, his actions and speech were slow and his speech was slurred. The prosecution adduced expert evidence that slurred speech was consistent with intoxication, rather than with the injuries he suffered in the accident.

Readings from partial breath specimens, indicating that the motorist was over the limit, were held not to be admissible in support of a charge of driving while unfit, because there was no evidence of their reliability or of their relevance: *Willicott v DPP* [2001] EWHC 415 (Admin), (2002) 166 JP 385. The Divisional Court pointed out that there was other evidence in the case on which the justices could have found that the defendant had been driving while unfit: his driving was erratic, he went through two sets of red traffic lights, his breath smelled of alcohol, his speech was slurred and his eyes were glazed.

The form MG DD/B (in the notes to para B1) suggests that in most impairment cases the evidence is likely to include:

- what witnesses (including police officers) say about the driving behaviour of the defendant. This may include observations of what took place at a preliminary impairment test, and a completed form MG DD/F;
- the analysis of a specimen showing the presence of alcohol or a drug, and, in the case of a drug, that it was capable of affecting the ability to drive.

7.4 'DRINK OR DRUGS'

To secure a conviction, it must be proved that the impairment was caused by drink or drugs. Suspects are therefore required to provide specimens for analysis. Road Traffic Act 1988, s 7(3)(bc) empowers a constable to require a specimen of blood or urine if, following a preliminary drug test, the constable has reasonable cause to believe that the person in question has a drug in the body. Section 7(3)(c) authorises requiring a blood or urine specimen where the offence suspected is under s 3A (causing death by careless driving when under the influence of drink or drugs – see Chapter 6), s 4 or s 5A (excess of a specified controlled drug – see Chapter 8), and a medical practitioner or registered health care professional has advised the constable that the suspect's condition might be due to some drug. See para 4.6.

As a result of the analysis of specimens, a suspect may be charged with an excess alcohol offence under s 5, excess of a specified drug under s 5A (or with failing to provide a specimen if that is the case) in addition to, or in place of, an offence under s 4. Where both offences are charged, one of them may be dropped on a guilty plea to the other. On the other hand, a person originally suspected of having excess alcohol or drugs may, following investigation, be charged with being unfit.

Road Traffic Offenders Act 1988, s 15 (evidence of the proportion of alcohol or any drug in a specimen to be taken into account) applies to offences under s 4. Likewise, the statutory assumption (that the concentration of alcohol or a specified controlled drug at the time of the alleged offence was not less than in the specimen) applies, unless the defendant can show that it was alcohol or a drug consumed after the alleged offence which explains the unfitness (see Chapter 8). In *R v Hunt* [1980] RTR 29, the Court of Appeal held that where the driver's alcohol concentration was nearly two and a half times the prescribed limit, the jury was entitled to infer that he was likely to be substantially intoxicated and that such intoxication was responsible for his impaired driving. It was common knowledge that a person with such an amount of alcohol in the body would be likely to be substantially intoxicated and expert evidence was not necessary. Nor was it significant that there was no evidence that the defendant had appeared to be drunk.

7.5 'DRUG'

Road Traffic Act 1988, s 11 defines 'drug' so as to include any intoxicant other than alcohol. While this appears to beg the question of the meaning of 'intoxicant', the cases decided before this definition was introduced may assist.

A drug is 'a medicament or medicine, something given to cure, alleviate or assist an ailing body'. It certainly includes insulin. See *Armstrong v Clark* [1957] 2 QB 391 (DC).

A diabetic could be guilty under s 4 if the unfitness takes the form of a hypoglycaemic attack which is a direct result of an injection of insulin: *R v Ealing Magistrates' Court ex parte Woodman* [1994] RTR 189. On the facts of the case, however, there was no evidence that any insulin remained in the applicant's body at the relevant time so as to lead to such an attack, or that any failure by the defendant to follow medical advice had caused the attack. In the earlier case of *Watmore v Jenkins* [1962] 2 QB 572, the Queen's Bench Division had also found, on the facts, that it was open to the justices to decide that injected insulin was no more than a predisposing or historical cause, and not the immediate cause, of a hypoglycaemic episode.

In *Bradford v Wilson* (1984) 78 Cr App R 77 (DC), the court found that, as a general rule, a substance taken into the body by whatever means – for example by inhalation, injection or by mouth – which is not a drink or food, but which does affect the control of the human body, is to be treated as a drug for these purposes. A particular example of such a substance is one which has a narcotic effect on the body. The substance in question in the case – toluene, found in glue which the defendant had been sniffing – was held to be a drug. The court dismissed Misuse of Drugs Act 1971, sch 2 (list of controlled drugs) as a guide to the meaning of the word 'drug' for road traffic purposes. Substances which are taken as medicines may be drugs, but equally substances not taken as medicines may be drugs. The provision is directed at preventing persons being in charge of vehicles when they have taken substances which could affect the control of their bodies in that activity.

7.6 POWER OF ARREST

Road Traffic Act 1988, s 6D(2)(b) confers on a constable the power to arrest a person without warrant if the person fails to co-operate with a preliminary test (see Chapter 2) and the constable reasonably suspects that the person has alcohol or a drug in his body, or is under the influence of a drug.

An arrest on suspicion of being unfit through drink or drugs may be made under PACE, s 24 (general power of arrest) (see para 2.8).

The fact that a roadside breath test is negative does not preclude arrest on suspicion of driving while impaired. In *DPP v Robertson* [2002] EWHC 542 (Admin), [2002] RTR 22, the Queen's Bench Division held that the power of arrest (then in s 4(6)) did not fall away because police had embarked on breath testing, although a negative test would bear on a decision to arrest on suspicion of driving while unfit. The driver had passed a roadside breath test but, in the ensuing conversation, police believed he slurred his speech. They arrested him, and breath analysis showed excess alcohol. The Queen's Bench Division upheld the arrest and ruled the evidence of the breath analysis admissible.

7.7 POWER OF ENTRY

There is a power of entry under PACE, s 17(1)(c)(iiia) to enter and search any premises to arrest a person on suspicion of an offence of driving or being in charge while unfit. The constable need not be in uniform.

7.8 NO LIKELIHOOD OF DRIVING

Road Traffic Act 1988, s 4(3) provides that a person is to be deemed not to have been in charge upon proof that at the material time the circumstances were such that there was no likelihood of driving while remaining unfit to do so through drink or drugs. This is discussed in para 9.4.

Chapter 8

The Excess Alcohol and Drugs Offences

8.1 INTRODUCTION

Road Traffic Act 1988, s 5 provides for the offences of driving, attempting to drive or being in charge of a motor vehicle with excess alcohol:

> (1) If a person—
>
> (a) drives or attempts to drive a motor vehicle on a road or other public place, or
> (b) is in charge of a motor vehicle on a road or other public place,
>
> after consuming so much alcohol that the proportion of it in his breath, blood or urine exceeds the prescribed limit he is guilty of an offence.

Section 5A, in force from 2 March 2015, provides for the offences of driving, attempting to drive, or being in charge with an excess of a specified controlled drug:

> (1) This section applies where a person ('D')—
>
> (a) drives or attempts to drive a motor vehicle on a road or other public place, or
> (b) is in charge of a motor vehicle on a road or other public place,
>
> and there is in D's body a specified controlled drug.
> (2) D is guilty of an offence if the proportion of the drug in D's blood or urine exceeds the specified limit for that drug.

As noted above (para 1.2.4), the offence under s 5A was introduced to tackle the growing incidence of drug-driving and to address the difficulties of proving impairment for the purposes of s 4 (see Chapter 7). The number of convictions for drug-driving is increasing rapidly, and in 2021 almost matched the number of convictions for drink-driving. The provisions on drug-driving largely mirror those on the excess alcohol offences, and the case law on drink-driving is expected to apply to drug-driving where relevant.

The offences in ss 5(1)(b) and 5A(1)(b), are dealt with in Chapter 9 on the 'in charge' offences.

Section 5(1)(a) creates six different offences (*R v Bolton Justices ex parte Zafer Alli Khan* [1998] EWHC 1040 (Admin), [1999] Crim LR 912):

- driving with excess alcohol in breath;
- driving with excess alcohol in blood;
- driving with excess alcohol in urine;
- attempting to drive with excess alcohol in breath;
- attempting to drive with excess alcohol in blood;
- attempting to drive with excess alcohol in urine.

The prosecution is aware of which specimen was analysed and the charge should be worded accordingly.

Where the defendant had been charged with driving with excess alcohol in the 'breath/blood/urine', the charge, as framed, was duplicitous. The prosecutor should simply have applied to amend the information which could have been done without prejudice to the defendant: *Zafer Alli Khan* (above). Compare the position under s 4 (see para 7.1), where it is the state of incapacity, whether caused by drink or drugs, which constitutes the offence, and s 7(6), which creates a single offence of failing to provide (see para 10.2.2 and *Shaw v DPP* [1993] 1 All ER 918, para 12.4.1) regardless of which type of specimen was required.

8.2 'DRIVES'

8.2.1 The meaning of 'drives'

The Court of Appeal considered the meaning of the word 'drive' in *R v MacDonagh* [1974] QB 448, which concerned driving while disqualified. The defendant had pushed the car, standing with his feet on the road, his shoulder against the door pillar, and one hand inside the car on the steering wheel. He appealed against conviction, arguing that he had not been driving. The Court of Appeal ruled that the essence of driving was the use of the driver's controls to direct movement, no matter how the movement was produced. The word 'drive' was to be given a wide meaning, but not so wide as to include activities which could not be said to constitute driving in any ordinary use of the word. There was a distinction between driving a car and pushing it. No ordinary meaning of 'drive' could extend to the appellant, who was not in the car, had both feet on the road and was making no use of the controls apart from an occasional adjustment of the steering wheel. The facts were close to the borderline, and the position might have been different had he had one foot in the car in order to make more effective use of the controls.

Where a passenger deliberately took hold of the steering wheel for a moment and assumed a degree of control over the car, that might amount to driving, but on the facts in *Jones v Pratt* [1983] RTR 54, it did not. In that case, the defendant had been a front seat passenger. An animal ran across the road and the defendant momentarily grabbed the steering wheel and jerked it, causing the car to go off the road. He was charged with driving with excess alcohol and without due care and attention. The Divisional Court held that he could not in the ordinary sense properly be described as driving. See also *DPP v Hastings* [1993] RTR 205 (DC).

That each case depends on its facts was emphasised in *Rowan v Chief Constable of the Merseyside Police*, *The Times*, 10 December 1985. The defendant had boarded a coach, which was parked on an obvious slope. For a joke, he knelt on the driver's seat and released the handbrake, but was then unable to control the coach and bring it to a stop. He appealed against conviction for driving with excess alcohol, arguing, *inter alia*, that he had not been driving. The Divisional Court concluded, with some hesitation, that it would be wrong to disturb the judgment of the court below. The court would not go so far as to say that, to establish driving, a person must have been using more than one control of the vehicle, although it must be shown that he was responsible for bringing about the movement of the vehicle. Every case depends on the circumstances and how sensible people look at it.

The Divisional Court again declined to interfere with the finding of the court below in *McKoen v Ellis* [1987] RTR 26 that the defendant had been driving. He had been pushing a motor cycle, deliberately setting it in motion and steering it. The lights were on; he used the brakes; the ignition had been turned on sufficiently to warm the exhaust pipe. When found by the police, he was astride the machine and was wearing a crash helmet and other motor cycling gear. Applying *R v MacDonagh* (above), the court found that, although the case might be thought close to the borderline, it was open to the justices, in all the circumstances, to reach the conclusion they did.

In *Gunnell v DPP* [1994] RTR 151, the Divisional Court found that there was ample material on which to find that a defendant had been driving a moped when, being unable to start it, he was astride it and set it in motion by propelling it with his feet for 60 or 70 yards.

It is not necessary for the vehicle to move to constitute driving. In *DPP v Alderton* [2003] EWHC 2917 (Admin), [2004] RTR 23, the defendant was sitting in his vehicle on a roadside verge, 'wheel-spinning'. The engine was running and the defendant was using the accelerator, clutch and steering wheel, with the vehicle in gear and the handbrake on. The Administrative Court found that he was using all the controls of the car. The fact that it was not moving because the handbrake was on did not preclude a finding that he had been driving. On the facts, the defendant's behaviour amounted to driving.

In cases concerning road traffic offences other than drink-drive offences, the following have been held to constitute driving:

- releasing the brake of a lorry which had no petrol in the tank, getting into the driving seat, and allowing it to go downhill, operating the brakes and the steering wheel: *Saycell v Bool* [1948] 2 All ER 83 (DC);
- sitting next to the driver with the left hand on the steering wheel and the right hand on the handbrake, while supervising a learner driver. It is not impossible for two people to be driving a vehicle at the same time: *Langman v Valentine* [1952] 2 All ER 803 (DC);
- sitting next to the driver, leaning across the person in the driving seat and steering, having access to the handbrake and ignition: *Tyler v Whatmore* [1976] RTR 83;
- steering, controlling and being able to apply the brakes of a vehicle which was being towed: *McQuaid v Anderton* [1981] 1 WLR 154 (DC);
- causing a vehicle to move by the voluntary act of depressing the accelerator in the mistaken belief that it was the brake: *Attorney General's Reference No 4 of 2000* [2001] EWCA Crim 780, [2001] 2 Cr App R 22 (CA);
- sitting in the driver's seat, using the brakes and steering, while the vehicle was being towed: *R (Traves) v DPP* [2005] EWHC 1482 (Admin).

On the other hand, sitting in the driving seat of a stationary car, switching on the engine, sitting up in the seat and placing the hands on the steering wheel did not of itself amount to driving in *Leach v DPP* [1993] RTR 161 (QBD).

8.2.2 Inference of driving

In *Planton v DPP* [2001] EWHC 450 (Admin), [2002] RTR 9, the defendant was found in the driver's seat of his car, which was stationary, on a man-made causeway linking an island in a river to the mainland. He was waiting for the tide to recede sufficiently to use the causeway. The engine was running and the lights were on. On appeal against conviction for driving with excess alcohol, he argued, *inter alia*, that he had not been driving. The Divisional Court found that it was a question of fact and degree whether the cessation of movement has been for so long and in such circumstances that it could not reasonably be said that the person in the driving seat is driving. On the facts found, the justices were entitled to hold that the defendant was driving the vehicle.

On the other hand, in *Huntley v DPP* [2004] EWHC 870 (Admin), justices were wrong to conclude that the defendant had been driving simply because he had been arrested on suspicion of driving with excess alcohol, and there was no evidence that he had been driving.

Where the identity of the driver is in issue, the relevant witnesses should be called and cross-examined: *Jones (Vivian Mary) v DPP* [2004] EWHC 3165 (Admin), [2005] RTR 15 (DC).

The fact that a person was driving on a public road may be inferred from the facts. In *DPP v Lloyd* [2002] EWHC 2977 (Admin), a van had become stuck in a ditch on a private road, the only access to which was via a public road. There was no dispute that the defendant had been driving the van when it became stuck, and no evidence that any route had been taken other than the public road, or that anyone else had driven. The necessary conclusion was to infer that the defendant had been driving on a public road.

Likewise, in *Premananthan v CPS* [2013] EWHC 3419 (Admin), the circumstances were such that the magistrates were entitled to infer that the defendant had been driving. The sole prosecution witness gave evidence that he had heard a crash, looked out of his window, and saw the defendant leaning against the bonnet of a car; no one else was in the vicinity. The defendant, who was over the limit, offered the witness £2,000 but did not say what it was for. The justices rejected a submission of no case to answer, drew an adverse inference from the accused's silence at trial, and, looking at all the circumstances, convicted the defendant of driving with excess alcohol. On his appeal, he did not dispute that he had been over the limit but argued that there was no evidence that the car had recently been driven; no finding concerning the whereabouts of the keys; no evidence to connect the car with the crash heard by the witness; and no evidence about how long the car had been in the place where it was found. There were various explanations for the offer of £2,000. The Divisional Court pointed out that questions of credibility and reliability, and of the weight to be attached to evidence, are for the court of trial to determine having regard to the whole of the evidence. Circumstantial evidence can be powerful. It is the whole picture that is important. The combination of all the facts and circumstances in this case entitled the court to reject the submission of no case to answer.

8.2.3 Admission of driving

It is sufficient that a defendant admits that he was driving; no corroboration is necessary: *Patterson v Charlton* [1986] RTR 18 (DC).

The admission must, though, be admissible in evidence. In *Whelehan v DPP* [1995] RTR 177, the motorist had been found, alone, in the driving seat of his stationary car. The keys were in the ignition. It was apparent to the officer that he had been drinking and, in reply to a question from the officer, he admitted that he had driven. The officer then cautioned him. The question was whether the officer should have cautioned him before asking him whether he had been driving, and if so, whether the oral admission that he had driven was therefore inadmissible. The Queen's Bench Division found that there was sufficient evidence, apart from his admission, that he had been driving. Even if the caution should have been given earlier, no properly directed court would have excluded the evidence of the reply. In any event, the Queen's Bench Division would not dissent from the justices' finding that the officer's obligation to caution did not arise until after he had administered the roadside breath test. See also *Charles v CPS* [2009] EWHC 3521 (Admin), [2010] RTR 34 (below).

In *CPS v O'Shea*, unreported, 11 May 1998 (DC), a road traffic accident had occurred. There were no witnesses, but nearby residents heard a loud bang and came out of their houses. They saw the defendant near his Volvo and thought he was drunk. Police were called. An officer said to the defendant 'An accident has just happened that is alleged was your fault. Were you driving your Volvo H569 WTV at the time of the accident?'. He replied 'yes'. The breath test procedure was then administered and showed excess alcohol. The justices accepted an argument that the officer's question constituted an interview as defined in PACE Codes of Practice, Code C. The defendant should therefore have been cautioned, but was not. The justices exercised their discretion under PACE, s 78 to exclude the admission. (Section 78 allows a court to exclude evidence which would have such an adverse effect on the fairness of the proceedings that the court ought not to admit it – see Chapter 11.) The Divisional Court recited the circumstances which amount to an interview (including questions put to a person in respect of whom there are grounds to suspect of an offence), and the circumstances which do not amount to an interview (including questions asked solely to establish identity or ownership of a vehicle). It found that when the officer asked the question, he knew the driver's identity and knew he owned the Volvo. The question was not solely to establish identity or ownership of the vehicle. It was also clear from the words 'an accident has just happened that is alleged was your fault', that there were grounds to suspect the defendant of having committed an offence. The thrust of the question was to seek an admission that the respondent was driving the Volvo at the relevant time and it was plain that the answer might be given in evidence. The question was therefore an interview, and the Divisional Court would not interfere with the justices' exercise of their discretion under s 78.

In *DPP v Davies* [2002] EWHC 1110 (Admin), the Administrative Court again upheld a decision by justices that an admission of driving was not admissible. Police had been called to the defendant's home. A car was parked nearby and the bonnet was warm. The defendant smelled of alcohol, his eyes were glazed and he was drinking tea. One of the officers asked if he had had anything else to drink since getting home. He replied that he had not, and, in answer to a further question, that he had been home for about 20 or 25 minutes. The officer cautioned him and told him he suspected he had driven his car home. The defendant admitted he had driven, and the officer required a sample of breath. It was argued that the evidence of the conversation at the defendant's home should be excluded under s 78 because Code C, para 11.13 had not been met. That paragraph requires that any comments made by a suspect outside the context of an interview, but which might be relevant, should be recorded in writing; the record is to be timed and signed by the maker, and, if practicable, the suspect is to be given the opportunity to read and sign the record. The justices found there was a significant and substantial breach of the Code in that the record was not timed or signed, and the defendant had not been given an opportunity to read it and sign it as correct, or indicate any respects in which he considered it inaccurate. They exercised their discretion to exclude the evidence and acquitted the defendant on the basis that it was not established that he had driven the vehicle. On the prosecutor's appeal, the Administrative Court ruled that the whole purpose of Code C, para 11.13 is to avoid the very kind of dispute of fact that there would have been had the evidence been admitted in the present case. The justices were entitled to conclude that the effect on the fairness of the proceedings was such as to require them not to admit the evidence.

Again, where the admission of driving was in the course of an interview conducted in breach of PACE, and without caution, it should not have been admitted in evidence pursuant to s 78: *Charles v CPS* [2009] EWHC 3521 (Admin), [2010] RTR 34, where police found the defendant slumped over the steering wheel of a parked car. The parking lights were on, the keys were in the ignition and he was asleep. He was arrested for being in charge while unfit through drink or drugs. At the police station, the lower breath specimen showed 74 microgrammes of alcohol in 100 millilitres of breath. The detainee was informed that he would be charged, but he was then interviewed, in breach of Code C, para 16.5. Paragraph 16.5 provides that a detainee is not to be interviewed about an offence after being charged with it, or after being told that he may be prosecuted for it, unless the interview is necessary. He was not cautioned. Nor was he told, at the outset of that interview, for what offence he was being investigated. During the interview he was asked if he had been driving and he admitted that he had. At the end of the interview, he was charged, not with being in charge, but with driving with excess alcohol, rendering him liable to compulsory rather than discretionary disqualification (see para 12.4.1). The prosecutor conceded that in the absence of the admission, there was no case against the defendant that he had been driving. The Divisional Court recognised that the two breaches were not in bad faith, but they showed scant regard for the clear requirements. In all the circumstances, the admission should have been excluded.

By contrast, in the earlier, unreported case of *Brown (Kevin Mark) v DPP*, 26 October 1993 (DC), the defendant attended the police station in connection with another matter. When an officer asked how he had got there so quickly, he said he had driven. The officer smelled intoxicating liquor and the defendant then denied having driven. The justices dismissed the defendant's argument that he should have been cautioned before being asked if he had driven and, since he was not, that his admission of driving should have been excluded under s 78. The Divisional Court upheld that decision. The question about driving was preliminary, not an interview. At that point the officer had no ground to suspect an offence so that a caution was not necessary. But even if there had been a breach of PACE, it was not of such substance as to justify excluding the admission.

The fact that a defendant was four times over the limit but nevertheless behaving purposefully and meaningfully when he admitted driving was no basis for excluding the admission under s 78: *McShane v DPP*, unreported, 8 December 1995 (DC).

See also *Ortega v DPP* [2001] EWHC 143 (Admin) and *Watson v DPP* [2003] EWHC 1466 (Admin), (2004) 168 JP 116, where, on the facts, the Divisional Court upheld decisions to allow in admissions of driving.

Where a person is required, pursuant to Road Traffic Act 1988, s 172(2), to say who was driving, the prosecution can rely on a resulting admission, and does not thereby breach the right to a fair trial in European Convention on Human Rights, art 6. Section 172(2)(a) provides that where the driver of a vehicle is alleged to be guilty of an offence to which the section applies, the person keeping the vehicle must give such information about the identity of the driver as may be required by or on behalf of a chief officer of police. It is usually used when an offence has been detected by a roadside camera, to ascertain who was driving at the time. In the Scottish case of *Brown v Stott* [2003] AC 681 (PC), a woman had been arrested for theft at a supermarket. She appeared to have been drinking, and pointed out a car in the car park, saying it was hers. The police, under s 172(2), required her to say who had been driving and she admitted it was her. She was breath tested and in due course convicted of driving with excess alcohol. On appeal, she argued that it was incompatible with her human rights for the prosecutor to rely on her admission. The Privy Council ruled that while the right to a fair trial under art 6 is absolute, the privilege against self-incrimination – one of the constituent rights under art 6 – is not. Limited qualification is acceptable if reasonably directed towards a clear and proper public objective and if representing no greater qualification than the situation calls for. Section 172 provides for the putting of a single simple question; the answer does not in itself incriminate the person answering. It does not represent a disproportionate legislative response to the problem of maintaining road safety. The manner in which the balance between the interests of the community at large and of the individual is struck is not unduly prejudicial to the latter and does not infringe a human right.

In *Ambrose v Harris* [2011] UKSC 43, [2011] 1 WLR 2435, the Supreme Court held that adducing evidence obtained in response to police questioning conducted under caution at the roadside, the suspect having had no access to legal advice, did not breach the right to a fair trial or the presumption of innocence. The defendant had been charged, in Scotland, with being in charge of a motor vehicle after consuming excess alcohol, contrary to s 5(1)(b). Officers found him sitting in the passenger seat of a car parked at the roadside. They thought he had been drinking. They cautioned him and asked three questions – where the keys were, whether he had driven, and whether he was going to drive. He gave incriminating answers. Breath analysis revealed excess alcohol. The answers to the questions were led at trial in the sheriff court and the defendant was convicted. He appealed, arguing that his rights under art 6(1) (the right to a fair trial) and art 6(3)(c) (the presumption of innocence) had been breached.

The Supreme Court ruled that the privilege against self-incrimination is not an absolute right. A person is therefore free to speak to the police and to answer questions if willing to do so, even after being cautioned. He can give self-incriminating answers, and those answers will be admissible if they are truly voluntary. The test is whether the will of the person to remain silent, if that is his will, has been respected. The correct starting point, when considering whether a person's Convention rights have been breached, is to identify the moment at which the person was charged for the purposes of art 6(1). The moment at which the individual is no longer a potential witness but has become a suspect provides as good a guide as any. Applying that test, the motorist was charged for the purposes of art 6 when he was cautioned and the officer had reason to think that the second and third questions were likely to elicit incriminating responses. The appellant was not entitled to a finding that this evidence was inadmissible because access to a lawyer should have been provided to him when he was questioned at the roadside. The Supreme Court left open the question whether, taking all the circumstances into account, it was fair to admit the whole or any part of this evidence.

8.3 ATTEMPTING TO DRIVE

Whether or not a person is attempting to drive appears to be a matter of interpretation based on the Road Traffic Act 1988. Criminal Attempts Act 1981, s 3(1) provides that a person is guilty of an attempt under a special statutory provision (which includes Road Traffic Act 1988, ss 4, 5 and 5A) if, with intent to commit the full offence, the person does an act which is more than merely preparatory to the commission of that offence. Under s 3(4), a person may be guilty of such an attempt even if the commission of the full offence is impossible.

In *R v Farrance* (1978) 67 Cr App R 136, the Court of Appeal (Criminal Division) held that a person sitting in the driving seat, attempting to start the car or to put it into gear, or using the accelerator in an effort to make it move, was attempting to drive it, and it made no difference that some intervening factor (in this case, mechanical failure) prevented the person from fulfilling the attempt.

In *Kelly v Hogan* [1982] RTR 352, the defendant had been sitting in the driving seat of a stationary car. He inserted various keys into the ignition, but the car would not start because none of the keys was the right key. It was accepted that the engine would have started if he had had the right key. He was convicted of attempting to drive while unfit through drink, and appealed. The Divisional Court found that putting a wrong key into the ignition was sufficiently proximate to the commission of the full offence of unlawful driving as to constitute an attempt to drive. Further, the commission of the full offence was not impossible; the defendant had failed to complete its commission through ineptitude, inefficiency, or insufficient means; he had it in mind to drive.

In the unreported case of *Elkarib v DPP*, 11 May 1995 (DC), it was held that driving on a private road, intending to proceed to a public road, amounted to attempting to drive. Likewise, in *Moore v DPP* [2010] EWHC 1822 (Admin), [2010] RTR 36, the defendant, who was over the limit, drove about 90 metres on a private car park to an open gate leading onto a public road. He would have driven onto the road if he had not been stopped by a police officer. The Divisional Court upheld his conviction for attempting to drive with excess alcohol. Following *Farrance*, it made no difference that an intervening factor had prevented him from fulfilling the attempt.

In *Mason v DPP* [2009] EWHC 2198 (Admin), [2010] RTR 11, the Divisional Court ruled that the defendant could not have embarked on driving until he did something which was part of the actual process of putting the car in motion. Turning on the engine would have been such a step, but starting to open the door of the car was not. The act of opening the car door was merely preparatory to the act of driving and did not constitute an attempt.

8.4 MOTOR VEHICLE

The offences under Road Traffic Act 1988, ss 5 and 5A can be committed only in respect of 'motor vehicles', while the offences under ss 3A (causing death by careless driving when under the influence of drink or drugs) and 4 (driving or in charge when under the influence of drink or drugs) may be committed in respect of the broader category of mechanically propelled vehicles. Motor vehicles are mechanically propelled vehicles intended or adapted for use on roads (s 185(1)(c)).

Road Traffic Act 1988, s 189 provides that the following vehicles are not to be treated as motor vehicles for these purposes:

- a lawnmower ('a mechanically propelled vehicle being an implement for cutting grass which is controlled by a pedestrian and is not capable of being used or adapted for any other purpose');
- any other mechanically propelled vehicle controlled by a pedestrian as specified in regulations; and
- an electrically assisted pedal cycle of a class prescribed by regulations.

Motor cycles, tractors, fork-lift trucks, earth-moving equipment and other construction plant, as well as cars, may all fall within the definition of 'motor vehicle'.

'Controlled by a pedestrian' means that the vehicle either is constructed or adapted for use only under such control, or is constructed or adapted for use either under such control or under the control of a person carried on it, but is not for the time being in use under, or proceeding under, the control of a person carried on it (s 189(2)).

The Electrically Assisted Pedal Cycles Regulations 1983 (SI 1983/1168), made under s 189 and amended by the Electrically Assisted Pedal Cycles (Amendment) Regulations 2015 (SI 2015/24), provide that certain electrically assisted pedal cycles are not to be treated as motor vehicles. To fall within the exception, they must be fitted with pedals by means of which they are capable of being propelled, and fitted with an electric motor only, which must be of a specified maximum wattage and incapable of propelling the vehicle at a speed greater than 15.5 miles per hour.

While many electric bicycles fall within the exception, in *Winter v DPP* [2002] EWHC 1524 (Admin), [2003] RTR 14, the Queen's Bench Division held that a 'City Bug' did not meet the condition concerning pedals and was therefore a motor vehicle. The vehicle was intended primarily to be powered by its motor. It was extremely difficult to propel it by its pedals and it would be impossible to use it safely on the roads by relying on the pedals alone. It was not reasonably capable of being propelled by the pedals.

In *Coates v CPS* [2011] EWHC 2032 (Admin), (2011) 175 JP 401, the Administrative Court ruled that a 'Segway' was a motor vehicle.

Riders of cycles which do not fall within the definition of 'motor vehicle' are subject to Road Traffic Act 1988, s 30, which makes it an offence to ride a cycle on a road or other public place while unfit to ride through drink or drugs. Unfitness is defined as being under the influence of drink or a drug to such an extent as to be incapable of having proper control of the cycle.

There appears to be no reported case law on the application or interpretation of s 30 in domestic law. It is suggested that the cases on unfitness to drive (Chapter 7) may well be relevant given the similarity between the definition of unfitness in s 30 and that under s 4(5), which refers to ability to drive being 'for the time being impaired'. In the extradition case of *Pieczewski v Judicial Authority of Poland* [2012] EWHC 969 (Admin), the Polish authorities sought the extradition of the appellant to serve a prison sentence for riding a bicycle on a pavement while intoxicated. In finding that the dual criminality test was met – that is, that the Polish offence also constituted an offence in domestic law as required by Extradition Act 2003, s 65(3)(b) – the Administrative Court said that 'there is no sensible distinction to be drawn between someone whose control is impaired and someone who is incapable of having proper control'. In another extradition case, the Administrative Court found that, taken by itself, a breath alcohol reading of 0.39 was not sufficient to 'impel the inference that the appellant was incapable of having proper control of the bicycle' for the purposes of s 30 and so the test was not met: *Brodziak v Circuit Judge in Lublin, Poland* [2013] EWHC 3394 (Admin), [2014] ACD 59.

A number of new personal transport devices – known as 'powered transporters' – have been developed in recent years. They are mechanically propelled by a motor, as well as, or instead of, being manually propelled. They include 'e-scooters, Segways, hoverboards, go-peds (combustion engine-powered kick-scooters), powered unicycles and u-wheels' (www.gov.uk/government/publications/powered-transporters/information-sheet-guidance-on-powered-transporters), but not electrically assisted pedal cycles (see above). The Department for Transport's advice is that, in the absence of specific regulation, these devices fall within the definition of motor vehicle. They may be used on private land, but not on roads, unless – as is unlikely – the regulations relating to motor vehicles (including insurance, technical standards, vehicle tax, licensing and registration) are met.

E-scooters may, however, be ridden on a road or cycle lane pursuant to government-sponsored trials (www.gov.uk/guidance/e-scooter-trials-guidance-for-users), subject to the conditions applying to the trials.

The definition of 'motor vehicle' in Road Traffic Act 1988, s 185(1)(c) is subject to Chronically Sick and Disabled Persons Act 1970, s 20, which makes concessions in respect of invalid carriages. Section 20(1)(a) and (b) provide that a mechanically propelled invalid carriage which complies with the prescribed requirements and is used in accordance with the prescribed conditions is not to be treated as a motor vehicle for the purposes of (among other provisions) the Road Traffic Act 1988 (apart from s 22A – causing danger to road users by interfering with motor vehicles, etc). The Use of Invalid Carriages on Highways Regulations 1988 (SI 1988/2268) define three classes of invalid carriage and prescribe the requirements and conditions applying to them for the purposes of s 20(1). The requirements concern unladen weight, means of stopping, lighting, speed indicators, width, audible warning instrument, vision and rear-view mirrors. The prescribed conditions (reg 4(a)) are that the invalid carriage is being used:

- (i) by a person falling within a class of persons for whose use it was constructed or adapted, being a person suffering from some physical defect or physical disability;
- (ii) by some other person for the purposes only of taking the invalid carriage to or bringing it away from any place where work of maintenance or repair is to be or has been carried out to the invalid carriage;
- (iii) by a manufacturer for the purposes only of testing or demonstrating the invalid carriage;
- (iv) by a person offering to sell the invalid carriage for the purpose only of demonstrating it; or
- (v) by a person giving practical training in the use of the invalid carriage for that purpose only.

Those provisions were considered in *Croitoru v CPS* [2016] EWHC 1645 (Admin), [2017] 1 WLR 1130. The appellant appealed against conviction for using a Motability scooter on a road with excess alcohol. He said he had bought the scooter for his elderly father, fitted it with a battery, and was testing it to see how far it would go. Police were called and he was found to be over the limit. He argued that the case fell within (ii) above, in that it was being used 'by some other person for the purposes only of taking the invalid carriage to or bringing it away from any place where work of maintenance or repair is to be or has been carried out to' it. On the facts, the Divisional Court found there was no evidence to support the contention that the use of the scooter fell within reg 4(a)(ii). The effect of s 20 of the 1970 Act was to create an exception in favour of a person accused of driving with excess alcohol and so there was an evidential burden on the appellant to show that he could come within the exception; he had not done so. The conviction was upheld. The Divisional Court said that the clear words of s 20(1)(b) are of general application to the whole of the Road Traffic Act 1988 (save for s 22A, which is specifically exempted). The exception therefore applies to all the drink- and drug- driving offences.

A person falling within the exception above may nonetheless be liable to prosecution under Licensing Act 1872, s 12, for being drunk in charge, on a highway or other public place, of a carriage (or a horse, cattle, or steam engine). Road Traffic Offenders Act 1988, s 5 provides that a person is not to be charged under s 12 of the 1872 Act if the person is liable to be charged with an offence under Road Traffic Act 1988, s 3A, s 4, s 5, s 7 or s 30.

8.4.1 Mechanically propelled vehicle

To be a motor vehicle, a vehicle must be both mechanically propelled and intended or adapted for use on roads. The offences under ss 3A and 4, however, can be committed in respect of a mechanically propelled vehicle which is not necessarily intended or adapted for road use.

Lawrence v Howlett [1952] 2 All ER 74 concerned an 'auto-pedal cycle', a pedal cycle with a motor which could be used or not as the rider chose. On the day in question, certain vital parts had been removed, such that the motor could not be used. The defendant was using it as a pedal cycle. The Divisional Court held that it was not, at that time, a mechanically propelled vehicle. It had two methods of propulsion, one mechanical and one non-mechanical, and to classify it, it was necessary to have regard to its working condition at the relevant time. The later cases of *R v Tahsin* [1970] RTR 88 (CA), *Binks v Department of the Environment* [1975] RTR 318 (QBD) and *McEachran v Hurst* [1978] RTR 462 (QBD) (below) suggest, however, that *Lawrence v Howlett* should be considered exceptional and confined to its own facts.

Where a similar cycle was in full working order and so was capable of being used as either a motor cycle or a pedal cycle, it was a mechanically propelled vehicle, even though the defendant was pedalling it at the material time: *Floyd v Bush* [1953] 1 WLR 242.

By contrast, a car is a mechanically propelled vehicle and has only mechanical means of propulsion, so that whether or not it is in working order, whether it is being free-wheeled or moved in some way with the engine disengaged, it is still being used as a mechanically propelled vehicle: *Lawrence v Howlett* (above).

In *Smart v Allan and Another* [1963] 1 QB 291, the engine in the car in question was incomplete, rusty and did not work, the tyres were flat, one tyre was missing; and there was no gear box or battery. It could not move of its own motion. The Queen's Bench Division held that it had ceased to be a mechanically propelled vehicle because there was no reasonable prospect that it would ever be mobile again.

In *Law v Thomas* [1964] Crim LR 415, the car could not be driven under its own power, but when a defective part was replaced, the defendant was able to drive it away. The Divisional Court found that it had not reached the stage that there was no reasonable prospect of ever making it mobile again. It could be and was repaired. It was therefore a mechanically propelled vehicle.

If a temporary defect in the engine prevents the vehicle (in this case, a moped) from starting, the vehicle does not cease to be a motor vehicle: *R v Tahsin* [1970] RTR 88 (CA).

In *Binks v Department of the Environment* [1975] RTR 318, the Queen's Bench Division applied the test in *Smart v Allan* – whether the stage has been reached that there was no reasonable prospect that the vehicle would ever be made mobile again – and found that the vehicle in question was still a mechanically propelled vehicle. It had suffered severe mechanical damage and needed a new engine. It had been in that state for some nine months, but the defendant intended to repair it so that the car could be driven.

The same rule applies to a moped. It is constructed as a mechanically propelled vehicle and remains such a vehicle until it reaches a stage where there is no reasonable prospect of its being mechanically mobile again: *McEachran v Hurst* [1978] RTR 462 (QBD), where the moped was not in working order and had no petrol in the tank. The defendant was pedalling it to a friend's house to have it repaired.

The burden of proving that a vehicle is a mechanically propelled vehicle is on the prosecution. In *Reader v Bunyard* (1987) 85 Cr App R 185, the Divisional Court found that justices had been wrong to convict on the basis that the defendant had not discharged a burden of showing, on the balance of probabilities, that the intended use of the vehicle was such that it had ceased to be a mechanically propelled vehicle.

8.4.2 Intended or adapted for use on roads

In deciding whether a vehicle is intended for use on the road, the intention of the user or of the manufacturer, wholesaler or retailer is not relevant. The test is whether a reasonable person looking at the vehicle would say that one of its uses would be some general use on the road: *Burns v Currell* [1963] 2 QB 433 (DC), where there was no evidence that a go-kart was intended for general use on the road. See also *Coates v CPS* [2011] EWHC 2032 (Admin), (2011) 175 JP 401 (para 8.4) and *DPP v Saddington* [2001] RTR 15 (below).

An earth-moving vehicle, the function of which is to move earth on building sites, but which moved from site to site under its own power, along roads, was intended or adapted for use on roads and was therefore a motor vehicle: *Childs v Coghlan* [1968] Crim LR 225 (DC).

In *Chief Constable of Avon and Somerset v F* (1987) 84 Cr App R 345 (DC), the question was whether a motor cycle, originally constructed and intended for use on roads, could be modified such that it ceased to be a motor vehicle. The court adopted the approach in *Burns v Currell* that the test is based on the view of the reasonable man as to the general user, and does not depend on the use adopted by the particular defendant. The court found that a vehicle originally manufactured for use on a road would require very substantial alteration before it could be said to be no longer a motor vehicle. It was improbable that the removal from a motor cycle of the lights, speedometer, number plates and reflectors would amount to such an alteration.

In *Nichol v Leach and Another* [1972] RTR 476, a Mini was being towed on a road, steered by one of the defendants. The other defendant was driving the towing vehicle. The Mini had been bought as scrap and adapted for racing under its own power on autocross circuits. The Queen's Bench Division ruled that it remained a vehicle intended for use on roads for insurance and vehicle licence purposes. It had been produced as an ordinary motor car intended to run on roads and did not cease to be so merely because the present owner saw no prospect of driving it on a road under its own power. This decision appears to run counter to that in the earlier case of *Brown v Abbott* (1965) 109 SJ 437, where the Divisional Court, on very similar facts, upheld the justices' finding that a vehicle which had been similarly modified was not intended or adapted for use on roads.

In *Newberry v Simmonds* [1961] 2 QB 345, the Divisional Court dismissed an owner's claim that his car was not a mechanically propelled vehicle for vehicle licence purposes because its engine had been stolen. The car did not cease to be mechanically propelled because the engine had been removed if the evidence admits the possibility that the engine would shortly be replaced. Its absence was not therefore conclusive either way. The court accepted that the meaning of the term for road licence purposes is the same as for road traffic purposes.

On the other hand, applying the test in *Burns v Currell*, a fork-lift truck was found, on the facts of the case, to be intended for use on roads in *Percy and Another v Smith* [1986] RTR 252 (QBD).

DPP v Saddington [2001] RTR 15 concerned a motorised scooter known as a Go-ped. It was accepted that a Go-ped is a vehicle, a motor cycle, and a mechanically propelled vehicle. The issue was whether it was intended for use on roads. The manufacturers stated that it was not. The Queen's Bench Division found that its design and capabilities, and its potential for getting through traffic quickly, were such that its use on roads was tempting, despite its limitations. A reasonable person would say that one of its uses would be some general use on the roads, not merely isolated use. A Go-ped was therefore a mechanically propelled vehicle intended for use on roads. On the same principle, a City Mantis scooter (another type of motorised scooter) was likewise a motor vehicle: *DPP v King* [2008] EWHC 447 (Admin), (2008) 172 JP 401. So too was an Italjet 22 cc motor cycle: *O'Brien v Anderton* [1979] RTR 388 (QBD).

8.5 ROAD

The word 'road' is defined in Road Traffic Act 1988, s 192 in relation to England and Wales, as 'any highway and any other road to which the public has access, and includes bridges over which a road passes'.

In *Lang v Hindhaugh* [1986] RTR 271, the Queen's Bench Division considered this definition, then contained in Road Traffic Act 1972, s 196(1). A motor cyclist had been convicted of driving with excess alcohol on a public footpath, which was 4 to 5 feet wide. It had once been surfaced but had deteriorated, with potholes in it and bushes growing between the fences on either side. It was not designed for motor vehicles and was not passable by a car. It had no street lamps or bollards. There was no indication that motor cyclists were forbidden from using it, and no barrier to prevent access. It was held to be a road for the purposes of the Act and it was irrelevant that it was not a 'road' within the ordinary meaning of the word.

The House of Lords considered the definition in *Cutter v Eagle Star Insurance Co Ltd* [1998] 1 WLR 1647 in the context of the liability of an insurer for personal injury sustained in a car park. It found that the question whether a car park constituted a 'road' within s 192 was a question of fact to be determined after consideration of its physical character and the function it served. On an ordinary use of language, a place that could reasonably be described as a car park does not qualify as a road. The proper function of a road is to enable movement along it to a destination, whereas the proper function of a car park is to enable vehicles to stand and wait. While a car might be driven across a car park, that was only incidental to the principal function of parking. In the absence of express provision, there were no grounds for construing 'road' so as to include a car park.

Cutter was considered in *Brewer v DPP* [2004] EWHC 355 (Admin), [2005] RTR 5 (DC), where the defendant appealed against conviction for being in charge with excess alcohol on a railway station car park. Access to the car park was via a button-operated barrier. Pedestrians walked through the car park to one of the station platforms. Staff drove through it to the staff car park. The Divisional Court reversed the justices' finding that the car park was a road, deciding that the only feature capable of rendering it a road was that staff drove cars through it on their way to the staff car park. That was insufficient, on the basis of *Cutter*, to render the car park capable of being a road. In *Dunmill v DPP* [2004] EWHC 1700 (Admin), justices decided the issue of whether a campsite was a 'road' by reference to whether or not the public had access to it. They were found to have been in error in finding that a campsite was a 'road'. In both *Brewer* and *Dunmill*, the defendants were charged with driving 'on a road', rather than the more usual 'road or other public place'. If the latter form of words had been used, the outcomes would no doubt have been different; see below.

Evidence of public use is necessary to establish that the place where an offence is said to have been committed is a 'road or other public place'. In *Hallett v DPP* [2011] EWHC 488 (Admin), the motorist had been driving on a service road running parallel to a main road; 20 houses led off the service road; 40 or more people had access to the houses; the service road was open at both ends; there were 'give way' markings at each end; it was not a cul-de-sac; the residents were responsible, by covenant, to maintain the road, but did not in fact maintain it; there was no signage indicating that the road was private or that access was prohibited; pedestrians had access to the road to reach a footpath and to cross the road to continue along the footpath. On appeal against conviction for driving with excess alcohol on the service road, the Administrative Court held that the key question was whether there was any evidence of public use of the unmade service road. In fact, there had been nothing to show that individuals other than householders and those in a special class used the service road, and it therefore fell outside the definition of a public road.

In *Cowan v DPP* [2013] EWHC 192 (Admin), (2013) 177 JP 474, the Administrative Court confirmed the need for evidence of public use, but could not tell, from the case stated, whether or not there had been such evidence before the court below. A motorist had been driving on an internal roadway in a university campus. A police officer gave evidence that the campus was accessed by an ordinary road; there was a barrier which opened using a pressure pad; no identification was needed to enter; anyone could go in; there were no 'private' signs, although there were signs about parking prohibitions; the grounds were accessible to students and visitors; the roads were of normal layout and had normal signs; the entrance was one-way and there was no barrier at the exit. The magistrates found that the place in question was used by members of the public at any time of day or night without restriction; access was not limited to a special class of members of the public. They decided it was a public place and convicted. On appeal, the Administrative Court found that the evidence, as set out in the case stated, was insufficient to support that conclusion.

Note, however, that in *R (Anastassova) v Northampton Magistrates' Court and DPP* [2023] EWHC 1586 (Admin) – an application for judicial review of a decision of magistrates not to state a case – the Administrative Court emphasised that in the case of a road, the statutory test is access by the public, not any particular level of public use. Access may be proved by showing that the public in fact uses the road, but that is not the only way.

Where part only of a vehicle encroached onto a public place, even though the wheels remained on private property, the driver was nevertheless 'on a road' for the purposes of the legislation. In *Avery v DPP* [2011] EWHC 2388 (Admin), [2012] RTR 8, the motorist had parked his car on his brother's drive. He had driven in, across the pavement, and parked the car so that the rear end faced the road. Later, he found that a neighbour's Ford Focus was also parked outside the same house, with the offside on the pavement and the onside on the road, but so that pedestrians could still pass along the pavement. He decided to adjust the position of his car. In so doing, the rear end of the defendant's car hit the Ford Focus. The wheels of the defendant's car did not leave his brother's property. The defendant was convicted of driving with excess alcohol. He appealed on the question whether he could have driven 'on a road' when the tyres did not leave private land. It was not disputed that the pavement was part of the road. The Divisional Court found that it was not necessary that there should be any contact between the vehicle and the road surface. The only issue was whether there was sufficient occupation of road space for the protective purposes of the statute to be engaged. That was the case here, where the encroachment on the road was sufficiently substantial to cause damage and to show a potential for causing injury. Any material encroachment on the air space vertically above the road was sufficient to justify concluding that the vehicle was on the road.

In cases concerning road traffic offences other than those dealt with in this volume, the following have been held to be roads:

- roads through a private housing estate where there were notices saying that it was private and that access was restricted to residents, but the part about restrictions on access had been deleted, and there was evidence that the roads were used by the general public: *Adams v Commissioner of Police of the Metropolis* [1980] RTR 289 (DC);

- Trafalgar Square: *Sadiku v DPP* [2000] RTR 155;
- roadways through a private caravan park which were used by the public to gain access to a public beach: *Barrett v DPP* [2009] EWHC 423 (Admin), [2010] RTR 2 (DC).

8.6 OTHER PUBLIC PLACE

Even if the place at which an alleged offence under Road Traffic Act 1988, s 4, s 5 or s 5A is committed does not fall within the meaning of 'road', it may nevertheless be a 'public place'. The interpretation of the phrase 'public place' is again a matter of fact and degree, but whether the material for consideration suffices to support one view or the other is a matter of law (see *DPP v Vivier* [1991] 4 All ER 18, below). The general rule appears to be that, for privately owned property to constitute a public place, it must be shown that the public uses the place, and uses it with the consent of, or at the invitation of, the owner, as in the case of a field to which the public was admitted for a point-to-point: *R v Collinson* (1932) 23 Cr App R 49 (CCA).

8.6.1 Car parks

Many of the cases concern car parks, as in *Cutter v Eagle Star Insurance Co Ltd* [1998] 1 WLR 1647 and *Brewer v DPP* [2004] EWHC 355 (Admin), [2005] RTR 5 (DC) in para 8.5 above. In *Bowman v DPP* [1991] RTR 263, a motorist was convicted of driving with excess alcohol on a car park. At the time, the barrier at the entrance was raised and the car park was accessible from the street. Other cars were parked there. The justices were aware that, at night, the barrier was left up and anyone could use the car park. The Divisional Court endorsed the justices' reliance on their own local knowledge. It found that, on the facts and the evidence, and given the justices' local knowledge, the appellant had failed to show that no reasonable bench could have concluded that the car park was a public place.

In *Havell v DPP* (1994) 158 JP 680, the defendant was convicted of being in charge when unfit. His vehicle was in the car park of a private club. The Divisional Court ruled that, as the appellant had used the car as a member of a *bona fide* club, and the car park was not of such size that the public would regard it as a public place, there were grounds for finding that he had not been in a public place.

The car park featuring in *Edwards v DPP*, unreported, 10 March 1994, on which the defendant was said to have driven with excess alcohol, was owned by a company. The company had not used it for about two years. It had given a taxi company, a school and a nightclub permission to use it. The justices found that it was in fact used by the local community at large. At the time of the alleged offence (2.05 am), it was three quarters full, members of the public were present and taxis were arriving. There were no signs, notices or effective barriers prohibiting any person from using the car park. The general public had been using the car park completely unhindered for the preceding 12 months. The Divisional Court upheld the justices' finding that the car park was a public place. It was not essential that members of the public should have rights (enforceable at law) to go there. The question was whether, as a matter of fact, they did use it with sufficient regularity that it had become *de facto* a public place, even though the owners could have stopped its use in that manner.

A hospital car park to which the public had access at any time was found to be a public place in *DPP v Greenwood*, unreported, 12 February 1997 (DC), a case concerning driving without due care and attention. There was nothing to distinguish those who used it from ordinary members of the public.

In *R v Spence* [1999] RTR 353, the defendant was convicted of dangerous driving in a car park. The car park was a yard outside a small office building. It was used by the staff and customers of, and visitors to, the company which owned it. The car park was bordered on three sides by a wall, a hedge and a fence. On the fourth side there were bollards preventing access from the road. Access was via a swing gate, which was open during the day and closed at night. The Court of Appeal found that those who used the car park were a special class as distinct from members of the general public and that there was no evidence of the general public using the car park. The car park was not therefore a public place.

In *R (Lewis) v DPP* [2004] EWHC 3081 (Admin), [2005] LLR 292, the Administrative Court ruled that the requirement for evidence that the public utilises a place may, in an appropriate case, be taken to mean that there must be evidence from which it can properly be inferred that the public utilises the place. On the facts of the case, it was proper to infer that a car park attached to a public house was a public place. There was no need for the prosecutor to adduce evidence of user.

A car park attached to a motor car dealership, which was intended for the use of customers only, but which was accessible from a public place, and to which entry was not restricted, was a public place: *May v DPP* [2005] EWHC 1280 (Admin), where the offence was driving without due care and attention. In *May*, the court again emphasised the need to examine the facts of each case in the light of the authorities to reach a conclusion.

Scott Richardson v DPP [2019] EWHC 428 (Admin), [2019] 4 WLR 46 concerned a car park which served several businesses. The appellant appealed against conviction for being in charge of his vehicle, which he had parked on the car park in question, when unfit through drink. There were various signs applying to most of the different parts of the car park. These included 'Private Property Strictly No Unauthorised Parking' and 'Private Car Park', indicating that parking by the public was not permitted in those parts. The prosecution had brought no evidence of where, in the car park, the appellant's car had actually been parked. Nor was there any evidence of use of the car park by the general public as opposed to those having business at the premises served by the car park. The absence of barriers did not of itself render the car park a public place. The appellant's appeal was upheld by the Administrative Court.

8.6.2 Other places

In *Pugh v Knipe* [1972] RTR 286 (DC), the defendant had been driving on land owned by a private members' club. The land was outside the front entrance to the club premises and not separated from the club's private car park. The court found that the land was *prima facie* private land. For it to be a public place, it would be necessary to establish that the public had access to the place. In the absence of evidence that the public in fact used the land, there was no evidence that the private land had become a public place.

In *DPP v Vivier* [1991] 4 All ER 18, the alleged offence had taken place at a privately owned campsite, of about 80 acres, with 3 to 4 miles of road. The campsite opened from spring to autumn and accommodated up to 3,500 people. It was surrounded by a ditch and had one main gate. Visitors were required to register and to have a car pass. Fees were charged and security services were employed. The justices decided that the site was not a public place and acquitted the defendant. The prosecutor appealed. The Divisional Court addressed the question whether the caravanners, campers and guests admitted to the site were to be regarded as members of the public, in which case the site would be a public place, or as a special class of members of the public, in which case the site would not be a public place. It found that, although those seeking entry to the site had to satisfy certain conditions, there was insufficient segregation or selection for them to cease to be members of the general public and to become instead a special class. The campsite was therefore a public place.

DPP v Coulman [1993] RTR 230 concerned a lorry driver with excess alcohol who had disembarked from a cross-channel ferry and was in the inward freight immigration lanes at Dover docks. The Divisional Court ruled that although persons entering those lanes from the landward side were permitted to do so only by reason of being employees of the occupier and in possession of passes, those entering from the seaward side did so simply to disembark and gain access to the shore. Such a common reason was insufficient to take those people out of the category of ordinary members of the public. The lanes were therefore a public place.

Robinson v DPP, unreported, 10 March 1995, QBD (DC) featured a lane of a rather different sort. The defendant was charged with driving with excess alcohol and with failing to provide a specimen for a breath test. The lane on which he had been driving was not made up, and had no road markings, pavements or tarmac. It was a cul-de-sac with nine houses, the last of which was the defendant's. It was approximately 70 yards long and unlit. There were no signs saying it was private, or indicating restricted access. There was no physical obstruction preventing access by the public, and a public footpath led off it. The Divisional Court upheld the justices' conclusion that the lane was in the nature of a road; even if it was not a road, it was a public place to which the general public had access.

On the other hand, a cul-de-sac marked 'Private Residents Only' was not a public place: *Taussik v DPP* [2001] ACD 10, where the defendant was said to have been in charge with excess alcohol. She had parked in an access road leading to a block of flats. The access road was a cul-de-sac, which led off the highway. At the entrance to the cul-de-sac there was a large sign, 'Private Residents Only'. Two police officers gave evidence that other people parked in the cul-de-sac. They did not say how many or how often, and this evidence appeared to be based partly upon what they had been told by other people. Two officials of the council were called, one on each side. Their evidence was similar – that the cul-de-sac was maintained by the Housing Department, not the Highways Department, and that it was private and for the use of residents only. Allowing an appeal against conviction, the Divisional Court found that the evidence was insufficient to establish that the cul-de-sac was a public place. The notice meant what it said: the public at large was excluded.

In *DPP v Neville* (1996) 160 JP 758 (QBD), it was held that the 'airside' part of an airport terminal was a public place.

In *Planton v DPP* [2001] EWHC 450 (Admin), [2002] RTR 9 (see para 8.2.2), justices found that a private causeway linking an island in the Blackwater River in Essex to the mainland was a public place. The causeway was sometimes passable and sometimes submerged by tidal water. Access to the causeway from the mainland was not prevented by any physical obstruction, but there was a barrier across part of the approach road. Signs by the entrance read 'Private Road Residents and Authorised Vehicles only'; 'Private Road No Parking'; and 'Danger Tidal Causeway Authorised vehicles only'. Overturning the decision of the justices, the Divisional Court found that there was insufficient evidence to establish that the causeway was a public place.

8.7 CONSUMING

'Consuming', for the purposes of Road Traffic Act 1988, s 5(1), is not confined to the act of drinking. In *DPP v Johnson* [1995] 1 WLR 728, a motorist was convicted of driving with excess alcohol. Some weeks before the offence, he had been injected with a slow-release painkiller which, unknown to him, contained alcohol. The Divisional Court was asked whether the word 'consuming' should be restricted to the act of drinking and to no other mode of introduction or injection of alcohol. The court accepted that Parliament probably did not specifically consider the possible modes of entry of alcohol into the body but found it possible, 'without doing violence to the chameleon-like qualities of this word', to construe it widely enough to embrace ingestion in any form. Given that the side note to s 5 read, 'driving or being in charge of a motor vehicle with alcohol concentration above prescribed limit', the answer to the question was 'no'. The word is not to be construed as confined to drinking.

On the other hand, in *Woolfe v DPP* [2006] EWHC 1497 (Admin), [2007] RTR 16 (see para 13.3), it was held that the word 'consume' does not include regurgitation of the contents of the stomach into the mouth or upper oesophagus and reabsorbing them.

The wording of s 5A – no doubt in view of the many ways in which drugs may be introduced into the body – avoids any such difficulty by making no reference to the means by which a drug may have come to be in a person's body, instead using the formulation 'and there is in [the person's] body a specified controlled drug'.

8.8 THE PRESCRIBED AND SPECIFIED LIMITS

The prescribed limit for alcohol is defined in Road Traffic Act 1988, s 11(2), as:

(a) 35 microgrammes of alcohol in 100 millilitres of breath,
(b) 80 milligrammes of alcohol in 100 millilitres of blood, or
(c) 107 milligrammes of alcohol in 100 millilitres of urine.

The subsection provides for the proportions to be amended by regulations made by the Secretary of State, but, as noted above (see para 1.4), there has been no change, in relation to England and Wales, since these limits were first introduced in 1967, although the limits in Scotland were reduced to 22 in breath, 50 in blood and 67 in urine with effect from 5 December 2014.

The specified controlled drugs for England and Wales are listed in the Drug Driving (Specified Limits) (England and Wales) Regulations 2014

(SI 2014/ 2868), as amended by the Drug Driving (Specified Limits) (England and Wales) (Amendment) Regulations 2015 (SI 2015/911):

Controlled drug	*Limit (microgrammes per litre of blood)*
Amphetamine	250
*Benzoylecgonine	50
†Clonazepam	50
*Cocaine	10
*Delta-9-Tetrahydrocannabinol	2
†Diazepam	550
†Flunitrazepam	300
*Ketamine	20
†Lorazepam	100
*Lysergic Acid Diethylamide	1
†Methadone	500
*Methylamphetamine	10
*Methylenedioxymethamphetamine	10
*6-Monoacetylmorphine	5
†Morphine	80
†Oxazepam	300
†Temazepam	1000

Note. The symbols * and † are described in the following paragraph.

In relation to alcohol, studies indicate that driving is impaired at well below the prescribed limit. The specified limits for drugs, by contrast, are far more restrictive. They were set following a report from a panel of experts commissioned by the Department for Transport: www.gov.uk/government/uploads/system/uploads/attachment_data/file/167971/drug-driving-expert-panel-report.pdf. The limits are said to reflect a 'zero tolerance' approach to eight controlled drugs (marked with asterisks in the list above) which are mostly associated with illegal use. To avoid catching those who have inadvertently consumed a very small amount of these drugs, the limits are set at the lowest concentration at which a valid and reliable analytical result can be obtained, yet above which issues such as passive consumption or inhalation can be ruled out – a 'lowest accidental exposure limit' – not quite 'zero tolerance'. In relation to eight drugs which have medical uses (marked † in the list above), the limits are based on a 'road safety risk' approach, which in most cases coincides with a level higher than would be expected of a person taking therapeutic doses. This reduces the risk of catching drivers who have taken medicine which has been properly prescribed or supplied, and who have taken it as directed or otherwise in accordance with the supplier's instructions. In relation to amphetamine, a separate approach has been adopted, said to balance its legitimate use for medical purposes against its abuse.

Limits in urine have not been set; the Consultation Document recites that it is not possible to establish evidence-based concentrations of drugs in urine which would indicate an effect on the nervous system, or which could be related to an increased risk of a road traffic accident. Nor is there any way of translating the concentration of a drug in blood to a concentration of that drug in urine.

The limits for both alcohol and drugs are expressed in terms of the concentration of alcohol or a drug in the body. In relation to alcohol, the concentration depends on the amount of alcohol consumed, the time over which it is consumed and the time which elapses before specimens are taken. Individual factors such as weight, gender, height, familiarity with alcohol and physical fitness are also in play, while eating as an accompaniment to drinking affects the rate of absorption of alcohol. It is therefore extremely difficult for an individual to know whether or not he or she has reached the limit. The official guidance acknowledges this difficulty, saying, for example:

- the best solution is not to drink at all when planning to drive (*The Highway Code*);
- the only safe option is not to drink any alcohol if you plan to drive (Department for Transport Road Safety website).

Research indicates that most drivers think the alcohol limit can be equated with drinking 2 or fewer units, the equivalent of rather less than a quarter of a bottle of wine of 12 per cent alcohol by volume, or one pint of beer of 4 per cent alcohol by volume. Other studies, however, suggest that the amounts which may be consumed without being over the limit may, in fact, be higher. As already noted (see para 1.4), for as long as it remains permissible to drink before driving, interpreting the limit is a problem of real practical significance.

On drugs, there is no official guidance on what amounts or dosage would equate to being over the specified limits. Different individuals metabolise drugs at different rates, and eating and drinking, among other factors, would also affect the resulting concentration. Drivers taking drugs medicinally, who take their medications as instructed, should rarely fall foul of s 5A, but if they do, the defence in s 5A(3) (see para 8.13) may be available. Those who take illicit drugs will have to deal with the question of which substances are on the list in s 5A – not necessarily straightforward given the host of alternative and informal names for many of the specified substances. In view of the virtual zero tolerance limits adopted in these cases, however, the question of how much may be consumed before reaching the limit should at least be clear. Less obvious, however, is how long an individual would have to wait for a drug to be eliminated before driving. In any event, regardless of s 5A, a concentration of a drug will constitute the offence under s 4 of unfitness to drive through drink or drugs (see Chapter 7) if driving is impaired.

8.9 THE STATUTORY ASSUMPTION

Road Traffic Offenders Act 1988, s 15 concerns the use of specimens in proceedings for offences under Road Traffic Act 1988, s 3A (causing death by careless driving when under the influence of drink or drugs), ss 4, 5 and 5A (driving, attempting to drive or in charge while unfit, with excess alcohol or with an excess specified controlled drug). Section 15(2) contains the 'statutory assumption' that the concentration of alcohol or of a drug at the time of an alleged offence is no less than in the specimen later analysed. Section 15(3) and (3A) provide that the assumption is not to be made if the defendant can prove having drunk alcohol, or taken the drug, after the time of the alleged offence, but for which the defendant would not have been over the limit. The statutory provisions are:

> (1) This section and section 16 of this Act apply in respect of proceedings for an offence under any of sections 3A to 5A of the Road Traffic Act 1988 (driving offences connected with drink or drugs); and expressions used in this section and section 16 of this Act have the same meaning as in sections 3A to 10 of that Act.
>
> (2) Evidence of the proportion of alcohol or any drug in a specimen of breath, blood or urine provided by or taken from the accused shall, in all cases (including cases where the specimen was not provided or taken in connection with the alleged offence), be taken into account and—
>
> > (a) it is to be assumed, subject to subsection (3) below, that the proportion of alcohol in the accused's breath, blood or urine at the time of the alleged offence was not less than in the specimen;
> >
> > (b) it is to be assumed, subject to subsection (3A) below, that the proportion of a drug in the accused's blood or urine at the time of the alleged offence was not less than in the specimen.

8.9.1 The application of the section

In *R v Ash* [1999] RTR 347, the Court of Appeal (Criminal Division) ruled that Road Traffic Offenders Act 1988, s 15(2) was specific to offences where the taking of drink or the quantity of drink (or, now, drugs) were constituents of the offence itself. Section 15 was concerned with proving offences of that kind and no others. It could not be extended to offences under s 1 (causing death by driving dangerously).

Section 15 is not engaged in respect of a preliminary breath test: *Smith (Stephen John Henry) v DPP* [2007] EWHC 100 (Admin), [2007] 4 All ER 1135, where the Divisional Court had no doubt that the assumption applies only to specimens taken under s 7. See also *Breckon v DDP* [2007] EWHC 2013 (Admin), [2008] RTR 8 (DC).

On the extent to which s 15 applies to offences under Road Traffic Act 1988, s 3A, see *R v Coe (Christopher Steven)* [2009] EWCA Crim 1452 (para 6.7).

8.9.2 The assumption is irrebuttable

The assumption in s 15(2) is irrebuttable: *Beauchamp-Thompson v DPP* [1989] RTR 54. In that case, the justices, on the basis of the statutory assumption, refused to allow the defendant to adduce expert evidence to show that at the time of driving he must have been below the limit. The Divisional Court upheld that decision, finding no ground for construing the assumption as rebuttable rather than irrebuttable. *Beauchamp-Thompson* was applied in *Millard v DPP* (1990) 91 Crim App R 108 (see para 8.10.3).

In *DPP v Williams* [1989] Crim LR 382, police came upon a suspect at 4 am. He said he had driven 'that night', and had had his last drink some five hours before. The justices dismissed a charge of driving with excess alcohol, finding that the evidence was incomplete. Police should have examined the car to see if the bonnet or engine was hot to show recent use, and should have established the time the defendant had last driven, and whether he had driven to the address at which he was found before or after drinking alcohol. The Divisional Court allowed the prosecutor's appeal, finding that the statutory assumption applied and it was for the defendant to displace it. There was no need for evidence of the kind referred to by the justices.

See also the cases concerning the assumption that the breath analysis device is reliable, in para 3.4.7.

The statutory assumption was challenged as incompatible with European Convention on Human Rights, art 6(1) and (2) in *Parker v DPP* [2001] RTR 16. It was argued before the Divisional Court that:

- to prevent a defendant from calling evidence to establish that he had been below the limit while driving could lead to the conviction of an innocent driver;
- the fact that the prosecution is entitled to calculate back to demonstrate guilt (*Gumbley v Cunningham* [1989] AC 281, see para 8.11), but that the defendant is not entitled to do the same to establish innocence, amounts to inequality of arms – an imbalance between the resources of the prosecutor and those of the defendant – which disadvantages the latter;
- the driver who had consumed alcohol before, but not after, driving is at a disadvantage compared with a driver who had taken alcohol after driving and invokes s 15(3) (below);
- s 15(2) should therefore be construed as giving rise to a rebuttable presumption only.

The court rejected all these arguments, confirming that s 15(2) provides for an irrebuttable presumption. It found that the legislation as a whole was aimed at preventing the consumption of alcohol before driving, and, given that context, there was no infringement of the Convention rights.

Parker v DPP [2001] RTR 16 was applied in *Griffiths v DPP* [2002] EWHC 792 (Admin), (2002) 166 JP 629, where the Administrative Court reiterated that the statutory assumption is wholly proportionate to the situation where a person has drunk alcohol and then drives.

8.9.3 Specimen not provided or taken in connection with the alleged offence

Section 15(2) includes words in brackets referring to specimens provided or taken otherwise than in connection with the alleged offence, and applies the statutory assumption to such specimens. These words were considered in *DPP v Carless* [2005] EWHC 3234 (Admin). Police took samples of blood from the inside of a car which had been involved in a road traffic accident; no driver was on the scene. They later came upon the defendant, who appeared confused and to have suffered a head injury. He said he had been abducted the previous evening. He was taken to hospital where police asked for specimens of blood and urine to ascertain whether or not he had been drugged. The blood specimen from the car matched the DNA of the person claiming to have been abducted, connecting him to the road traffic accident. The procedure under Road Traffic Act 1988, s 7 was not followed, but analysis of the blood specimen taken at hospital revealed excess alcohol. The defendant was charged with driving with excess alcohol. The justices excluded the evidence of the blood analysis under PACE, s 78 (discretion to exclude evidence which would have such an adverse effect on the fairness of the proceedings that the court ought not to admit it; see para 11.9).

The Divisional Court reversed that decision, accepting the Crown's argument that the words added to s 15(2) meant that the blood sample was properly admitted, even though it had been provided otherwise than in connection with the alleged offence and in a manner at variance with the procedure in s 7. The court went on to emphasise that where the specimen is provided in connection with the alleged offence, then all the procedural requirements of the Road Traffic Act 1988 apply and those requirements must be strictly complied with. The Divisional Court concluded that the words added in s 15(2) of the 1988 Act created a new set of circumstances in which samples may be admitted in prosecutions for excess alcohol offences. The court left open the question whether Road Traffic Offenders Act 1988, s 15(4) (on consent to the taking or analysis of a specimen – see para 4.12) would apply so as to exclude from evidence a specimen obtained otherwise than in connection with the alleged offence if it was not taken in accordance with the circumstances set out there.

R v Coe (Christopher Steven) [2009] EWCA Crim 1452 (see para 6.7) again concerned the words 'including cases where the specimen was not provided or taken in connection with the alleged offence'. The judgment of the Court of Appeal in *Coe* does not mention *Carless*, but suggests that *Carless* – in so far as it endorsed the admission of the blood specimen in a prosecution for driving with excess alcohol – is to be confined to its own exceptional facts.

Coe was an appeal against conviction for the offence under Road Traffic Act 1988, s 3A(1)(c) – causing death by careless driving and failing without reasonable excuse to provide a specimen. Police obtained a court order for the hospital to produce blood samples taken at hospital by a member of the hospital staff. Analysis showed excess alcohol. The analysis was admitted in support of the prosecution case. The reasoning of the Court of Appeal in dismissing an appeal against conviction is set out in para 6.7 above: all the prosecution had to prove was that the defendant was driving without due care and attention and had no reasonable excuse for failure to provide specimens, not that he had taken drink, or how much. The court went on to say, *obiter* ('although it is not necessary for our decision'), that the evidence of the blood analysis was rightly admitted as it was relevant to whether the defendant had driven without due care and attention, and to the reason he refused to provide specimens. The reference in s 15 to s 3A must have been intended to apply only to offences contrary to paras (a) (unfit through drink or drugs) and (b) (excess alcohol), not to para (c) (failing to provide a specimen) or (d) (failing to give permission for testing a blood specimen) – in effect, that provisions relating to the admissibility of the analysis of specimens have no relevance where no specimen was in fact provided.

The court emphasised that, in concluding that the evidence of the blood analysis was admissible, it was not intending to set a precedent for cases in which it is sought to admit such evidence. Each case must turn on its own facts and circumstances.

Again, an argument that the blood analysis should be excluded under PACE, s 78 was rejected.

In *Carless*, the blood specimen taken outside the drink-drive regime was admitted to prove the offence of driving with excess alcohol; in *Coe*, it was admitted to prove driving without due care and attention and went to the reasons for failing to provide. *Coe* did not confirm the finding in *Carless* that the words in question 'have created a new set of circumstances in which samples may be admitted in prosecutions for excess alcohol offences'. Nor does either case suggest that the usual procedural requirements to be followed in a drink- or drug-drive investigation are in any way undermined; indeed, in *Carless*, they are specifically confirmed.

8.10 THE EXCEPTION TO THE STATUTORY ASSUMPTION

While the statutory assumption is irrebuttable, Road Traffic Offenders Act 1988, s 15(3) and (3A) provide that it is not to be made in certain circumstances:

> (3) The assumption in subsection (2)(a) above shall not be made if the accused proves—
>
> (a) that he consumed alcohol before he provided the specimen or had it taken from him and—
>
> (i) in relation to an offence under section 3A, after the time of the alleged offence, and
> (ii) otherwise, after he had ceased to drive, attempt to drive or be in charge of a vehicle on a road or other public place, and
>
> (b) that had he not done so the proportion of alcohol in his breath, blood or urine would not have exceeded the prescribed limit and, if it is alleged that he was unfit to drive through drink, would not have been such as to impair his ability to drive properly.

(3A) The assumption in subsection 2(b) above is not to be made if the accused proves—

(a) that he took the drug before he provided the specimen or had the specimen taken from him and—

(i) in relation to an offence under section 3A, after the time of the alleged offence, and

(ii) otherwise, after he had ceased to drive, attempt to drive or be in charge of a vehicle on a road or other public place, and

(b) that had he not done so the proportion of the drug in his blood or urine—

(i) in the case of a specified controlled drug, would not have exceeded the specified limit for that drug, and

(ii) if it is alleged that he was unfit to drive through drugs, would not have been such as to impair his ability to drive properly.

For many years, this exception was known as the 'hip-flask' defence, after the receptacle from which a driver might take a draught upon being stopped by police. It is now generally referred to as the 'post-incident consumption' defence.

8.10.1 Proof of drinking or taking the drug after driving

A series of cases – all concerning alcohol rather than drugs – illustrate how the provisions operate. In the first place, the court must have before it evidence of drinking after the alleged offence. It is not sufficient that the defendant asserted having done so, or that a police officer accepted that assertion, or that the defendant had the time and opportunity to consume alcohol: *Thynne v Hindle, R v Newcastle upon Tyne Justices* [1984] 1 All ER 770 (DC). See also *DPP v Sangha*, unreported, 28 January 1998 (DC) and *DPP v Ward (Kevin William)*, unreported, 2 October 1998 (DC).

8.10.2 The burden of proof

The Divisional Court has placed the burden of proof, in accordance with the normal rule of criminal law, on the accused, on the balance of probabilities: *Dawson v Lunn* [1986] RTR 234 and *Patterson v Charlton* [1986] RTR 18 (DC).

In *DPP v Chambers* [2003] EWHC 2142 (Admin), (2004) 168 JP 231, there was agreed expert evidence relating to two scenarios. The first was based on the amount the defendant told the police she had drunk before and after an accident, as recorded by the police; the second was based on later instructions from the defendant in which she said she had consumed a greater amount of alcohol after the accident. The justices found no case to answer and the prosecutor appealed. The Administrative Court found that the justices were in error in failing to consider the defendant's admission to the police about what she had consumed before the accident. They should not have taken into account the scenario presented to the experts by the defendant herself which was merely a hypothesis. They should not have found that the burden of proof in s 15(2) had been discharged.

In *R v Drummond* [2002] EWCA Crim 527, [2002] Cr App R 25, the Court of Appeal examined the compatibility of s 15(3) with the European Convention on Human Rights. Although the case concerned Road Traffic Act 1988, s 3A (causing death by careless driving when under the influence of drink or drugs – see Chapter 6), the court made clear that what it had to say applies equally to the offences under ss 4 and 5 (and now, presumably, s 5A). The court found that the legislative interference with the presumption of innocence in s 15 imposes on the defendant a persuasive burden, requiring proof on a balance of probabilities. Such interference is not only justified, but is no greater than necessary. It found no reason to read down the reverse burden from a persuasive to the less onerous evidential burden. The court characterised driving while over the limit as a social evil which Parliament had sought to minimise by the legislation.

The case of *DPP v Tooze* [2007] EWHC 2186 (Admin) again illustrates where the burden of proof lies. There was a gap of two and a half to two and three-quarter hours between the time of driving and the time breath specimens were analysed. The justices found that, although it was likely the motorist had been over the limit when he drove, the assumption in s 15(2) should not be made because of the large amount of alcohol consumed since driving, and the length of time before the breath analysis. The analysis could not be an accurate reflection of the alcohol in the defendant's system at the time of driving. They were not sure beyond reasonable doubt that the motorist had been over the limit and acquitted him. The Divisional Court allowed the prosecutor's appeal on the basis that the justices had made a fundamental error about the burden of proof. It was for the accused to prove the matter in s 15(3). Furthermore, he had produced no evidence in that respect.

8.10.3 Proving the effect of the alcohol consumed or drug taken after driving

In *Dawson v Lunn* [1986] RTR 234, the Divisional Court provided guidance on the nature of the evidence required to show that the alcohol consumed after driving, attempting to drive or being in charge had the effect of taking the defendant over the limit. Medical or scientific evidence is almost always required 'unless the case really is an obvious one'. There appear to be no reported cases on what is 'really obvious' in relation to s 15(3). But cases concerning 'laced drinks' in the context of special reasons for not disqualifying (see Chapter 13) provide some guidance. Thus, in *Pugsley v Hunter* [1973] 1 WLR 578, it was held that medical evidence is usually necessary to establish that drinks were laced and that the excess alcohol in a defendant's body was attributable to the additional drink unknowingly consumed. The court acknowledged that there are some cases where it can be said to be obvious to a layman that the added drink, when its nature and quality are known, caused the commission of the offence. The example given was where the statutory limit is only just exceeded and the court is satisfied that the added drink unknowingly taken was substantial. But, the court went on, to dispense with expert evidence, the case must be a really obvious one.

In *Lloyd v Knight*, *The Times*, 8 February 1985, the justices found that the exception in s 15(3) was made out on the basis of an expert report concerning breath alcohol levels after drinking certain amounts of alcohol. The prosecutor had not questioned the admission of the report. The Divisional Court could find no grounds for interfering with the justices' decision, but remarked that if the report had not been agreed, and the expert had been examined and cross-examined, doubt about his evidence might have arisen.

In *Rynsard v Spalding* [1986] RTR 303, justices convicted a person of driving with excess alcohol on the basis that he had not proved he was no longer in charge of the vehicle when he consumed two large whiskies which took him over the limit. On appeal, the Divisional Court found that the justices' approach was in error. The defendant had been charged with driving with excess alcohol, and he therefore had to prove that it was alcohol he had drunk after driving, not after ceasing to be in charge, which took him over the limit.

The fact that expert evidence is usually required to make out the exception is further illustrated in *Oxford v Fairhurst*, unreported, 21 May 1986 (DC) and *DPP v Singh* [1988] RTR 209 (DC). In *DPP v Lowden* [1993] RTR 349, the prosecutor adduced expert evidence that if the defendant had drunk the amount he claimed to have drunk after driving, he would still have been over the limit when driving. The defendant then gave oral evidence that he had in fact drunk more after driving than he first said, and that this accounted for his having been over the limit. The justices accepted that and acquitted him. The Divisional Court dismissed the prosecutor's appeal, finding that the justices had had sufficient expert assistance, and it was for them to decide whether or not the defendant's evidence was to be accepted.

In *Millard v DPP* (1990) 91 Crim App R 108, the Divisional Court upheld the justices' decision that they could hear evidence only about what the defendant had drunk after driving; the statutory assumption precluded their hearing evidence about what he had drunk before driving.

In *R v Drummond* [2002] EWCA Crim 527, [2002] Cr App R 25 (para 8.10.2), the Court of Appeal indicated that the evidence which the accused must adduce includes the following, all of which are within the knowledge, or means of access, of the accused rather than the Crown:

- the amount drunk after the incident;
- the 'blood-breath' ratio, used to calculate the rate at which the body absorbs alcohol;
- the rate at which the body eliminates alcohol over time;
- the accused's body weight.

In *DPP v Ellery* [2005] EWHC 2513 (Admin), the Divisional Court rejected an argument that the decision in *Drummond* should be revisited in the light of *DPP v Sheldrake* [2004] UKHL 43, [2005] 1 AC 264 (see para 9.4.1).

The justices disbelieved the amount the defendant said he had drunk since ceasing to drive in *Lonergan v DPP* [2002] EWHC 1263 (Admin), [2003] RTR 12. They gave as their reason that they would have expected his breath alcohol to have been much higher than it was if his story had been true. There was no expert evidence. On appeal against conviction, the Administrative Court found that the justices were not entitled to convict on this basis.

In *DPP v Bolton* [2009] EWHC 1502 (Admin), the need for expert evidence was again emphasised. Blood analysis showed 155 milligrammes of alcohol in 100 millilitres of blood. The motorist said he had drunk three pints of lager topped up with lemonade over a period of almost six hours before driving, and one and a half pints of cider, and a cup of tea with a small whiskey in it, after driving. He argued that it would be obvious that the amount drunk before driving would not be sufficient to put him over the limit, and that the matter was so obvious that medical evidence was not necessary. The Administrative Court disagreed, ruling that the magistrates had fallen into error in accepting the defendant's assertions without scientific support.

In *DPP v Dukolli* [2009] EWHC 3097 (Admin), the Divisional Court ruled that where the credibility of the defendant is in question, expert evidence concerning alcohol said to have been taken after driving is essential. When giving breath specimens, and in interview, the defendant said he had not had a drink after he had stopped driving, but at the trial he said he had taken a shot of vodka after stopping his car but before the police reached him. He adduced no expert evidence. The Divisional Court ruled that this was precisely the kind of case where expert evidence is important to test whether the defendant's account was consistent with the readings. Further, even if the defendant had taken a shot of vodka, it was not at all obvious that it could have explained the excess. The justices were wrong to have found that the defendant had discharged the burden of proof under s 15(3).

What is not clear is the time at which it is to be shown that, but for the alcohol consumed after the incident, the defendant would not have been over the limit or unfit. The overall purpose of the legislation suggests that what is to be proved is that the defendant would not have been over the limit or unfit at the time of the alleged offence, rather than at the time the specimen was taken.

Form MG DD/D contains guidelines on police investigations where it is believed (among other possibilities) that the suspect may argue that the excess was a result of alcohol consumed after the alleged offence. Officers are advised to record anything said by the suspect, whether on arrest, during the investigation or in interview, about having taken any drink after the incident in question; and to ascertain, in interview, in as much detail as possible, exactly what the suspect claims to have drunk and when.

8.11 BACK-CALCULATIONS

The statutory assumption is that the alcohol concentration at the time of the offence was *no less* than in the specimen. Consequently, there is nothing to prevent a prosecutor from adducing evidence that at the time of the offence the accused's alcohol concentration was *higher* than in the specimen, a process known as 'back-calculation' or 'back-tracking'. In *Gumbley v Cunningham* [1989] AC 281, a motorist had been involved in a fatal accident and a blood specimen was taken some four hours later. Analysis of the specimen showed 58 milligrammes of alcohol in 100 millilitres of blood – below the limit. Medical evidence was adduced to the effect, *inter alia*, that at the time of the accident the blood alcohol level would have been between 120 and 130 milligrammes – over the limit. The House of Lords upheld the admissibility of such evidence.

That the prosecution is entitled to calculate back to demonstrate guilt, but that the defendant is not entitled to do the same to establish innocence, does not amount to inequality of arms: *Parker v DPP* [2001] RTR 16 (see para 8.9.2).

A person guilty of driving with excess alcohol who drank after driving, but who cannot establish that it was that drink which took him over the limit, is nevertheless entitled, for the purposes of the penalty, to adduce evidence that the reading at the time of driving was lower than that shown on the printout: *Goldsmith v DPP* [2009] EWHC 3010 (Admin), [2010] RTR 20. Likewise, back-calculations by the defence are permissible in support of a 'laced drinks' argument that there are special reasons why the defendant should not be disqualified from driving, or should be disqualified for a shorter period than would otherwise be appropriate (see para 13.7.3).

For the approach of the Crown Prosecution Service to back-calculations, see www.cps.gov.uk/legal-guidance/road-traffic-drink-and-drug-driving.

Investigating officers use form MG DD/D in cases where, among other matters, back-calculation may be appropriate, for example, where several hours have elapsed between the incident in question and the breath analysis, and the breath analysis shows the subject to be below the limit. The notes to the form suggest that back-calculation is to be confined to serious cases. Officers are advised to collect certain details under interview conducted in accordance with PACE. Those details include the subject's age, gender, height, weight and build, what the subject has eaten (if anything) before the incident, any medical condition and any medication taken.

See also *R v Hodnitt* [2003] EWCA Crim 441 (para 6.2).

8.12 AIDING AND ABETTING

A person supervising a learner driver was held to have aided and abetted driving with excess alcohol in *Carter v Richardson* [1974] RTR 314 (QBD), where the supervisor knew that the driver had consumed alcohol to such an extent that it was probable that he was over the limit. This was so even though the supervisor did not know the driver's exact blood alcohol concentration.

A person who surreptitiously laces the drinks of another, whom he knows is going to drive, causing the other's blood alcohol to exceed the prescribed limit, is guilty of procuring the offence: *Attorney-General's Reference No 1 of 1975* [1975] QB 773 (CA (Crim)). That case was distinguished in *Blakely v DPP* [1991] Crim LR 763, where the necessary intention to constitute procuring was not present. A driver's friends did not want him to go home, and laced his drinks intending to tell him they had done so, and believing that he would not then drive. In fact, he did drive and was found to have excess alcohol. The Court of Appeal ruled that the offence of procuring was not committed because the friends did not intend the offence to be committed.

Two people were arrested having run away from a car, both were found to have excess alcohol, and each claimed that the other had been driving in *Smith v Mellors* (1987) 84 Cr App R 279. They were both charged with driving with excess alcohol, as principals, on the basis that each was either driving, or was aiding and abetting the other. The Queen's Bench Division held that either could be charged as a principal even if only a passenger, provided it could be shown that he was aiding and abetting the driver. The prosecution did not have to show which defendant drove and which aided and abetted, so long as the defendants were involved in a joint enterprise and both knew that the other was unfit to drive.

In *DPP v Anderson* [1990] RTR 269, a motor cyclist had been convicted of driving with excess alcohol, and his pillion passenger was accused of aiding and abetting, counselling or procuring the offence, contrary to Magistrates' Courts Act 1980, s 44(1). The justices dismissed the case. The Divisional Court allowed the prosecutor's appeal. The prosecution had to show that:

- the principal offender had committed the offence;
- the defendant was aware that the principal offender had consumed excess alcohol, or was reckless as to the possibility that he had; and
- the defendant had aided, abetted, counselled or procured the commission of the offence.

On the facts of the case, all those elements were made out. The passenger knew how much the motor cyclist had had to drink (half a bottle of wine, half a bottle of cider, and a mixed spirit) and nevertheless encouraged him to drive.

8.13 EXCESS DRUGS: THE MEDICAL DEFENCE

Road Traffic Act 1988, s 5A(3) provides for a defence to a charge of driving, attempting to drive or in charge with a concentration of a specified controlled drug above the specified limit. The intention is to avoid convicting drivers who have taken prescribed or over-the-counter drugs as directed, and in accordance with any manufacturer's or supplier's instructions. Under section 5A(3), it is a defence for a defendant ('D') to show that:

(a) the specified controlled drug had been prescribed or supplied to D for medical or dental purposes,

(b) D took the drug in accordance with any directions given by the person by whom the drug was prescribed or supplied, and with any accompanying instructions (so far as consistent with any such directions) given by the manufacturer or distributor of the drug, and

(c) D's possession of the drug immediately before taking it was not unlawful under section 5(1) of the Misuse of Drugs Act 1971 (restriction of possession of controlled drugs) because of an exemption in regulations made under section 7 of that Act (authorisation of activities otherwise unlawful under foregoing provisions).

Since most of the specified limits equate with levels slightly above what would be expected in persons taking normal therapeutic doses (see para 8.8), the defence is likely to arise rarely. At the time of writing (January 2024), there have been no reported cases on the medical defence, and it is difficult to see how it will work in practice. Section 5A(5) addresses the burden of proving the defence, providing that if a defendant adduces evidence that is sufficient to raise an issue with respect to the defence, the court must assume that the defence is satisfied unless the prosecution proves beyond reasonable doubt that it is not. The consultation document leading to the enactment of s 5A recognised that the requirement to adduce evidence sufficient to raise an issue amounts to a reverse burden, but it is of the less onerous 'evidential' type, rather than a 'legal' or 'persuasive' burden (see *R v Drummond*, [2002] EWCA Crim 527, [2002] Cr App R 25 (CA) (para 8.10.2); see also para 10.4). It is not a burden of proof, but it must amount to 'an issue as to the matter in question fit for consideration by the tribunal of fact': *Sheldrake v DPP* [2004] UKHL 43, [2005] 1 AC 264 (see para 9.4.1).

To 'raise an issue' under s 5A(3) would presumably require something more than a simple assertion that the drug was prescribed or bought over the counter. It may not be easy to adduce evidence that a drug was prescribed, as the prescription will have been handed in to the dispensing pharmacy, so that a defendant may have to go back to the prescriber. A defendant who still has the packaging, showing the date the drug was dispensed, to whom it was dispensed, and directions for taking it, may be better placed. A defendant who had taken an over-the-counter drug may be able to satisfy section 5A(3) by producing the packaging and a dated receipt for the purchase.

Section 5A(4) goes on to provide that the defence is not available if the defendant's actions were:

> (a) contrary to any advice, given by the person by whom the drug was prescribed or supplied, about the amount of time that should elapse between taking the drug and driving a motor vehicle, or
>
> (b) contrary to any accompanying instructions about that matter (so far as consistent with any such advice) given by the manufacturer or distributor of the drug.

Disproving the defence, or proving any of the matters under s 5A(4), seems an almost impossible task for a prosecutor, particularly as the defendant is under no obligation to assist. Since the limits equate with a small excess over normal therapeutic doses, anything substantially over the limit might be accepted as evidence in itself that the drug was not taken in accordance with the relevant directions and/or instructions, but the difficulty would be to pinpoint quite how far over the specified limit would be enough to disprove the defence. Any question of failure to comply with advice concerning the time lapse between taking a drug and driving is likewise likely to give rise to problems of establishing when a drug was taken, the time which elapsed before driving, and exactly what directions (over and above, or in contradiction of, those appearing on the pharmacy label or product information leaflet) were given.

The original offence of unfitness to drive through drink or drugs continues alongside the new offence. If there is evidence of impairment, there seems nothing to prevent a person who is taking medication fully in accordance with all directions and advice from being charged with the offence of driving while unfit under s 4; see Chapter 7. Such a person would be disadvantaged compared with someone charged under section 5A, in that the defence under section 5A(3) would not be available.

8.14 THE DEFENCE OF DURESS OR NECESSITY

The defence of duress may be available to a defendant charged with a drink- or drug-driving offence, although the case law suggests that it is rarely successful. In *R v Conway* [1989] QB 290, a case of reckless driving, the Court of Appeal held that it was immaterial whether duress of circumstances was termed duress or necessity. The defence would be available only if, viewed objectively, the defendant could be said to have been acting to avoid a threat of death or serious injury.

The defence was available to a person charged with reckless driving, but the court should consider whether the driver acted under duress during both of two stages of the driving complained of: *R v Willer* [1987] RTR 22 (CA). The same point was made in *DPP v Jones (David Alan)* [1990] RTR 33, where there had been an altercation in a pub car park and the defendant was hit on the head. He got into his car, then drove 2 miles home. He did not check to see whether he was being followed. He was later convicted of driving with excess alcohol. The Divisional Court found that, while a defence of necessity might have been available for the initial part of his journey (presumably, until he had escaped the threat), it was not available for the entirety of his journey. He could have stopped the car and completed the journey on foot.

But where the defendant drove away in fear of personal injury, and there was nothing to suggest that he had driven for longer than was necessary, the defence of duress was upheld: *DPP v Bell (Derek)* [1992] RTR 335 (DC), another case which began with trouble in a car park and ended with a charge of driving with excess alcohol. The court also pointed out that, once a defence of duress is raised, it is for the prosecutor to negative it.

Duress is to be assessed objectively. On the facts in *DPP v Davis, DPP v Pittaway* [1994] Crim LR 600, duress was not made out. In *Davis*, the defendant had been drinking with an acquaintance and they returned together to the acquaintance's flat, where the acquaintance made an unwelcome sexual advance. The defendant resisted and, fearing for his life, ran out of the flat; the other man chased him and was abusive. The defendant drove away and was later charged with driving with excess alcohol. In *Pittaway*, the defendant was at a party with a man, but they argued and he threatened her. The defendant ran to her home which was about 200 yards away, but decided to hide in her car. She then drove the car a short distance before being stopped. She too was charged with driving with excess alcohol. In both cases, the justices found that the defence of duress was made out. The Divisional Court ruled that the defence of duress has an objective element in that there must be a threat of such a degree of violence that a person of reasonable firmness in the defendant's position and with the defendant's characteristics could not be expected to resist. In neither case had the test been properly applied, the justices instead having adopted a subjective test. The justices were also in error in having approached the question of the distance driven on the basis of reasonableness rather than necessity. Duress was not made out in either case.

Likewise, in *DPP v Rogers* [1998] Crim LR 202, justices failed to apply the objective test and ask whether the perceived danger was such that the defendant could not reasonably have been expected to act otherwise than he did. The defendant had driven away from his home following an argument with his wife. He believed his wife had gone to a neighbour and that the neighbour was following him, and would cause him serious physical harm. The justices found that the defence of duress to a charge of driving with excess alcohol was made out. The Divisional Court overturned their decision, finding that they had focused only on the subjective element – the defendant's own belief. They had not applied the objective test of whether the perceived danger was such that the defendant could not reasonably have been expected to act otherwise than he did, for example by taking some other form of evasive action such as escaping on foot.

The justices again failed to apply the correct test in *DPP v Tomkinson* [2001] EWHC 182 (Admin), [2001] RTR 38. The defendant had had an argument with her husband who had assaulted her, causing injury. He threatened her and put her in fear. He damaged the telephone and took the defendant's mobile phone and her money and credit cards. The husband had also injured himself, and left the house to go to hospital. Some time later, the defendant decided to drive some 72 miles to the town where she used to live. She was stopped by police and found to have excess alcohol. The justices found the defence of duress made out. The Divisional Court allowed the prosecutor's appeal against acquittal, finding that there was no longer any threat to her when she set off, and that the justices had been wrong to find that a sober woman of reasonable firmness would have reacted to the situation in the same way.

Where a defendant's child had become ill and the defendant drove to a pharmacy to buy the medicine Calpol, the defence of necessity to a charge of driving with excess alcohol was not, on the facts, made out. The defendant had considered telephoning a doctor but feared a doctor would not see the child immediately. He had no access to a telephone and did not have money for a taxi. No one else could have driven him. See *DPP v Hicks* [2002] EWHC 1638 (Admin), where the Administrative Court gave a useful summary of the conditions for making out the defence of necessity:

- the driving must be to avoid consequences that could not otherwise be avoided;
- those consequences must be inevitable and involve serious harm to the driver or to some other person the driver is bound to protect;
- the driver must do no more than reasonably necessary to avoid the harm; and
- the danger of driving a motor vehicle with excess alcohol must not be disproportionate to the harm sought to be avoided.

Again, duress was not made out on the facts in *DPP v Mullally* [2006] EWHC 3448 (Admin). The defendant was at her sister's home with her daughter. She was assaulted and threatened by her sister's partner. She called the police, then left with her daughter. The police arrived just as they got to their car. The motorist nevertheless drove away. She was stopped and found to have excess alcohol in breath. The Divisional Court reiterated the two-stage test. First, the accused must have been driven to act as she did because she genuinely (even if mistakenly) believed that otherwise death or serious injury would result to herself or someone for whose safety she would reasonably regard herself as responsible. Second, if so, it must then also be shown that a sober person of reasonable firmness, sharing the characteristics of the accused, would have acted as she acted. If the answer to both questions is 'yes', the court must acquit so long as the threat was effective at the time the offence was committed and there was no available escape route or other means of dealing with the situation that a reasonable person in the defendant's situation would have taken. On the facts, the first part of the test was satisfied and not disproved by the prosecution. But the second part was not satisfied. From the moment the defendant was aware that the police had attended at the premises, it ceased being necessary for her to continue to drive to avoid a serious assault. A reasonable person would have concluded that the officers would provide appropriate protection.

Nor, on the facts, was the defence of duress available in *CPS v Brown (Christopher)* [2007] EWHC 3274 (Admin). A motorist had invited three men, whom he had just met, into his home. One of them began to flirt with the motorist's girlfriend and he asked them all to leave. They did, but later the motorist received a threatening telephone call. He was afraid and decided to drive to his grandmother's home. As he left his house, he saw the three men but believed they did not see him; they did not follow him. He was stopped by police, having covered about 3 miles, and was found to have excess alcohol in breath. The magistrates accepted a plea of duress, finding that it was reasonable for him to have driven away rather than to have called the police. The prosecutor appealed against the dismissal of the charge of driving with excess alcohol. The Divisional Court referred to *DPP v Jones* (above) to the effect that the defence of necessity is not available to a defendant who drives for a period longer than necessary. In the present case, the defence ceased to be available long before the motorist was stopped by the police. He was not being pursued and had no grounds to think that he was being pursued.

More recently, in *Stevens v DPP* [2017] EWHC 2839 (Admin), an argument of duress again failed. The defendant admitted driving while disqualified, driving with excess alcohol, failing to stop when required to do so, driving while uninsured and dangerous driving. She said she had a genuine fear that if she did not do as instructed by her partner (who was in the car with her at the time of the offences), he would kill her or cause serious injury to her children. There was a history of violent conduct by her partner against her. The justices ruled that a reasonable and sober person would have stopped the vehicle and told the police that she was acting under duress; in fact, the issue was not raised until after her first court appearance, and her own description of the incident was that it was 'not as bad as the others'. The justices found that the defence of duress was not made out. On appeal, the Divisional Court found that the justices should have asked, did the appellant behave in the way she did because she believed her partner would seriously assault or kill her because he had behaved in that way in the past; and would a reasonable woman of her age have responded to those threats in the way she did. In so far as the justices misdirected themselves, it was in the appellant's favour. Her appeal was dismissed.

8.15 THE DEFENCE OF INSANITY

Insanity can be a defence in the magistrates' court, but only if the offence charged is one in which *mens rea* is required. A defendant is assumed to have been sane at the time of an alleged offence, and the burden is on the defendant to establish insanity. Since the offences of driving with excess alcohol or excess of a specified drug are strict liability offences and no *mens rea* is required, the defence of insanity is not therefore available: *DPP v Harper* [1997] 1 WLR 1406. The decision in *Harper* has, however, been criticised (see Tony Ward, 'Magistrates, Insanity and the Common Law' [1997] Crim LR 796; and see *R v Norman* [2023] EWCA Crim 1112).

Chapter 9

The 'In Charge' Offences

9.1 INTRODUCTION

Road Traffic Act 1988, s 4(2) provides for the offence of being in charge when unfit:

> Without prejudice to subsection (1) above, a person who, when in charge of a mechanically propelled vehicle which is on a road or other public place, is unfit to drive through drink or drugs is guilty of an offence.

Section 5(1)(b) creates the corresponding offence of being in charge with excess alcohol. If a person:

> is in charge of a motor vehicle on a road or other public place after consuming so much alcohol that the proportion of it in his breath, blood or urine exceeds the prescribed limit he is guilty of an offence.

In relation to specified drugs, s 5A(1)(b) and (2) make it an offence for a person to be in charge of a motor vehicle on a road or other public place with a specified controlled drug in his or her body which exceeds the specified limit.

All three offences are subject to an exception where there is no likelihood of driving, although the statutory wording is slightly different. In respect of the s 4 offence:

> a person shall be deemed not to have been in charge of a mechanically propelled vehicle if he proves that at the material time the circumstances were such that there was no likelihood of his driving it so long as he remained unfit to drive through drink or drugs. (s 4(3))

And under s 5(2):

> It is a defence for a person charged with an offence under subsection (1)(b) above to prove that at the time he is alleged to have committed the offence the

> circumstances were such that there was no likelihood of his driving the vehicle whilst the proportion of alcohol in his breath, blood or urine remained likely to exceed the prescribed limit.

Section 5A(6) provides a defence to a charge of driving, attempting to drive, or in charge with an excess of a specified drug; it is in the same terms as for alcohol, in s 5(2) above.

In respect of all three offences, the court may, in determining whether there was such a likelihood, disregard any injury to the accused and any damage to the vehicle (ss 4(4), 5(3) and 5A(7)).

The offence under s 4 may be committed in respect of a mechanically propelled vehicle, while the 'in charge' offences relating to alcohol and excess drugs may be committed in relation to motor vehicles only. For the distinction, see para 8.4.

In this chapter, the concepts of 'in charge' and 'no likelihood of driving' are examined.

9.2 IN CHARGE

There is no statutory definition of the expression 'in charge'. Its interpretation is a question of fact: *R v Harnett* [1955] Crim LR 793. In *Haines v Roberts* [1953] 1 WLR 309, the Divisional Court ruled that a person remains in charge of a vehicle until such time as the person puts it into the charge of someone else. The respondent was drunk in the car park of a pub. His friends arranged for another friend to come and ride his motor cycle back to the respondent's house, but the respondent was not aware of these arrangements. He remained in charge of the motor cycle, having not put it in anyone else's charge.

The Divisional Court restated the principle that once a person takes a vehicle onto a public road, that person remains in charge of it until it is off the road again or put into the charge of someone else: *Woodage v Jones (No 2)* (1974) 60 Cr App R 260. Whether a person is in charge is a matter of fact and degree in every case. A driver who had been driving erratically stopped on a garage forecourt in response to requests from other motorists. He learned that police had been called and walked away without locking the car. Officers found him some half a mile away. The court found that he had not abandoned his vehicle and remained in charge of it. His conviction for being unfit with excess alcohol was upheld.

In *DPP v Watkins* [1989] QB 821, the Divisional Court again emphasised that whether or not a person is in charge of a vehicle is a matter of fact and degree. While exhaustive guidance probably could not be given, the court nevertheless identified certain principles. It recognised two classes of case. First, where the defendant is the owner or lawful possessor of the vehicle or has recently driven it, that person is in charge of it unless it is shown that he is no longer in charge. Such a person would no longer be in charge if that person:

- has put the vehicle in someone else's charge; or
- has ceased to be in actual control and there is no realistic possibility of resuming actual control while unfit. The court gave as examples where the person is at home in bed for the night, is a great distance from the car, or the vehicle is taken by someone else.

The second class of case is where the accused is not the owner, lawful possessor or recent driver, but is nevertheless sitting in the car or is otherwise involved with it. Here the question is whether the person has assumed being in charge. Such a person is in charge of the vehicle if:

- voluntarily in *de facto* control of it; or
- given the circumstances, such as the person's position, intentions and actions, the person may be expected imminently to assume control. Usually, this would take the form of having gained entry to the vehicle and evinced an intention to take control of it, although gaining entry may not be necessary if there is some other manifestation of intention, such as stealing the keys in circumstances indicating an intention presently to drive it.

The court provided a list of circumstances which would usually be relevant:

- whether the defendant was in the vehicle (and if so, where in the vehicle), or, if not in the vehicle, how far from it the defendant was;
- what the defendant was doing at the relevant time;
- whether the defendant was in possession of a key fitting the ignition;
- whether there was evidence of an intention to take or assert control by driving or otherwise;
- whether anyone was in or near the vehicle at the time, and, if so, the like particulars in respect of that person.

The facts in *DPP v Watkins* [1989] QB 821 were that the defendant was in the driving seat of a Mini which did not belong to him. It was parked in the street in the early hours of the morning. He was holding a bunch of keys, with a key marked 'Honda' between his thumb and forefinger. The key could be inserted into the ignition but there was no evidence that it would actually start the engine. It was not known whether the defendant had the owner's permission to be in the Mini. The court found that these circumstances were sufficient to show that the defendant had assumed, or intended to assume, control, and that he was therefore in charge of the vehicle. The court below, however, had found that because the prosecutor had failed to show that the key would start the car, it had not been proved that there was a likelihood of driving, and the defendant was acquitted. The Divisional Court emphasised that it is not for the prosecution to prove that there was a likelihood of driving.

Where the driver of a vehicle holds a provisional licence only, the person supervising the learner is, in normal circumstances, in charge of the vehicle. That does not necessarily mean that the driver is not also in charge; it is perfectly possible for more than one person to be in charge: *DPP v Janman* [2004] EWHC 101 (Admin), [2004] RTR 31 (DC).

In *CPS v Bate* [2004] EWHC 2811 (Admin), a police officer saw a motorist approaching his car with the keys in his hand. He stumbled as he approached the driver's door. When the officer reached him, he was sitting in the driver's seat although he had not started the engine. The Divisional Court found that he had manifestly been in charge of the vehicle.

The place at which a person is in charge is the place where the vehicle is, not the place where the defendant is, and the charge should be framed accordingly. In *DPP v Webb* [1988] RTR 374, the defendant, in a road called Park Avenue, was seen tampering with parked cars, smoking two cigarettes at the same time and fumbling with keys, apparently thinking one of the cars was his own. Police arrived and found the defendant in possession of the keys to his own car, which was in fact parked one-fifth of a mile away in Seaton Road. He was prosecuted for being in charge in Park Avenue, not Seaton Road, and for failing to provide specimens for analysis. The Divisional Court found that the wording of the provision, 'in charge of a motor vehicle which is on a road or other public place' makes the geographic place critically the place where the vehicle is, not where the defendant is. The vehicle was not in Park Avenue, the information was flawed, and the defendant could not therefore be convicted of the 'in charge' offence. But the same did not apply to the offence of failing to provide, where all that is required is that there should be an investigation into whether an offence has been committed.

9.3 LIKELIHOOD OF DRIVING

There seems little doubt that the 'in charge' offences consist solely in the act of being in charge while unfit, with excess alcohol or, now, with an excess of a specified drug; they include no element of likelihood of driving and it is not for a prosecutor to prove such likelihood: *DPP v Watkins* [1989] QB 821 (see para 9.2). The House of Lords in *Sheldrake v DPP* [2004] UKHL 43, [2005] 1 AC 264 confirmed that the prosecutor must prove the elements of the offence – the being in charge, coupled with the impairment or excess alcohol, but not likelihood of driving. This reflects the fact that the offence was first created without the 'no likelihood of driving' escape route. *Hansard* (HL Deb, vol 191, col 584, 28 February 1955) records that the original purpose was that a person in charge of a car should not be under the influence such as to render him incapable of controlling it. Such a person might have no intention of driving but might, for example, inadvertently release the brake, causing the vehicle to roll away.

9.4 NO LIKELIHOOD OF DRIVING

As noted in para 9.1, the provisions in Road Traffic Act 1988, s 4 concerning the likelihood of driving are couched in somewhat different terms from those in ss 5 and 5A. Under s 4(3) a person is to be *deemed* not to have been in charge upon proving no likelihood of driving; under ss 5(2) and 5A(6), it is a *defence* to prove no such likelihood. In *DPP v Frost* [1989] RTR 11, the Divisional Court decided that, at least for the purposes of that case, 'the essential problems to which those two provisions give rise are not significantly different'. In *Sheldrake v DPP* [2004] UKHL 43, [2005] 1 AC 264 at [40], Lord Bingham remarked that there appeared to be 'no very good reason (other than history) for the adoption of these different legislative techniques, but the outcome is effectively the same'. For practical purposes, the difference in drafting likewise appears of no significance.

There may be circumstances in which it would be extremely difficult to prove no likelihood of driving. One commentator has counselled, 'don't ever wash your car when drunk: you may be convicted of this offence' (N Padfield, 'The burden of proof unresolved' [2005] CLJ 17). Another difficult situation might be where, following a domestic dispute, a person simply resorts to sitting in the car as a place of refuge, not as a means of transport.

9.4.1 The burden of proof

In *Morton v Confer* [1963] 1 WLR 763, the Divisional Court applied the general criminal law principle that when a burden of proof falls on a defendant, the standard of proof is on the balance of probabilities. It was for the defendant to prove, to that standard, not only that he had no intention of driving until he felt fit to do so, but also that there was no likelihood of departing from that intention.

Sections 4(3), 5(2) and 5A(6) all feature a reverse burden of proof, placing the onus on the defendant rather than the prosecutor. The burden in s 5(2) and its relationship with the presumption of innocence in European Convention on Human Rights, art 6(2) were examined by the House of Lords in *Sheldrake v DPP*

[2004] UKHL 43, [2005] 1 AC 264. The motorist argued that the defence of no likelihood of driving while remaining over the limit infringed the presumption of innocence in art 6(2) if interpreted as imposing on the defendant a legal burden of proof. A legal burden would require the defendant to prove the absence of likelihood on the balance of probabilities. Instead, it was argued, the provision should be interpreted as imposing only an evidential burden. This would require a defendant to raise a reasonable doubt, and it would then be for the prosecution to negative the defence beyond reasonable doubt. The House of Lords found that while s 5(2) indeed infringes the presumption of innocence, it is aimed at the legitimate objective of preventing death, injury and damage, and meets the tests of acceptability for a presumption of fact identified by the jurisprudence of the European Court of Human Rights. The legal burden of proof is reasonable and in no way arbitrary; the defendant has every opportunity to show that there was no likelihood of driving while over the limit. Furthermore, the House of Lords found that the likelihood of driving was a matter so closely conditioned by the defendant's own knowledge and state of mind that it is more appropriate for the defendant to prove unlikelihood of driving, than for the prosecutor to prove likelihood. The imposition of a legal burden did not go beyond what was necessary.

Thus it is for the defendant to prove, on the balance of probabilities, that there was no likelihood of driving while remaining unfit or while likely to be over the limit – a challenging series of probabilities and likelihoods.

9.4.2 Expert evidence

In certain circumstances, expert evidence is necessary. In *DPP v Frost* [1989] RTR 11, the defendant was charged with both being in charge while unfit and being in charge while over the limit. The Divisional Court emphasised the distinction between the two offences, finding that it is open to justices, without expert evidence, to conclude that there was no likelihood of driving while the defendant remained unfit. But, the court went on, the position is entirely different in respect of being in charge while over the limit, where the question is the rate of elimination of alcohol from the body over a given period. In view of the lapse of time before the defendant, Frost, next planned to drive (at most, some six hours), and the high breath alcohol reading (nearly three times the limit), the court concluded that it was not possible to discharge the burden of no likelihood of driving while over the limit without expert evidence. What would be required would be, 'clear, cogent and reliable evidence as to the relative rate at which the particular defendant would have been likely to lose the alcohol found on testing to have been present in his body'.

9.4.3 Likelihood and intention

In the case of *CPS v Bate* [2004] EWHC 2811 (Admin) (see para 9.2), the Divisional Court recognised that a defendant's intention or otherwise to drive was not necessarily relevant to the question whether or not the defendant was in charge of the vehicle, but it might be relevant to the question whether or not there was no likelihood of driving while unfit.

In *CPS v Thompson* [2007] EWHC 1841 (Admin), [2008] RTR 5, police had found the defendant asleep across the front seats of his van. The reversing lights were illuminated but the engine was not running. The keys were in the ignition, the heater fan was on, the gear stick was in the reverse position and an opened bottle of wine was on the front passenger seat. Breath analysis showed 106 microgrammes of alcohol in 100 millilitres of breath. The justices accepted the defendant's argument that he had had no intention of driving when he got into the vehicle, or when he was woken by the police officers. They dismissed the charge. On the prosecutor's appeal, the Divisional Court found that while the defendant's intention may well be a factor to be considered, the principal question is whether or not the defendant has shown no *likelihood* of driving while over the limit. A defendant's subjective intention cannot be decisive where he was affected by drink, was well above the prescribed level, intended to drive when he felt 'alright', would have no way of knowing when his blood alcohol level would fall below the prescribed limit, and put forward no scientific evidence to indicate when that point might be reached. While there might be circumstances in which evidence of intention could satisfy the statutory defence, such circumstances would most likely arise where evidence of intention is accompanied by other compelling circumstantial evidence, or by expert scientific evidence.

9.4.4 Supervisors of learner drivers

In *Sheldon v Jones* [1970] RTR 38, the Queen's Bench Division had found that there may be circumstances in which the supervisor of a learner driver could show no likelihood of driving and so avoid conviction for being in charge. But in *DPP v Janman* [2004] EWHC 101 (Admin), [2004] RTR 31, the Divisional Court said that the likelihood of driving extends to operations which the supervisor might have to undertake if the learner were to get into difficulties, and a supervisor who is in charge of the vehicle would usually have a difficult task to prove that there was no likelihood of driving. Certainly, the competence of the learner driver is not sufficient to establish no likelihood of driving.

9.4.5 Disregard of injury or damage

Sections 4(4), 5(3) and 5A(7) provide that, in determining whether there was or was not a likelihood of driving, a court may disregard any injury to the defendant or damage to the vehicle. These provisions – presumably intended to prevent a defendant from invoking any such injury or damage in support of an argument that there was no likelihood of driving – have been subject to little judicial interpretation. In *Drake v DPP* [1994] RTR 411 (DC), it was held that there was no likelihood of driving a vehicle which had been wheel-clamped. The presence of the wheel clamp did not constitute 'damage' for the purposes of s 5(3).

Chapter 10

The 'Failing' Offences

10.1 INTRODUCTION

In this chapter, the 'failing' offences are examined. They fall into three categories:

- failing without reasonable excuse to co-operate with a preliminary test, which may be a breath test, an impairment test, or a drug test, and is usually administered at the roadside;
- failing without reasonable excuse to provide a specimen of breath, blood or urine for analysis, traditionally at a police station; and
- failing without reasonable excuse to permit the testing of a blood specimen taken while incapable of consenting.

10.2 THE OFFENCES

10.2.1 Failing to co-operate with preliminary tests

Road Traffic Act 1988, s 6(6) provides that:

> A person commits an offence if without reasonable excuse he fails to co-operate with a preliminary test in pursuance of a requirement imposed under this section.

This subsection was substituted, and other provisions inserted, by the Railways and Transport Safety Act 2003, with effect from 30 March 2004. These changes introduced preliminary impairment testing and preliminary drug testing in addition to breath testing (see Chapter 2). Section 6(6) now also extends to preliminary drug tests. The provision in force before 30 March 2004 was s 6(4), which was as follows:

> A person who, without reasonable excuse, fails to provide a specimen of breath when required to do so in pursuance of this section is guilty of an offence.

Although the wording has now been amended from 'fail to provide' to 'fail to co-operate', in the absence of anything to suggest otherwise, the case law under the old s 6(4) appears to remain relevant.

Preliminary tests are governed by s 6 and are described in Chapter 2. Most of the case law, however, relates to alcohol testing, and mainly arises out of requirements for evidential specimens rather than for co-operation with a preliminary test.

10.2.2 Failing to provide specimens for analysis

Road Traffic Act 1988, s 7(6) provides that:

> A person who, without reasonable excuse, fails to provide a specimen when required to do so in pursuance of this section is guilty of an offence.

Where causing death by careless driving when unfit or over the limit (under s 3A) is suspected, it is likewise an offence to fail, without reasonable excuse, to provide a specimen if so required within 18 hours of driving: s 3A(1)(c).

Section 7(6) (and now, presumably, s 3A(1)(c) also) creates a single offence of failing to provide, whether the specimen in question is one of breath, blood or urine. See *Worsley v DPP*, unreported, 11 November 1994 (DC), where the court held that the reference in the information to 'breath/blood/urine' did not render it duplicitous.

In *Martiner v DPP* [2004] EWHC 2484 (Admin), the Administrative Court could:

> see absolutely no consideration of policy or sense which might give rise to a different argument depending … upon whether the specimen sought to be provided, but refused to be or failed to be provided … is breath on the one hand, or blood or urine on the other hand.

The fact that the penalties are different according to which offence is being investigated when the requirement for specimens is made has no bearing; see *Shaw v DPP* [1993] 1 All ER 918, and *DPP v Butterworth* [1995] 1 AC 381 (para 12.4.1).

10.2.3 Failing to permit testing of a blood specimen

Road Traffic Act 1988, s 7A(6) provides that:

> A person who, without reasonable excuse, fails to give his permission for a laboratory test of a specimen of blood taken from him under this section is guilty of an offence.

In the context of the offence under s 3A (causing death by careless driving when unfit or over the limit), it is likewise an offence to fail without reasonable excuse to permit the laboratory testing of a blood specimen taken while the subject was incapable of consenting: s 3A(1)(d).

These provisions came into force on 1 October 2002 by virtue of the Police Reform Act 2002, which introduced a new regime for taking specimens of blood from persons incapable of consenting following an accident (see Chapter 5). At the time of writing (January 2024) there has been no case law on this provision. As shown below, 'reasonable excuse' has been interpreted, in relation to failing to provide, as a physical or mental inability. Since the failure contemplated in s 7A(6) is a failure to give permission, rather than to give a specimen, the Divisional Court may be called upon to elaborate the term 'fail to give permission', and there may be scope for arguing a different interpretation of 'reasonable excuse' in this context.

10.2.4 Relationship to the substantive offences

A person charged under any of the above provisions should not also be charged with driving with excess alcohol or, now, with driving with an excess of a specified drug. Failing to provide a specimen, and driving with excess alcohol, are intended to be alternatives, and the legislation is to be construed to the effect that they are mutually exclusive: *Cracknell v Willis* [1988] AC 450 (HL).

10.3 THE ELEMENTS OF THE OFFENCES

For any of the three offences to be made out, the following must be established:

- the failure to co-operate, provide or permit;
- the absence of reasonable excuse;
- that the requirement was properly made; and
- that the suspect was warned of the consequences of failure (see para 10.9) and understood the warning.

10.4 THE BURDEN OF PROOF

The normal rule applies to the 'failing' offences and the prosecution must prove all the elements of the offence beyond reasonable doubt. The absence of reasonable excuse is an element of the offence, not a defence: *Piggott v DPP* [2008] EWHC 305 (Admin), [2008] RTR 16 (see para 10.6.5). A defendant wishing to argue that he had a reasonable excuse must raise the issue. The onus is then on the prosecution to negative the argument: *Rowland v Thorpe* [1970] 3 All ER 195. The court must be satisfied to the criminal standard – beyond reasonable doubt – that the defendant had no reasonable excuse: *R v Harling* [1970] 3 All ER 902.

In *DPP v Szarzynski* [1993] RTR 364, the Crown Court had not been satisfied that the prosecution had negatived a reasonable excuse advanced by a motorist, and overturned his conviction for failing to provide. The Divisional Court upheld that decision.

In *Mckeon v DPP* [2007] EWHC 3216 (Admin), [2008] RTR 14, the Divisional Court reiterated that the burden as to reasonable excuse is on the defendant to raise the issue on the evidence, and once that is done it is for the prosecution to prove the absence of reasonable excuse to the criminal standard. The defendant had adduced medical evidence, but the magistrates were of the opinion that he had failed to make out a reasonable excuse. On appeal, the Divisional Court found a clear suggestion that the justices considered there was a burden on the appellant to make out, that is to prove, a reasonable excuse, and quashed the conviction.

In *R (Cuns) v Hammersmith Magistrates' Court* [2016] EWHC 748 (Admin), the Administrative Court again acknowledged that it is for the prosecution to prove the absence of reasonable excuse, but only if the defendant provides some evidential basis to bring the issue into play. Here, the defendant, while at the police station, said he suffered needle phobia, but adduced no evidence in support of that assertion and did not himself give evidence at his trial. The Administrative Court found that the magistrates had been right to convict him and dismissed his appeal against their refusal to state a case.

Thus the burden of proof on the defendant is evidential only, in the sense that the task is to raise only a reasonable doubt as to the matter in question, rather than the more onerous legal or persuasive burden, where a defendant must prove something on the balance of probabilities. Since the burden is evidential only, it is compatible with the presumption of innocence in European Convention on Human Rights, art 6(2): *R v DPP ex parte Kebilene* [2000] 2 AC 326, *per* Lord Hope and *R v Lambert* [2001] UKHL 37, [2002] 2 AC 545, *per* Lord Steyn. See also paras 8.10.2 and 8.13 on evidential and legal burdens of proof.

As explained in para 10.6.3, the defendant is almost always required to adduce medical or other expert evidence to raise reasonable excuse. While the burden is evidential only, it is not necessarily a light one. The Crown Prosecution Service advises crown prosecutors, if reasonable excuse based on medical evidence is raised, to require the defence to provide the evidence before the hearing, or seek an adjournment for the purpose.

10.5 THE MEANING OF 'FAIL'

Road Traffic Act 1988, s 11(2) provides that 'fail' includes 'refuse'. An abundance of case law elaborates the meanings of these words.

10.5.1 Absence of device

The fact that the appropriate device is not presented, or visible, to the suspect when the requirement is made is irrelevant. In *R v Wagner* [1970] RTR 422, an officer required a motorist to take a roadside breath test. After about three minutes waiting for the equipment to be brought, the motorist pushed the officer aside, said he was not going to wait, and that he was going for a drink of water. He walked away. The Court of Appeal (Criminal Division) held that the motorist's behaviour amounted to refusal. In *DPP v Swan* [2004] EWHC 2432 (Admin), the Divisional Court found that the physical production of the breath test device was not a prerequisite to a proper requirement for a breath test and was not therefore a precondition for an offence of failing to provide a roadside specimen.

The same applies at the police station. In *Campbell v DPP* [1989] RTR 256, the suspect was silent in response to the requirement for breath specimens. He was in a room where no breath analysis device was present, and no device was presented to him. On appeal against conviction for failing without reasonable excuse to provide specimens, the Divisional Court found that he could reasonably be expected to know that a device was present and available. He had an opportunity to supply specimens and failed to do so.

10.5.2 Insufficient breath provided

As noted elsewhere (see para 4.5.1), the approved devices for gauging breath alcohol in drink-drive investigations are designed to measure the alcohol in 'deep lung air'. To ensure that the specimen includes deep lung air, a minimum amount of breath must be provided into the device before a measurement for evidential purposes can be made. Road Traffic Act 1988, s 11(3) reflects this, providing that a person does not co-operate with a preliminary test or provide a specimen of breath for analysis unless the person's co-operation or the specimen:

(a) is sufficient to enable the test or the analysis to be carried out, and
(b) is provided in such a way as to enable the objective of the test or analysis to be satisfactorily achieved.

In *Anderton v Waring* [1986] RTR 74, the suspect put the mouthpiece to his mouth and blew, but no sample was recorded. The justices dismissed a charge of failing without reasonable excuse to provide specimens of breath for analysis, finding that if the device recorded that no sample had been provided, the display would have shown the word 'aborted'. The prosecutor appealed. The Divisional Court found that, in the absence of evidence on the point, the device should have been assumed to be in good working order and the justices should not have made the assumption they did.

Where a motorist held the mouthpiece to his mouth, but the device registered no breath, the Divisional Court found, without reference to s 11(3), that he had failed to provide: *DPP v Radford* [1995] RTR 86.

In *DPP v Heywood* [1998] RTR 1, a motorist was required to provide a roadside specimen. She blew hard enough to illuminate one, but not both, of the lights on the device. The consequence was that, if the officer had pressed the 'read' button, the device would have provided either a reliable positive reading, or an unreliable negative reading. The Divisional Court found that the motorist had failed to provide a specimen. The objective of s 11(3) was to obtain a reliable reading one way or the other.

Where the motorist blew so little into a roadside device that neither light illuminated, but the officer nevertheless pressed the 'read' button and the reading was positive, the motorist had failed to provide a specimen: *Chand v DDP; DPP v Chand*, unreported, 19 October 1998 (DC).

In *DPP v Darwen* [2007] EWHC 337 (Admin), the same principle was applied in respect of the requirement for evidential breath specimens at the police station. The suspect had blown insufficient amounts of breath, withdrawing the mouthpiece even though the officer told him to keep blowing. He provided a number of such partial specimens. In each case the device recorded that the specimen was incomplete, but nevertheless provided an analysis. Each partial specimen showed excess alcohol. The justices acquitted the defendant of failing to provide; the prosecutor appealed. The Divisional Court found that the issue turned on s 11(3). Citing *DPP v Heywood* [1998] RTR 1, it decided that the respondent had not provided a specimen in accordance with s 11(3), in that he had not provided a specimen as directed, and the machine made clear that the amount of air produced was insufficient for its purposes. He did not therefore provide a specimen for the analysis to be carried out, and he did not provide it in such a way that the analysis could be satisfactorily achieved.

In *Rweikiza v DPP* [2008] EWHC 386 (Admin), the suspect had again blown partial specimens and was charged with failing to provide, contrary to s 7(6). The Divisional Court rejected an argument that *Darwen* had been wrongly decided, finding that the requirements of s 11(3) were not met.

In *Hussain v DPP* [2008] EWHC 901 (Admin), [2008] RTR 30, a motorist provided a first specimen, but the device registered 'ambient fail' and would not allow a second specimen to be provided. The process was repeated with the same result. The investigating officer believed the device had not produced a reliable indication and took the motorist to another police station, where, in response to a requirement by a different officer, the motorist refused to provide breath specimens. On appeal against conviction for failing without reasonable excuse to provide breath specimens, the Divisional Court found that the officer had been entitled to require two further specimens and that the motorist's refusal to do so constituted the offence.

10.5.3 Single breath specimens

Providing a single breath specimen for evidential analysis, rather than two, amounts to failure to provide: *Stepniewski v Commissioner of Police for the Metropolis* [1985] RTR 330 (DC). This is so even where the reason the second specimen was not provided was that the machine's three-minute cycle came to an end while the motorist was disputing the need for a second specimen; there is no duty on the officer to explain the time limit: *DPP v Thomas* [1996] RTR 293 (DC).

Several short blows, rather than a single long continuous blow, likewise constitute failing to provide: *Oldfield v Anderton* [1986] RTR 314 (DC).

In *DPP v Thomas (Elwyn Kenneth)* [1996] RTR 293, the suspect provided a first specimen, which produced a reading of 52. When asked for a second specimen, he questioned the purpose when he had already given a specimen showing 52. He did then begin to give a second specimen, but the breath analysis device ran out of time and aborted before he had done so. The justices dismissed a charge of failing to provide, on the basis that the officer did not clearly indicate the need to provide a second specimen within three minutes, with the result that the motorist did not have a proper opportunity to provide the second specimen. On the prosecutor's appeal, the Divisional Court ruled that there is no obligation to explain that the second specimen must be given within three minutes or within any other period of time. The only reason the defendant did not provide two specimens was that he chose, instead of providing the second specimen within a reasonable period, to argue that the second test was unnecessary.

Where a single breath specimen was given, but it was unclear to the Divisional Court whether the officer had decided that the suspect had refused to provide a second specimen, or had decided there were medical reasons why breath could not be provided or should not be required (see para 4.3), the case had to go back to the justices for re-hearing: *May v DPP* [2000] RTR 7. In *May*, the suspect provided a breath specimen which revealed excess alcohol. He declined several opportunities to provide a second specimen, saying that he wished blood to be taken. A blood specimen was taken, but the suspect was prosecuted for failing without reasonable excuse to provide breath specimens. The Divisional Court remarked that, had the matter ended with the refusal to provide a second specimen of breath, it may very well have been that there was no answer to the charge of failing to provide.

See also *Sykes v DPP* [1988] RTR 129 (see para 4.7), where evidence of failure to provide a second breath specimen remained admissible despite the fact that the officer had, in error, then gone on to require a blood specimen.

10.5.4 Theft of specimen

Where a suspect provided a blood specimen but then stole it back from the police, that did not amount to failing to provide, although he was imprisoned for the theft: *R v Rothery* (1976) 63 Cr App R 231 (CA).

10.5.5 Time for providing

In accordance with the requirements for type approval specified by the Home Office, the breath analysis devices are designed to allow three minutes for the subject to provide specimens. In the unreported case of *Patel v DPP*, 30 November 1988, the defendant was told he had 'three blows' to produce specimens. He argued that what he should have been told was that he had three minutes. The court was satisfied that he had deliberately not provided adequate breath and convicted him. The Divisional Court upheld his conviction, finding that it was quite impossible to see how he could have been prejudiced by being told he had three blows, rather than three minutes. Nor is there any requirement that the suspect be told there is a three-minute time limit: *Cosgrove v DPP* [1997] RTR 153 (DC), *Stepniewski v Commissioner of Police for the Metropolis* [1985] RTR 330 (DC) (see para 10.5.3) and *DPP v Thomas* [1996] RTR 293 (DC).

Not only is the officer not obliged to explain the three-minute time limit, but the three minutes need not be allowed in full. In *Cosgrove v DPP* [1997] RTR 153, a motorist first blew past the mouthpiece, then blew hard enough but not for long enough. When then asked whether there was a medical reason why he had failed to provide the specimens, he said there was not. He was not given another opportunity to provide a specimen, although two minutes of the cycle remained. He appealed against conviction for failing without reasonable excuse to provide specimens of breath. The Divisional Court found that there is no principle of law that the full three minutes must necessarily be allowed. If the officer concludes that the person is not making proper attempts to provide specimens, the officer is entitled to reach such a conclusion part-way through the three-minute period, although the risk might then be that the court could find reasonable excuse. On the facts of this case, the court below was justified in finding that the defendant was deliberately avoiding giving the specimen and in convicting him.

Cosgrove was followed in *Watson v DPP* [2006] EWHC 3429 (Admin), where the suspect had provided a first breath specimen, then insisted he wished to use the lavatory before providing the second. The investigating officer indicated that if the suspect did not provide the second specimen immediately his refusal to do so would constitute failure to provide. The second specimen was not provided, and the defendant's appeal against conviction for failing to provide was dismissed by the Divisional Court. It found the decision of the officer, and its endorsement by the justices, unimpeachable.

See also *Hingley-Smith v DPP* [1997] EWHC 952 (Admin) (para 3.4.7) and *DPP v Thomas (Elwyn Kenneth)* [1996] RTR 293 (para 10.5.3).

10.5.6 Non-co-operation

Rude and aggressive behaviour, delaying tactics and demanding to have a photograph taken amounted to a refusal to provide specimens: *DPP v Swan* [2004] EWHC 2432 (Admin).

10.5.7 Retracting a refusal

Failure to provide a specimen is complete upon a first refusal. It is immaterial that the suspect has a change of mind and offers a specimen before being charged: *Procaj v Johnstone* [1970] RTR 49 (QBD), where there were 26 minutes between the refusal and the change of mind. In *DPP v Lawrence* CO/1576/98, the suspect declined to provide blood specimens, saying he was afraid of needles, then changed his mind between 35 and 40 minutes later, after speaking to the doctor. The Divisional Court held that the change of mind was too late. The offence of failing to provide was complete.

But where the suspect, in response to the requirement for breath specimens, at first said 'no', but changed his mind within five seconds, that was not taken as a refusal and he had not failed to provide: *Smyth v DPP* [1996] RTR 59 (DC).

In *Plackett v DPP* [2008] EWHC 1335 (Admin), (2008) 172 JP 455, the motorist at first refused to provide an evidential breath specimen. He then left the room to speak to the duty solicitor by telephone. While the motorist was out of the room, the investigating officer started a new operating cycle of the breath analysis device. The motorist returned to the room and indicated he would now provide specimens; about one minute of the machine's three-minute cycle remained. At the first attempt to provide specimens, the mouthpiece came off; at the second, the amount of breath was insufficient. No further opportunity to provide specimens was given. The motorist appealed against conviction for failing without reasonable excuse to provide specimens. The Divisional Court found that the officer might well have considered the offence complete when the motorist left the room. But instead he had, by his conduct, agreed to allow a further opportunity, and should have allowed a full cycle. The motorist's appeal succeeded.

If the suspect fails to provide specimens at the first attempt, and the officer allows a second attempt, the initial failure may nevertheless be relied upon as the basis of the charge of failing to provide: *Hingley-Smith v DPP* [1997] EWHC 952 (Admin) (see para 3.4.7).

Where the defendant failed to provide breath specimens, then asked to provide a blood specimen but was not allowed to, the Divisional Court ruled that even if a blood specimen might have shown he was below the limit, it would have been irrelevant to the offence of failing to provide breath specimens. His conviction for that offence would stand: *Perkins v DPP* [2004] EWHC 255 (Admin).

See also *Oberoi (Yash) v DPP*, unreported, 23 November 1999 (para 10.7.3).

10.5.8 Urine specimens

Road Traffic Act 1988, s 7(5) stipulates that a specimen of urine is to be provided within one hour of its being required, and after the provision of a previous specimen of urine.

In *DPP v Baldwin* [2000] RTR 314, the Divisional Court found that if a suspect fails to provide the specimen within that time limit he may 'there and then be charged with the offence of failing to supply a specimen'. But the officer had allowed extra time and the specimen was provided 15 minutes after the hour expired. Evidence of its analysis was held admissible in a prosecution for driving with excess alcohol.

An argument that the court should, when calculating the hour, take into account seconds, was dismissed in *Walters v DPP*, unreported, 18 March 1997. The evidence was that the requirement for a urine specimen had been made at 2.10 and the procedure was abandoned at 3.10, no specimen having been provided. It was argued that the requirement could have been made as late as 2.10 and 59 seconds, and the procedure abandoned on the dot of 3.10, so allowing something less than the full 60 minutes. The Divisional Court found that, since seconds had not been referred to in evidence, the court was not obliged to take them into account.

In *Robertson v DPP* [2004] EWHC 517 (Admin), a motorist was providing a urine specimen pursuant to the statutory option (now repealed; see para 1.3.4). The officer delayed, possibly for up to half an hour, allowing him to produce the first specimen, and he was unable to provide the second until 75 minutes after the decision that the specimen would be of urine. The officer rejected it as too late. The Divisional Court held that the motorist had not been allowed the full time to provide the specimen. He had been deprived of the safeguard in the old option and the breath analysis was not admissible. It seems likely that this case survives the repeal of the option.

Merely passing urine does not amount to providing a specimen. The police officer must have the opportunity to take charge of it, and must in fact take charge of it. Where the suspect dropped the container as the officer was reaching for it, and the specimen was spilled, no specimen was provided: *Ross v Hodges* [1975] RTR 55 (DC). It was immaterial whether the jar was dropped deliberately or accidentally.

To constitute a 'specimen' of urine, the amount provided must be large enough to be divided into two parts by a constable in a police station, and each part must be capable of analysis: *R v Coward* (1976) 63 Cr App R 54 (CA).

10.6 'REASONABLE EXCUSE'

It is a question of law whether a particular circumstance is capable of constituting a reasonable excuse for failing to provide a specimen. If it is, it is then a matter of fact and degree whether or not that circumstance amounts to such an excuse: *Law v Stephens* [1971] RTR 358.

10.6.1 The test in *Lennard*

Over the years, defendants have advanced a multiplicity of arguments in their attempts to establish reasonable excuses for failing to provide. The classic statement of what constitutes a reasonable excuse remains that in *R v Lennard* [1973] 1 WLR 483, where the Court of Appeal said that:

> no excuse can be adjudged a reasonable one unless the person from whom the specimen is required is physically or mentally unable to provide it or the provision of the specimen would entail a substantial risk to his health.

The courts have applied this test rigorously, and attempts to widen the scope of reasonable excuse have largely failed. This is despite the fact that, in *R v Reid (Philip)* [1973] RTR 536, the Court of Appeal referred to the possibility that a future court might find *Lennard* too restrictive in its interpretation. In *R v John* [1974] RTR 332, the Court of Appeal suggested that the court in *Lennard* 'did not intend to lay down something rigid and exhaustive', while the case of *DPP v Varley* [1999] Crim LR 753 (see para 10.7.1) has been said to illustrate 'the established narrow limits of the notion of reasonable excuse … and the minimal scope for innovation'.

At the time of the decision in *R v Lennard* [1973] 1 WLR 483, the only types of specimen which could be taken were blood or urine. The introduction of evidential breath analysis, in addition to the analysis of blood or urine, pursuant to the Transport Act 1981, did not lead to any relaxation of the test; see, for example, the 'trying hard' cases cited in para 10.7.9. While the introduction of s 7A(6) might have provided scope for renewed argument, that appears, at the time of writing (January 2024), not to have been the case.

Facts which do not amount to a reasonable excuse may nevertheless be sufficient to constitute special reasons for not disqualifying, or for disqualifying for a shorter period than would otherwise be appropriate. See Chapter 13.

10.6.2 The *Lennard* test compared with medical reasons for not taking breath or blood

The matters which may amount to a physical or mental inability to provide specimens within the test in *Lennard* are not necessarily on all fours with the matters which may amount to medical reasons why breath cannot be provided or should not be required, entitling the investigating officer to require a blood or urine specimen instead (see para 4.3.2). Nor are they necessarily the same as the medical reasons why blood cannot or should not be taken under s 7(4A) (see para 4.8.2). The relationships between these different situations may be significant. For example, as will be seen, intoxication does not amount to a reasonable excuse for failing to provide specimens under s 7(6), but it may amount to a medical reason why breath cannot be provided or should not be required under s 7(3)(a): *Young (Paula) v DPP* [1992] RTR 328 (DC) (see para 10.7.4).

In *Woolman v Lenton* [1985] Crim LR 516, the suspect responded to the requirement for breath specimens by saying he had difficulty in breathing through his nose. He argued that, although he had not been physically unable to provide a specimen of breath and had no reasonable excuse, the officer had reasonable cause to believe that for medical reasons a breath specimen could not be provided or should not be required, and so should not have required a breath specimen. The Divisional Court found that the sole relevant question was whether the suspect had reasonable excuse for failure to supply a specimen. Since he had not, the question of medical reasons was irrelevant.

In *DPP v Shuker* [1995] CLY 4420, the motorist, when taken to the breath analysis device, clutched his chest as though having an attack. When asked if there was any medical reason why he could not provide specimens, he replied, 'bronchitis'. The officer administering the procedure thought he was feigning the attack, and when the police surgeon arrived nearly an hour later, the defendant immediately said he would blow into the machine if the doctor gave him a certificate saying he was fit to do so. He provided no specimen for analysis. The justices accepted the motorist's submission that the procedure had been suspended pending medical advice and should have been restarted when the doctor said the motorist was fit. They concluded that there had been no requirement to provide a breath specimen and dismissed the information. On the prosecutor's appeal, the Queen's Bench Division highlighted an incontrovertible finding in the case stated that the motorist had been required to provide a breath sample and failed to do so. If the justices' decision was correct, it would give recalcitrant motorists a virtual charter to play the system. On the facts, the respondent had been required to provide breath specimens and had failed to do so. He raised no reasonable excuse and so was guilty of the offence. See also *Atkinson v DPP* [2011] EWHC 706 (Admin) (para 10.6.5), where the suspect feigned falling and banging his head.

Even if the investigating officer has reasonable cause to believe that for medical reasons a breath specimen cannot be provided or should not be required, that does not of itself furnish the suspect with a reasonable excuse, or preclude prosecution for failing to provide breath specimens. In *DPP v Boden* [1988] RTR 188, the motorist had declined to provide breath specimens, saying there was a medical reason, but not elaborating. The officer, believing there were medical reasons against breath specimens, went on to require a blood specimen instead, but the motorist refused. The motorist appealed against conviction for failing without reasonable excuse to provide specimens of breath. The Divisional Court found no reason at all why a request for blood should eliminate penal consequences for a refusal to give breath without reasonable excuse. The request for blood was not determinative on the question of reasonable excuse. On the facts, there was no reasonable excuse and the appeal failed.

In *Pattison v DPP* [2005] EWHC 2938 (Admin), [2006] 2 All ER 317, the investigating officer accepted a motorist's statement that he had asthma as a medical reason for not supplying breath specimens, and went on to require a blood specimen. The motorist then refused, saying, 'no one is sticking any needles in me, it's against my religion to give blood'. The Administrative Court upheld his conviction for failing to provide breath specimens, finding that the justices were entitled to consider all the evidence, including the motorist's behaviour after saying he had asthma, and his stated reasons for refusing to give blood. Having done so, they were entitled to conclude that what the motorist had said about his asthma was incredible, and that he had no intention of providing any form of specimen.

On the facts in *Oladimeji v DPP* [2006] EWHC 1199 (Admin), the court was entitled to find that the motorist had no medical reason for not supplying breath specimens and that he therefore had no reasonable excuse. His first specimen of breath produced a reading of 72 and he failed to provide a second specimen. He did not answer the question whether there was any medical reason for this failure. When asked about medication, he said he had suffered from asthma in the past. The Divisional Court upheld the justices' finding that he had no medical reason for failing to provide breath. He had not had any difficulty in providing a roadside breath specimen; he had successfully provided a first specimen at the police station; he did not suggest at the time that there was any medical reason for his failure to provide a second one; he had not been coughing at the time; and all that against the background of evidence that he had not had any asthma problems for a number of years.

In *Longstaff v DPP* [2008] EWHC 303 (Admin), [2008] RTR 17, a motorist failed to provide breath specimens, saying he could not breathe properly because of back pain. The officer therefore required a blood specimen and called a doctor. The doctor examined the motorist and found no medical reason for failure to provide breath, and the procedure for taking a blood specimen was abandoned. The motorist was convicted of failing to provide breath specimens. On appeal, the Divisional Court found nothing in the legislation to suggest that the mere fact that the officer later sought a blood test debars the prosecution from alleging failure without reasonable excuse to provide breath specimens.

10.6.3 Evidence

To establish physical or mental inability to provide, appropriate evidence must be before the court. In *DPP v Daley* [1992] RTR 155, a driver simply failed to provide breath specimens at the roadside and at the police station. When asked if there was any medical reason, he answered that there was nothing wrong with his lungs. At his trial he could not account for his failure. On appeal against acquittal, the Divisional Court held that there was no evidence on which the justices should have assumed or inferred that he was incapable of providing the specimens. In *DPP v Curtis* [1993] RTR 72, the Divisional Court reiterated that justices must not go beyond the evidence before them to find reasonable excuse.

Evidence of physical or medical disability to satisfy the test in *Lennard* would normally be the evidence of a medical practitioner, but it need not be, and, in some circumstances, the evidence of the defendant himself might suffice: *Grady v Pollard* [1988] RTR 316 (see para 10.7.9).

In *DPP v Ambrose* [1992] RTR 285 (see para 10.7.9), the court said that a finding of physical or mental inability is achievable only on evidence, which, in almost all imaginable cases, is of a medical character. In *Smith (Nicholas Paul) v DPP* [1992] RTR 413, the Divisional Court rejected an argument of reasonable excuse based on nervousness and stress where there was no medical or other expert evidence that the nervousness was at least a possible explanation for the failure to provide. See also *DPP v Simpson (Ian William)*, unreported, 18 January 2000, where the Divisional Court said that, almost always, if medical evidence is not adduced, the defendant does not satisfy the evidential burden such that the prosecution must negative it to the criminal standard.

Exceptionally, in *DPP v Crofton* [1994] RTR 279, medical reasons were made out without expert evidence. The Divisional Court identified the relevant matters:

- the need for evidence of physical or mental incapability to provide the specimen;
- that medical evidence is normally required to support such a claim; and
- the necessary causative link between the physical or mental conditions and the failure to provide the specimen.

The justices had properly addressed these issues and had believed the defendant on those issues by unimpeachable findings of fact. The appellate court would not overturn those findings since it had not itself had the benefit of seeing and hearing the witnesses.

See also *DPP v Pearman* [1992] RTR 407 (para 10.7.4), a case in which the causal connection was established even in the absence of medical evidence.

10.6.4 Causative link

The defendant must establish a causative link between the condition claimed and the inability to provide the specimen(s): *DPP v Brodzky* [1997] RTR 425, where the Divisional Court said that the most important reason for medical evidence is to show such a link.

In *DPP v Furby* [2000] RTR 181, the defendant had failed even to try to provide breath specimens. It later transpired that he suffered from reduced lung capacity and would have been unable to provide the specimens even if he had tried. The court held that there must be a direct relationship between the excuse relied upon and the failure to provide. The appellant could not rely on his impaired lung capacity unless he had made a genuine attempt to provide the specimens. His conviction was upheld.

In *Falzarano v DPP* [2001] RTR 14, the justices found, *inter alia*, that the defendant had done her best to provide a specimen, but that shortness of breath resulting from a panic attack prevented her. The Divisional Court was satisfied that the findings of the court below disclosed a causative link between the defendant's physical and/or mental condition and her failure to provide a specimen. It dismissed the prosecutor's appeal against acquittal.

Where the motorist refused to provide a specimen because he had a sore ear, but the medical examiner found there was no reason why he could not give a breath specimen, the motorist did not have a reasonable excuse for failing to provide specimens: *McMahon v CPS* [2001] EWHC 180 (Admin).

On the facts in *DPP v Grundy* [2006] EWHC 1157 (Admin), no causative link between the defendant's distress and her failure to provide a specimen was established and she did not therefore have a reasonable excuse for failing to provide. The Administrative Court reiterated the three points to be considered, as set out in *DPP v Crofton* [1994] RTR 279 (above), and that, while medical evidence is not always necessary, it is generally necessary to determine whether or not there is a causative link between the condition and the failure to provide. The justices had dismissed the charge on the basis that the defendant's state of distress gave her a reasonable excuse, even though she adduced no medical evidence to relate the distress to the failure to provide. The Administrative Court ruled that the material before the justices was insufficient to establish a causative link, and it was not therefore necessary for the Crown to call any evidence to negative it.

10.6.5 Time for raising the excuse

A number of cases concern the time at which, or the manner in which, the question of reasonable excuse must be raised. If the suspect does not even attempt to provide a breath specimen, no question of reasonable excuse arises. In *Teape v Godfrey* [1986] RTR 213, the motorist had made no effort to blow into the breath analysis device. He was not permitted, at his trial, to argue that he had a medical condition, of which he had been unaware at the time, which would have constituted a reasonable excuse. See also *DPP v Furby* [2000] RTR 181 (para 10.6.4).

Where the defendant told the officer who had arrested him, but not the officer who later conducted the breath analysis procedure at the police station, that he suffered from bronchitis, he was found not to have a reasonable excuse: *DPP v Lonsdale* [2001] EWHC 95 (Admin), [2001] RTR 29. There is some suggestion in the judgment that he may not even have tried to provide specimens, although that is not borne out by the recitation of the facts.

In *Martiner v DPP* [2004] EWHC 2484 (Admin), the Administrative Court reiterated that if a suspect makes no effort to provide specimens and offers no reason, particularly if he has an excuse but chooses not to invoke it, he cannot later seek to excuse himself.

In *Piggott v DPP* [2008] EWHC 305 (Admin), [2008] RTR 16, however, the Divisional Court found that there is no *obligation* on a suspect to communicate a reasonable excuse at the time the specimens are required. But if a defendant knows of a medical condition and does not mention it at the time the specimens are required, the risk is that the justices will conclude that the failure was wilful and that there had been no genuine attempt to provide them. The court dismissed as *obiter* comments in *Teape v Godfrey* to the effect that a person who knows he has a medical condition has a duty to inform the investigating officer, remarking that cases in which *Teape v Godfrey* had been followed featured failure or refusal to provide, rather than a genuine attempt to provide breath specimens, as in the present case. While the Administrative Court in *Martiner* had approved those *dicta*, the court in *Piggott* found persuasive the approach adopted in the Scottish case of *McClory v Owen-Thomas* 1990 SLT 323. In *McClory*, the High Court of Justiciary was clear that there is nothing in the statutory language imposing an onus on a motorist to disclose anything to the investigating officer, or to relieve the prosecutor of the burden of proving the absence of reasonable excuse. The absence of such an excuse was, the court emphasised, part of the definition of the offence, not a defence.

In *Atkinson v DPP* [2011] EWHC 706 (Admin), during the police station procedure, the motorist twice fell to his knees and claimed to have banged his head. He did so in a controlled manner and the officer conducting the procedure, and another officer, were sure he was feigning injury. A nurse saw the suspect an hour later, found his pulse and blood pressure high and called an ambulance, but the suspect declined to go to hospital. The nurse gave evidence that a panic attack could not be ruled out. On appeal against conviction for failing to provide specimens, the Administrative Court noted that the high pulse and high blood pressure had been recorded *after* the procedure had been carried out. The crucial time is the time the procedure is being carried out; at that time, the two officers were of the view that the motorist was feigning a condition which disabled him from understanding the procedure. The magistrates were entitled to find that the motorist did not have a reasonable excuse for failing to provide.

10.7 CIRCUMSTANCES WHICH CONSTITUTE REASONABLE EXCUSE

A substantial number of judgments concern attempts by defendants to bring themselves within the test in *Lennard*.

10.7.1 The defendant's state of mind

Many arguments based on what the defendant had in mind have been found not to fall within the mental inability to provide identified in *Lennard*. Thus the fact that the suspect did not agree that he had committed a traffic offence is not a reasonable excuse: *R v Downey* [1970] RTR 257. See also *Williams v Osborne* [1975] RTR 181.

Where the officer told the suspect that the consequences of failing to provide would be a fine, disqualification, and (incorrectly) imprisonment, that did not excuse failure to provide in *Bryant v Morris* [1972] RTR 214 (DC).

Nor did a sincerely held personal belief which did not allow the subject to comply with the requirement to provide a blood specimen: *R v John* [1974] 1 WLR 624, where the defendant believed he was possessed of certain faith-healing powers derived from the presence in his blood of divine gifts.

In *McGrath v Vipas* [1984] RTR 58, a genuine but mistaken belief that the preconditions for requiring the specimen had not been met, and that the requirement was therefore invalid, did not provide the defendant with a reasonable excuse. The defendant thought the officer had not been acting *bona fide*, and had not had reasonable cause to believe that the defendant had been driving. The Divisional Court remarked that a person who declines a request because he believes one or more of the preconditions is not satisfied does so in the peril of being wrong.

A motorist's belief that he is entitled to see a solicitor before providing a specimen cannot in law amount to a reasonable excuse: *Grennan v Wescott* [1988] RTR 253 (DC) and *DPP v Varley* [1999] Crim LR 753. A motorist's belief that he is entitled to consult the codes of practice under PACE likewise could not constitute a reasonable excuse: *DPP v Whalley* [1991] RTR 161 (DC). See also the cases cited in para 10.7.3.

A defendant's belief that he had not drunk enough to take him over the limit does not provide a reasonable excuse: *Cracknell v Willis* [1988] AC 450 (HL) (see para 3.4.7). Nor does the fact of having drunk only non-alcoholic lager, as the defendant claimed in *DPP v Fountain* [1988] RTR 385 (DC).

Having already supplied a blood specimen for medical purposes was not a reasonable excuse for failing to provide a blood specimen for evidential purposes: *Kemp v Chief Constable of Kent* [1987] RTR 66 (DC). The defendant, who was in hospital at the time, was not physically incapable of providing a further blood specimen and there was no medical objection to his doing so.

Thinking he had a choice between giving a blood or a urine specimen did not amount to a reasonable excuse in *DPP v Lawrence (Scott James)* [1998] COD 371 (DC).

In *DPP v Mukandiwa* [2005] EWHC 2977 (Admin), [2006] RTR 24, the motorist refused to provide a blood specimen 'for spiritual reasons'. At his trial he said he originated from Zimbabwe and was a licensed healer and spirit medium. The sight of blood could induce a trance during which he would become violent and create a risk of injury to himself and others. The Divisional Court held that, on the facts, it was not open to the court below to make a finding that there was a substantial risk to the motorist's health.

10.7.2 Conditional agreement: taking the specimen

It is for the practitioner taking a blood specimen to use professional discretion to decide from which part of the body to extract it. A defendant who insisted that the specimen be taken from his big toe was guilty of failing to provide: *Solesbury v Pugh* [1969] 1 WLR 1114.

10.7.3 Conditional agreement: advice

A series of cases concerns the suspect's desire for advice before responding to the requirement to provide specimens. In *Grennan v Wescott* [1988] RTR 253 (DC) (see para 10.7.1), a belief that there was an entitlement to advice before providing a specimen was not a reasonable excuse.

Conditional agreement to provide a specimen amounts to failure to provide, although, as the cases illustrate, the line between conditional and unconditional agreement may be fine, as may the distinction between refusal and agreement. In *Pettigrew v Northumbria Police Authority* [1976] RTR 177 at 182, it was said:

> the motorist … refuses to comply with the request if he gives an acceptance which is subject to a condition … in practice there will be many cases in which the motorist will wish not immediately to give a specimen. Sometimes it is because he wants a solicitor … a distinction must be made between the motorist who says 'I will not unless –' and the motorist who says 'I will but may I do so-and-so beforehand?' In the second instance there is no refusal …

Where it appeared that the suspect had simply asked to speak to his solicitor before deciding whether to provide a specimen, and the investigating officer consented, the suspect spoke to the solicitor and then provided the specimens, there was no failure to provide: *Smith v Hand* [1986] RTR 265 (DC). But in *Chief Constable of Avon & Somerset v O'Brien* [1987] RTR 182 (DC), desiring to see a doctor and a solicitor before providing specimens was not a reasonable excuse.

In *Francis v Chief Constable of Avon and Somerset* [1988] RTR 250, the suspect declined to provide a specimen of blood until he had spoken to his solicitor. The investigating officer told him he could not consult a solicitor but allowed him to make a telephone call, following which the suspect was willing to provide the specimen. The delay was of no more than five minutes. The Divisional Court found that a conditional acceptance of this kind, even where there was no unreasonable delay, could not amount to a reasonable excuse for failing to provide a sample.

In *DPP v Billington* [1988] 1 WLR 535, the Divisional Court ruled that the procedure for taking breath specimens for analysis is not an 'interview' for the purposes of PACE. PACE Code of Practice, Code C, para 6.3 (providing that a person who asks for legal advice may not be interviewed or continue to be interviewed until he has received such advice) does not therefore apply. A suspect may not delay the procedure so as to speak to a solicitor, and the right to consult a solicitor does not afford a suspect a reasonable excuse for failing to provide a specimen.

The parts of the *pro forma* containing questions and answers do not constitute an interview for the purposes of Code C. Requesting breath specimens from a juvenile does not amount to an interview covered by Code C so as to require the presence of an appropriate adult. See *DPP v Rous and D (A Minor)* [1992] RTR 246 (DC). But see *Miller v DPP* [2018] EWHC 262 (Admin), [2018] RTR 19 (para 11.9.1). See also para 3.2.2 on the non-application of PACE.

The rule that conditional agreement amounts to refusal was applied in a number of later cases: *DPP v Skinner; DPP v Cornell* [1990] RTR 254 (DC); *Salter v DPP* [1992] RTR 386 (DC); *DPP v Kirk* [1993] COD 99 (DC); *DPP v Smith*, *The Times*, 1 June 1993; *DPP v Varley* [1999] Crim LR 753 and *DPP v Noe* [2002] RTR 351 (DC).

But in *Hudson v DPP* [1992] RTR 27, on the facts – the information given to the suspect, and delay in starting the breath testing procedure following his request for a solicitor – the Divisional Court did not interfere with the decision of the court below that there was material upon which to exercise the discretion under PACE, s 78. Section 78 provides for the discretion to exclude evidence which would have such an adverse effect on the fairness of the proceedings that the court ought not to admit it – see para 11.9.

In *DPP v Kirk* [1993] COD 99, the defendant argued that he had not given breath specimens because he had wished to wait for advice from his solicitor, and to take his medication, before doing so, but had not been allowed. He also said that he thought the reading might be affected by medication he had taken before arrest. The Divisional Court dismissed all these arguments; none amounted to a reasonable excuse.

Where the suspect said he would provide a blood specimen only if it were taken by his own doctor, that again amounted to a refusal: *DPP v Smith (Alan Robert), The Times*, 1 June 1993 (DC). A decision on similar facts, but where the suspect's own doctor was present at the police station when the specimen was required, went the other way in the earlier case of *Bayliss v Chief Constable of Thames Valley* [1978] RTR 328.

In the unreported case of *Oberoi (Yash) v DPP*, 23 November 1999, the Divisional Court again found that the defendant had been rightly convicted of failing to provide. On arrival at the police station, he asked to speak to a solicitor. The sergeant told him that the procedure would not be delayed for that purpose. The defendant repeatedly said that he could not supply a specimen until he had spoken to a solicitor. The sergeant started up the machine but the defendant declined to blow into it, and the machine closed down. The defendant was then allowed to speak to the duty solicitor by telephone. The duty solicitor told him that the law required him to blow into the breath analysis device and that he could not choose to give a blood or urine sample instead. The defendant then offered to provide specimens of breath but was told it was too late.

Billington (above) was applied in *Campbell v DPP* [2002] EWHC 1314 (Admin), [2004] RTR 5, where a motorist at a police station had asked for a solicitor, and refused to provide evidential breath specimens in the meantime. He appealed against conviction for failing without reasonable excuse to provide breath specimens. His argument was that evidence of the procedure at the police station should be excluded under PACE, s 78 (above), on the ground that he had the right to legal advice under PACE, s 58, and under European Convention on Human Rights, art 6(3). Section 58 entitles a person arrested and held in custody at a police station to consult a solicitor, upon request, as soon as is practicable.

Article 6(3) is on the right to legal assistance. The appeal was dismissed, the Administrative Court finding that art 6(3) did not impose a blanket requirement that a detained person was entitled to legal advice before being asked to say or do anything. Any restriction on the right under art 6(3) must be proportionate to the aim. Delay would prejudice the legitimate aim of suppressing drink-driving. Procedures were in place to avoid prejudice to the suspect. By contacting the duty solicitor, the police had complied with their obligations.

Similar issues on similar facts arose in *Kennedy v DPP* [2002] EWHC 2297 (Admin), [2004] RTR 6, except that in *Kennedy*, police had delayed contacting a solicitor to the extent that the magistrates found that there had been a breach of s 58. The outcome was, though, the same. A conviction for failing without reasonable excuse to provide breath specimens was upheld. The breach of s 58 was neither significant nor substantial. In *Kennedy*, the court remarked that:

> If there happens to be a solicitor in the charge office whom the suspect says that he wants to consult for a couple of minutes before deciding whether or not to provide specimens of breath he must be allowed to do so. Similarly, if the suspect asks at that stage to speak on the telephone for a couple of minutes to his own solicitor, or the duty solicitor, and the solicitor in question is immediately available.

In *Myles v DPP* [2004] EWHC 594 (Admin), [2004] 2 All ER 902, it was argued that it should be permissible to delay the procedure for some short defined period for obtaining advice; 15 minutes was canvassed. The Divisional Court rejected this, reiterating that the process should not be delayed to any significant extent. This was a full and sufficient explanation of the position in law, which would serve as a practical guide to those who have to deal with such matters.

In *R (Forde) v DPP* [2004] EWHC 1156 (Admin), the suspect requested a solicitor part-way though the procedure and the officer did not relay that request for 20 minutes. The Administrative Court found that this had not prejudiced the defendant, and was not a sufficiently significant or substantial breach of s 58 to justify exclusion of the evidence from the blood specimen under s 78.

A seven-minute delay in contacting a solicitor 'only just' breached s 58 and the relevant code of practice, and was neither significant nor substantial. It was correct not to exclude the evidence of the request for breath specimens. See *Kirkup v DPP* [2003] EWHC 2354 (Admin), (2004) 168 JP 255.

In *Whitley v DPP* [2003] EWHC 2512 (Admin), a delay of 13 minutes between the request for a solicitor and the police telephone call for a duty solicitor was found to breach Code C, but not s 58. Again, the Divisional Court found the breach insignificant and insubstantial. It was right not to exclude evidence of the procedure.

Justices were in error to find that a suspect's solicitor should have been contacted in the four minutes between her request for a solicitor and beginning the breath testing procedure: *CPS v Rice* [2004] EWHC 508 (Admin).

A 14-minute delay was neither significant nor substantial, and the evidence of the breath testing procedure was not to be excluded under s 78: *Causey v DPP* [2004] EWHC 3164 (Admin), (2005) 169 JP 331. In *Causey*, the Divisional Court reviewed *Kennedy*, *Kirkup*, *Whitley* and *Myles*, distilling the following principles:

- there is no general duty on the police to delay taking a specimen at the police station until the detainee has obtained legal advice;
- whether, in contacting a solicitor at the detainee's request, the custody officer has acted without delay and has permitted the detainee to consult a solicitor as soon as is practicable is always a question of fact and degree depending on the circumstances;
- a custody officer has no way of knowing how long it will take to receive a response from the duty solicitor or public defender service, especially at night;
- if the custody officer knows a solicitor is immediately available, and particularly if there have been no other significant delays in the procedures up to that point, he should, if the suspect so requests, be allowed to consult the solicitor before deciding whether or not to provide specimens;
- specimens must be taken as close to the time of the alleged offence as possible, and the default position is there should be no delay. The process should not be delayed to any significant extent;
- a short and unwarranted delay in contacting a solicitor when requested may constitute a breach of s 58 and the Code of Practice, but not such as to merit excluding the evidence of the refusal to provide specimens.

In *Gearing v DPP* [2008] EWHC 1695 (Admin), [2009] RTR 7, a motorist had failed a roadside breath test and had been arrested. At the police station, she said, several times, that she wished to speak to a solicitor before providing breath specimens. Some 18 minutes after her first such request, she declined to provide specimens, and four minutes later an officer telephoned the duty solicitor call centre. The motorist spoke to a solicitor, and, 23 minutes after the duty solicitor call centre had first been contacted, the motorist indicated that she was willing to provide specimens, but was not given a further opportunity to do so. She was charged with failing to provide and convicted. On appeal, the Divisional Court found that the delay in contacting the duty solicitor call centre breached s 58. It was argued that the evidence of the refusal to provide should therefore be excluded under s 78. The Divisional Court, without reference to *Causey*, highlighted the public interest in prompt testing of those who had failed a roadside breath test, that the procedure carried with it its own safeguards, the practicability of obtaining prompt legal advice, and the extent of the delay and its significance, if any. On the facts, the judge in the court below had been entitled to exercise his discretion to refuse to exclude the evidence of the breath test procedure.

In *Cowper v DPP* [2009] EWHC 2165 (Admin), the Divisional Court confirmed that the advent of the Criminal Defence Service Direct telephone advice system does not make any difference to the principles above. It was argued that since the new system was designed to be more efficient than the old system, the officer should have waited for the solicitor to telephone the police station before beginning the procedure, or should have interrupted the procedure when the solicitor telephoned just after it had begun. Neither argument found favour.

In *CPS v Chalupa* [2009] EWHC 3082 (Admin), (2010) 174 JP 111, a motorist had been arrested and, at the police station, confirmed that he required legal advice. The police called the duty solicitor 20 minutes later. Meantime, they started the breath analysis procedure. The motorist would not provide specimens even though he was told he could not delay for legal advice. He was charged with the offence under s 7(6). When the duty solicitor was called, he returned the call within two minutes, but was told, in error, that the motorist was then undergoing the breath analysis procedure. The Divisional Court found that this was not, as the motorist had argued, an exceptional case where a solicitor was immediately available, such that it could be said that any delay would necessarily have been minimal, as in *Kennedy v DPP* (above). Although the duty solicitor did respond within two minutes of being contacted, there would not always be such a speedy response, and the response may not have been so fast if the solicitor had been contacted earlier. While there was a breach of PACE, s 58, that did not justify excluding the evidence of failure to provide under s 78.

Lastly, and perhaps surprisingly, being advised by a solicitor not to provide a specimen has also been found not to be a reasonable excuse: *Dickinson v DPP* [1989] Crim LR 741. It may seem unduly severe that reliance on professional advice, albeit misguided, should not exonerate a defendant, and the steadfast application of *Lennard* has been described, in the context of this decision, as a 'harsh gloss on the wording of the Act' (Case Comment [1989] Crim LR 741). On the other hand, of course, any such advice might advantage a suspect who has an exceptionally high level of alcohol, such that the penalty if the alcohol level is ascertained might be higher than the penalty for failing to provide.

10.7.4 Drunkenness and distress

In *Timothy v DPP* [1989] Crim LR 893, the appellant appealed against conviction for failing to provide a specimen of breath. His arguments included that the evidence of the request for the specimen should have been excluded under PACE, s 78 because he had been unfit through drink and in need of medical treatment for a cut to the forehead. The Divisional Court found that there was no evidence that the cut affected his state of mind, nor was he so drunk as to be incapable. His appeal failed.

Self-induced drunkenness such that the defendant could not understand the instructions for providing specimens, or the consequences of non-compliance, cannot amount to a reasonable excuse for failing to provide: *DPP v Beech* [1992] RTR 239. It has, however, been suggested that the result might have been different had the suspect lapsed into a state of total unconsciousness (Case Comment [1992] Crim LR 64).

On the other hand, the Divisional Court has upheld a finding that the defendant's emotional distress was a reasonable excuse, on the basis that it made her mentally unable to provide a specimen: *Spalding v Paine* [1985] Crim LR 673. While it may be difficult to distinguish the effects of severe distress from the effects of drunkenness, it is obvious that, as a matter of policy, 'a drunk cannot be acquitted of a drink-driving offence on grounds of intoxication' (see *Timothy v DPP*, Case Comment [1989] Crim LR 893). Where the suspect is so drunk as to be unable to blow into the device, that is unlikely to amount to a reasonable excuse: see *Young (Paula) v DPP* [1992] RTR 328 (DC), although it may amount to a reason why breath cannot be provided or should not be required. See para 4.3.2.

Both *Beech* and *Young* left open the question whether inability to blow because of self-induced drunkenness may, in itself, amount to a reasonable excuse. In *DPP v Camp* [2017] EWHC 3119 (Admin), [2018] Crim LR 406, the driver understood the instructions to provide breath specimens, and was given a number of opportunities to do so, but was too drunk to comply. The investigating officer was of the view that he did not have a medical reason why breath specimens could not be provided or should not be required. The magistrates' court accepted that he had a reasonable excuse for failing to provide and acquitted him. The prosecutor appealed. The Divisional Court emphasised that the scope of reasonable excuse is a question of fact in each case. While voluntary intoxication may explain inability to provide a specimen, that does not mean that the driver has a reasonable excuse for not doing so. There is a distinction between reasonable excuse for failing to provide, and medical reasons why a specimen of breath cannot be provided or should not be required. The case of *Young* concerned the latter. It would be unattractive if a defendant whose self-induced intoxication was so great as to prevent him from providing a specimen could take advantage of the defence of reasonable excuse which is not available to a defendant whose level of intoxication was not such as to render him incapable of providing a specimen of breath. Although *Lennard* established that a reasonable excuse must arise from a physical or mental inability to provide, such an inability does not of itself afford the driver a reasonable excuse; the excuse must be inherently reasonable, and that was not the case here. Nor was there any requirement on the police to terminate the breath testing procedure and proceed to require blood or urine specimens.

Where intoxication and distress were shown to render the defendant physically incapable of providing a breath specimen, even without medical evidence, a reasonable excuse was, perhaps exceptionally, made out in *DPP v Pearman* [1992] RTR 407. Although the Divisional Court acknowledged in this case that medical evidence would normally be needed, it was satisfied that the connection between the condition of the defendant and the inability to provide had been established, and was not prepared to interfere with the justices' assessment of the evidence. It is difficult to reconcile this decision with the general trend in the case law, particularly since the defendant in question had provided a first specimen without difficulty. The judgment seems to conflate the issues of distress and drunkenness, although there is a suggestion that the state of distress may have been more influential than the drunkenness.

Where the condition alleged was insufficient to render the suspect incapable of providing specimens or understanding the requirement, the reasonable excuse argument failed. In *DPP v Meller* [2002] EWHC 733 (Admin), where the motorist was anxious and agitated, but capable of providing specimens and understood the requirement, she did not have a reasonable excuse for failing to provide a blood specimen. See also *Smith (Nicholas Paul) v DPP* [1992] RTR 413 (see para 10.6.3).

10.7.5 Fears and phobias

In the early case of *R v Harding* (1974) 59 Cr App R 153, the Court of Criminal Appeal found that where fear of a needle truly incapacitated the appellant from submitting to the taking of a blood specimen, this could amount to a reasonable excuse. Stephenson LJ went on to remark that no fear short of a phobia recognised by medical science to be as strong and inhibiting as, for instance, claustrophobia, can be allowed to excuse failure to provide a specimen for a laboratory test. In most, if not all, cases where the fear of providing it is claimed to be invincible, the claim must be supported by medical evidence.

In *Alcock v Read* [1980] RTR 71, the suspect declined to provide a blood specimen, claiming mental incapacity. He had previously fainted when giving blood and had a terror of blood. He called a witness in support. The justices accepted that the defendant's refusal to supply blood was reasonable. The Divisional Court dismissed the prosecutor's appeal against acquittal, finding that there was evidence upon which the justices could have reached their conclusion. A mental incapacity or invincible repugnance to providing blood would amount to a reasonable excuse.

Dislike of the sight of blood, leading to light-headedness, does not amount to a phobia constituting physical incapacity to provide a blood specimen. Nor does an irrational belief that discomfort at the sight of blood might be interpreted as evidence of intoxication: *Sykes v White* [1983] RTR 419.

Mere embarrassment at having to provide a urine specimen is not a reasonable excuse: *Palmer v Killion* [1983] RTR 138.

The use of mouthpieces and syringes in the provision of specimens gave rise to a spate of arguments concerning the risk of contracting HIV. In *DPP v Fountain* [1988] RTR 385, the defendant's words, 'in view of the danger of AIDS, I'd rather not give blood', was held to amount to a refusal to provide a blood specimen which was not capable of constituting a reasonable excuse. It has, however, been suggested that this conclusion is too wide (Case Comment [1988] Crim LR 123). Where a fear of contracting AIDS from contact with the mouthpiece of the evidential breath testing device was so great as to amount to a phobia, reasonable excuse was, 'uniquely', made out: *De Freitas v DPP* [1993] RTR 98. Doubtless similar claims arose in relation to COVID-19, although no cases have been reported.

See also *R (Cuns) v Hammersmith Magistrates' Court* [2016] EWHC 748 (Admin) (para 10.4) on the need for evidence to support a claim of a phobia.

10.7.6 Irregularity in the procedure

Defendants have not fared well by alleging procedural irregularity. In *Hartland v Alden* [1987] RTR 253 (DC), the fact that the suspect had been unlawfully arrested did not provide him with a reasonable excuse for failing to provide. In *Thomas v DPP* [1991] RTR 292, a motorist was, in error, arrested without the roadside breath test having been administered. His arrest was therefore unlawful, but the Divisional Court found that the justices were nevertheless right to admit evidence of his subsequent failure to provide specimens at the police station.

In *DPP v Coyle* [1996] RTR 287 (see para 10.7.9), the fact that the three-minute time limit for providing breath specimens was not explained until part-way through the cycle was not a reasonable excuse, there being no obligation on the officer to indicate a time limit.

10.7.7 Limited command of English

The subject's failure to understand the procedure because of his limited English was accepted as a reasonable excuse in *Beck v Sager* [1979] RTR 475. The Divisional Court found that it could bring the circumstance of the case within the spirit, if not the letter, of the principle in *Lennard*, in that the defendant's failure to understand rendered him mentally incapable of providing the specimen. See also *R (Matara) v Brent Magistrates' Court* [2005] EWHC 1829 (Admin), (2005) 169 JP 576 (para 11.10).

In *Bielecki v DPP* [2011] EWHC 2245 (Admin), a motorist was charged with failing without reasonable excuse to supply specimens of breath. He was a Polish national who spoke little or no English. The procedure at the police station was conducted with an interpreter in the usual way. The officer conducting the procedure told the motorist that she required him to provide two specimens of breath, and warned him more than once that if he did not provide them he might be prosecuted. The magistrates were satisfied that the testing procedure had been properly explained via the interpreter and that the motorist understood the requirement. They convicted him for failing without reasonable excuse to provide the specimens. On appeal, he argued that it was not permissible to infer that what had been said had been translated properly and understood by the appellant, and that direct evidence from the interpreter was necessary before reaching such a conclusion. The Administrative Court rejected that argument, finding a court may draw the inference, if the evidence supports it, that someone being asked to do something in a police station by a police officer with the assistance of an accredited interpreter of the relevant language has been asked the correct question, understands it and also the consequences of not responding to it.

10.7.8 Physical awkwardness

Physical awkwardness in the facilities for providing a specimen, again, have not been fruitful grounds for arguing reasonable excuse. The subject's position in the back of a police car, such that he could not see the lights on the screening device (having been instructed to blow long and hard enough so that the lights came on and stayed on) did not amount to physical inability to provide and did not provide a reasonable excuse: *Dawes v Taylor* [1986] RTR 81 (DC).

10.7.9 'Trying hard'

Applying *Lennard*, in *Grady v Pollard* [1988] RTR 316, the Divisional Court found that (even if accepted) trying 'as hard as he could', but failing to produce breath specimens, could not amount to a reasonable excuse in the absence of some physical or mental disability.

The defendant's argument that he had tried his best but failed to provide a second breath specimen was accepted by justices in *DPP v Eddowes* [1991] RTR 35, and he was acquitted. The reading from the first specimen was 126. The prosecutor's appeal to the Divisional Court succeeded, Watkins LJ urging that, 'justices must be very careful not to be so gullible ... as to accept propositions of this kind'. The court in *Eddowes* disapproved *Cotgrove v Cooney* [1987] RTR 124, where the Divisional Court had endorsed the justices' finding of reasonable excuse on the basis that the defendant had tried his best but failed to provide breath specimens. In *DPP v Coyle* [1996] RTR 287, the Divisional Court reiterated that, 'it is not a reasonable excuse in law simply that the motorist was doing his best, or trying as hard as he could, without succeeding' in providing a specimen.

In *DPP v Ambrose* [1992] RTR 285, it was held that trying to provide a breath specimen, but failing because of distress, did not amount to a physical or mental inability and was not a reasonable excuse.

10.7.10 Summary

In summary, for a defendant to escape conviction by virtue of reasonable excuse:

- the defendant must raise the issue of reasonable excuse, and will fare better if the issue was raised at the time of the requirement and, in the case of breath specimens, if the defendant attempted to provide them;
- the circumstances raised must be capable in law of amounting to a reasonable excuse (see below);
- the circumstances must as a matter of fact and degree amount to such an excuse;
- the defendant must almost certainly adduce medical or other expert evidence;
- there must be a causative link between the condition claimed and the inability to provide specimens; and
- the prosecution must be unable to negative the claimed reasonable excuse to the criminal standard.

The case law provides many more illustrations of what does not constitute a reasonable excuse than of what does. In so far as it is possible to deduce general principles, the following, it is suggested, do *not* in law amount to reasonable excuses:

- personal beliefs and perceptions, even if genuine and/or mistaken;
- conditionally agreeing to provide specimens;
- agreeing to provide specimens once legal advice has been received, unless, possibly, the investigating officer agrees to delay the procedure for the purpose, or a solicitor is immediately available;

- being advised by a solicitor not to provide specimens;
- drunkenness;
- emotional distress, unless severe enough to render the suspect mentally unable to provide a specimen or understand the requirement for it;
- fears and embarrassment about the process for providing specimens, unless amounting to a medically recognised phobia or otherwise highly exceptional;
- unlawful arrest;
- failure of the investigating officer to explain the three-minute time limit;
- physical awkwardness when undergoing a screening test;
- 'trying hard' but failing, unless there is a physical or mental disability.

10.8 WHETHER REQUIREMENT MADE

A person cannot be convicted of any of the 'failing' offences unless the requirement was correctly made in the first place. Road Traffic Act 1988, ss 6 to 7A confer the relevant powers and are discussed in detail elsewhere. Further, it must be shown that a requirement was in fact made. Where an officer said, 'I suspect you have driven this car with an alcohol level above the …', but the suspect interrupted him, shouting and swearing, and becoming violent, the requirement had not been made: *Maudling v DPP*, unreported, 4 December 1996 (DC).

To prove that a requirement for a blood or urine specimen has been made, it is not necessary to show that the officer specified that blood or urine would be required, or that he asked whether the suspect would be willing to provide the specimen. In *Burke v DPP* [1999] RTR 387, in response to the officer's words, 'I require you to provide a specimen of blood or urine for a laboratory test', the suspect said 'no, no, no', questioned the legality of the request and mentioned the European Court of Justice before the officer could go any further. The Divisional Court found that the requirement had indeed been made.

In *Cawley v DPP* [2001] EWHC 83 (Admin), the officer, reading from a *pro forma*, made the requirement, explained the procedure, gave the warning about failing to provide, and asked whether there were medical reasons why a blood specimen could or should not be taken by a doctor. He did not mark on the *pro forma* that he had actually required a blood specimen, but he did record that the motorist refused to supply such a specimen. The Divisional Court found that, on the facts, it was proper to infer that a lawful requirement had been made. There is no obligation on the officer to complete the *pro forma*.

In *DPP v Karamouzis* [2006] EWHC 2634 (Admin), a preliminary breath test was carried out at the roadside, using a mobile device which gives a reading of the breath alcohol level. It showed excess alcohol, and the suspect was arrested and required to provide further specimens at the police station. She refused and was charged with failing without reasonable excuse to provide specimens. The motorist argued that the roadside breath test had been an evidential breath test for the purposes of s 7. The officer had no power to take her to a police station and require further specimens of breath, because the conditions in s 7(2D) (power to require specimens at a police station following the provision of evidential specimens elsewhere) for requiring such further specimens had not been met. The prosecutor successfully appealed against her acquittal. The Divisional Court found that the roadside test could only have been a preliminary breath test under s 6. The evidential breath testing procedure at the roadside, under s 7(2D), was not yet effective, as no breath devices had been approved for the purpose.

10.9 WARNING OF THE CONSEQUENCES OF FAILURE

Road Traffic Act 1988, s 7(7) provides that a constable 'on requesting any person to provide a specimen in pursuance of this section, must warn him that a failure to provide it may render him liable to prosecution'. Failure to administer the warning defeats a prosecution for failing to provide, as well as for the offences in ss 4, 5 and 5A (see Chapters 7 and 8). Section 7A(5) likewise provides that a warning must be given when requiring permission for the laboratory testing of a specimen taken from a person incapable of consenting. In *Simpson v Spalding* [1987] RTR 221, Ralph Gibson LJ remarked that even many police officers, lawyers and judges would not know that failure to provide a specimen would lead to prosecution.

The requirement to warn does not, however, apply to roadside breath testing: *Worsley v DPP*, unreported, 11 November 1994 (DC). Nor is there any provision in the current s 6, s 6A, s 6B or s 6C for a warning in relation to preliminary testing.

In the leading case of *DPP v Jackson; Stanley v DPP* [1999] 1 AC 406 (see para 4.13), the House of Lords made clear (among other matters) that, when making a requirement for a blood or urine specimen, the warning of the risk of prosecution for failure to provide must be given. If it is not, the accused is entitled to be acquitted.

In *Murray v DPP* [1993] RTR 209, the motorist was charged with driving with excess alcohol in breath. The justices accepted that he had not been warned of the consequences of failing to provide, but found this had not prejudiced him. They admitted the breath analysis and convicted him. On appeal, the Divisional Court found that the evidence of the breath analysis should not have been admitted since the warning had not been given, and that it was not possible to make out an exception where no prejudice results.

Where the defendant did not understand the warning because of his inability to understand English, his acquittal for failing without reasonable excuse to provide breath specimens was upheld: *Chief Constable of Avon & Somerset v Singh* [1988] RTR 107 (DC). See also *Beck v Sager* [1979] RTR 475.

Self-induced drunkenness such that the defendant could not understand the warning is not a reasonable excuse for failing to provide: *DPP v Beech* [1992] RTR 239 (see para 10.7.4).

Justices were wrong to accept the prosecutor's submission that no warning was necessary because the defendant was compliant: *R (Cox) v DPP* [2009] EWHC 3595 (Admin), [2010] RTR 18.

The warning must be given by the officer, not by a doctor: *Beatrice v DPP* [2004] EWHC 2416 (Admin), where the Divisional Court said that the statutory procedure 'must be strictly observed and a failure to warn in accordance with subsection (7) would lead to inevitable acquittal'. The motorist's conviction for driving with excess alcohol was quashed.

Justices were entitled to conclude that the defendant had been properly warned where there had been no cross-examination of the investigating officer, who had followed a *pro forma* when conducting the breath analysis procedure and had given evidence of the procedure: *Braham v DPP* [1996] RTR 30 (DC). Where the officer followed the standard *pro forma*, justices were entitled, in the absence of challenge, to use their own knowledge of the form to find that the officer had given the warning: *Whitfield v DPP* [2006] EWHC 1414 (Admin).

See also *Malcolm v DPP* [2007] EWHC 363 (Admin), [2007] 1 WLR 1230 (para 11.12) on evidence that the warning was given.

Where the defendant understood the request for breath specimens and the penal consequences of failing to provide them, it made no difference that he had been detained under the Mental Health Act 1983. In *Francis v DPP* [1997] RTR 113, when the police came upon the motorist, they formed the view that he was suffering a mental disorder, and detained him under Mental Health Act 1983, s 136. That section confers the power to remove to a place of safety a person in a public place who appears to be suffering mental disorder and to be in immediate need of care and control. At the police station, the officer concluded that the motorist had calmed down and appeared to understand the request for breath specimens. The motorist refused to supply the specimens and in due course appealed against conviction for failing without reasonable excuse to provide them. The Divisional Court rejected an argument that the request for specimens should not have been made. It found that when the defendant was asked for the specimens he understood what was being asked and the penal consequences of failure. There was no reason to exclude the consequences of the investigation simply because the police had parallel obligations in relation to the defendant's detention under the Mental Health Act 1983. See also *Miller v DPP* [2018] EWHC 262 (Admin), [2018] RTR 19 (para 11.9.1).

It is a matter of fact and degree whether the warning should be repeated if there is a delay. In *Edmond v DPP* [2006] EWHC 463 (Admin), [2006] RTR 18, the analysis of two breath specimens was not satisfactory and the officer invited further breath specimens. The motorist appealed against conviction for driving with excess alcohol. The Divisional Court found that Road Traffic Act 1988, s 7(7) does not apply when a person is invited, rather than required, to provide breath specimens. Failure to provide a specimen when invited does not render a person liable to prosecution. The only consequence of failing to provide would be that the officer would go on to require a blood or urine specimen instead.

On the other hand, in *DPP v Palmer*, unreported, 21 March 1997, the investigating officer gave the warning and breath specimens were given, but the device then broke down. The officer took the suspect to another police station, 6 miles away, and there was a time lapse of 39 minutes. The warning was not repeated, but further specimens were provided and the motorist was charged on the basis of the second set of specimens. On the prosecutor's appeal against acquittal, the Divisional Court declined to overturn the magistrates' finding that the chain of events had been broken by the transfer to the second police station and that the warning should have been repeated. Since it had not been, the analysis of the specimens was inadmissible.

Chapter 11

Trial, Evidence, Procedure

11.1 MODE OF TRIAL

The offence under Road Traffic Act 1988, s 3A of causing death by careless driving when unfit through drink or drugs or with excess alcohol or drug(s) is triable on indictment only. The remaining drink- and drug-drive offences are triable summarily. See Road Traffic Offenders Act 1988, sch 2.

11.2 THE INFORMATION

In cases featuring an error in the information, which the prosecutor has corrected by issuing a fresh information, defendants have sought to invoke the principle that a person cannot be tried more than once for the same, or substantially the same, offence, arguing that the doctrine of *autrefois acquit*, or the rule against double jeopardy, applies. As noted in the judgments referred to below, a plea of *autrefois acquit* can be raised only in a trial on indictment, but the same principles apply in the magistrates' courts. The issue is usually whether the second offence charged is the same as, or substantially the same as, the first offence charged.

11.2.1 Correcting an error

In *Broadbent v High* [1985] RTR 359, the information was in error in alleging that the defendant had driven with excess alcohol in blood, as ascertained by a specimen of breath. Rather than amend the information, the prosecution issued a new information, which correctly referred to a specimen of blood. Before the trial, the defendant put the prosecution to an election as to which information should be proceeded on. The prosecutor elected the second, and the justices dismissed the first. The defendant invoked the doctrines of *autrefois acquit* and *res judicata*, arguing that he had been acquitted on the first information and that the court was therefore debarred from trying him on the second. The Divisional

Court rejected that argument, finding that *autrefois acquit* and *res judicata* did not apply. There had been no trial of the first information on its merits. This was not a case in which the prosecutor was seeking to resurrect a charge which had already been heard and dismissed. The prosecution had quite properly been put to an election, although it would have been preferable for the justices to have dealt with the second information before dismissing the first.

See also *Williams (Alan Davies) v DPP* [1991] 1 WLR 1160, where, on similar facts, the Divisional Court ruled that the defendant was never in jeopardy of conviction on the first charge, the charge having been dismissed before the defendant entered a plea.

In similar vein, in *DPP v Porthouse* [1989] RTR 177, the Divisional Court ruled that *autrefois acquit* does not arise where the court dismissed an information which alleged an offence unknown to law. The information had been wrongly worded and the prosecutor invited the justices to substitute a corrected information. No evidence was offered on the first information and it was dismissed. The Divisional Court found that there was no risk to the defendant arising out of the first information. Since it alleged an offence unknown to law, the defendant could not validly have been convicted.

Where a defendant sought to argue that an information was defective because it did not state which of two failures to provide a specimen was relied upon, the Divisional Court found she knew perfectly well what the case against her was, and was in no way embarrassed by the lack of particularity: *Hingley-Smith v DPP* [1997] EWHC 952 (Admin).

In a case where the information said that the accused had 'used' a vehicle with excess alcohol, rather than that he had 'driven' it in such a condition, the justices refused to allow the prosecutor to amend the information to bring it into line with the wording of Road Traffic Act 1988, s 5(1)(a). On the prosecutor's successful appeal, the Administrative Court ruled that the information was to be looked at as a whole. The defect was not so fundamental that it could not be corrected. The information referred to the correct statutory provision. The court had a wide discretion under Magistrates' Courts Act 1990, s 123 to amend an information where there was no injustice to the defendant, and the defendant had been aware of the nature of the case against him. See *DPP v Short* [2001] EWHC 885 (Admin).

Where the information referred to a section of the Road Traffic Act 1972 'as amended', rather than 'as substituted', the information would not mislead and was not defective. It satisfied Magistrates' Courts Rules 1981 (SI 1981/552), r 100 (specifying the contents of an information). See *Jones v Thomas* [1987] RTR 111 (DC).

On the facts in *Crann v CPS* [2013] EWHC 552 (Admin), a late amendment was allowed. A motorist, when asked to provide breath specimens had said he was 'not right in the head', and was apparently threatening to self-harm. He did not provide breath specimens. The officer accepted this as a valid reason for not providing breath and went on to request a specimen of blood. The motorist refused, saying he was terrified of needles. The next day, the motorist was charged with failing without reasonable excuse to provide a specimen of breath for analysis (see para 10.2.2). At the first hearing, the motorist's advisers pointed out that the charge should refer to blood, not breath. After a number of hearings and adjournments, the charge was eventually amended, on the grounds that the amended charge arose out of the same, or substantially the same, facts as the original charge and that the accused would not face a more serious charge than had already been charged; he would not therefore be prejudiced by the amendment. The motorist pleaded guilty to the amended charge, but appealed against the decision to allow the amendment. The Administrative Court noted that every case depended upon its own facts. The magistrates had taken into account that the amendment would not prejudice the appellant; they were entitled so to decide and the appellate court would not interfere. On whether they addressed the need to ensure that justice was dispensed with promptitude as suggested in *Williams v DPP* [2009] EWHC 2354 (Admin) (see para 11.6.2), they did not say expressly that they took this into account, but the whole of the case was drawn to their attention and it would be difficult to believe that considerations such as the requirement for justice to be dispensed expeditiously were not well and truly in their minds. While not every bench of magistrates would have granted the amendment at such a late stage, the decision was within the band of reasonable responses to the issues that fell to the magistrates to consider, and was therefore upheld.

The amendment of an indictment, however, is a serious matter, not a mere formality. *R v Leeks* [2009] EWCA Crim 1612, [2010] 1 Cr App R 5 concerned a defendant initially charged with causing death by reckless driving and failing without reasonable excuse to provide a specimen of breath. The Crown wished to add a charge of causing death by careless driving when unfit through drink, contrary to Road Traffic Act 1988, s 3A(1)(a). A fresh indictment was prepared but no formal application was ever made to add the second count, and no order for amendment was ever made. The defendant pleaded guilty to the offence under s 3A. It was later realised that the indictment had not been amended, and the driver appealed against conviction. The Court of Appeal ruled that Indictments Act 1915, s 5(a) required the court to exercise its discretion and make an order for amendment if the indictment was defective. Although all the parties believed that such an order would be made, but it was not, that was a fundamental error, not a minor irregularity. The defendant's plea and conviction were founded on a nullity and were quashed.

11.2.2 Multiple charges

In *DPP v Gane* [1991] Crim LR 711, the defendant was charged both with driving with excess alcohol, and with being in charge with excess alcohol. Both charges arose out of the same facts. The justices convicted him of the driving offence and dismissed the other charge without consulting the prosecutor. The Divisional Court found that it was inappropriate to dismiss the second information. The justices should instead have adjourned it *sine die*, or convicted and imposed a nominal fine with concurrent disqualification, to avoid the possibility that the defendant might successfully appeal against conviction for driving with excess alcohol and so escape altogether.

In *R v Truro & South Powder Justices ex parte McCullagh* [1991] RTR 374, the defendant was accused of being in charge with excess alcohol. He established that there was no likelihood of driving while he remained over the limit and was acquitted. Police then discovered that he had been driving on the occasion in question, earlier than the time at which he had been in charge, and charged him with driving with excess alcohol. The motorist pleaded *autrefois acquit*. The Divisional Court ruled that the acquittal on the first charge did not lead automatically to acquittal on the second charge. He had been acquitted on the first charge by reference to the statutory defence. The evidence in relation to the first charge related to a later time than the period during which it is alleged that the applicant was driving. The defence of *autrefois acquit* was not available.

In *Macphail v DPP*, unreported, 1 July 1996, justices acquitted a motorist of driving with excess alcohol, but convicted him of driving while unfit, both allegations having arisen out of the same episode. The justices accepted that the defendant had drunk three large glasses of wine before driving, and that that would not have put him over the limit, but would have impaired his ability to drive. The Crown Court rejected his appeal against conviction for driving while unfit, finding that he had consumed far more alcohol before driving than he had stated, and did not accept what he said about the amount he had drunk after driving. The motorist appealed further and succeeded. The Divisional Court found that the Crown Court was bound by the justices' acquittal on the drink-drive charge and could not make any finding which ran counter to the acquittal or undermined it. By finding that the appellant must have had more than three glasses of wine before driving, the Crown Court effectively found that he had been over the limit, in direct contradiction of the acquittal by the justices.

On the other hand, where a motorist pleaded guilty to drink-driving, it was an abuse of process, in the absence of special or exceptional circumstances, later to charge him with dangerous driving arising out of the same incident: *R v Phipps* [2005] EWCA Crim 33, where the motorist had been driving in the wrong direction on a dual carriageway and collided head-on with another vehicle, causing injury. He pleaded guilty to driving with excess alcohol and was sentenced. Some weeks later, apparently in response to press reports of the case, he was charged with dangerous driving in relation to the same incident. On appeal against conviction for dangerous driving, the Court of Appeal (Criminal Division) found that both prosecutions arose out of the same or substantially the same facts, and accepted the argument that it was an abuse of process for the Crown to proceed with the charge of dangerous driving. The Crown should decide at the outset, or at the latest before the conclusion of the first set of proceedings, what charges it wishes to bring arising out of the incident. Any other approach is unfairly oppressive to a defendant. The burden of establishing special or exceptional circumstances is on the Crown.

Charges of failing to provide a specimen of breath for analysis, and failing to provide a specimen for a laboratory test, are not inconsistent with each other. If both offences are charged arising out of the same facts, they should be tried together, as was the case in *White & Gaskell v Proudlock* [1988] RTR 163: *R v Chichester Justices ex parte DPP* [1994] RTR 175. In the *Chichester Justices* case, the second charge had been brought in case the defendant had a defence to the first. The Divisional Court found that the justices were wrong to order that the two matters be tried separately by differently constituted benches. The facts and circumstances relating to the two charges were so inter-related that no justice, in the true sense of the word, could be done unless they were heard together.

In *Ankrah v DPP* [1998] RTR 169, the motorist had been charged with driving with excess alcohol, and with failing without reasonable excuse to provide a specimen. He pleaded guilty to the second charge and was sentenced. He pleaded not guilty to driving with excess alcohol, no evidence was offered and the charge was dismissed. He then appealed to the Crown Court arguing that his guilty plea had been equivocal, on the basis that the procedure required by *DPP v Warren* [1993] AC 319 (see para 4.13) had not been followed in full. Alternatively, the plea was entered as a result of a mistake of law. The appeal was dismissed and the motorist appealed further. The Divisional Court found that the plea was not equivocal. The facts actually put before the court included nothing about the procedure. Nor was there anything to suggest that he had entered his plea under a mistake of law.

As mentioned in para 4.15.2, the Crown Prosecution Service acknowledges that where more than one drug is detected, the decision whether to pursue two or more charges depends on the circumstances. As there are different limits for different drugs, it could be argued that a single charge based on two or more drugs would be bad for duplicity, such that separate charges for separate drugs may be preferable. See www.cps.gov.uk/legal-guidance/road-traffic-drink-and-drug-driving.

11.3 DOCUMENTARY EVIDENCE CONCERNING SPECIMENS

Road Traffic Offenders Act 1988, s 16 contains provisions on documentary evidence concerning specimens in proceedings for an offence under ss 3A, 4, 5 or 5A.

11.3.1 A statement and a certificate of proportion of alcohol or drug

Road Traffic Offenders Act 1988, s 16(1) relates to evidence of the analysis of a specimen for alcohol or drugs, either by way of a printout from a breath analysis device, or by way of an analyst's certificate. A printout from a breath analysis device must include or be accompanied by a certificate signed by a constable, linking the statement to a specimen provided by the accused person. The subsection provides as follows:

> Evidence of the proportion of alcohol or a drug in a specimen of breath, blood or urine may, subject to subsections (3) and (4) below and to section 15(5) and (5A) of this Act, be given by the production of a document or documents purporting to be whichever of the following is appropriate, that is to say—
>
> (a) a statement automatically produced by the device by which the proportion of alcohol in a specimen of breath was measured and a certificate signed by a constable (which may but need not be contained in the same document as the statement) that the statement relates to a specimen provided by the accused at the date and time shown in the statement, and
>
> (b) a certificate signed by an authorised analyst as to the proportion of alcohol or any drug found in a specimen of blood or urine identified in the certificate.

Section 16(1) is permissive only and does not preclude evidence of these matters being given by other means. The most common situations are where public analysts give evidence pursuant to s 16, and where private analysts give evidence by statement under Criminal Justice Act 1967, s 9. Section 9 provides that a written statement is admissible as if it were oral evidence as long as the relevant conditions in s 9 are met.

In *R (Byrne, Simon David) v DPP* [2003] EWHC 397 (Admin), the blood analyst was not authorised for the purposes of s 16(1)(b), so that a certificate signed by him would not have been admissible under s 16(1)(b). But the evidence had in fact been adduced in a statement made pursuant to Criminal Justice Act 1967, s 9. Given the witness's qualifications and experience, his evidence was admissible as expert evidence under s 9. The Administrative Court said that s 16 is not a comprehensive or exclusive means of evidencing a blood analysis.

Oral evidence in place of the document

There is nothing to prevent the prosecution from proving the results of breath analysis by oral evidence in the ordinary way, rather than by producing the printout from the device: *Chief Constable of Avon & Somerset v Creech* [1986] RTR 87, where the prosecutor relied on the oral evidence of the police sergeant of his observations of the device and its readings. No printout was adduced. The Divisional Court ruled that proof by production of the printout is a way of avoiding the inconvenience of providing oral evidence. But if the prosecutor does not wish to make use of that procedure, there is nothing to prevent proof of the results of the analysis by oral evidence in the ordinary way.

See also *Castle v Cross* [1984] 1 WLR 1372 (DC), *Morgan v Lee* [1985] RTR 409 (para 4.4.2), *Thom v DPP* [1994] RTR 11, *Brett v DPP* [2009] EWHC 440 (Admin), [2009] 1 WLR 2530 and *Leong v DPP* [2006] EWHC 1575 (Admin). In *Leong*, the printout had not been served, but the officer who conducted the procedure instead gave oral evidence of what had been done and of the contents of the printout. The Administrative Court upheld the admissibility of his oral evidence, adding that there is no provision limiting the forms of admissible evidence relating to the alcohol concentration in a specimen.

In *R (Olajide) v Stratford Magistrates' Court* [2018] EWHC 2159 (Admin), it was argued that the printout had not been given to the applicant when it was produced, nor served before the trial, and so should not have been admitted at the hearing. The Administrative Court again affirmed that the certificate *may* be used to demonstrate the proportion of alcohol in the breath, but that there are other routes. The court below had evidence from a police officer that he had been present when the applicant blew into the breath analysis device, producing readings of 97 and 90. The officer's evidence alone was enough to prove the level of alcohol in the breath was in excess of the legal limit. It was not necessary to decide whether or not the printout had been properly served.

The printout

The printed test record produced by a breath analysis device and signed by the operator is a document purporting to be a statement and a certificate for these purposes; the document could not be split into two parts: *Gaimster v Marlow* [1984] QB 218 (DC). It was further held that an officer who is a trained operator of the device may give evidence to explain the printout.

Justices were wrong to refuse to admit the printout in evidence on the basis that it would be hearsay: *Chief Constable of Kent v Ellis*, unreported, 15 May 1985 (DC).

The production of the printout showing that a specimen was insufficient for a proper analysis is not an essential prerequisite for a conviction for failing without reasonable excuse to provide breath specimens: *Teape v Godfrey* [1986] RTR 213 (DC).

Section 16(1)(a) and (3) (below) are not engaged in relation to a printout where a defendant is charged with excess alcohol in blood rather than breath: *Jubb v DPP* [2002] EWHC 2317 (Admin), [2003] RTR 19, where the printout was adduced solely as evidence that the device had given an unreliable indication of the breath-alcohol concentration.

Where the defendant pleaded guilty to driving with excess alcohol, the court's insistence on the production of the original printout was an improper exercise of discretion: *R v Tower Bridge Magistrates' Court ex parte DPP* [1988] RTR 193, where the original printout was not available, but a copy was. After an unfruitful adjournment for one day to produce the original, the motorist, at the stipendiary magistrate's invitation, changed his plea from guilty to not guilty. The magistrate then invited the prosecutor to proceed. He was unable to do so and the magistrate dismissed the case. The Divisional Court noted the practice at Tower Bridge Magistrates' Court of inspecting the printout to check all the details, but ruled that it was not necessary to do so. The court should have proceeded to sentence on the basis of the guilty plea.

In *Hasler v DPP* [1989] RTR 148, the police officer who administered the breath testing procedure gave oral evidence that the printout was available in court should the justices wish to see it. He did not adduce it as evidence, and gave no oral evidence concerning calibration. On the motorist's appeal against conviction, the Divisional Court said that it is the task of the prosecution to adduce all necessary evidence. It would have been open to them to have done so otherwise than by producing the printout, as by calling the officer. But it would then be necessary for the officer to give evidence not only of the actual reading from the breath specimen, but also that the device was properly calibrated, and other details. None of those was proved before the justices and so the prosecution had not established the case against the defendant. Compare *R v Pydar JJ ex parte Foster* (1996) 160 JP 87 (DC) (see para 3.4.3).

But where the failure to produce the printout was simply an oversight and defence counsel did not take the point at the time, the justices were entitled to take into account the printout handed up after the prosecution had closed its case and the defence had invited them to dismiss the case because there was no evidence of calibration: *Leeson v DPP, Leeson v Haringey Justices* [2000] RTR 385 (DC).

The fact that the printout was not signed by the investigating officer does not necessarily defeat a prosecution. The printout is admissible at common law independently of s 16: *Garner v DPP* (1990) 90 Cr App R 178 (QBD), where the officer produced the printout to the court and gave oral evidence linking it to the defendant. The purpose of the statutory provision is to enable the certificate to be tendered to establish the facts stated in it without anyone having to attend to prove the document.

Where there was simply no evidence at all before the court of the defendant's having been over the limit, his conviction could not stand: *Hawke v DPP* [2011] EWHC 1345 (Admin). His representatives at the hearing before the justices perfectly properly requested the attendance of an officer whose evidence was crucial to establishing that the Intoximeter used was accurate and had been properly calibrated. Without that, there was no admissible evidence on this crucial issue. The officer was not available to give evidence when required and a prosecution application for adjournment to secure his attendance was rejected. No further application was made to treat the printout as hearsay evidence, and thus possibly admissible by that route. The justices should have acceded to the submission of no case and should have acquitted the appellant.

11.3.2 Certificate of consent

Section 16(2) relates to blood specimens and evidence by the person who took the specimen that the accused consented:

> Subject to subsections (3) and (4) below, evidence that a specimen of blood was taken from the accused with his consent by a medical practitioner or a registered health care professional may be given by the production of a document purporting to certify that fact and to be signed by a medical practitioner or a registered health care professional.

For the meaning of 'registered health care professional', see para 4.8.

Again, this provision is permissive not mandatory. In both *Steward v DPP* [2003] EWHC 2251 (Admin), [2004] 1 WLR 592 (see para 11.12) and *Rathbone v DPP*, unreported, 20 January 2005 (DC), the investigating officer's oral evidence of the taking of the blood specimen was sufficient, in the absence of a doctor's certificate contemplated in s 16(2).

11.3.3 Service

Section 16(3) concerns service, requiring that a printout from a breath analysis device is to be handed to the accused when it is produced, or served on the accused not later than seven days before the hearing. Other documents are to be served not later than seven days before the hearing. Section 16(3) is as follows:

Subject to subsection (4) below—

(a) a document purporting to be such a statement or such a certificate (or both such a statement and such a certificate) as is mentioned in subsection (1)(a) above is admissible in evidence on behalf of the prosecution in pursuance of this section only if a copy of it either has been handed to the accused when the document was produced or has been served on him not later than seven days before the hearing, and
(b) any other document is so admissible only if a copy of it has been served on the accused not later than seven days before the hearing.

By contrast with s 16(1) and (2) above, s 16(3) is mandatory in that failure to comply renders the document in question inadmissible in evidence. See *Tobi v Nicholas* [1988] RTR 343 (DC), *Badkin v DPP* [1988] RTR 401 (DC) and *CPS v Sedgemoor Justices* [2007] EWHC 1803 (Admin). In *Wooldridge v DPP* [2003] EWHC 1663 (Admin), the Administrative Court affirmed that a medical certificate is not admissible unless served in accordance with s 16(3), going on to say that it is not possible to waive service, although it is possible to waive formal proof of service. In *Wooldridge*, it was also held that a police officer's witness statement which was signed below the opening declaration, rather than at the end, was admissible under Criminal Justice Act 1967, s 9. The irregularity was a matter of form, not of substance.

'Hearing', for the purposes of the seven-day limit, means the hearing at which the evidence is to be given, not a preliminary hearing: *Williams (Alan Davies) v DPP* [1991] RTR 214 (DC).

Leaving a copy of the printout on the counter at which the defendant was standing does not constitute 'handing' it to the defendant. In *Walton v Rimmer* [1986] RTR 31, three printouts were produced, the suspect signed two of them and the third was simply left on the counter. The Divisional Court ruled that while a defendant cannot render evidence inadmissible by refusing to take a document which is handed to him, the fact that he signed the printout did not necessarily mean that it had been handed to him. There was no finding that it had been indicated to the defendant that one of the copies was for him to take away. On the other hand, in *McCormack v DPP* [2002] EWHC 173 (Admin), [2002] RTR 20, the printout was offered to the suspect but he declined to take it. The Administrative Court found that s 16(3)(a) was complied with even though there had been no physical transfer of the printout to the defendant. The printout was therefore admissible in evidence.

Where the copy printout handed to a suspect had not been signed by the investigating officer, the copy was nevertheless served: *Chief Constable of Surrey v Wickens* [1985] RTR 277 (DC).

Objection to certificate

Section 16(4) provides for the accused to object to a certificate:

> A document purporting to be a certificate (or so much of a document as purports to be a certificate) is not so admissible if the accused, not later than three days before the hearing or within such further time as the court may in special circumstances allow, has served notice on the prosecutor requiring the attendance at the hearing of the person by whom the document purports to be signed.

Method of service

Section 16(6) provides for service in accordance with the Criminal Procedure Rules (in England and Wales), personal service, or service by registered post or recorded delivery. Part 4 of the Rules allows for service of a document by handing it to the person concerned; by leaving it at, or posting it to, that person's address; by document exchange; or by electronic means. Service may be on a legal representative.

These provisions are permissive and do not preclude service under Criminal Justice Act 1967, s 9: *DPP v Stephens* [2006] EWHC 1860 (Admin). In that case, a witness statement by the doctor who took the specimen, and the analyst's certificate, were posted to the accused. He did not receive them, so they were served on him personally six days before the trial. The justices found that neither document had been served as required by s 16 and dismissed the case. On the prosecutor's appeal, the Divisional Court ruled that the doctor's witness statement had been validly served under s 9, and could be so served as an alternative to service under s 16. On the other hand, the analyst's certificate was not in the correct form to comply with s 9, and so could be admitted only under s 16. Since it had not been served by any of the three methods in s 16(6), the justices were right to rule it inadmissible.

Likewise, service may be effected under Criminal Justice Act 2003, s 116 (admissibility of hearsay evidence when the witness is not available): *Brett v DPP* [2009] EWHC 440 (Admin), [2009] 1 WLR 2530, where the analyst was living abroad and had not been warned, and it was not practicable to secure her attendance. Service under s 116 was effective even though notice had been given under Road Traffic Offenders Act 1988, s 16(4) that the witness was required to attend, on the basis that s 16(4) restricts admissibility by the s 16 route only.

In *Anderton v Kinnard* [1986] RTR 11 (DC) and *Penman v Parker* [1986] 1 WLR 882, service on the defendants' legal representatives was held to be good service. Such situations are now specifically provided for in Criminal Procedure Rules, r 4.3(1)(c).

In *Hawkins v DPP* [1988] RTR 380, the prosecutor sought to establish service of documents sent by recorded delivery by the sender's endorsements of posting marked on the certificates, in accordance with Magistrates' Courts Rules 1981, r 67(2) (proof of service by a certificate signed by the person who effected service or posted or registered the letter), and Interpretation Act 1978, s 7 (service deemed effective by properly addressing, pre-paying and posting, etc). The defendant claimed not to have received the documents, although the letter had not been returned by the Royal Mail. The prosecutor did not produce the record of delivery. An adjournment notice sent by recorded delivery had been returned marked 'not called for'. The defendant had attended court in response to another adjournment notice sent by recorded delivery. The justices were satisfied of service and convicted. The Divisional Court found that there had been *prima facie* evidence of service; it was open to the defendant to persuade the justices that the certificates had not been served, but he had failed to do so. His conviction was upheld.

Where the only evidence of service of the analyst's certificate was that of a police officer who had not been present at the time when service was said to have taken place, that evidence was hearsay. The justices were not entitled to conclude that the certificate had been properly served, and it was therefore inadmissible in evidence: *Whyte v DPP* [2003] EWHC 358 (Admin).

Errors in the documents

Where the certificates of consent to the taking of a blood specimen, and of the blood analysis, contained errors, but were re-served in corrected form, in time, service was good: *Ramsey (Jennifer) v DPP* [1996] EWHC 39 (Admin). The errors were that the doctor's statement was illegible in parts, and the analyst's certificate mis-recited the analyst's forenames. The fact that a certificate of service of blood analysis was unsigned did not affect its admissibility: *Louis v DPP* [1998] RTR 354 (DC).

Authorised analyst

Road Traffic Offenders Act 1988, s 16(7) defines an 'authorised analyst' as:

> (a) any person possessing the qualifications prescribed by regulations made under section 27 of the Food Safety Act 1990 as qualifying persons for appointment as public analysts under those Acts, and
> (b) any other person authorised by the Secretary of State to make analyses for the purposes of this section.

In *CPS v Sedgemoor Justices* [2007] EWHC 1803 (Admin), the prosecution sought to rely on the evidence of an analyst who was not authorised as defined above. The justices ruled the evidence inadmissible. On the prosecutor's appeal, the Divisional Court held that the definition relates only to a certificate contemplated by s 16(1); since s 16(1) is permissive, evidence of analysis can be given in other ways. The prosecution's evidence of a professional toxicologist by way of statement under Criminal Justice Act 1967, s 9 was admissible. See also *Khatibi v DPP* [2004] EWHC 83 (Admin), (2004) 168 JP 361 (para 11.12).

11.4 DISCLOSURE

See para 3.4.7 under '*Disclosure of documents and witness summonses*'.

11.5 THE MG DD FORMS

The contents of an MG DD form may be admitted in evidence in various ways. The investigating officer present in court may seek the court's permission to refer to the form as a contemporaneous note of the procedure. Alternatively, the form itself being inadmissible under the hearsay rule, the contents may be recited in a statement pursuant to Criminal Justice Act 1967, s 9 or the defendant may make a formal admission under s 10. In the unreported case of *Williams v DPP*, 4 December 1995 (Queen's Bench Division), the officer who had administered the procedure gave evidence, referring to the record of the procedure to refresh his memory, and the court had sight of the document. The Divisional Court rejected an argument that the court should not have seen it, finding that, on the contrary, it would have been a matter of criticism if the court had not seen it.

See also *Whitfield v DPP* [2006] EWHC 1414 (Admin) (para 5.2.3), where again the officer refreshed his memory from the record and the justices found that he had followed the procedure as set out in the booklet 'to the letter'. The defence objected to the justices seeing the booklet, but the Divisional Court found that the justices were entitled to use their knowledge of its contents to conclude that it referred to the statutory warning of the consequences of failing to provide a specimen, and that, the officer having followed the procedure to the letter, the warning had been given.

In *Cummings v CPS* [2016] EWHC 3624 (Admin), (2017) 181 JP 269, a police sergeant conducted the breath testing procedure in the presence and hearing of a police constable. The two officers together completed the form MG DD/A, although the constable did not countersign it. The sergeant did not appear at the trial. Instead, the constable gave evidence, and was allowed to refresh her memory from the form. The motorist appealed on the ground that the magistrates should not have allowed the constable to refer to the form because she had not herself completed it. The Divisional Court rejected that argument, finding that the constable had given evidence of what she had witnessed, and was properly entitled to refresh her memory from the form.

A copy of the form may be used to refresh the memory, although the defence may then raise the question of any likelihood or risk that the copy differs from the original: *DPP v Sugden* [2018] EWHC 544 (Admin), [2018] RTR 17. The court stressed that this was not to be taken to encourage a lax approach to the production of original documents, nor as any encouragement to defendants to seek the exclusion of memory-refreshing documents on flimsy grounds where there is no reason to suppose that they differ from the originals.

11.6 ADJOURNMENTS

11.6.1 The principles

Magistrates' Courts Act 1980, s 10(1) provides that a magistrates' court may at any time, whether before or after beginning to try an information, adjourn the trial. Guidance on the exercise of the discretion to adjourn is to be found in the body of case law on the point (much of it in the context of the drink- and drug-driving offences) and the Criminal Procedure Rules 2020 (SI 2020/759).

The Divisional Court has cautioned that:

> the decision to adjourn is discretionary; challenges to such a decision will be difficult to mount and should only be commenced if the circumstances are exceptional. (*Balogun v DPP* [2010] EWHC 799 (Admin), [2010] 1 WLR 1915, below)
>
> The grant or refusal of a request for an adjournment involves an exercise of discretion on the part of the tribunal. This court will not interfere with such an exercise of discretion unless it can be shown that no reasonable tribunal would have found in that way. (*Stevens v DPP* [2017] EWHC 2839 (Admin))

Applications for adjournments are to be subject to rigorous scrutiny by the courts. The prosecution is expected to proceed with appropriate expedition, and if it fails to do so, it must bear the consequences. In *R (Walden) v Highbury Corner Magistrates' Court; R (Stern) v Highbury Corner Magistrates' Court* [2003] EWHC 708 (Admin), the motorist Walden was charged with being in charge of a motor vehicle with excess alcohol on 10 November 2001. In *Stern*, the motorist was charged with driving with excess alcohol on 22 April 2001. Both pleaded not guilty and their cases were adjourned to await the decision in *DPP v Brown; DPP v Teixeira* [2001] EWHC 931 (Admin), [2002] RTR 395 (see para 3.4.2) and other cases. Trial dates were then fixed for 3 September 2002 and 26 September 2002, respectively. On both trial dates, the prosecution witnesses had not been warned and so were not present. The prosecution sought adjournments. The justices asked for an outline of the facts of the allegations but did not ask why the witnesses had not been warned. The magistrates granted the adjournments, citing the seriousness of the charge in the case of *Walden*, and without giving reasons in the case of *Stern*. The defendants sought judicial review of the decisions to adjourn, but at the hearing of the application neither the magistrates' court nor the Crown Prosecution Service was represented. The magistrates' court had filed no evidence and the Crown Prosecution Service had made no submissions. The Administrative Court recited the duty of the court below formally to examine the circumstances leading to an application for an adjournment, the reasons for it, and the consequences, both to the prosecution and to the defence, and to subject such applications to rigorous scrutiny. In fact, all the court had done was ask for an outline of the prosecution's case. It did not ask the prosecutor to investigate the non-attendance of witnesses. It did not exercise rigorous scrutiny. The orders for adjournment were quashed. The Administrative Court was highly critical of the kind of inefficiency which led to the non-appearance of the witnesses in these cases. Such delays were scandalous and were not to be tolerated. The prosecution was the author of its own misfortune.

In *Essen v DPP* [2005] EWHC 1077 (Admin), a motorist was charged with driving when unfit and with careless driving. Her application to vacate the trial date on the grounds that it was inconvenient for her witnesses was refused. On the trial date, the prosecution sought an adjournment because it had failed to warn its witnesses and they had not attended. The defendant opposed the application, but the justices granted it, although they did not give reasons. The motorist was in due course convicted. She appealed, arguing that having refused the defence application to adjourn the original trial date, it was *Wednesbury* unreasonable, and an inequality of arms, for the justices to have granted the equivalent application by the prosecution. The Divisional Court found that inconvenience to a party is not of itself a reason for an adjournment. The mere fact that the defence application had been refused does not affect the justices' decision on the prosecution's application. But the Divisional Court had no information on which it could be satisfied that the justices took into account relevant considerations and excluded irrelevant considerations. They may simply have wished to avoid allowing the case to collapse. Since applications for adjournments must be subjected to rigorous scrutiny, the decision of the justices to allow the prosecution's adjournment was, reluctantly, reversed. In his concurring judgment, Sedley LJ indicated that if the reason for granting the adjournment was to rescue the prosecution from the consequences of its own neglect, it should have been refused.

Balogun v DPP [2010] EWHC 799 (Admin) is a further example of a case where an adjournment was granted without appropriate scrutiny. The trial date was adjourned because the prosecution had failed to identify a particular police officer as a relevant witness and warn her to attend. The reasons given for the adjournment were that:

- although other prosecution witnesses could have given evidence and the case could then have been adjourned part heard, the parties urged against doing so; these witnesses were police or other professional people and questions of loss of memory of relevant events were therefore unlikely;
- this was the first listing for trial and neither party had sought further directions concerning the service of evidence since the case management hearing;
- it was proper to decide whether or not to grant an adjournment before identifying a new trial date;
- once the defendant had a reasonable expectation that his case would be concluded on the trial date, it was open to him to apply for costs if he was acquitted, or for wasted costs of the day originally set for trial;
- there was a legitimate public interest that the charge would be adjudicated on.

The Divisional Court found each of these reasons, if not flawed, then at least open to challenge.

See also *R (Jenkins) v Hammersmith Magistrates' Court* [2015] EWHC 3961 (Admin), where again the Crown Prosecution Service had failed to prepare for trial, and the district judge's decision to allow them an adjournment was overturned on appeal. Likewise in *Decani v City of London Magistrates' Court and CPS* [2017] EWHC 3422 (Admin), justices erroneously allowed an adjournment. The Crown Prosecution Service had simply failed to warn the vital witness in a drink-drive case and thereafter to get him to court, despite having known for some time that his attendance was necessary. The Divisional Court ruled that this was an error at the more serious end of the spectrum. The principles had not been properly applied by the justices. See also *R (Kharaghan) v City of London Magistrates and CPS* [2018] EWHC 229 (Admin) (para 11.6.5).

The judgments in *Balogun*, *Jenkins* and *Decani* (and *Visvaratnam* – see para 11.6.2) all cite the case of *CPS v Picton* [2006] EWHC 1108 (Admin), (2006) 170 JP 567, where the charge was assault. In *Picton*, the Divisional Court reviewed the case law on adjournments and distilled the following principles:

(a) A decision whether to adjourn is a decision within the discretion of the trial court. An appellate court will interfere only if very clear grounds for doing so are shown.

(b) Magistrates should pay great attention to the need for expedition in the prosecution of criminal proceedings; delays are scandalous; they bring the law into disrepute; summary justice should be speedy justice; an application for an adjournment should be rigorously scrutinised.

(c) Where an adjournment is sought by the prosecution, magistrates must consider both the interest of the defendant in getting the matter dealt with, and the interest of the public that criminal charges should be adjudicated upon, and the guilty convicted as well as the innocent acquitted. With a more serious charge the public interest that there be a trial will carry greater weight.

(d) Where an adjournment is sought by the accused, the magistrates must consider whether, if it is not granted, he will be able fully to present his defence and, if he will not be able to do so, the degree to which his ability to do so is compromised.

(e) In considering the competing interests of the parties the magistrates should examine the likely consequences of the proposed adjournment, in particular its likely length, and the need to decide the facts while recollections are fresh.

(f) The reason that the adjournment is required should be examined and, if it arises through the fault of the party asking for the adjournment, that is a factor against granting the adjournment, carrying weight in accordance with the gravity of the fault. If that party was not at fault, that may favour an adjournment. Likewise if the party opposing the adjournment has been at fault, that will favour an adjournment.

(g) The magistrates should take appropriate account of the history of the case, and whether there have been earlier adjournments and at whose request and why.

(h) Lastly, of course the factors to be considered cannot be comprehensively stated but depend upon the particular circumstances of each case, and they will often overlap. The court's duty is to do justice between the parties in the circumstances as they have arisen.

By contrast, *R (Parashar) v Sunderland Magistrates' Court and CPS* [2019] EWHC 514 (Admin), [2019] 2 Cr App R 3 is an example of a successful challenge to the refusal of a defence application to vacate a trial date. The defence sought judicial review of the magistrates' court's refusal of an advance application to vacate the date for trial of an allegation of driving with excess alcohol. The trial had been set for a date on which the prosecution expert (who had been instructed late) could attend, but the defence expert (whose report had been served in good time) could not. The Divisional Court held that that was clearly wrong; the defendant's ability to present his defence would have been seriously compromised and the trial would have been unfair. This was therefore an exceptional case in which the Divisional Court should intervene. The case was to proceed to trial; the prosecution was to seek permission to rely on the report of its expert. If granted, the trial was to be on a date when both experts could attend.

In *Saunders v Bristol Magistrates' Court v CPS* [2022] EWHC 2544 (Admin), [2023] 1 Cr App R 8, a driver was charged with failing to provide a specimen of blood for analysis. The custody doctor had been unable to take a specimen. The circumstances were contentious, the defendant arguing that she had been willing, but had suffered a panic attack. The prosecution planned to call as witnesses two police officers and the custody doctor, and was directed to serve a statement from the doctor. The defence required the doctor (and there was initially confusion about the doctor's identity) to attend, but the doctor was not warned. Three days before the trial date, the prosecution sought an adjournment. The application was heard by two lay justices, who granted the adjournment, saying it was in the interests of justice to do so, but without giving further reasons other than that 'the failure on the admin side should not affect the interests of justice'. It later transpired that one of the justices had told the legal adviser, in the retiring room, that the defendant 'can't get away with it because there has been an admin error'; they maintained that view despite being asked by the legal adviser to check their thinking. Such was the legal adviser's concern about their approach, that she spoke to the defendant's representative about it. There was then a further case management hearing, at which the Crown Prosecution Service said it would prove the case by the evidence of the two police officers, without the doctor.

On the driver's appeal, the Administrative Court found that, despite the inadequate reasons and appearance of bias, and despite the procedural failure by the prosecution, the justices could have adjourned the case on the basis that the offence had taken place less than four months before and there was every prospect that an adjourned trial could be accommodated shortly; the police officers had attended court and there was a body of other material about the defendant's conduct. But, taken together, the lack of adequate reasons for the adjournment, the justice's comment about 'getting away with it', and the reaction of the very experienced legal adviser tipped the case over the line so that the test for apparent bias was met. The decision to adjourn was quashed and the case remitted to the justices with a direction to acquit.

See also *Parish v DPP* [2000] RTR 143 (para 4.15.4).

11.6.2 The Criminal Procedure Rules

The coming into force of the Criminal Procedure Rules 2005 (SI 2005/384) in April of that year (see now the Criminal Procedure Rules 2020 (SI 2020/759), in force from 5 October 2020) has strengthened the robust views of the appellate courts on applications for adjournments, especially when made late in the proceedings. In *R (DPP) v Chorley Magistrates' Court* [2006] EWHC 1795 (Admin), the Divisional Court said that the rules effected a sea change in how cases should be conducted. The court recited the overriding objective of dealing with criminal cases justly, the court's duty to further that overriding objective by actively managing cases, and the early identification of the real issues. The days of ambushing and taking last-minute technical points are gone.

In *Williams v DPP* [2009] EWHC 2354 (Admin), a motorist had failed to provide a specimen of urine, but, in error, was charged with failing to provide specimens of breath. Following a case management hearing at which the question of the charge was not raised, and some seven months after the date of the alleged offence, the Crown Prosecution Service wrote to the defendant indicating that it would, on the date set for trial, seek to amend the charge. On the trial date, the justices allowed the amendment and adjourned the trial for a further three and a half months. The Divisional Court held that in principle it was permissible to amend the charge out of time, since both offences arose from the same facts, but in the absence of any compelling reason, an adjournment for such a long period following the amendment was not in the interests of justice. The Divisional Court stressed that the Criminal Procedure Rules 2005 require proper attention to case management duties by both prosecution and defence, and was highly critical of the delays which had occurred. The case was remitted to the justices with a direction to refuse leave to amend the charge. See also *Crann v CPS* [2013] EWHC 552 (Admin) (para 11.2.1).

The next case in this series was one of failing to provide breath specimens: *Writtle v DPP* [2009] EWHC 236 (Admin), [2009] RTR 28. At the case management hearing, the court had before it a letter from the defendant's solicitors indicating that no novel or complex issues arose. The defence would be factual and the intention was to put the prosecution to proof of its case. At the trial, the court heard the prosecution witnesses, and watched a CCTV recording of the procedure. The prosecution closed its case and the hearing was adjourned for lack of time to hear the defence. Some six weeks later, the defence served an additional report from an expert concerning the handling of the investigation as shown in the CCTV recording. At the resumed hearing, the justices decided not to admit that report on the basis that it was not relevant to the issues in the case and dealt with wholly new issues. The Divisional Court held that Criminal Procedure Rules 2005, r 24(1) sets out the requirement to disclose expert evidence as soon as is practicable and r 24(3) states that a party seeking to adduce expert evidence but failing to comply with r 24(1) may not adduce the evidence without the leave of the court. Either the defence knew the nature of the defence which was later set out in the report in question but failed to raise it appropriately, or it did not, and contrived the defence after the prosecution case had closed. Neither approach was acceptable. The case management regime should in general ensure that the issues in the case are identified well before a hearing. The court repeated that the days when the defence can assume that it can ambush the prosecution are over.

Visvaratnam v Brent Magistrates' Court [2009] EWHC 3017 (Admin), (2010) 174 JP 61 was a case of serious failure by the prosecution to prepare for trial, where the Divisional Court quashed the justices' decision to adjourn. The allegation was of being in charge when unfit through drugs. The prosecution had failed to serve the medical evidence of unfitness on the defence and failed to warn the witness. Nor had it reacted to ample notice that the analyst of the blood specimen would not be available on the date set for trial. The Divisional Court delivered a robust judgment on the failings of the prosecution.

11.6.3 Delay

Both defence and prosecution must proceed diligently. In *R v Bishop's Stortford Justices ex parte DPP* [1997] EWHC 379 (Admin), the defendant himself was responsible for the delay. He was charged with driving with excess alcohol in August 1993 and was bailed to appear before magistrates on 9 September 1993. On 9 September he failed to appear and the justices issued a warrant for his arrest, which remained unexecuted until either 29 February or 1 March 1996. Meanwhile, the defendant was before a magistrates' court on 21 September 1994 and thought the drink-drive offence in question had been dealt with then. In fact it had not. The case was eventually listed for trial in July 1996. On that date, the defendant applied for a stay of the proceedings on the basis that to continue would be an abuse of process in view of the length of time since the date of the alleged offence. He argued that the delay had prevented him from providing adequate instructions to his lawyers, and his own failure to surrender to custody was partly explained by the fact that in September 1994 when he had been at a court on other matters, he had been told by a police officer that there were no outstanding warrants against him. The magistrates stayed the prosecution and acquitted the defendant. On the prosecutor's appeal, the Divisional Court found that the decision to stay the proceedings was wrong. The defendant had himself contributed to the delay and the chances of prejudice were remote. His identification was not in dispute and the evidence against him was largely documentary.

In *Murphy v DPP* [2006] EWHC 1753 (Admin), some four years elapsed between the date of the alleged offence and the trial date, during which time there were 44 appearances before the justices. On the trial date, the defendant sought a stay of proceedings on the grounds, *inter alia*, of delay. The Divisional Court held that the district judge was right to refuse that application, and was highly critical of the delay. See also *Rose v DPP* [2010] EWHC 462 (Admin), [2010] RTR 25, where, on the facts, a fair trial was still possible despite delay.

In *Filmer v DPP* [2006] EWHC 3450 (Admin), [2007] RTR 28, a defendant charged with driving with excess alcohol on the parking area of commercial premises had been allowed to vacate his guilty plea to argue that the area was not a public place. At his trial, the justices heard evidence from a police officer concerning the features of the car park and its use. At the close of the prosecution case, the defendant sought an adjournment to gather more evidence about the parking area, claiming that he had been ambushed by the prosecution. The Divisional Court upheld the justices' decision to refuse the application, rejecting the motorist's complaint that he had received insufficient details of the case that the car park was a public place so as to enable him to gather evidence in rebuttal. His guilty plea had been vacated for that very purpose.

In *Cherpion v DPP* [2013] EWHC 615 (Admin) (see para 5.2.4), on the facts, the magistrates were right to refuse an adjournment. On the adjourned trial date, the prosecution first sought an adjournment because its three witnesses, although correctly warned, had not appeared. The defence asked the court to proceed, but it then became clear that the witnesses were in fact on their way; they had been told to go to the wrong court. The defence then sought an adjournment on the basis that a hospital doctor who saw the defendant was not present; she had not been asked to attend, even though the prosecution had indicated, at an earlier hearing, that she would be called. The magistrates refused the adjournment on the basis of the already lengthy history of the case; that the other witnesses were present and ready to give evidence; that the defence had at first itself cited delay as a reason not to adjourn; that the prosecution had agreed not to rely on certain matters said to be hearsay; that the attendance of the doctor had not been identified as necessary until late in the case and in any event the defence could have called her; and that no defence statement had been served. On appeal, the Divisional Court held that, having said it would do so, the prosecution was plainly at fault in not requesting the doctor to attend. That said, the magistrates had to deal with the position as it was before them. They were entitled to refuse to adjourn. The case had already taken far too long. The magistrates had taken the view that the delayed request for the doctor to attend was no more than a speculative attempt to see whether the appellant might avoid the consequences of having driven with excess alcohol.

See also *R (Gatenby) v Newton Ayecliffe (sic) Magistrates' Court* [2017] EWHC 3772 (Admin) (para 13.2).

11.6.4 Delegation of power of adjourn

As part of its case management responsibilities under the Criminal Procedure Rules, a court may nominate a judge, magistrate or justices' legal adviser to manage a case (r 3.5). This includes power to adjourn a hearing (para (2)(f)). In the drink-drive case of *Bourne v Scarborough Magistrates' Court* [2017] EWHC 2828 (Admin), [2018] 4 WLR 29, the Divisional Court held that a justices' legal adviser so nominated may rule on a contested application to adjourn a hearing. On the facts of the case, however, the legal adviser's decision to allow the prosecution's application to vacate the trial date was quashed. He had insufficient information on which to assess the prosecution's culpability for the delay; he appeared not to have considered whether the delay thereby caused would be short or comparatively lengthy; the circumstances were such that it was not appropriate to deal with the matter on the papers; and neither party knew that the correspondence they had submitted would be treated as the entirety of their representations on the application.

In *DPP v Woods* [2017] EWHC 1070 (Admin), (2017) 181 JP 395, the legal adviser, acting under delegated authority, granted the prosecution's application to vacate the date for trying charges of driving when unfit through drink or, in the alternative, driving with excess alcohol. The next day (the trial date), however, a district judge reversed that decision. On the prosecutor's appeal, the Divisional Court upheld the district judge's decision that there was to be no adjournment, on the basis that the prosecutor's application for adjournment was misleading in suggesting the defence was not ready, whereas in fact the prosecution, having earlier failed to comply with orders to serve its evidence, had failed to warn its principal witness, whose attendance had been required from the start.

11.6.5 Judicial review

While the usual routes of appeal are by way of re-hearing in the Crown Court, or, on a point of law, by way of case stated to the Administrative Court (see para 11.15.1), there may be circumstances where judicial review of a decision to adjourn is appropriate.

In *Balogun v DPP* [2010] EWHC 799 (Admin) (see para 11.6.1), the Divisional Court distinguished *Hoar-Stevens v Richmond Magistrates' Court* [2003] EWHC 2660 (Admin) (see para 11.13) and *CPS v Sedgemoor Justices* [2007] EWHC 1803 (Admin) (see para 11.3.3), in which attempts to challenge interlocutory decisions of justices by way of judicial review had been deprecated. It found that different considerations may apply when the issue of adjournment is raised:

> not only because of the unsatisfactory nature of quashing a conviction which is not itself before the court but also because, in the interim, considerable expense has been incurred, not merely by the parties but also by the court in conducting a hearing which in the event has proved entirely nugatory and thereafter setting aside the original decision.

In such a case, a challenge should be way of judicial review rather than by case stated. But the court went on to caution that a claim for judicial review must be pursued as a matter of extreme urgency, so as not to affect the continued progress of the case if permission is not granted, or, if permission is granted, to prevent the prosecution continuing while the matter is being investigated.

The judgment in *Parashar* (see para 11.6.1) contains a discussion of the case law on the availability of judicial review to challenge discretionary decisions of justices, leading to the conclusion that, while the Divisional Court will only exceptionally consider an interlocutory challenge once a trial is under way, the threshold for exceptionality is lower where the decision subject to challenge was a refusal to vacate a trial date.

In *R (Hi) v Willesden Magistrates' Court and Crown Prosecution Service* [2016] EWHC 1760 (Admin), a person convicted of driving with excess alcohol sought judicial review of the district judge's decision to refuse her application for an adjournment and proceed to trial without disclosure of the CCTV footage of the custody suite. The original application for judicial review was dismissed on the basis that the claim was totally without merit, and the appellant sought to have that decision reconsidered at an oral hearing. The Administrative Court found that there is no such right to appeal where the decision which it was sought to have judicially reviewed was made in criminal proceedings. The court went on, however, to revisit its reasons for having found the initial application totally without merit. There was clearly an adequate alternative remedy in the form of an appeal to the Crown Court. Further, the CCTV had been identified as disclosable in the schedule of unused material, but the defendant had not relied on its non-disclosure as a reason for seeking an adjournment, nor brought it to the attention of the court; the application for the adjournment had been made on different grounds. Further, the suggestion that the CCTV might undermine the prosecution case or assist the defence was wholly speculative.

See also *R (Clarke) v Ipswich Crown Court* [2013] EWHC 1129 (Admin) – a drink-drive case where the Divisional Court refused a claim for judicial review on the basis that the challenge should have been brought by case stated; it was effectively an appeal from the Crown Court's decision on the evidence.

On the facts in *R (Usman) v Reading Magistrates' Court* [2017] EWHC 2153 (Admin), judicial review was not appropriate. The applicant had been charged with driving with excess alcohol. He disputed the allegation. On the date set for trial, his solicitor asked for a half-hour adjournment to read and take instructions on additional evidence he had just received from the prosecution. The magistrates refused the application and the solicitor withdrew from the case. The case proceeded and the defendant was convicted. He sought judicial review on the ground that it was wrong to insist on proceeding when he had expected to be represented by a specialist solicitor.

His application was refused on the basis that, while an allegation that a hearing was unfair would normally justify judicial review, the applicant had also lodged an appeal to the Crown Court and thereby obtained a suspension of the disqualification from driving which had been imposed by the magistrates; judicial review is to be used only where no alternative is appropriate. On renewal of the application, the Administrative Court emphasised that the grant of permission is always a matter of discretion. While agreeing that the applicant had at least an arguable case, it was necessary to take into account the suspension of disqualification; that the appeal to the Crown Court had been served promptly, while the application for judicial review was not issued until the relevant time limit had almost expired; and that there was a conflict of evidence between the applicant and his solicitor concerning the sequence of events on the trial day. Refusal of permission would not leave him without a remedy; he could still pursue his Crown Court appeal. His renewed application was refused.

The judgment in the joined cases of *R (DPP, Hanson) v Sunderland Magistrates' Court; R (Kharaghan) v City of London Magistrates and CPS* [2018] EWHC 229 (Admin) provides an extensive review of the case law and the Criminal Procedure Rules concerning mistakes of fact in relation to contested applications to adjourn in magistrates' courts. The Divisional Court held that material mistake of fact resulting in unfairness may be a ground of challenge by way of judicial review not only in civil proceedings (as in *E v Secretary of State for the Home Department* [2004] EWCA Civ 49, [2004] QB 1044), but also in criminal proceedings, providing the five preconditions set out in *E v Secretary of State for the Home Department* are met:

(1) all participants had a shared interest in co-operating to achieve the correct result;
(2) there was a mistake as to an existing fact (which could include a mistake as to the availability of evidence on a particular matter);
(3) the fact or evidence has been 'established' – in the sense that it is uncontentious and objectively verifiable;
(4) the person relying on the mistake, and/or his advisers, was not responsible for the mistake;
(5) the mistake played a material (not necessarily decisive) part in the court's reasoning.

On the facts in the *Sunderland* case, which concerned a charge of criminal damage, all five conditions were met.

In the *City of London* case, a motor cyclist was charged with driving with excess alcohol. At the first hearing, he pleaded not guilty, and the court made an order for the prosecution to disclose its evidence and any unused material by a given date. Although the motor cyclist's solicitor contacted the prosecution about disclosure following the expiry of the deadline for service, he did not point out that the order as to service had not been met. Nor did he provide a secure email address, so the prosecution had to send its documents by post. The documents were eventually served over a month late and only some 12 days before the trial date. CCTV footage and the custody record were not served. The defendant's solicitor did not tell the court that the disclosure requirements had not been met and that the defence was not ready for trial. On the trial date, the prosecutor and the justices mistakenly understood that the prosecution had done nothing at all to comply with the order for disclosure. The prosecution applied for an adjournment to enable it to serve its case, which was granted.

The motor cyclist's challenge of that decision failed. The Divisional Court held that, although it appeared that the prosecution had not complied with the order as to service and disclosure, the claimant's advisers had themselves failed to comply with their duties under the Criminal Procedure Rules to bring that to the attention of the court at an early stage, and to warn the court that the defendant was not ready for trial. The justices had given the application to adjourn the appropriate degree of scrutiny, and had considered the relevant authorities, the conduct of the parties and the real issues involved, including the strength of the evidence and the seriousness of the allegation (the high breath readings and the fact that the breath analysis device had recorded no error in its operation); the public interest in criminal charges being adjudicated upon; and the lack of prejudice to the claimant in the length of the proposed adjournment. There was a public interest in those charged with driving while intoxicated being prosecuted, and with that being done not only efficiently but fairly. While there had been a failure by the prosecution to serve evidence and to disclose unused material, that material, save for the CCTV footage and the custody record, could all have been made available in hard copy on the day of the hearing, and the witnesses were at court. The justices had therefore been right to conclude that the claimant could have been tried that day, and were also correct to note that no specific order had been made as to the disclosure of the CCTV footage. The decision to grant the adjournment was upheld; it was not necessary to consider the five-point test in *E v Secretary of State for the Home Department*.

See also *R v Wilson, Walmsley, York and Senior* [2019] EWCA Crim 2410 (para 4.15.5), where the Court of Appeal, after reviewing the statutory authorities, did not have jurisdiction, on the facts of the cases, to hear appeals against the summary convictions; nor would appeal by way of case stated be appropriate because the convictions were neither wrong in law nor in excess of jurisdiction. But, reconstituting itself as a Divisional Court, the Court of Appeal Criminal Division granted permission to apply for judicial review, abridged the procedures and quashed the drug-driving convictions.

11.7 VIDEO RECORDINGS

A motorist charged with failing to provide specimens of breath for analysis disputed that the record of the procedure had been completed in his presence, and that he had been warned of the consequences of failing to provide specimens under Road Traffic Act 1988, s 7(7) (see para 10.9). He sought disclosure of a video recording of the custody area, but the recording had been over-written. The justices found that there was no abuse of process and declined his application to stay the proceedings. The officer who had conducted the procedure gave evidence that he had completed the contemporaneous record in the presence of the defendant, and the justices took note of a number of initialled responses on the record, including the defendant's response to the warning under s 7(7). They accepted the police evidence and convicted the defendant. The Divisional Court found that it was entirely open to the justices, on the evidence, to conclude that the prosecution was not an abuse of process. See *Roberts v DPP* [2008] EWHC 643 (Admin).

The question of video recordings cropped up again in *Morris v DPP* [2008] EWHC 2788 (Admin), (2009) 173 JP 41. The motorist had been convicted by justices of driving with excess alcohol in blood and appealed to the Crown Court. At a pre-trial review he said the issue at trial would be a challenge to the statutory procedure and to the reliability of the blood analysis, giving no further details. At trial, he argued that the statutory warning had not been given and that the blood analysis was therefore inadmissible. The investigating officer, who had completed the contemporaneous record of the procedure, on which was recorded the s 7(7) warning, mentioned in cross-examination that there was CCTV in the custody suite. In accordance with usual procedure, the video tape had been kept for three months, then, in the absence of anyone wanting to look at it, it had been destroyed; nobody had thought it relevant or significant. The Crown Court thought it highly unlikely that the precise detail of what had been said would be audible from the tape; there was a single microphone covering a custody area with a number of ports at which people were interviewed. The Crown Court found that a fair trial was possible and there was no abuse of process. The procedure had been correctly followed and the appeal was dismissed. The Administrative Court upheld the decision of the Crown Court. The prosecution is not automatically required to retain CCTV evidence which might record the giving of the warning. The Crown Court had considered the appropriate question, which was whether the appellant could have a fair trial in the circumstances.

For other cases concerning CCTV footage, see *Writtle v DPP* [2009] EWHC 236 (Admin), [2009] RTR 28 (para 11.6.2); *R (Kharaghan) v City of London Magistrates and CPS* [2018] EWHC 229 (Admin) (para 11.6.5); *R (Hi) v Willesden Magistrates' Court and Crown Prosecution Service* [2016] EWHC 1760 (Admin) (para 11.6.5); *Ivic v DPP* [2006] EWHC 1570 (Admin) (para 11.13); *DPP v Petrie* [2015] EWHC

48 (Admin) (para 11.3); *DPP v Spalluto* [2015] EWHC 2211 (Admin) (para 11.13); and *Ho-Shing v CPS* [2022] EWHC 3137 (Admin) (para 12.6).

11.8 IDENTIFICATION

Some of the cases concerning the drink-drive provisions have given rise to questions concerning the identification of the defendant.

In *Barnes v Chief Constable of Durham* [1997] 2 Cr App R 505, the defendant had been involved in a road traffic accident and was later arrested and taken to a police station. He gave his name as John William Hawkins, born on 10.9.64. His name was in fact John William Barnes, born on 9.10.64. He was charged with failing without reasonable excuse to provide a specimen for analysis, and at the hearing argued that there was insufficient evidence that he was the man who had been arrested and taken to the police station. The only evidence that the defendant was the driver concerned, and the person who was required to provide a specimen, was that of a police officer who had attended the scene of the accident and was present at the interview. He was certain that the man in the dock was the man he had interviewed that night. The Divisional Court found that while dock identification is not permissible in the Crown Court, it is customary in the magistrates' courts, to deal with the problem of defendants such as those charged with driving offences, who make no statement and, in the absence of identification, submit that it is not proved that they were the driver. It was fair, on the facts, to allow a dock identification, as the defence had given no indication that identification was an issue, and no identification parade had been asked for.

In *Porceddu v DPP* [2001] EWHC 597 (Admin), the Administrative Court again found, on the facts, that it was fair to admit identification evidence. The defendant's vehicle had collided with a stationary car in a well-lit street. An independent witness said there was only one occupant of the car and that he saw him get out, look back at the vehicle and stagger towards the end of the street, before returning to the vehicle. The witness telephoned the police, giving a description, and, shortly after, identified the appellant as he was being led from the passenger seat of his car, having been arrested. The justices acknowledged that where identification is an issue, an identification parade should be held (PACE Code of Practice, Code D2), but found that the breach of the Code was not sufficiently significant and substantial that the evidence should be excluded. On the defendant's appeal against conviction for driving with excess alcohol, the Administrative Court said that the breach was an important issue, but that the driver must have been either the defendant, or another person in the vehicle, and the witness had given evidence that there was in fact only one occupant. Furthermore, this was a recognition case rather than a true identification case, because the witness had a clear view of the appellant in good light over a significant period of time shortly before he made the identification. Although there was a breach of the Code, it was fair to admit the evidence of identification.

See also *Davis (Karl) v DPP* [2001] EWHC 1129 (Admin), another case in which identification evidence was admitted even though there had been no identification parade. And in *R (Marsh) v DPP* [2006] EWHC 1525 (Admin), evidence of identification was admissible even though, contrary to PACE, no note of the witness's description had been made before the witness identified the accused.

11.9 THE DISCRETION TO ADMIT OR EXCLUDE EVIDENCE

PACE, s 78(1) provides that:

> In any proceedings the court may refuse to allow evidence on which the prosecution proposes to rely to be given if it appears to the court that, having regard to all the circumstances, including the circumstances in which the evidence was obtained, the admission of the evidence would have such an adverse effect on the fairness of the proceedings that the court ought not to admit it.

This provision has been invoked in a number of cases mentioned throughout this work. The appellate courts have declared themselves loath to interfere with the exercise of discretion under s 78, and do so only if the lower court has taken into account matters which are irrelevant, or has failed to take into account matters which are relevant, or otherwise has come to a conclusion that could not have been reached by a reasonable bench of magistrates properly directed. See, for example, *DPP v Davies* [2002] EWHC 1110 (Admin), and *DPP v Corthine*, unreported, 25 November 1999, where the Divisional Court said that an appellate court would be slow to conclude that the discretion was improperly exercised.

If the discretion in s 78 is not invoked before the justices, it cannot be raised on appeal: *Braham v DPP* [1996] RTR 30 (DC).

Daniels v DPP [1992] RTR 140 was a case of failing to provide breath specimens for analysis. Police had come upon the defendant in circumstances that led them to believe he may have stolen the motor cycle he was riding. They also suspected he had drunk alcohol but did not require a roadside breath test. They arrested him for theft. Some time after his arrival at the police station, the officers were satisfied that he had not stolen the cycle, but did not tell him. He was then asked to provide specimens of breath for analysis, but refused. On appeal against conviction, he argued, *inter alia*, that the evidence of the breath analysis procedure should have been excluded under s 78. The Divisional Court noted that the application of s 78 is not confined to cases of *mala fides*, although the police, in failing to tell him they no longer suspected theft, had not behaved properly. Nevertheless, the defendant had been warned of the consequences of failing to provide and it was not unfair to admit the evidence of failure.

For a case where there was no evidence of any substantial and significant breach of PACE, or that the motorist did not understand the procedure, such that the justices should not have excluded evidence of blood analysis, see *DPP v Preston* [2003] EWHC 729 (Admin). And where justices erroneously found that the police had acted in bad faith, again their decision to exclude evidence was unlawful: *DPP v Corthine*, unreported, 25 November 1999 (DC).

In *R (CPS) v Wolverhampton Magistrates' Court* [2009] EWHC 3467 (Admin), police officers were following a car on foot. It collided with a bank and a hedge and came to a stop. One of the officers saw that the driver's eyes were glazed and he could smell intoxicants on his breath. The officer did not carry out a preliminary breath test because he did not have the equipment with him. Nor did he carry out a preliminary impairment test because he had not been trained to do so. The driver was arrested for driving while unfit through drink, and analysis of a blood specimen showed excess alcohol. The defendant was charged with driving with excess alcohol, but submitted there was no case to answer because his arrest was unlawful. The district judge severely criticised the police for not having trained sufficient officers to conduct preliminary impairment testing (see Chapter 2). He excluded the evidence of the blood analysis under s 78 and allowed the defendant's submission of no case to answer. On the prosecutor's application for judicial review of that finding, the Divisional Court ruled that the real issue was that the district judge had not considered the critical question, which was whether admission of the blood analysis would have such an adverse effect on the fairness of the proceedings that it should not be admitted. In all the circumstances, it would not have been unfair to admit it. Further, the officer had power to arrest the defendant upon reasonable cause to suspect that he had committed a s 4 offence (driving when unfit; see Chapter 7).

Where officers did not make contemporaneous notes, and, at trial, could not remember all the details of the incident in question, that did not of itself render their evidence inadmissible: *Moore v Preston Crown Court* [2011] EWHC 3780 (Admin). Two officers had been on patrol in connection with burglaries in the area. Neither was familiar with the area or knew the names of the roads. They followed a black Peugeot which stopped at a T-junction. The driver, who was stumbling and intoxicated, got out and approached the officers, asking why they had followed him. A roadside breath test was positive and in due course breath analysis revealed excess alcohol. The officers' evidence was that they had followed the motorist until his car stopped and he got out. The motorist admitted he had been drinking, in a nearby pub, but said he had simply got into the car and gone to sleep. He denied having driven. The officers did not make their notes until some time after the incident, and at the trial, they had difficulty recalling details of the roads and the roundabout. The court rejected the motorist's version of events and convicted him.

On his appeal, the Divisional Court acknowledged that the Crown Court had recognised that there were some inconsistencies and variation in the police officers' accounts, but accepted their core evidence that they had followed the vehicle for some considerable distance before it came to a stop. Crucially, the officers were adamant and consistent that the vehicle which they had followed was the same vehicle in which they found the appellant. The Crown Court rejected the appellant's wholly different version of events as implausible and untrue. On the material before it, that conclusion could not be considered without foundation or perverse, even if there was force in some of the criticisms of the officers' overall evidence. There were no grounds for excluding any part of the officers' evidence under PACE, s 78. While it was perhaps regrettable that no contemporaneous note was made and that the initial statements were made so long after the date of the offence, there is no requirement that police make contemporaneous notes of incidents that they deal with. The absence of any contemporaneous notes was relevant only to the weight and not to the admissibility of the evidence. The Crown Court was fully aware of the lack of notes and took that absence into account in weighing the oral evidence of the officers. The appeal was dismissed.

11.9.1 Appropriate adults

A number of cases on whether or not evidence is rightly admitted or disallowed under PACE, s 78 concern failure to arrange for the attendance of an appropriate adult where PACE so requires.

In *R (DPP) v Evans (Brychan Gethin John)* [2002] EWHC 2976 (Admin), there had been a breach of PACE Code of Practice, Code C, which requires that where the suspect is a juvenile, the custody officer must contact an appropriate adult as soon as possible. The suspect was aged 16. Before requiring breath for analysis, it was not possible to contact his parents, and the officer did not contact the local social services department because it was close to the time at which their shifts changed. The justices excluded the evidence of the breath analysis under s 78 and dismissed the charge. The Administrative Court referred to the consistent theme running through the cases that time is of the essence (see para 10.7.3). It is not necessary to delay the procedure to allow the detainee time to read the Codes of Practice or to obtain brief telephone advice, or to await the arrival of a solicitor. It would be contrary to this principle to require the attendance of an appropriate adult in the circumstances of this case. While there had been a breach of PACE, the justices were wrong to exclude the evidence because of that breach.

Where, again, the absence of an appropriate adult caused the motorist no unfairness, evidence of breath analysis remained admissible: *Stanesby v DPP* [2012] EWHC 1320 (Admin). Here the motorist appeared to understand the police station procedure and responded coherently to questions. He was taking medication for depression (a mental illness). Under PACE Code of Practice, Code C, para 1.4 (circumstances in which a person is to be treated as mentally disordered or otherwise mentally vulnerable) an appropriate adult should therefore have been called to advise and assist, but was not. The Crown Court found that there was no unfairness as a result. Even if an appropriate adult had been present, the breath testing procedure would have gone ahead anyway. The motorist was convicted of driving with excess alcohol. On his appeal, the Administrative Court held that, on the facts found, the decision of the court below was clearly right. The breach of the Code made no difference and the court was right to conclude under s 78 that the admission of the result of the breath test procedure would not have such an adverse effect on the fairness of the proceedings that the court ought not to admit it.

By contrast, in *Miller v DPP* [2018] EWHC 262 (Admin), [2018] RTR 19, police stopped a driver on suspicion of driving under the influence of drugs. He was arrested and, at the police station, behaved erratically and aggressively. It seemed he was known to police as a person with learning difficulties and autism, and an appropriate adult had assisted on earlier occasions when the suspect had been interviewed by police. The custody record recited that he was a suicide risk, had mental health issues and learning difficulties, and had himself said that he suffered from Asperger's Syndrome. He asked for solicitors and an appropriate adult, saying he was not 'feeling well in the head'. PACE Code of Practice, Code C requires that, if a detainee is mentally disordered or otherwise mentally vulnerable, an appropriate adult be informed of the reason for the detention and the whereabouts of the person, and asked to come to the police station. An appropriate adult was not contacted. The detainee refused to provide a blood specimen, and was charged with failing without reasonable excuse to provide such a specimen. The justices agreed that there had been a breach of Code C, but declined to exclude the evidence of the police station procedure under PACE, s 78; they convicted the driver. He appealed.

The Divisional Court highlighted that, among the reasons for requiring the presence of an appropriate adult, is that he or she is independent of the police authorities, and able both to safeguard the welfare of the detained person and to provide an independent perspective. The appropriate adult is likely to have a significant role in providing a calming influence on a minor or vulnerable adult who may have become, as in the present case, distressed and agitated. In a failing to provide case, the person under investigation must understand the nature of the request and the consequences of failing to comply. The appropriate adult is likely to play a key role in explaining both. That is very different from the role which an appropriate adult might have played in *Evans* (above), where a freely given sample demonstrates an alcohol reading in excess of the legal limit. Here, the presence of an appropriate adult was an important procedural safeguard for the appellant and the failure to summon such an adult had a clear adverse impact on the fairness of permitting the evidence of the drug-drive procedure to be admitted. The magistrates exercised their discretion under s 78 wrongly, and should not have admitted the evidence.

11.10 ADVICE, ASSISTANCE AND REPRESENTATION

Qualification for legal aid depends not only on means, but on the application of the 'interests of justice' test. Now set out in Legal Aid, Sentencing and Punishment of Offenders Act 2012, s 17(2), the test requires that the following be taken into account:

> (a) whether, if any matter arising in the proceedings is decided against the individual, the individual would be likely to lose his or her liberty or livelihood or to suffer serious damage to his or her reputation;
> (b) whether the determination of any matter arising in the proceedings may involve consideration of a substantial question of law;
> (c) whether the individual may be unable to understand the proceedings or to state his or her own case;
> (d) whether the proceedings may involve the tracing, interviewing or expert cross-examination of witnesses on behalf of the individual; and
> (e) whether it is in the interests of another person that the individual be represented.

The provisions formerly in force (Legal Aid Act 1988, s 22; Access to Justice Act 1999, sch 3, para 5) were in substantially the same terms and the cases decided pursuant to that section likely remain relevant.

An inability to understand English may well bring a defendant within the above criteria, as in *R (Matara) v Brent Magistrates' Court* [2005] EWHC 1829 (Admin), (2005) 169 JP 576. The defendant was charged with failing without reasonable excuse to provide specimens for analysis. His defence was that he had not understood what was being required of him because his English was poor, and that he therefore had a reasonable excuse. His appeal against the refusal of representation succeeded on the question whether he might be unable to understand the proceedings or to state his case. The fact that the court would provide an interpreter was not sufficient. He needed to demonstrate that he had been unable to understand what was being said at the time of his arrest. That went to the heart of the case, his ability to state his own case, and the overall fairness of the trial.

In *R v Richmond Magistrates' Court ex parte Gawel*, unreported, 22 November 1994, the motorist was charged with driving with excess alcohol and with driving when unfit. He applied for legal aid to defend the charges, saying, *inter alia*, that he was in real danger of a custodial sentence and of losing his job. His application was refused. The justices found no real risk of a custodial sentence because the alcohol level was not high and there were no previous convictions. On the risk of losing his job, they said that disqualification was compulsory on conviction unless a defence or special reasons were made out. The Divisional Court reversed its decision. Although there might have been no real risk of a custodial sentence for the offence of driving with excess alcohol, the possibility of such a sentence for driving when unfit depended on the facts as they would emerge, which would bear on seriousness. The justices' decision about the risk to the defendant's job appeared not to take account of the length of the possible disqualification – again, the facts would indicate the degree of danger posed by the defendant's driving and consequent seriousness of the offence of driving with excess alcohol.

In *R v Slough Magistrates' Court ex parte Noble*, unreported, 3 December 1997, the Divisional Court found it appropriate that legal aid should be granted. The defendant was charged with being in charge when unfit, and with failing without reasonable excuse to provide two specimens of breath for analysis. Conviction could damage her reputation as a foster parent. A number of difficult legal points arose, including the question whether the parking place where the car was found was a public place. The defendant's case was that she was only in the car as a means of avoiding her ex-partner. There was a question of the admissibility of the evidence of the manager of a public house. Expert cross-examination of police officers could well have been necessary, and it might have been necessary to cross-examine the ex-partner and his son. The combination of difficulties and complications were such that the refusal of legal aid could not be justified.

A defendant who intended to plead guilty to driving with excess alcohol, but argued special reasons for not disqualifying on the basis that her drinks had been spiked, was refused legal aid and appealed. The Queen's Bench Division found that legal aid should be allowed because an expert would have to be consulted to ascertain whether the driver's evidence was consistent with the scientific facts, and whether the amount she admitted drinking would have put her over the limit in any event. An expert would also be needed to assist in the cross-examination of any expert called by the prosecution. Further, witnesses had to be found and interviewed. See *R v Gravesham Magistrates' Court ex parte Baker* [1998] RTR 451.

In *R v Cheshire Justices ex parte Rolt*, unreported, 24 February 1998, the defendant was a lorry driver who was found to be nearly four times over the limit. He wished to argue that he had not consumed sufficient alcohol to explain the breath analysis readings, and that the breath analysis device must have been faulty. His appeal against the refusal of his application for legal aid succeeded. The Divisional Court agreed that, in light of the reading, he would, if convicted, be at grave risk of imprisonment, and that, if convicted and disqualified, he would lose his livelihood. The nature of the defence was such that the applicant's evidence would need to be corroborated or supported by other witnesses of fact, who would have to be traced and interviewed. Expert evidence would also be required. There was a real risk that the denial of legal aid would cause significant injury to the applicant. The refusal of legal aid went beyond the justices' broad, but not unfettered, discretion.

In *R v Dean Thomas* [2020] EWCA Crim 117, [2020] 4 WLR 66, a driver had been convicted of causing death by careless driving when over the limit for drugs. His appeal against conviction was based on the court's refusal of his application for the appointment of an intermediary to assist him, as a vulnerable defendant, throughout his trial; the court's finding that he was fit to plead; and the court's refusal to use its inherent power to appoint an intermediary to assist him for his evidence alone. His difficulties included inability to concentrate or focus for any length of time and difficulty retaining information, exacerbated by medication for pain. The Court of Appeal reviewed the relevant provisions of the Criminal Practice Directions 2015, and went on to dismiss the appeal, finding that, although the appellant had a range of significant difficulties:

> the issues on which he would have had to concentrate whilst giving evidence were few in number and straightforward in nature. With clear, precise questioning and with appropriate breaks, these subjects could have been addressed successfully without the assistance of an intermediary, albeit the latter would no doubt have assisted in the process if retained.

11.11 THE JUSTICES

A number of cases have concerned the role, independence and powers of the justices.

11.11.1 Personal knowledge

As noted above (*Jarvis v DPP* [1996] RTR 192, para 4.4.6), justices were in error to use personal knowledge that only one breath analysis device was available at a particular police station. But the position was otherwise in *Owen v Jones* [1988]

RTR 102, where the defendant, a serving police officer, was convicted of being in charge with excess alcohol. The justices ordered his licence be endorsed with 10 penalty points. He already had 3 penalty points and so was liable for disqualification under what is now Road Traffic Offenders Act 1988, s 35 (12 or more penalty points). The justices were told by the motorist's solicitor that police policy was that the defendant would lose his job and his home if disqualified. Already aware of this policy themselves, the justices declined to hear mitigating evidence on the point. They found exceptional hardship and did not disqualify. The Divisional Court could find no reason why justices should not rely on their own knowledge of the consequences of disqualification, without evidence, as long as they are confident that the knowledge is well founded on facts positively known to them from a past event.

11.11.2 Bias

Justice must not only be done, it must be seen to be done, and in *R v Downham Market Magistrates' Court ex parte Nudd* [1989] RTR 169 there was a risk that it was not. The defendant was convicted of failing without reasonable excuse to provide a specimen for a breath test, and of failing without reasonable excuse to provide a specimen of breath for analysis. He had applied, unsuccessfully, for his case to be tried by a different bench because the chairman of the trial bench had recently, with other justices, imposed a suspended prison sentence on him for threats to kill, had sentenced him for failing to leave licensed premises when required to do so and for using abusive language, and had seen his criminal record, including a previous conviction for driving while unfit. The application was refused and he was convicted. His appeal to the Divisional Court was successful. While mere knowledge of previous convictions did not necessarily preclude a court from trying a case, justices should not proceed where the previous convictions were disclosed in a way which might lead to bias or a suggestion of bias in the minds of the public. On the facts, the public could not conclude otherwise than that the chairman, despite his efforts and experience, might have been unable to put out of his mind what he knew about the applicant.

On the other hand, knowledge of a previous conviction for driving with excess alcohol did not give rise to a serious danger of bias by a bench hearing a special reasons argument in *Huchard v DPP* [1994] COD 459. A motor cyclist pleaded guilty to driving with excess alcohol, but argued, unsuccessfully, that there were special reasons for not disqualifying (see Chapter 13). He appealed to the Crown Court against disqualification. The documents provided for the Crown Court revealed a previous conviction for driving with excess alcohol. He submitted that such knowledge would prejudice the bench. The bench rejected that argument, and dismissed the appeal. The Divisional Court held that there is no absolute rule that justices with knowledge of previous convictions should not sit. The question is whether there was concern about any sort of bias. All the court below knew was that the motor cyclist had on a previous occasion driven with excess alcohol, and that was not an issue in the present case because he had pleaded guilty. It was therefore difficult to see how knowledge of that conviction would seriously bias the justices when considering whether there were special reasons. Second, the court below addressed the question of potential for bias, said that they did not find the matter to be prejudicial, and that they had considered the appeal on the evidence before them and on that evidence alone. On those facts, the Divisional Court was not prepared to find any real danger of bias.

See also *Saunders v Bristol Magistrates' Court v CPS* [2022] EWHC 2544 (Admin), [2023] 1 Cr App R 8 (para 11.6.1).

11.12 RE-OPENING THE PROSECUTION CASE

Among the many challenges raised by defendants is the question of the circumstances in which the prosecution may rectify minor errors or omissions once it has closed its case. See, for example, *Leeson v DPP* [2000] RTR 385 (DC) (para 11.3.1) and *Greenaway v DPP* [1994] RTR 17 (para 3.4.3).

The general rule is that the court has a discretion to allow the prosecution to re-open its case in exceptional circumstances, usually to adduce rebuttal evidence, or to deal with a mere formality. While the essence of a discretion is that it remains flexible, the discretion to allow the prosecution to re-open its case other than in these two circumstances should be exercised rarely. See *R v Francis* (1990) 91 Cr App R 271 at 275. The discretion must be exercised with caution, and the strictly adversarial system in which the prosecution and defence cases are presented consecutively and in their entirety should be followed unless justice really demands otherwise: *Khatibi v DPP* [2004] EWHC 83 (Admin), (2004) 168 JP 361 (below).

In the early case of *R v Tate* [1977] RTR 17, the Court of Appeal (Criminal Division) ruled that a trial judge has a discretion to allow the prosecution, after the close of its case, to call further evidence relating to the analysis of a blood specimen, particularly if it does not prejudice the defendant.

In *MacDonald v Skelt* [1985] RTR 321, the motorist was charged with driving with excess alcohol in his blood. At the close of the prosecution case, he submitted there was no case to answer since the evidence did not show that the specimen of blood which had been analysed was the one taken from him. The justices accepted this argument, saying that there was insufficient evidence to show the defendant had been over the limit, but went on to grant the prosecution's application to re-open its case to call the necessary linking evidence. The Divisional Court found that this decision was neither perverse nor wrong in principle, and the justices' exercise of discretion could not be faulted.

By contrast, in *R v Aylesbury Crown Court ex parte Lait*, unreported, 13 March 1998, the Crown Court went outside the reasonable bounds of its discretion. The forensic analyst of a blood specimen failed to give evidence that the computer which was used was operating correctly (as then required by PACE, s 69(1)). After the prosecution had closed its case, and after defence counsel's closing speech, the Crown Court allowed the prosecution to re-open its case, to recall the analyst to give further evidence. The Crown Court then adjourned the case because the analyst was no longer available and it was late in the day. The motorist succeeded in an application for judicial review of that decision. The Divisional Court recognised that each case depends on its circumstances, but it is for the prosecution to prepare the case, identify the points upon which evidence is to be given, and to call evidence on those points. Prosecution evidence must be called at the appropriate time. Once the prosecution closes its case, ordinarily it is not permitted to re-open it.

On similar facts in *Jolly v DPP* [2000] Crim LR 471, however, the decision went the other way. The magistrate allowed the prosecutor to recall the forensic scientist, who gave further evidence about the computers in question. On the defendant's appeal against conviction, the Divisional Court said that any trial court must recognise that it is the duty of the prosecution to call its evidence before closing its case. But it was beyond argument that there is a general discretion to permit evidence to be called at a later stage. Before exercising the discretion, the court should look carefully at the interests of justice overall, and, in particular, the risk of any prejudice to the defendant. On the facts, the magistrate was within his powers to allow the prosecution to re-open its case. The judgment in *Jolly* contains a comprehensive review of the case law. The critical difference between *Jolly* and *Lait* appears to be that the witness in *Jolly* was available to give the missing evidence straightaway. In *Lait*, the witness had left the courthouse and the case was adjourned for re-hearing.

The matter was considered again in *R v Cook ex parte DPP* [2001] Crim LR 321. The Divisional Court said that a prosecution application to re-open its case and recall a witness to deal with evidence previously omitted by oversight may properly be granted, but the prosecutor must be in good faith, there must be no possible material prejudice to the defendant, and the defendant must be given the opportunity to deal with the evidence heard following the re-opening. The effect of the decision in *Jolly*, according to the court in *Cook*, was further to limit the opportunities to ambush the prosecution.

Another example of a case in which the Divisional Court endorsed re-opening the prosecution case for further evidence is *Steward v DPP* [2003] EWHC 2251

(Admin), [2004] 1 WLR 592. The prosecution's analyst gave evidence (by way of witness statement), producing his certificate of the proportion of alcohol in a blood specimen. At the end of the prosecution case, the defence argued there was no case to answer in that there had been no oral evidence or a certificate from the doctor who took the specimen (see para 11.3.2). The magistrates found no case to answer, but it then became clear they had confused the analyst's certificate with the doctor's certificate. All parties agreed this, and the magistrates reversed their decision. They went on to accept the police officer's evidence that the specimen had been taken with the defendant's consent by a medical practitioner. They convicted the defendant and he appealed. The Divisional Court found that this was not a case of a bench being persuaded to re-open a case and, in effect, hear further submissions as to the evidence. An error had been identified and admitted by the magistrates, and the defendant's solicitor agreed. The proceedings had not reached a point where the process of adjudication had been completed. The justices were correct to permit the prosecution to complete its evidence.

On the facts in *Khatibi v DPP* [2004] EWHC 83 (Admin), (2004) 168 JP 361, the justices were entitled to allow the prosecution to re-open its case. *Khatibi* was another case of driving with excess alcohol in blood. The defendant submitted, *inter alia*, that the forensic scientist's evidence was inadmissible since it depended in part on the evidence of his assistant. The prosecutor then applied to re-open its case and adjourn to allow the assistant to be called. The justices agreed and adjourned the case for some five months, when the assistant gave evidence that she had analysed the specimen under the supervision of the analyst. She was not cross-examined. On the defendant's appeal against conviction, the Divisional Court found there had been no prejudice to the defendant, and upheld the decision of the justices.

Malcolm v DPP [2007] EWHC 363 (Admin), [2007] 1 WLR 1230 is an example of a finding of special circumstances such that a witness could be recalled even after the justices had retired to reach their verdict. The police officer who conducted the breath analysis procedure gave evidence but was not cross-examined. In her closing speech, counsel for the defendant submitted that the warning required by Road Traffic Act 1988, s 7(7) (of the consequences of failing to provide, see para 10.9) had not been given, and that there was therefore no admissible evidence of the breath analysis or that the correct procedure had been followed. The justices retired to consider this. When they returned to court they announced that they accepted there had been no evidence that the warning had been given. At the prosecutor's request, the justices allowed the police officer to be recalled, and heard further evidence from him. They concluded that the motorist had been properly warned and convicted her. On her appeal, the Divisional Court found that justices have a discretion to receive further evidence after they have retired to consider a verdict, but the discretion is to be exercised only in special circumstances. It is the duty of the defence to make clear its defence and the issues it raises, to the prosecution and to the court, at an early stage, as is implicit in Criminal Procedure Rules 2005 (now the Criminal Procedure Rules 2020), r 3.3, but the defence had not raised the matter of the warning until counsel's closing speech. She did not cross-examine the officer on the point or object to the admission of evidence of the proportion of alcohol in the appellant's breath. She should not therefore have been permitted to raise the issue of the warning in her final speech unless the prosecution was allowed to call evidence to deal with the point. To take the s 7(7) point in the final speech was a classic and improper defence ambush of the prosecution. These factors amounted to special circumstances justifying the recall of the police officer even though the justices had retired and had partially announced their decision. There was no injustice to the motorist, who was available to be recalled if the officer's further evidence was disputed.

In *R (Cox) v DPP* [2009] EWHC 3595 (Admin), [2010] RTR 18, the Administrative Court ruled that the exercise of the discretion to order a new trial depends on the circumstances of an individual case. It is most often exercised where there has been some misconduct or infraction of the rules of procedure by the defence which has resulted, or may have resulted, in unfairness or injustice. On the facts, however, that was not so and the prosecutor was not allowed a new trial. The defendant was charged with driving with excess alcohol. In its closing submissions, the defence raised, for the first time, that the investigating officer had not warned the defendant, as required by Road Traffic Act 1988, s 7(7), that failure to provide specimens would render him liable to prosecution, arguing that the specimens were therefore inadmissible. The prosecutor declined the justices' invitation to recall the officer, saying that there had been no need for the warning as the defendant had been fully compliant with the procedure. The justices convicted the defendant, and he appealed, successfully. The Administrative Court found that the justices were in error in agreeing that there was no need for the warning. The court highlighted the obligation on the defence to make its defence clear to the prosecution and to the court at an early stage. To raise the point about the warning in the final speech was improper. At that stage, the prosecution could have recalled the officer, or could have asked for an adjournment to consider the position. The prosecutor further argued that there was evidence that the warning had been given and that the decision of the justices should be quashed, allowing the prosecutor to apply for a new trial. The Administrative Court found it was impermissible for the prosecution to make a bad submission of law, fail to call relevant evidence, accept on appeal that the decision was, for that reason, flawed, but nevertheless contend that the prosecution should be allowed a new trial on the basis of evidence which could and should have been adduced before the justices.

Where an issue was not raised in the court below, it could not be raised on appeal: *Santos v Stratford Magistrates' Court* [2012] EWHC 752 (Admin). A motorist had been charged with driving with excess alcohol. When the trial opened, defence counsel identified as one of the issues the accuracy of the device, on the basis that the motorist had not consumed enough to put him over the limit. The sergeant who conducted the breath analysis procedure gave evidence, but, possibly because of an interruption, did not give evidence that the device was working correctly at the relevant time. Defence counsel cross-examined the officer, but the district judge did not allow her to put questions relating to the accuracy or proper functioning of the device, on the ground that there was no issue concerning the functioning of the device, and that in any event the officer was not an expert. The motorist gave evidence suggesting he had consumed insufficient alcohol to account for the reading, and on that basis it was submitted that the evidence of the Intoximeter should not be relied on. There was no submission based on the absence of evidence that the device was functioning properly. At the end of the case, the defence did not submit that there was no case to answer. The motorist was convicted and appealed.

The Divisional Court held that the district judge was in error in disallowing the questions about the correct functioning of the device; there had been a challenge to its accuracy, and the sergeant would have been entitled to give evidence that it was working normally. Had the point been raised in the court below by means of a submission of no case to answer, or in a properly formulated closing submission, the court would have acceded to a prosecution application to re-open the case in the interests of justice. The accuracy of the Intoximeter would then have been demonstrated by the evidence of the custody officer, and/or by the production of the printout, which on its face showed that the machine was functioning normally. The technical defect in the prosecutor's case was not allowed to avail the appellant and his conviction was upheld.

In *DPP v Chajed* [2013] EWHC 188 (Admin), [2013] 2 Cr App R 6, the magistrates found the motorist guilty of failing without reasonable excuse to provide specimens of breath for analysis. Immediately after the verdict was announced, defence counsel rose, arguing that there had not been a lawful requirement to provide a specimen since the question about regurgitation of stomach contents (see para 4.5.1) had not been put. Without giving the prosecutor any opportunity to make submissions on this point, and without saying they were going to reconsider their verdict, the bench retired. They returned soon after and substituted a verdict of not guilty. On the prosecutor's appeal, the Divisional Court found that the only power under which magistrates could reconsider a decision was Magistrates' Courts Act 1980, s 142 (powers of magistrates' court to re-open cases to rectify mistakes, etc). The section was, however, limited, and did not enable a convicted defendant to make further submissions with a view to persuading the bench to change its mind; nor did it empower the court to hear such submissions with a view to their mind being turned. It would be antagonistic to the principle of finality in justice for a defendant, in the face of a pronounced guilty verdict, to seek to re-argue a point in that way. If the magistrates make a wrong decision, the appropriate course for the offended party is to appeal.

11.13 STAY OF PROCEEDINGS

The power to stay proceedings is to be used sparingly, and only in exceptional circumstances. If proceedings are to be stayed because of the conduct of the prosecution, that conduct must amount to a manipulation or misuse of the process of the court so as to deprive a defendant of the protection provided by the law or to take unfair advantage of a technicality. See *DPP v Garrety*, unreported, 11 December 2000 (below).

In *R v Beckford* [1996] 1 Cr App R 94, a driver appealed against conviction for causing death by careless driving when unfit. The car had been scrapped without having been examined, and the driver was unable to show that a mechanical failure (the locking of the steering) had caused the accident. The Court of Appeal (Criminal Division) acknowledged that it had power to stay proceedings where it concludes that the defendant could not have a fair trial or that it would be unfair to try the defendant, but each case was to be considered on its own facts. In the present case, there was no evidence that there had been any difficulty steering the car and there were no marks on the road indicating that the wheels had locked or even that the brakes had been applied. On these and other facts in the case, the absence of the car did not affect the fairness of the trial and there were no grounds for setting aside the verdict.

In *DPP v Garrety*, unreported, 11 December 2000, the motorist was charged with driving while unfit through drugs. She had been in a road traffic accident. An officer who attended marked his accident report book, in error, to the effect that there was video evidence. On the trial date, the Crown had not served any primary disclosure material, or stated that no such material existed, under Criminal Procedure and Investigations Act 1996, s 3(1), but the prosecutor said that there was in fact no video. He also said that all material that did exist had been served. The justices concluded that the absence of the video and the Crown's non-compliance with its disclosure obligations had prejudiced the defendant, to the extent that a fair trial was not possible. They stayed the proceedings as an abuse of process. On the prosecutor's appeal, the Divisional Court found that the prosecutor had rectified its omission by confirming that it had disclosed all its evidence. The justices could have dealt with the matter by calling the officer to clarify whether or not a video existed. The officer could have appeared that day, but the accused objected to exploring that possibility. Further, the relevance of any video evidence, if it existed, was entirely speculative. The justices exceeded the reasonable exercise of their discretion in staying the proceedings as an abuse.

Proceedings should not be stayed unless the defendant will suffer such prejudice that a fair trial is not possible. In *DPP v Meakin* [2006] EWHC 1067 (Admin), a case of driving with excess alcohol, the prosecution did not disclose to the defence the name of a witness who had called police to the scene of an accident, where they found the defendant. At the trial, the defence complained about the non-disclosure of the woman's identity, but did not apply for disclosure. The court found that the defendant could not have a fair trial and that there had been an abuse of process, and stayed the proceedings. The prosecutor appealed. The Divisional Court agreed, as conceded by the prosecution, that the name of the caller should have been disclosed, but the real issue was whether she could give any material evidence. That was unclear, but unlikely. Since she was not a witness on whom the prosecution intended to rely, the prosecution had no duty to secure her attendance or tender her for cross-examination. If the defence intended to call her, the defence should have made proper enquiries about her name and address and applied for a witness summons. The failure was as much that of the defence as of the prosecution. There was no question of bad faith or serious misconduct. The justices were in error to find that the defendant could not have a fair trial and that there had been an abuse of process, and to stay the proceedings.

Ivic v DPP [2006] EWHC 1570 (Admin) is another example of circumstances in which a stay of proceedings on the ground of abuse of process was inappropriate. A motorist had been charged with driving with excess alcohol. The date of the alleged offence was 3 November 2001. There were various applications and adjournments and the trial did not take place until March 2005. The district judge was first asked to stay the proceedings as an abuse of process because of the delays. She declined. Nor would she order a stay on the ground that a CCTV video of the procedure had not been provided to the defendant, or exclude evidence of the breath analysis because a police officer had had his radio on during the procedure. The defendant appealed against conviction. The Divisional Court upheld the decisions of the district judge. On the issue of delay, the case would turn on expert evidence about the breath analysis device, which would not be affected by the passage of time. A fair trial was possible. It was unclear whether the CCTV tape, which was missing, would have recorded relevant events, but two police officers were available to be cross-examined about these matters, and one of them completed a contemporaneous record of the procedure and the results. There was evidence that the fact the police radio was switched on would not affect the accuracy or reliability of the breath analysis.

Nor should proceedings in the magistrates' court be stayed for guidance from a higher court: *Hoar-Stevens v Richmond Magistrates' Court* [2003] EWHC 2660 (Admin), a driving with excess alcohol case. Issues concerning disclosure arose. The district judge found that the prosecution had not fully complied with its duty of disclosure. She was asked to consider excluding material under PACE, s 78 (see para 11.9). She decided it was not appropriate to consider the question until after the closing submission for the defence, and invited the parties to test her decision by judicial review because the issue of disclosure had arisen in several cases and there was no guidance from a higher court. The Divisional Court stressed that the course of a criminal trial in the magistrates' court should not be punctuated by applications for an adjournment to test a ruling in the higher court, especially when, if the case proceeds, the ruling may turn out to be of little or no importance. Even when an important point arises during a trial, the Divisional Court cannot intervene. The proper course is to proceed to the end of the trial in the lower court and then to test the matter.

See, however, *Balogun v DPP* [2010] EWHC 799 (Admin) (para 11.6.5) where the Divisional Court distinguished *Hoar-Stevens*, finding that different considerations may apply where a decision to adjourn is challenged; there was no fetter to the higher court's intervention. See also para 11.6.5 on the availability of judicial review.

In *DPP v Petrie* [2015] EWHC 48 (Admin), the defendant was charged with driving with excess alcohol. It was agreed that CCTV footage recorded at the police station was required at the trial. It was produced, but in a format such that it could not be viewed. The prosecutor applied for an adjournment to enquire whether viewable footage could be obtained that day; the defendant applied for a stay of proceedings. The magistrates refused the adjournment and granted the stay on the ground of abuse of process in that the defendant would not have a fair trial in the absence of the CCTV footage. The Divisional Court found that the bench was not disentitled from deciding to refuse the adjournment, remarking that this may well have been a robust case management decision, but was not justified in staying the proceedings. It was not known whether anyone had, in fact, viewed the footage or whether it contained anything relevant. The magistrates' decision that the defendant could not have a fair trial without it was therefore without foundation. Second, the trial could have proceeded on the basis of the available evidence. Even if the magistrates believed that the interests of justice required that the footage be viewed, they could, at the end of the live evidence, and as a last resort, have revisited the refusal of the adjournment.

Petrie was followed in *DPP v Spalluto* [2015] EWHC 2211 (Admin), where the CCTV footage was defective in that there was no sound.

See also *Roberts v DPP* [2008] EWHC 643 (Admin) (para 11.7), *Morris v DPP* [2008] EWHC 2788 (Admin), (2009) 173 JP 41 (para 11.7) and *R v Boyd* [2002] EWCA Crim 2836, [2004] RTR 2 (para 4.15.4).

11.14 ALTERNATIVE VERDICTS

Road Traffic Offenders Act 1988, s 24(1), as amended, provides for alternative verdicts in certain instances. A person charged with causing death by careless driving when under the influence of drink or drugs (Road Traffic Act 1988, s 3A), who is found not guilty of that offence, may instead be convicted of:

- causing death by careless or inconsiderate driving under s 2B, or of careless and inconsiderate driving under s 3;
- driving when unfit (s 4(1)) or with excess alcohol (s 5(1)); or
- failing to provide a specimen (s 7(6)) or to permit a specimen to be laboratory tested (s 7A(6)).

Section 24(1) does not allow for the alternative verdict of driving with an excess of a controlled drug (s 5A) when the s 3A offence is not made out. The general provision in Criminal Law Act 1967, s 6(3), however, applies to trials on indictment for offences other than treason and murder where the jury finds the defendant not guilty of the offence specifically charged. If the allegations in the indictment amount to or include (expressly or by implication) an allegation of another offence falling within the jurisdiction of the trial court, the jury may find the defendant guilty of that other offence.

Section 24(1) goes on to provide that persons charged with driving or attempting to drive when unfit, with excess alcohol or with an excess of a specified controlled drug may, if found not guilty, instead be convicted of the equivalent 'in charge' offence under s 4(2) or s 5(1)(b), or s 5A(1)(b) and (2).

Those charged with driving when unfit, with excess alcohol or with an excess of a specified drug may, if found not guilty, instead be convicted of attempting to drive in such a condition.

11.15 APPEALS

11.15.1 Case stated

Any party to proceedings in a magistrates' court may challenge a conviction, determination or other proceeding on the ground that it is wrong in law or in excess of jurisdiction, by applying to the justices to state a case for the opinion of the High Court on the point of law or jurisdiction in question (Magistrates' Courts Act 1980, s 111). Likewise, an appeal by way of case stated may be made against any order, judgment or other decision of the Crown Court (Senior Courts Act 1981, s 28). The High Court may reverse, affirm or amend the decision challenged, or remit the matter to the court which stated the case, with its opinion, and make such other order as it thinks fit (Senior Courts Act 1981, s 28A).

Although an application to state a case debars an appeal to the Crown Court, there is no corresponding provision that lodging an appeal to the Crown Court debars an appeal by way of case stated: *R v Fylde and Wyre Justices ex parte Gornall* [1996] COD 434 (DC).

11.15.2 Judicial review

In certain circumstances, judicial review of a decision complained of may be appropriate; see para 11.6.5.

11.15.3 *Certiorari*

The Divisional Court has jurisdiction to quash a conviction following an unequivocal guilty plea only where the conduct of the prosecution was analogous to fraud. In *R v Dolgellau JJ ex parte Cartledge; R v Penrith JJ ex parte Marks* [1996] RTR 207, motorists had pleaded guilty to driving with excess alcohol, but sought orders of *certiorari* to quash their convictions on the grounds that the police had not observed in full the procedure set out in *DPP v Warren* [1993] AC 319 (see para 4.13). The prosecution accepted that the correct procedure had not been followed. The Divisional Court found nothing to suggest that the conduct of the prosecution in either case was analogous to fraud, and there had been no injustice to the applicants. Evidence had not been falsified or suppressed, and there was nothing to suggest that the blood analyses were open to doubt. There had simply been a procedural error in obtaining the evidence. The applications were dismissed.

See also *R v Kingston upon Thames Justices ex parte Khanna* [1986] RTR 364 (para 3.4.3), *R v Bolton Magistrates' Court ex parte Scally and Others* [1991] 1 QB 537 (para 4.14.4) and *R v Bolton Justices ex parte Khan* [1998] EWHC 1040 (Admin), [1999] Crim LR 912, where *certiorari* was granted in favour of defendants who had pleaded guilty, to correct an 'overwhelming wrong' (*Khanna*), because the swabs used before taking blood specimens had contained alcohol (*Scally*), and because the charge was duplicitous (*Khan*). See also *R v Downham Market Magistrates' Court ex parte Nudd* [1989] RTR 169 (para 11.11.2) and *R v Wilson, Walmsley, York and Senior* [2019] EWCA Crim 2410 (para 4.15.5).

Chapter 12

Penalties

12.1 THE PENALTIES

The maximum penalties for the offences discussed in this book are set out in Road Traffic Offenders Act 1988, sch 2. The principles by which sentences are to be decided appear in the Sentencing Act 2020 ('the Sentencing Code'), a consolidating measure applying to convictions on or after 1 December 2020. The general provisions concerning sentencing apply. A sentencing court must have regard to the purposes of sentencing in Sentencing Act 2020, s 57, and must follow the guidelines issued by the Sentencing Council, unless satisfied that it would be contrary to the interests of justice to do so (s 59(1)). Sentencing guidelines have been issued for all the offences considered in this book, and are online at www.sentencingcouncil.org.uk. Seriousness, in terms of culpability and harm, is to be taken into account (ss 59(2)(a) and 63), as are whether or not the offender was on bail at the relevant time, and previous convictions (ss 64 and 65). A guilty plea is also relevant (s 73). Courts must give reasons for sentences, and explain their effects (s 52).

12.1.1 Causing death by careless driving when under the influence or having failed to provide a specimen or to permit analysis

Road Traffic Offenders Act 1988, sch 2 provides for a maximum penalty, for an offence under Road Traffic Act 1988, s 3A, of life imprisonment, an unlimited fine, or both. Disqualification, an extended re-test and the endorsement of the driving licence are obligatory, but if the offender establishes special reasons for not disqualifying (see Chapter 13), 3 to 11 penalty points are imposed. The maximum custodial sentence was increased from 14 years to life, and the minimum period of disqualification increased from three to five years, with effect from 28 June 2022 (Police, Crime, Sentencing and Courts Act 2022, s 86).

The s 3A offences are triable on indictment. They are specified offences for the purposes of Sentencing Act 2020, s 306 and sch 18 (extended sentence for certain violent, sexual or terrorism offences).

The sentencing guideline for causing death by careless driving when under the influence of drink or drugs, etc applies to those aged 18 or over, who are sentenced on or after 1 July 2023. Before that date, the guideline had not been updated to reflect the increase in the maximum penalty for offences committed after 28 June 2022. Nor was there any guideline relating to the offence in para (ba) of s 3A(1) – causing death by careless driving while the proportion of a specified controlled drug in the blood exceeds the specified limit. This gave rise to a number of challenges concerning sentencing; see *R v Mohamed (Ahmed)* [2018] EWCA Crim 596, [2018] 4 WLR 1; *R v Myers* [2018] EWCA Crim 1974, [2019] RTR 12; *R v Roberts* [2018] EWCA Crim 2965, [2019] 1 CR App R (S) 49; *R v Wilson* [2019] EWCA Crim 1141; *R v Marcus Wood* [2019] EWCA Crim 2078; *R v Adebisi* [2020] EWCA Crim 1446; and *R v Redding* [2021] EWCA Crim 1502. The position has now been clarified by the introduction of a revised guideline.

In determining the seriousness of a s 3A offence, the sentencing court must first establish the offence category by determining the standard of driving by reference to a number of specified factors. Matters relevant to the alcohol or drug(s), or refusal to provide a specimen, are then considered. The loss of life in a s 3A offence makes it always of the utmost seriousness. The guideline provides a table of starting points and sentencing ranges, by reference to specific levels of blood alcohol concentration and to deliberate refusal to provide a specimen. In relation to drugs, the appropriate category range is to be identified by reference to: evidence of substantial impairment; multiple drugs or a combination of drugs and alcohol; any quantity of a single drug above the legal limit; a single drug below the legal limit. The guideline sets out a non-exhaustive list of aggravating and mitigating factors specific to these offences.

The guideline refers to blood alcohol concentration in terms of microgrammes per 100 millilitres, but, in relation to drugs, to impairment, multiple drugs and combination of drugs and alcohol, as well as simply to being over or under the limit for the drug in question. The guideline in place before 1 July 2023 referred to high, moderate or medium levels of drugs as indicators of seriousness. As pointed out in *Redding* (above), there was no definition of what constituted a high or moderate quantity. What was clear, however, was that the multiples which can be interpolated into alcohol cases are not to be applied in drugs cases. For example, an alcohol concentration of 71 microgrammes or over puts the offender at a minimum of twice the limit and so at the highest level of seriousness. But a drug concentration of two or more times the relevant limit does not necessarily indicate a high quantity.

In *R v Jordan* [1995] RTR 201, a decision which predated the 2008 sentencing guideline for the s 3A offences, the Court of Appeal had found it unhelpful to consider guideline cases relating to drink-driving when sentencing for an offence of causing death by careless driving when unfit through drugs. The sentencing appeal was dealt with solely on the basis that the appellant had consumed an unlawful drug which was likely to have, and did have, an adverse effect on the manner of driving.

R v Bond [2017] EWCA Crim 2329 was a reference by the Solicitor General of a sentence for causing death by careless driving while unfit through drugs, on the basis that it was unduly lenient. The Court of Appeal accepted expert evidence that 'the sort of correlation that can be made between quantities of alcohol consumed and levels of impairment cannot be made in relation to the specified limits for drugs'. The presence of benzoylecgonine (BZE, the main metabolite of cocaine), even at 2.5 times the specified limit, which was inactive, had no adverse effects on driving ability. The level of impairment caused by the drugs taken would depend on when the drugs were used and the offender's tolerance to the drugs. Low levels of different drugs, not exceeding the specified limits, in combination, would be a factor in causing impairment.

In *R v Benjamin Norman* [2022] EWCA Crim 1738, [2023] 1 Cr App R (S) 38, a driver was convicted of causing death by careless driving when over the limit for a controlled drug. He was almost three times over the limit for cannabis. The sentencing judge, in assessing seriousness, took the starting point at its highest, on the basis that in an alcohol case, being twice or more over the alcohol limit would take the case into that category. On appeal, the Court of Appeal referred to Parliament's zero tolerance approach to the drug-drive offences (see para 8.8), and to the Sentencing Council's then guidance relating to the s 5A offence (see para 12.1.4) to the effect that it would be wrong to rely on the guideline for driving with excess alcohol when sentencing for an excess drugs offence. The sentencing judge erred in comparing the excess of cannabis over the specified level with the level of excess alcohol over the prescribed limit in a drink-drive case. On the facts, however, the judge was entitled to treat the appellant as having been substantially impaired by the cannabis he had used. See *R v Norman* [2023] EWCA Crim 1112 for the dismissal of the driver's appeal against conviction.

See also *R v Keilan Roberts* [2023] EWCA Crim 1023.

While it is not necessary to establish impairment to make out the offence under s 3A(1)(ba), the degree of impairment is relevant to sentencing: *R v Myers* [2018] EWCA Crim 1974, [2019] RTR 12; *R v Karl Roberts* [2018] EWCA 2965; *R v Adebisi* [2020] EWCA Crim; *R v Keilan Roberts* [2023] EWCA Crim 1023.

12.1.2 Driving or attempting to drive when unfit or with excess alcohol

The maximum penalties for driving or attempting to drive when unfit through drink or drugs (Road Traffic Act 1988, s 4(1)), with excess alcohol (s 5(1)(a)), or with an excess of a specified controlled drug (s 5A) are the same: imprisonment for six months, a level 5 fine (up to £5,000), or both. Disqualification and the endorsement of the driving licence are obligatory, but if the offender establishes special reasons for not disqualifying (see Chapter 13), 3 to 11 penalty points are imposed.

The relevant sentencing guidelines require that the seriousness of an offence is to be assessed taking account of the level of impairment or the alcohol concentration, and the presence or absence of aggravating features. The suggested starting point penalties for first-time offenders who plead not guilty are a band C fine at the lowest level of seriousness, up to 12 weeks' imprisonment for the most serious, but with an overall sentencing range of up to 26 weeks' imprisonment. The suggested periods of disqualification start at the minimum 12 months and go up to three years for the most serious offences.

The guidelines include non-exhaustive lists of factors, specific to these offences, indicating higher culpability or greater seriousness. On the other hand, certain matters may go to reduce culpability in an excess alcohol case, even though insufficient to amount to special reasons for not disqualifying.

A person guilty of driving with excess alcohol who drank after driving, but cannot establish that it was that drink which took the person over the limit, is nevertheless entitled, for the purposes of the penalty, to adduce evidence that the reading at the time of driving was lower than that shown on the printout: *Goldsmith v DPP* [2009] EWHC 3010 (Admin), [2010] RTR 20 (see para 8.11).

12.1.3 In charge when unfit or with excess alcohol

The offences of being in charge carry lower maximum penalties than those of driving or attempting to drive. The maximum penalty for being in charge when unfit (s 4(2)), with excess alcohol (s 5(1)(b)), or with an excess of a specified controlled drug (s 5A(1)(b) and (2)) is imprisonment for three months, a level 4 fine (up to £2,500), or both. Disqualification is discretionary, but the licence must be endorsed. If the driver is not disqualified, 10 penalty points are imposed.

Again, the relevant sentencing guidelines shed further light on the penalties to be expected by a first-time offender who pleads not guilty. The starting points range from a band B fine and 10 penalty points at the lower end of seriousness, up to a high level community order with disqualification or 10 penalty points. Sentencing ranges go up to 12 weeks' imprisonment.

For being in charge when unfit, suggested penalties relate to the degree of impairment – a less straightforward basis than the measured alcohol concentration in the excess alcohol cases (see Chapter 7).

Factors listed as likely to indicate higher culpability or seriousness include that there was a high likelihood of driving. Conversely, a low likelihood of driving makes for lower culpability.

12.1.4 Driving or attempting to drive with an excess of a specified controlled drug

Although the s 5A offence was introduced in 2015, it was not until 1 July 2023 that a sentencing guideline was available. Before that, sentencing courts were using a guidance document, which did not have the formal status of a guideline, but seems to have been widely used. *R v Hussain* [2018] EWCA Crim 2361, [2019] RTR 19 was an appeal against the period of disqualification for two offences of drug-driving. The recorder who sentenced the appellant set the period taking into account matters mentioned in the guidance: the presence of more than one drug made the offence more serious; it was further aggravated in that the offender was carrying a passenger, and, at the time of the offence, was subject to a suspended sentence for conspiracy to supply cannabis. The Court of Appeal, while acknowledging that the guidance did not have the same status as a sentencing guideline, found that it had been appropriately followed and upheld the decision of the court below.

Under the new guideline, factors indicating higher culpability are that the vehicle in question was a large goods vehicle, a heavy goods vehicle or a public service vehicle or was being driven for commercial purposes; or that there was another specified drug or alcohol present. Indicators of harm are obvious signs of impairment and evidence of an unacceptable standard of driving. The guideline emphasises that it is not possible to make a connection between the level of a drug and the level of harm, reciting that the limits are set on the modified zero tolerance approach described in para 8.8, rather than the approach taken to alcohol, which is based on the effect certain amounts of alcohol would be expected to have on driving ability. The guideline penalties range from a band C fine with 12 to 16 months' disqualification for a first offence, up to six months' imprisonment and 29 to 36 months' disqualification. Aggravating and mitigating features are given.

12.1.5 In charge with an excess of a specified controlled drug

For the 'in charge' offence under s 5A, the factors indicating higher culpability are that there was a high likelihood of driving; that the vehicle in question was a large goods vehicle, a heavy goods vehicle or a public service vehicle, or there was some commercial purpose; or that there was another specified drug or alcohol present. Obvious signs of impairment suggest greater harm. The sentencing range is from a band B fine and 10 penalty points, up to 12 weeks' imprisonment and disqualification.

12.1.6 Failing to co-operate with a preliminary test

The maximum penalty for failing to co-operate with a preliminary test (Road Traffic Act 1988, s 6(6)) is a level 3 fine (up to £1,000). Disqualification is at the discretion of the court. Endorsement of the licence with 4 penalty points is obligatory. The sentencing guidelines suggest a band B fine as the starting point.

12.1.7 Failing to provide specimens

To avoid the situation where a defendant might escape more lightly simply by refusing to provide evidential specimens, the penalties for failing to provide evidential specimens are the same as those for the substantive offences. On the other hand, it is possible that a person who is greatly over the limit might receive a lighter sentence by refusing to supply a specimen than if the alcohol level is ascertained.

The penalties for failing to provide specimens of breath, blood or urine (s 7(6)), or for failing to allow a specimen to be laboratory tested (s 7A(6)) depend on the offence which was being investigated when the specimen(s) was required or taken. The penalties are higher where the specimen was required in an investigation into whether the defendant was unfit or over the limit when driving or attempting to drive, rather than where the investigation was into whether the defendant was only in charge in such a condition.

In assessing the penalty for refusing to provide a specimen of breath, justices are entitled to take into account any evidence of how much the motorist had consumed. This would include the result of the analysis of a single breath specimen where the first, but not the second, specimen was provided. See *Cracknell v Willis* [1988] AC 450 (HL) (para 3.4.7).

Driving or attempting to drive

Where the offence under investigation was driving or attempting to drive when unfit or with excess alcohol, the maximum penalty is imprisonment for six months, a level 5 fine (up to £5,000), or both. Disqualification and the endorsement of the driving licence are obligatory, but if the offender establishes special reasons for not disqualifying, 3 to 11 penalty points are imposed.

The relevant sentencing guidelines again provide a table of sentence starting points, and ranges, depending on seriousness in terms of culpability and harm, for first-time offenders who pleaded not guilty. The lower end is a band C fine, and the maximum, up to 12 weeks' imprisonment. Deliberate refusal or failure to provide would indicate greater culpability, while a high level of impairment would suggest greater harm. Examples of factors indicating higher seriousness are provided.

In charge

In an 'in charge' case, the maximum penalty is imprisonment for three months, a level 4 fine (up to £2,500), or both. Disqualification is discretionary, but the licence is to be endorsed with 10 penalty points if the offender is not disqualified. The relevant sentencing guidelines give a starting point of a band B fine, up to a maximum of a medium level community order, together with up to 12 months' disqualification. The examples of factors making for higher culpability are a deliberate refusal or failure to provide. On the other hand, an honest but erroneous belief that the defendant had a reasonable excuse, or a genuine attempt to comply, would reduce culpability. A high level of impairment would indicate greater harm. Aggravating factors include a high likelihood of driving.

12.2 PERSONAL MITIGATION

The sentencing guidelines should enable a court to assess the seriousness of an offence and to reach a preliminary view concerning the appropriate sentence. Factors personal to the offender may then operate to mitigate the likely penalty. Such factors include remorse.

12.3 GUILTY PLEAS

Further, a reduction in sentence may be available in response to a guilty plea, depending on the point at which the guilty plea was entered. The sentencing guidelines indicate that a reduction of one-third is appropriate where a guilty plea was entered at the first stage of the proceedings, while a one-quarter reduction may be allowed for a guilty plea entered after that point. The concession reduces to 10 per cent for a guilty plea entered on the trial date, and ceases to be available if the guilty plea is entered during the course of the trial. The reduction applies to the punitive element of the sentence only, and not to the period of disqualification.

12.4 ANCILLARY ORDERS

12.4.1 Disqualification

Discretionary or obligatory

Road Traffic Offenders Act 1988, sch 2 provides that disqualification from driving is obligatory for the following offences:

- causing death by careless driving when under the influence of drink or drugs (Road Traffic Act 1988, s 3A);
- driving or attempting to drive when unfit (s 4(1));
- driving or attempting to drive with excess alcohol (s 5(1)(a));
- driving or attempting to drive with an excess of a specified controlled drug (s 5A(1)(a) and (2));
- failing to provide a specimen for analysis or for a laboratory test, or failing to allow a specimen to be subjected to a laboratory test, if the specimen was required or taken to ascertain ability to drive or the proportion of alcohol when driving or attempting to drive (ss 7(6) and 7A(6)).

Disqualification is a matter for the discretion of the justices in respect of the following offences:

- being in charge when unfit (s 4(2));
- being in charge with excess alcohol (s 5(1)(b));
- being in charge with an excess of a specified controlled drug (s 5A(1)(b) and (2));
- failing to provide a specimen for analysis or for a laboratory test, or failing to allow a specimen to be subjected to a laboratory test, where the specimen was required or taken other than to ascertain ability to drive or the proportion of alcohol when driving or attempting to drive (ss 7(6) and 7A).

In cases of failing to provide specimens, or of failing to allow specimens to be tested, the context in which the requirement was made is significant, because there is scope for a person who was being investigated for one of the 'in charge' offences to argue against disqualification. Before sentencing a person for failing to provide under s 7(6) (and presumably, now, under s 7A(6) also), justices must ascertain whether the person was driving or attempting to drive, or simply in charge, to establish whether disqualification is obligatory or discretionary. It is for the prosecution to prove beyond reasonable doubt that a defendant was driving or attempting to drive: *Crampsie v DPP* [1993] RTR 383.

In *George v DPP* [1989] RTR 217, police found the defendant asleep in the back of his car. Although he admitted he had driven, he was prosecuted for failing to provide specimens on the basis that he had been in charge. He pleaded guilty. The justices found that at the time he was required to provide specimens he had been driving or attempting to drive, and disqualified him on the basis that it was obligatory to do so. His appeal against disqualification succeeded, the Queen's Bench Division ruling that although there was just enough evidence to conclude that he was driving or attempting to drive, that was not the basis on which the prosecution had proceeded, and the justices should have approached the question of disqualification on the basis that it was discretionary. See also *Gardner v DPP* [1989] RTR 384 (DC), to the same effect.

Where the circumstances in which specimens were required do not emerge from the trial, or are not admitted, they should be independently ascertained, by a *Newton* hearing (*R v Newton (David)* [1974] RTR 451) if necessary. In *Shaw v DPP* [1993] 1 All ER 918, the appellants challenged their convictions for failing to provide specimens for analysis, contrary to s 7(6). They argued that because the Act provided different penalties according to the offence being investigated, there were in fact two offences under s 7(6). Since the charges did not specify which, they were bad for duplicity. The Divisional Court rejected that argument. There is only one offence under s 7(6), which stands apart from the circumstances before or after commission.

The decision in *Shaw* was approved by the House of Lords soon after, in *DPP v Butterworth* [1995] 1 AC 381, where it was held that the central test for establishing the offence under s 7(6) is whether the officer is investigating whether a person has committed any offence under s 4 or s 5. It is not necessary to show that the officer had in mind a specific offence under either section, or to specify a specific offence in the charge. The substance of the offence is the refusal in the course of a general investigation for the purposes of ss 4 and 5. Any other interpretation would mean the officer would have to decide what offence is under investigation even before knowing whether or not the suspect is over the limit. The question whether the person was driving or attempting to drive, or in charge, is relevant only after conviction when the penalty is being considered. At this point the defendant needs to know which offence was being investigated. That is usually clear from the trial on the s 7(6) offence, but there must be an inquiry and a distinct decision on the point after conviction, by means of a *Newton* hearing if necessary.

In *Cawley v DPP* [2001] EWHC 83 (Admin), the defendant gave evidence that he had not been driving, but that another person had. He called no evidence in support, and the prosecutor called no evidence that the defendant had been driving. The Divisional Court found, however unmeritorious the submission, there was no evidence before the court on which to conclude that the defendant had been driving rather than in charge. The justices therefore had a discretion to disqualify; disqualification was not mandatory.

Obligatory disqualification

Road Traffic Offenders Act 1988, s 34(1) provides that those convicted of offences which carry obligatory disqualification must, in the absence of special reasons (see Chapter 13), be disqualified for a minimum period of 12 months.

Longer minimum periods of disqualification apply to repeat offenders. The minimum is three years for a person who has, within the preceding 10 years, committed any of the drink- and drug-drive offences which carry obligatory disqualification (except the s 3A offence) (s 34(3)). For an offence under s 3A, the minimum period of disqualification is five years (s 34(4ZA)), and six years if such an offence is repeated within 10 years (s 34(3)).

The minimum period is two years rather than 12 months where the offender has been disqualified more than once for a fixed period of 56 days or more within the three years immediately preceding the commission of the offence under consideration (s 34(4)). Certain disqualifications, specified in s 34(4A), are, however, disregarded for this purpose.

The sentencing guidelines contain suggested periods of disqualification for each of the offences and are considered above.

A plea of guilty amounts to conviction for the purposes of s 34(3). In *DPP v Haddigan*, unreported, 27 May 1994, the defendant pleaded guilty, on 5 June 1992, to driving with excess alcohol and the case was adjourned for a pre-sentence report. The defendant failed to appear for sentence. On 23 September 1993 he had still not been sentenced, but was involved in a road accident and was again over the limit. He pleaded guilty to the second offence on 24 September 1993. The question was whether he had been convicted of the earlier offence, so that he had to be disqualified for a minimum of 12 months for the earlier offence, and a minimum of three years for the second. The Divisional Court held that he had.

For the purposes of s 34, the word 'convicted' means 'found guilty of an offence' and does not include the imposition of a sentence.

In *R v Rivano* (1993) 14 Cr App R (S) 578, an offender who had nine previous convictions for driving with excess alcohol was found driving while disqualified and, again, with excess alcohol. The Crown Court disqualified him for life, but the Court of Appeal reduced the disqualification to 10 years, finding that there were no very exceptional circumstances to suggest that the driver would be a danger to the public indefinitely.

Extended disqualification

Disqualification from driving must be served while the offender is at liberty in the community, rather than being allowed to run while the offender is in custody. Road Traffic Offenders Act 1988, s 35A, introduced in April 2015, provides for a disqualification from driving to be extended if a custodial sentence is imposed at the same time, so that the period of disqualification does not begin to run until the offender is released The disqualification must be for the period which would be imposed under s 34 or s 35 ('the discretionary period'), plus an 'extension period', usually equal to half the custodial sentence. In *R v McDonagh* [2022] EWCA Crim 759, [2023] RTR 2, the use of the word 'discretionary' was said to be apt to confuse, because in some cases disqualification is obligatory under Road Traffic Offenders Act 1988, s 34 and sch 2, whereas in others it is discretionary in the different sense that it is not obligatory.

Section 35B applies where the offender is already serving a prison sentence and the court then disqualifies and imposes a custodial sentence for a further offence. Here the court, when determining the period of disqualification, must have regard, if and to the extent that it is appropriate to do so, to the diminished effect of disqualifying as a distinct punishment if the person is also in custody.

See *R v Needham and Others* [2016] EWCA Crim 455, [2016] 1 WLR 4449, where the Court of Appeal set out a checklist for applying ss 35A and 35B, and *R v Holmes* [2018] EWCA Crim 131.

In *R v Anderson* [2021] EWCA Crim 1796, a driver had been convicted of dangerous driving, two offences of driving with excess drugs, and driving without insurance, all committed on the same occasion. For dangerous driving, he was sentenced to 14 months' imprisonment, consecutive to a prison sentence he was already serving for unrelated matters, and disqualified for 31 months (24 months discretionary with a seven-month extension). For each of the drug-drive offences, he was disqualified from driving for 18 months. It appeared from the record that the disqualifications for drug-driving had been ordered to run consecutively to the

31 months for dangerous driving. On appeal, the Court of Appeal acknowledged that disqualification must run from the date it is imposed. Referring to s 35B, to achieve the sentencing judge's objective that the offender serve two years' disqualification on release from custody, the period of disqualification should have been extended by nine months to take account of the unexpired balance of the sentence being served. The Court of Appeal directed that the 18-month period of disqualification be served concurrently with the 31 months' disqualification, so that on release from custody the appellant would have about 15 of the 31 months' disqualification left to serve. It could not impose a further extension because that would result in the appellant's being dealt with more severely on appeal than in the court below, contrary to Criminal Appeal Act 1968, s 11(3).

Criminal Procedure Rules, Part 29 sets out matters which the court must explain to the defendant when convicting of an offence leading to obligatory disqualification, and invite representations concerning special reasons or mitigating circumstances if such representations have not already been made.

Discretionary disqualification

Disqualification is a matter for the discretion of the court for the 'in charge' offences, and for failing to provide a specimen (or to allow a specimen to be laboratory tested) in an 'in charge' investigation. If the court does not disqualify, it must order that the offender's licence be endorsed, and impose a number of penalty points appropriate to the seriousness of the offence. Again, the sentencing guidelines contain suggested numbers of penalty points.

Where justices exercised their discretion to disqualify a defendant for 18 months for failing to provide specimens, the Divisional Court declined to interfere: *Tucker v DPP* [1992] 4 All ER 901. It would do so only if the sentencing court had acted in excess of jurisdiction or otherwise wrongly in law. The correct course for challenging a sentence imposed by justices is to appeal to the Crown Court.

Interim disqualification

Road Traffic Offenders Act 1988, s 26 permits a court to order interim disqualification in certain circumstances, notably where the offender is convicted but the case is adjourned for sentence. The disqualification is until the offender is dealt with for the offence, subject to a maximum of six months.

Reduced period of disqualification

Road Traffic Offenders Act 1988, ss 34A, 34B and 34C contain provisions under which the period of disqualification for any of the drink-driving (but not drug-driving) offences may be reduced if the offender satisfactorily completes an approved course. The intention is that offenders may benefit from training about the problems associated with drink-driving, so as to reduce the risk of re-offending. The provisions apply where the offender is disqualified for at least 12 months, for any of the drink-drive offences considered in this work. The reduction may be for no less than three months and no more than one quarter of the remaining period of the disqualification. The court must be satisfied that a place on a course is available. It must explain the effect of the order, the cost of the course, and that the offender must pay for it in advance. The offender must agree to the making of the order. The course must be completed by a specified date, which must be at least two months before the reduced period of disqualification would expire. Section 34B contains provisions concerning the mechanics for certifying completion of courses. The Driver and Vehicle Standards Agency's Drink-drive Rehabilitation Scheme Course Syllabus gives further details: https://assets.publishing.service.gov.uk/media/5a7edac9e5274a2e87db2543/drink-drive-rehabilitation-scheme-course-syllabus.pdf.

Road Safety Act 2006, ss 15 and 16 introduced an alternative way of reducing the period of disqualification. When they come into force (at the time of writing, January 2024, they are not in force), these provisions empower courts to offer an offender the opportunity to participate in an alcohol ignition interlock programme. The central feature of such a programme is a device designed to prevent the offender from driving without first providing a satisfactory breath specimen. Section 15 inserts ss 34D to 34G into the Road Traffic Offenders Act 1988, which govern the operation of the scheme, and Road Safety Act 2006, s 16 provides for an experimental period.

Application to remove disqualification

Road Traffic Offenders Act 1988, s 42 contains provisions enabling an offender to apply to the magistrates' court for the removal of a disqualification in certain circumstances.

The possibility that the period of disqualification may be reduced pursuant to s 42 is not to be taken into account when sentencing. In *R (Corner) v Southend Crown Court* [2005] EWHC 2334 (Admin), the defendant was convicted of driving with excess alcohol and sentenced to 24 months' community rehabilitation and disqualified for four years. The Crown Court dismissed his appeal against sentence, deciding not to alter the period of disqualification because, after two years, the offender could apply to have it removed. The offender appealed further, arguing that the Crown Court had been wrongly influenced by the potential to invoke s 42. The Divisional Court agreed. If the proper period of disqualification was two years, then that should have been the sentence and no reference should have been made to any possible reduction. But in the unusual circumstances of the case – the defendant had not set out to drink and drive and had displayed minimal culpability – the appropriate period of disqualification was two years.

12.4.2 Endorsement of the driving licence

Road Traffic Offenders Act 1988, sch 2 provides that an offender's driving licence is to be endorsed in respect of all the offences discussed in this work. But when a person is disqualified from driving, penalty points should not also be imposed in respect of offences committed on the same occasion. See *Martin (Ross) v DPP* [2000] 2 Cr App R (S) 18, where the justices disqualified for driving with excess alcohol, but were in error in imposing eight penalty points for driving without insurance on the same occasion. Section 44(1) provides that:

> Where a person is convicted of an offence involving obligatory endorsement, the court must order there to be endorsed on his driving record particulars of the conviction and also—
>
> (a) if the court orders him to be disqualified, particulars of the disqualification, or
> (b) if the court does not order him to be disqualified—
>
> (i) particulars of the offence, including the date when it was committed, and
> (ii) the penalty points to be attributed to the offence.

The Divisional Court in *Martin* ruled that s 44(1) is to be interpreted as meaning that a court is not to impose penalty points in relation to an offence if it orders disqualification in respect of another offence of which the offender is convicted on the same occasion.

For all the offences discussed in this work, except failing to co-operate with a preliminary test, the endorsement is effective for 11 years from the date of conviction (s 45A(5)). For failing to co-operate with a preliminary test, the period is four years from the date of the offence, or four years from the date of conviction if the offender is disqualified (s 45A(3)).

Disqualification pending further driving test

Road Traffic Offenders Act 1988, s 36(4) empowers courts, when endorsement is obligatory, to disqualify the offender until the offender passes a driving test. Such a driving test may be an extended driving test if the offence was one carrying obligatory disqualification (s 36(5)(a)). The court must take into account the safety of road users when deciding whether or not to make such an order (s 36(6)).

Further, the sentencing court must order an extended test where the offence is one of causing death by careless driving when under the influence of drink or drugs, contrary to Road Traffic Act 1988, s 3A: see Road Traffic Offenders Act 1988, s 36 and the Driving Licences (Disqualification until Test Passed) (Prescribed Offence) Order 2001 (SI 2001/4051).

12.4.3 Property deprivation order

Powers of Criminal Courts (Sentencing) Act 2000, s 143 empowers a court to make an order depriving an offender of property used in committing or facilitating the commission of an offence. It may do so in addition to any other penalty. The power is available in respect of offences under the Road Traffic Act 1988 which are punishable by imprisonment (that is, all the offences considered in this work except the offence of failing to co-operate with a preliminary test). The vehicle is regarded as having been used for the purpose of committing the offences of driving, attempting to drive, or being in charge. It is also regarded as having been used for the purpose of committing the offences of failing to provide a specimen, or to permit a specimen to be tested, where the failure was in the course of an investigation into an offence of driving, attempting to drive, or being in charge. Before making such an order, the court must have regard to the value of the property and to the likely financial and other consequences on the offender of making the order.

12.4.4 Forfeiture or suspension of liquor licence

The Licensing Act 2003 provides that a person who holds a personal licence to supply liquor must, if charged with certain offences, tell the court of its existence, or produce the licence to the court, no later than the defendant's first appearance before the court. The offences to which this applies include the offences of driving, attempting to drive, or being in charge when unfit or with excess alcohol. If the defendant is convicted, the court may order that the liquor licence be forfeit, or suspended for up to six months. If it decides not to do so, the court must nevertheless notify the licensing authority of the conviction and the sentence. See Licensing Act 2003, ss 128 to 132.

12.4.5 High risk offenders

Special provisions apply to 'high risk offenders', such that the issue of a driving licence at the end of the period of disqualification is not automatic. Motor Vehicles (Driving Licences) Regulations 1999 (SI 1999/2864), reg 74 (as amended) defines 'high risk offenders' as:

- a drink driver who has been disqualified for being two and a half times (or more) over the limit;
- a person convicted and disqualified for failing to provide a specimen under s 7;
- a person who has been disqualified on two or more occasions within any 10-year period for driving with excess alcohol or while unfit; or
- a person who has been disqualified for failing without reasonable excuse to give permission for a laboratory test of a specimen of blood taken under s 7A.

Following disqualification, the Driving and Vehicle Licensing Agency (DVLA) contacts such drivers explaining that, upon re-applying for a licence at the end of the disqualification, the question whether the conviction indicates a medical disability and, if so, whether the offender has brought the drinking problem under control, is addressed. The DVLA advises the offender to seek help and advice during the period of disqualification. The offender must satisfy the Medical Advisory Branch at the Department for Transport that he does not have an alcohol problem before a licence is issued. To do so, the offender is interviewed, medically examined, and a blood specimen is taken. See the Motor Vehicles (Driving Licences) Regulations 1999, and Road Traffic Act 1988, ss 92 and 93.

At the time of writing (January 2024), a comparable scheme in relation to drug drivers has been proposed (Department for Transport, 'Proposals for a High Risk Offenders Drug Driving Scheme', August 2020, https://assets.publishing.service.gov.uk/government/uploads/system/uploads/attachment_data/file/1061738/proposals-for-a-high-risk-offenders-drug-driving-scheme.pdf), but is not in place.

12.5 PURPORTED RESCISSION OF SENTENCE

In *R v Highbury Corner Magistrates' Court ex parte Tann* [1994] RTR 5, a motorist pleaded guilty, on 27 November 1990, to driving with excess alcohol. He was fined and disqualified. Later the same day he came back before the magistrate and asked for an adjournment to enable him to advance further mitigation, and an adjournment was granted. The motorist then changed his mind and decided to accept the original sentence. On the adjournment date, he handed in to the court a letter to that effect, but did not stay until the case was called on. When it did come before the magistrate, the magistrate took the view that the motorist had yet to be sentenced, and issued a warrant for his arrest. The motorist thought the original fine and disqualification would stand and refrained from driving for the period of disqualification. About a year later, the motorist applied for the return of his licence. The police then executed the warrant. On 6 February 1992, he was brought back before the court and the magistrate imposed a fine of

£100 and disqualification for 12 months, to run from 6 February 1992. On his appeal, the Divisional Court found that, on the facts before the magistrate on 27 November 1990, there was nothing to suggest that the applicant would later seek to advance any special reasons why he should not be disqualified for the minimum period, or that he had any particular concern about the fine imposed. It was not therefore a case such as to justify the exercise of the statutory power (under Magistrates' Courts Act 1980, s 142 – to rectify mistakes, etc) to rescind the sentence. The magistrate's purported exercise of the power of rescission was inappropriate as a route to possible future variation and, on the particular facts, *Wednesbury* unreasonable. The original sentence of 27 November 1990 was to stand, and the purported sentence of 6 February 1992 was quashed.

On s 142, see also *DPP v Chajed* [2013] EWHC 188 (Admin), [2013] 2 Cr App R 6 (para 11.12).

12.6 COSTS

In *Ivic v DPP* [2006] EWHC 1570 (Admin), the defendant appealed unsuccessfully against (among other matters) a costs order of £4,000. The Divisional Court recited the normal rule that costs should not be grossly disproportionate to the fine, which in this case was £500. It nevertheless upheld the order, stressing that defendants must understand that if they instruct lawyers, or are unwise enough to accept advice, to pursue hopeless technical defences which inflate the costs, they will have to pay those costs if they fail. Those who cause the costs must pay them.

See also *Cox v DPP* [2010] EWHC 3589 (Admin), where the motorist's application for a costs order was rejected on the grounds that the issues he planned to raise were not made clear to the prosecution and to the court at an early stage.

In *Ho-Shing v CPS* [2022] EWHC 3137 (Admin), the appellant had been charged with failing without reasonable excuse to provide specimens for analysis. Before appearing at court, she agreed to pay her solicitors a total of £1,600 plus VAT to represent her up to and including her first appearance at court. At the first hearing she made clear her defence would be that, at the time she was asked for specimens, she was asleep in a police cell. The police had CCTV footage of the cell showing that she was indeed asleep, but did not provide it to the Crown Prosecution Service until after a number of requests and a case management meeting. The Crown Prosecution Service then discontinued the case. The appellant applied for her costs.

The district judge hearing the application proceeded on the basis of the Costs in Criminal Cases (General) Regulations 1986 (SI 1986/1335) and the case law arising from them, applying the test of whether there had been an unnecessary or improper act or omission, as a result of which costs were incurred by another party such that the court would have a discretion to order the party responsible to meet those costs. Quoting *Evans v Serious Fraud Office* [2015] EWHC 263 (QB), such awards are 'generally restricted to those exceptional cases where the prosecution has acted in bad faith or made a clear and stark error'. Here, the Crown Prosecution Service should have reviewed the CCTV footage before the first appearance, so that the case could have been discontinued much earlier, but the failure did not meet the test in *Evans*, since it was only at the first appearance that the nature of the defence was made clear. By that time, the appellant's costs had already been incurred. On appeal, the Administrative Court considered the judge's reasons were intelligible, coherent and sufficient to explain why he considered the line between an error simpliciter and a clear and stark error of the kind needed to justify an award of costs was not crossed until after the first appearance. That conclusion was properly open to him and the appeal was dismissed.

Chapter 13

Special Reasons for Not Disqualifying

13.1 INTRODUCTION

Road Traffic Offenders Act 1988, s 34(1) provides that:

> Where a person is convicted of an offence involving obligatory disqualification, the court must order him to be disqualified for such period not less than twelve months as the court thinks fit unless the court for special reasons thinks fit to order him to be disqualified for a shorter period or not to order him to be disqualified.

As seen in Chapter 12, disqualification is obligatory for most of the drink-drive offences discussed in this book, but discretionary for the 'in charge' offences and for failing to co-operate with a preliminary test. Unsurprisingly, the prospect of avoiding disqualification by arguing special reasons has given rise to a wealth of case law. Much of it is in the context of driving with excess alcohol, although some judgments concern failing without reasonable excuse to provide specimens.

There are two stages to a successful special reasons argument. First, the special reason must be established, and, second, the court must be persuaded to exercise its discretion in favour of the offender. These are distinct elements, and the fact that a special reason is made out does not necessarily mean that the offender avoids disqualification.

If the justices make a finding of special reasons, they must give their reasons in open court, and record them in the court register: Road Traffic Offenders Act 1988, s 47. Failure to do so, however, is not of itself a ground for appeal by the prosecutor: *Brown v Dyerson* [1969] 1 QB 45.

A matter which does not amount to a reasonable excuse for failing to provide specimens (see Chapter 10) may nevertheless amount to a special reason.

13.2 EVIDENCE

It is for the defendant to show special reasons for not disqualifying, and the justices should hear evidence on the point: *Jones v English* [1951] 2 All ER 853. In that case, the defendant's advocate made a statement to the justices that the vehicle had broken down and had been towed to the position in which it was found. The respondent then drank a number of beers, and went to sleep in the vehicle rather than leave it unattended. The Divisional Court found that the defendant should have given evidence himself to discharge the burden of proof, and that the justices should not simply have accepted the statement.

The facts said to constitute a special reason must be supported by evidence: *Brown v Dyerson* [1969] 1 QB 45.

Nebulous evidence is not sufficient. In *Park v Hicks* [1979] RTR 259, the defendant said his wife had suffered a brain haemorrhage and had been advised not to become excited. They were at a party and a disturbance of some kind occurred. The defendant considered he had no option but to drive his wife home for her own safety. He was stopped and found to have excess alcohol. The wife did not give evidence and there was no other evidence about her condition. The Divisional Court ruled that, before it could be inferred that there had been a medical emergency, the wife's medical condition should have been set out in far greater detail and with far greater force. The finding that the defendant believed his wife might suffer a recurrence of brain damage was 'wholly insufficient'.

The burden of proof is on the balance of probabilities: *Pugsley v Hunter* [1973] 1 WLR 578 (see para 13.7).

In *R (Gatenby) v Newton Aycliffe (sic) Magistrates' Court* [2017] EWHC 3772 (Admin), the applicant for judicial review had been charged with failing without reasonable excuse to provide a specimen of breath for analysis. He pleaded guilty on the basis that he had not been driving or in charge at the relevant time, such that disqualification would be discretionary rather than obligatory. On the hearing day, neither the prosecutor nor the court's legal adviser accepted that if the accused had not been driving or attempting to drive at the material time, that could amount to a special reason. They had before them an extract from *Wilkinson's Road Traffic Offences*, but not the report of *McCormick v Hitchins* (see para 13.9). The court declined a request for a short adjournment to obtain a copy of the report. The offender was fined, his licence was endorsed with 10 penalty points and he was ordered to pay costs and a victim surcharge. The court found nothing to suggest there was a special reason not to endorse the licence at all. On judicial review, the Administrative Court found that the procedural unfairness to the applicant was such that the sentence had to be quashed and the matter remitted to the magistrates for a fresh sentencing hearing; it:

> beggar[ed] belief ... that the prosecution, and the Legal Adviser, and ... the court, the magistrates, were not aware of their responsibility to ensure that the law governing special reasons was properly before the court.

13.3 SPECIAL TO THE OFFENCE: THE FOUR CRITERIA

The four criteria to be met to make out a special reason were set out in *Whittall v Kirby* [1947] KB 194 (DC). The case concerned an offence under Road Traffic Act 1930, s 15, of driving when under the influence of drink or drugs so as to be incapable of having proper control of the vehicle. The court emphasised that the limited discretion not to disqualify is to be exercised judicially, and that 'special' is the antithesis of 'general'. To be special, a reason must be special to the offence, and not to the offender. In other words, it must be:

- a mitigating or extenuating circumstance;
- not amounting in law to a defence to the charge; yet
- directly connected with the commission of the offence; and
- one which the court ought properly to take into consideration when imposing punishment.

On the facts – the defendant had no previous convictions and needed his licence for his livelihood – there was no special reason.

The Court of Appeal followed the principles enunciated in *Whittall v Kirby* in *R v Wickins* (1958) 42 Cr App R 236, another case under Road Traffic Act 1930, s 15. While these two cases are still both cited as authority for the four criteria, *Wickins* is almost certainly no longer good authority on its facts. In *Wickins*, the defendant was suffering from diabetes, but was unaware of it. He had consumed a small amount of beer, which would not have affected his driving but for the diabetes. Although the court recognised that this was a 'rather difficult' case, it found that there was a special reason.

Whittall v Kirby was again followed in *R v Jackson; R v Hart* [1970] 1 QB 647 (CCA). The appellant Hart had pleaded guilty to failing to provide a specimen for a laboratory test contrary to Road Traffic Act 1967, s 3(3). The appellant Jackson had driven with excess alcohol, contrary to s 1(1). Mr Hart was a polio victim whose lower right arm had been amputated. He was unable to get home without his invalid car, unless he hired a taxi or had assistance from a friend. Mr Jackson's liver was, unknown to him, malfunctioning, which, when combined with his blood pressure, caused alcohol to be retained in the body longer than usual. The court ruled that none of these facts constituted a special reason, and went on to say that any general state of health of an offender or bodily defect is peculiar to the offender and not to the offence. It makes no difference whether or not the defendant is aware of that state of health or its effect. Nor was it relevant that in neither case was the appellant's driving ability impaired.

At first sight it is difficult to reconcile *Jackson and Hart* with *R v Wickins*. In *Jackson and Hart*, however, the court pointed out that the considerations may vary depending on the offence committed, and that a matter which might be relevant to impaired capacity, as in *Wickins*, would not necessarily apply in respect of the offences of driving with excess alcohol and of failing to provide a specimen. Consequently, 'the difficult and borderline decision' in *Wickins* was not authority as regards cases arising under the later Act. And in *Jarvis v DPP* (2001) 165 JP 15, a case of dangerous driving in which special reasons were argued, the Divisional Court confirmed *Whittall v Kirby* as the guiding authority. It followed *Jackson and Hart* in finding that the hypoglycaemia brought on by diabetes was peculiar to the defendant and was not part of the offence. It could not therefore constitute a special reason.

In *Bullen v Keay* [1974] RTR 559, a motorist had driven to a lay-by where he took barbiturates, intending to commit suicide, but later resumed driving. He pleaded guilty to driving while unfit through drugs. The justices found that he had not intended to drive after taking the drug and that when he did drive he was not in control of his actions. They found special reasons and did not disqualify. The Queen's Bench Division ruled that the justices' finding that he had not intended to drive after taking the tablets was not relevant because he had in fact driven, but in any event it was a reason peculiar to the offender and not to the offence. The unreported cases of *DPP v Hyland*, 6 July 1987 (DC), *DPP v Crawford*, 22 June 1994 (DC) and *DPP v Phillips*, 22 June 1994 (DC) all further illustrate that depression, despair, domestic problems and anxiety relate to the offender rather than to the offence, and do not justify a finding of special reasons.

In *Lodwick v Brow* [1984] RTR 394, the defendant lost his portion of the blood specimen and argued that this amounted to a special reason not to disqualify. There had been an accident and the blood specimen had been taken in a hospital. Later, the defendant could not remember having given the specimen and his portion of it could not be found. The Divisional Court found that the blood testing took place after the offence had been completed and could not therefore relate to the commission of the offence.

In *Stewart v DPP*, unreported, 14 December 1998, the defendant was registered disabled, having had a leg amputated following an accident. He argued that if he had had both legs, he would have had a greater proportion of water in his body and therefore would have been under the limit. The Divisional Court upheld the court below in finding that his was a state of affairs special to the offender and not the offence, and so was not a special reason.

In *DPP v O'Meara* [1989] RTR 24, some 12 hours had elapsed between the respondent's last drink and the offence. The Divisional Court ruled that the fact that the defendant did not think he would still be over the limit the next morning was a matter connected with the offender and not directly connected with the commission of the offence. It could not therefore be a special reason. Likewise in *Bryant v DPP*, unreported, 9 June 1988 (DC), the defendant's belief that he would not be over the limit was not a matter to be taken into account in relation to penalty, and was peculiar to the offender rather than to the offence.

In *Jarvis v DPP* (2001) 165 JP 15, a dangerous driving case, the defendant was, at the time of the offence, suffering from hypoglycaemia brought on by diabetes, and argued that this amounted to a special reason. The court considered *Wickins*, *Jackson and Hart* and *Stewart*, and held that the physical condition of the offender was a condition special to her, not to the offence. It was not therefore a special reason. Likewise, in *Kinsella v DPP* [2002] EWHC 545 (Admin), abnormal alcohol metabolism was not capable of being a special reason.

In *Woolfe v DPP* [2006] EWHC 1497 (Admin), [2007] RTR 16 (see para 4.5.1), the justices found that, because the defendant's medical condition – his susceptibility to regurgitation – was not a defence, it could not be the basis for arguing a special reason either. The Divisional Court, quite correctly, found that they had erred in this. *Whittall v Kirby* is to the contrary effect, that a matter cannot ground a special reason if it amounts to a defence. On the basis of the case law discussed above, however, it seems unlikely that the medical condition in question would be found to amount to a special reason.

Woolfe was considered in *Ng v DPP* [2007] EWHC 36 (Admin), [2007] RTR 35, where the motorist argued that the breath analysis was affected by eructation (belching), and that if the reading had thereby been artificially inflated, that would amount to a special reason. The Administrative Court agreed, ruling that these facts went directly to the commission of the offence, and could explain why the appellant had been over the limit even though the alcohol he had consumed would not have had that effect. The court drew an analogy with the laced drinks cases (see para 13.7). The distinction between *Woolfe* and *Ng* is that *Woolfe* concerned the underlying medical condition which gave rise to frequent eructation, while *Ng* focused on the contamination of the breath specimen by alcohol brought from the stomach.

13.4 THE SEVEN-POINT CHECKLIST

In *Chatters v Burke* [1986] 1 WLR 1321, without reference to either *Whittall v Kirby* or *R v Wickins*, the Divisional Court provided a seven-point checklist for assessing whether special reasons exist:

1. how far the vehicle was driven;
2. the manner in which it was driven;
3. the state of the vehicle;
4. whether it was the intention of the driver to drive any further;
5. the prevailing conditions with regard to the road and the traffic upon it;
6. whether there was any possibility of danger by contact with other road users; and
7. the reason for the vehicle being driven at all.

Item 6 was highlighted as the most important, the court pointing out that the distance driven is of itself not a sufficient determinant of special reasons. On the facts of the case, the court found that there was enough evidence to justify finding special reasons. The defendant had been to a party. On leaving, he thought he had had too much to drink and asked someone else to drive. The driver lost control, the car left the road and stopped in a field. The defendant then drove the car off the field and back onto the road. He immediately stopped the car, which now had a flat tyre, got out and waited for the police.

13.5 THE DISTANCE DRIVEN AND THE DEGREE OF DANGER

Where the defendant drove only a few yards to move his car into a friend's driveway, but was stopped and found to have excess alcohol, he had a special reason not to be disqualified: *James v Hall* [1972] 2 All ER 59 (QBD). The reason was special to the offence. On the other hand, where the driver moved his vehicle 200 yards to re-park it, but in so doing collided with two stationary vehicles, he did not have a special reason: *Coombs v Kehoe* [1972] 1 WLR 797, in which the Queen's Bench Division said that *James v Hall* was a special case and was not to be extended. In *Haime v Walklett* (1983) 5 Cr App R (S) 165, the defendant intended to drive about 200 yards to park his car. The lights were not on as they should have been, the engine stalled twice and the car twice mounted the pavement before coming to a stop close to a police officer. The Queen's Bench Division applied *Coombs v Kehoe* to find that the defendant did not have a special reason. The justices were in error in confining their attention to the distance actually driven. The distance the defendant had intended to drive was significant, on a road which was likely to be carrying traffic; he was a potential danger. By contrast, in *DPP v Rose* (1988) 156 JP 733, the distance driven was only two feet, but the defendant, convicted of failing to provide specimens, did not have a special reason.

In *Redmond v Parry* [1986] RTR 146 (DC), the defendant had been at a dinner with his wife. His wife was to have driven home, but was reluctant to reverse the car out of its parking position and the defendant did so, but collided with another car. It was held that the shortness of the distance driven could, in the circumstances, amount to a special reason. The circumstances included that he intended to drive no further, he drove in a car park where there were no pedestrians at the time, and he believed he was committing no offence.

On the facts in *DPP v Corcoran* [1991] RTR 329, the short distance driven and the absence of danger justified a finding of special reasons. The motorist had been going to the theatre, intending to leave his company car in a car park overnight, to be collected by a colleague the next morning. But he was late, and parked on the street. At the end of the performance he drank alcohol while still in the theatre, then drove his car to the car park. On the way, he was stopped by police and found to be driving with excess alcohol. Given that he had driven only about 40 yards, and there was no danger to other road users, the Divisional Court found that the justices were entitled to find special reasons.

By contrast, in *Costello v DPP*, unreported, 8 March 1995, there was a possibility of danger, and the distance driven was not short enough to give rise to a special reason. The appellant saw a van belonging to his companion's father being reversed into the road. The driver decamped, leaving the van in the middle of the road. The defendant then drove it at least 80 yards to a more secure, brighter place. The Divisional Court found that the justices had been correct to take into account that the appellant need not have driven as far as he did. He could simply have driven the van back into the space from which it had been taken. The final category in *Chatters v Burke* [1986] 1 WLR 1321 – the reason the vehicle was being driven at all – was also relevant.

In *DPP v Elsender* [1999] EWHC 529 (Admin), the Divisional Court held that where there was no emergency or other good reason for driving in the first place, the shortness of the distance driven (about half a mile) and the absence of danger were irrelevant; there was no special reason.

In *CPS v Humphries* [2000] 2 Cr App R (S) 1, the defendant intended to steal a car, but could not start the engine. His passenger pushed the car a few feet. The defendant admitted he had been extremely drunk, wished to get home and decided to steal the car. He was convicted of attempting to drive with excess alcohol. The

Divisional Court held that what mattered was that he had intended to drive on the public highway with all the danger attendant upon his unfitness. The shortness of the distance moved was irrelevant and there was no special reason.

DPP v Conroy [2003] EWHC 1674 (Admin), [2004] 1 Cr App R (S) 37 illustrates the degree of danger which does not justify finding special reasons. The motorist had driven, over the speed limit and erratically, for nearly a mile, including half a mile through the centre of Congleton at 3 am. He intended to drive a further 200 yards beyond the place at which he was stopped by police. The Divisional Court ruled that the justices had been in error to find special reasons.

All the circumstances are relevant, and the shortness of the distance driven does not of itself necessarily justify a finding of special reasons. In *DPP v Oram* [2005] EWHC 964 (Admin), the respondent drove his van 350 yards along a residential cul-de-sac, from a pub car park to his home, because he had valuable tools in it. The Administrative Court found that there was no question of any emergency. The respondent's difficulties were entirely of his own making. A sober, reasonable and responsible friend (see para 13.6.5) would have advised against driving. There was no special reason.

The shortness of the distance driven is not available to ground a special reasons argument where the offence charged is one of failing to provide specimens, because it cannot be directly connected with the commission of that offence: *DPP v Williams (Shane)*, unreported, 22 June 1994 (DC).

In *DPP v Harrison* [2007] EWHC 556 (Admin), there were again no grounds to find special reasons. The respondent had suffered harassment from a gang of youths, who verbally abused him, damaged his vehicle and threw bottles into his property. On the evening in question, he was woken by breaking glass and verbal abuse, and saw youths attacking a neighbour's property. He telephoned the police who told him to stay at home. The youths then went to the defendant's property, broke the back gate and threw a brick through his patio doors. The respondent got into his car and drove after the youths. His breath alcohol reading was 54. The Divisional Court ruled that the distance driven – some 446 yards – was significantly greater than could justify a finding of special reasons. The respondent drove on a major arterial road such that there must have been a real prospect of danger to other road users. The breath alcohol level, and the fact that there were alternative courses of action (asking one of the neighbours to drive or giving chase on foot) also militated against a finding of special reasons, as did the fact that the respondent had not followed the advice from the police that he should stay at home. Taking those facts individually or cumulatively, special reasons could not properly be found.

See also *DPP v Craddock*, unreported, 2 April 1996 (para 13.6.3).

In *DPP v Cove* [2008] EWHC 441 (Admin), the motorist, at about 3 am, drove 250 metres to avoid incurring an excess parking charge. The Divisional Court found there could be no special reason. Given the location, other road users, including pedestrians, could have been about. The respondent drove around a roundabout, without lights, and had drunk a significant amount of alcohol. There was a possibility of danger by contact with other road users, and there was no emergency.

13.6 EMERGENCIES

Where a person drives in response to an emergency, having not intended to drive, and is found to have excess alcohol, there may be a special reason. In *Taylor v Rajan; Fraser v Barton* [1974] QB 424, the Divisional Court laid down the principles:

- The court must consider whether the emergency was sufficiently acute to justify driving, taking into account all the circumstances, including:
  - the nature and degree of the crisis or emergency,
  - whether there were alternative means of transport or methods of dealing with the crisis,
  - the manner in which the defendant drove, and
  - whether the defendant acted responsibly or otherwise.
- The matter is to be considered objectively.
- If the defendant's alcohol level is very high, that is a powerful reason against exercising the discretion in favour of the defendant, and if the reading exceeds 100 milligrammes of alcohol in 100 millilitres of blood, justices should rarely, if ever, refrain from disqualifying.
- A distinction is to be made between an outward journey to deal with an emergency and the return journey; generally, the latter is more difficult to justify than the former.

On the facts of the two cases, special reasons were not made out. In *Taylor v Rajan*, the respondent was a restaurant manager. He had influenza and was at home, drinking brandy. He learned that there was no responsible person at one of the restaurants he managed to secure the premises and remove the cash. He therefore drove to the restaurant. He could have asked his father, who owned the restaurant, to go, but preferred not to trouble him. The respondent stayed at the restaurant for an hour and a half, and did not drink while there. He was stopped while driving home and was found to have excess alcohol. The Divisional Court found it extremely unlikely that, viewed objectively, this was an emergency at all.

In *Fraser v Barton*, the respondent, who had consumed a large amount of alcohol, received a telephone call from a friend who said she was having serious domestic trouble and asked him to go and see her at once. He telephoned for a taxi but could not get one. He called the only minicab number he had, but there was no answer. He then drove to his friend's home. He was stopped while driving back, and was found to have excess alcohol. The Divisional Court ruled that the degree of emergency was wholly insufficient to amount to a special reason, and that it was out of the question that anyone who drove with such a high alcohol concentration (230 milligrammes in blood) should be in any way excused.

13.6.1 The nature and degree of the emergency

Whether an emergency justifies driving is to be considered objectively: *Jacobs v Reed* [1974] RTR 81. The defendant was at an airport awaiting a flight and, not expecting to drive, was drinking. He learned in a telephone call that his daughter had not arrived at school, and decided to abandon his travel plans and drive home. He was stopped and found to have excess alcohol. The Divisional Court ruled that the test is objective, taking into account the degree and character of the emergency and the extent to which alternative transport might be used. The evidence of emergency was nebulous and the defendant had not even considered alternative transport. His special reasons argument failed.

Again, in *Evans v Bray* [1977] RTR 24, it was emphasised that, to constitute an emergency, the conduct must be justified in all the circumstances, taking into account any alternative responses. The defendant's wife, who was on holiday some 40 miles from home, telephoned saying she had been taken ill and urgently needed her medication, which she had left at home. The defendant decided to take it to her. He was stopped while driving and found to have excess alcohol. The justices found there had been a dire emergency which might have been a life-or-death situation, the defendant's response was understandable, and there were special reasons for not disqualifying. The Queen's Bench Division was less certain that the emergency was dire, but ruled that the more dire it was, the more obvious was the alternative of contacting one of the emergency services, rather than driving. The high level of alcohol (171 milligrammes in blood) also militated against the course of action the defendant took. The question was not whether the defendant's actions were understandable, but whether there was no alternative. He had not considered any alternative, and the justices were wrong to find special reasons.

Likewise, in *Powell v Gliha* [1979] RTR 126, the circumstances did not amount to an emergency. The defendant and her husband, who was a paraplegic, went to a party 30 miles from their home, intending to stay the night. At about midnight, the husband had to use the lavatory, but needed a specially adapted lavatory and there was not one at the party venue. The defendant drove him home. The Divisional Court found no special reason for not disqualifying. A crisis can provide a special reason if sufficiently compelling, but an invented crisis should not be accepted. The defendant had made no provision for the possibility that her husband would need to use the lavatory during the night and the situation was partly of her own making.

See also *Park v Hicks* [1979] RTR 259 (para 13.2).

In *Thompson v Diamond* [1985] RTR 316, the defendant had been giving a family lunch party at home and had consumed alcohol. His sister telephoned to say their mother had been admitted to hospital as an emergency patient. Without inquiring the nature of his mother's indisposition, he immediately set off in his car to drive from the Wirral to collect his sister and go on to the hospital in Torbay. Public transport was not available. He did not inquire about hiring a taxi or seek private assistance. He was stopped by police, and found to have excess alcohol. The Divisional Court found there had been no emergency. The defendant had not even inquired whether he needed to go to the hospital that day, or immediately. He did not even know the reason for his mother's admission.

By contrast, on the facts in *Williams v Tierney* [1988] RTR 118, the Divisional Court found that the justices' finding of special reasons was not open to challenge. The defendant had been at a public house with his wife, intending to stay the night with his wife's sister who lived nearby. On leaving the public house, the ex-husband of the defendant's wife, who had a history of violence against his former wife, ran towards them. The defendant and his wife were afraid for their safety. They got into their car and the defendant drove home. Another car, which they believed contained the ex-husband and others, followed them. The defendant drove about four and a quarter miles and pulled into a driveway, so shaking off the car which had been following. He then drove a further three-quarters of a mile home. The justices found that the only means of immediate transport was the car. The defendant initially drove in an emergency, which continued until he and his wife were no longer being followed. The vehicle was then driven a very short distance without danger to others. The defendant intended to drive no further than to his home. A reasonable person would not have considered other means of transport at that time of night and in the circumstances.

In *DPP v Thomas*, unreported, 20 June 1989, the Divisional Court held that driving away from home after a row, albeit for less than half a mile, did not amount to an emergency.

In another unreported case, *DPP v Bird*, 24 February 1994, driving to see a suicidal friend, drinking while there, and then driving home, did not give rise to a special reason. A friend telephoned the defendant. The friend was in distress, saying she did not want to live any more. She had in the past attempted suicide. The defendant went to her home, as he had done on earlier occasions. While there, he drank gin. Normally, he would have stayed the night at the friend's home, but she became angry, threatened to take an overdose, and told him to leave. She would not let him use the telephone to call a taxi and there was no telephone box in the immediate vicinity. He considered walking home, but it was a 6-mile journey along unlit country roads. He drove away, taking the tablets with him, but was stopped by police and found to be over the limit. The Divisional Court ruled that, to find a special reason, there has to be an emergency acute enough to impel the defendant to drive. While disposing of the pills might have been a matter of emergency, driving them away was not.

Where a woman cried rape and demanded money, and the defendant drove with her to a cash machine and back, the Divisional Court upheld the justices' finding that there was a special reason: *DPP v Enston* [1996] RTR 324. The defendant and a woman whom he knew went to a public house, then to the defendant's flat. The defendant thought he would not be driving again that night, the woman having said she would stay at his flat. He drank two and a half cans of strong lager. The woman became aggressive, demanding £25 and saying she would accuse him of rape if he did not drive her home. The defendant was frightened; he suggested ordering a taxi. She refused and threatened to scream if he did not do as she asked. He drove with her to a cash machine where he withdrew £30, giving £25 to the woman. On the return journey he was stopped by police and was found to have excess alcohol. The justices found that the facts amounted to mitigating or extenuating circumstances, did not amount to a defence, and were directly connected with the commission of the offence. Applying an objective test, they found there had been an emergency, which continued up to the time the defendant was stopped by the police, and that there were special reasons not to disqualify. On the prosecutor's appeal, the Divisional Court found that the justices had gone through the various stages in an impeccable fashion. While justices should be on the alert not to be taken in by hard luck stories, their conclusion could not be found to be perverse.

In *DPP v Cox* [1996] RTR 123, the defendant was the steward of a golf club which had its premises about 300 yards from his home. About half that distance was on a public road. The premises had been burgled several times. On the day in question, the defendant had finished work and was at home. He had been drinking and did not intend to drive. The alarm company telephoned to say the burglar alarm had been activated. Without thinking of the amount he had drunk, alternative methods of transport, or contacting other key holders, he drove to the club. No traffic was on the road other than police vehicles *en route* to the club. The justices found there had been an emergency which amounted to a special reason, and did not disqualify. The Divisional Court considered that the respondent could have walked to the club, although he would not then have arrived as quickly; the situation was not static and could have been worsening. With some hesitation, it found that the justices were entitled to conclude that there had been an emergency. *DPP v Tucker*, unreported, 6 November 1996 (DC) is a similar case concerning the response to an intruder alarm.

In *DPP v Knight* [1994] RTR 374 (DC), driving home because the baby-sitter had received a number of threatening telephone calls, in the light of the defendant's various efforts to get home other than by driving herself, amounted to a special reason.

In the unusual case of *Tottman v DPP* [2004] EWHC 258 (Admin), the defendant's girlfriend had telephoned him late at night, saying she was walking home and was being followed. Considering this an emergency, the defendant drove to meet her, but was stopped and found to have excess alcohol. The justices found special reasons, decided not to disqualify, and imposed 11 penalty points. Unknown to the justices, the offender already had 3 penalty points on his licence and so became liable to disqualification for six months under the 'totting up' provisions in Road Traffic Offenders Act 1988, s 35. He appealed to the Crown Court, arguing that he should not have been given 11 penalty points. Counsel for both sides agreed that no evidence need be called, and the prosecutor did not seek to challenge the finding of special reasons or to extend the period of disqualification. The Crown Court did not indicate that it was considering increasing the sentence, but asked counsel whether the defendant had telephoned 999; whether the person said to have been following his girlfriend was ever caught; whether the justices knew that the defendant already had 3 penalty points (to all three of which the answer was 'no'); and whether, in counsel's view, the amount the defendant said he had drunk would result in the reading given, which counsel declined to answer. The Crown Court accepted that there were special reasons but went on to disqualify for 12 months for the drink-drive offence, taking into account that the driver had not called 999, that his girlfriend was quite near the house at the time, and that the police were near. On further appeal, the Administrative Court found that the Crown Court had delved further into the case than it should have done given that there was no re-hearing and no fresh evidence. The driver had no opportunity to seek to dissuade the Crown Court from increasing the sentence; indeed, the whole complaint was that the justices had never intended him to be disqualified. The Administrative Court quashed the Crown Court's ruling and remitted the case for re-hearing.

In *DPP v Heathcote* [2011] EWHC 2536 (Admin), (2011) 175 JP 530, the motorist drove his van in pursuit of someone who had stolen his quad bike. He drove for about 10 minutes, covering a distance of about a mile and a half. He then saw police officers and attempted to report the theft. They smelled alcohol on him and asked if he had been drinking. Breath analysis revealed 57 microgrammes alcohol in 100 millilitres of breath. The justices found there had been an emergency in that a crime was in progress and there was a realistic prospect of recovering the quad bike and a possibility of apprehending the perpetrator(s); the defendant acted instinctively; there was little other traffic and few pedestrians; and the defendant had not planned to drive that night. They concluded that there was a special reason for not disqualifying. On the prosecutor's appeal, the Administrative Court held there had been no emergency. The respondent had had a considerable amount to drink; the danger to road users must have been obvious; the distance to be driven was uncertain; a chase in itself imports more risk than normal driving; the respondent drove for one and a half miles for some 10 minutes. The problem was theft, not imminent fear or threat to life and limb. A normal friend advising the respondent might well have considered that property of this nature was likely to be insured and the matter should be left to the police. No consideration seemed to have been given to the alternatives.

In *Key v CPS* [2013] EWHC 245 (Admin), the defendant had been to a party, five minutes' walk from his home. He drove there, intending to walk back. There was a fight at the party; he was attacked by six young men. When he left the party he saw two of them outside. He got into his car. The two men came up to him and screamed and shouted as he drove off. He argued that his fear of being attacked amounted to an emergency and that there was therefore a special reason for not disqualifying. The district judge found that his fear was, not that he would be assaulted, but that his car would be damaged, and that he drove it to avoid its being damaged. Even if he was in fear for his own safety, alternatives were open to him; he could have gone back into the party, or to any of the nearby houses, to ask for help; he had a phone but did not use it. The district judge said he did not consider these because he was impaired by drink, and rejected the special reasons argument. On the motorist's appeal, the Administrative Court stressed that the test is indeed an objective one. The district judge was entitled to make the findings of fact she did, and that would be quite sufficient to justify the decision not to find special reasons. Although the district judge went on to say that the alternatives were not considered because of impairment by drink, that did not detract from the fact that the proper objective test had been applied.

13.6.2 Alternative means of transport

Where a 17-year-old drove his injured friends to hospital, having been told no ambulances were available and having tried unsuccessfully to get a taxi, the justices' finding of special reasons could not be faulted: *DPP v Upchurch* [1994] RTR 366. The defendant went on foot to a restaurant with three friends. They expected to be drinking. A serious disturbance took place in the town, and the defendant and his friends became innocently caught up in it. The friends were all injured on the head. The defendant asked a police officer to call an ambulance, but none was available. They walked back to their accommodation. The friends were seriously unwell. The defendant telephoned for a taxi, but the taxi company would not send a car, in view of the disturbance. The defendant then drove his friends three miles to a hospital. He drove at 62 mph when the limit was 30 mph, but otherwise drove perfectly properly. He was stopped by police and his breath alcohol reading was 45. On these facts, the Divisional Court upheld the justices' finding of special reasons and their decision not to disqualify.

By contrast, in *DPP v Ellis*, unreported, 2 November 1998, the respondent drove his wife home from a dinner because she was in pain. The person who was to have taken them home was not prepared to leave early. The respondent did not telephone for a taxi or inquire if anyone else could drive them. His breath alcohol reading was 67. The Divisional Court reiterated that the test is an objective one. It found it impossible to say that there had been an emergency, since the respondent did not investigate alternatives to driving and his wife's pain was not such that a doctor had to be called.

13.6.3 Objective approach

In *DPP v Whittle* [1996] RTR 154, the justices were wrong to have found a special reason. The defendant had been out drinking. His wife was driving, but complained of dizziness and blurred vision and the defendant took over the wheel. He drove in a suburban area of Manchester and there was a telephone in the car. He argued that he had panicked, thinking there was a medical emergency. The Divisional Court found no suggestion that the defendant thought his wife was in need of urgent medical attention. The justices had approached the matter on a subjective rather than an objective basis. Their finding that there was a special reason was perverse.

In *DPP v Craddock*, unreported, 2 April 1996, the respondent and his wife were at her father's home. The wife attacked the respondent, demanding that he leave the house. He went and sat in his car. His wife followed, threatening to break the window unless he left. The respondent drove some 12 to 15 miles. Police found him asleep in his car and his breath alcohol reading was 52. The justices found special reasons and did not disqualify. The Divisional Court ruled that the justices had not considered, objectively, what other steps a reasonable person could have taken to deal with the emergency. It was impossible to justify driving 12 to 15 miles. If the emergency did justify removing the car from outside the house, the respondent could have driven a short distance and found somewhere to park for the night. Furthermore, the justices should have taken into account the high reading.

In *DPP v Ubhi* [2003] EWHC 619 (Admin), the respondent had been awoken by his sister, who had fallen and was screaming. Her boyfriend tried to call an ambulance, then a taxi, but without success. The brother decided to drive her to hospital, but was stopped on the way and found to be driving with excess alcohol. The justices found special reasons, but the Administrative Court overturned that finding, ruling that the justices should have considered whether a reasonable person would have believed there was a medical emergency, and should have considered whether other ways of getting help had been explored. If an alternative was available, it would be rare indeed that special reasons could be found.

In *R (Khan) v DPP* [2004] EWHC 2505 (Admin), the justices correctly applied the objective test. The appellant heard that there had been a road traffic accident near his home and feared his sons might be involved. He tried to rouse his wife, who had not been drinking, to take him there, but she did not wake and he drove himself to the scene of the accident. He was arrested and found to be some two and a half times over the limit. The Administrative Court upheld the justices' decision that there was no special reason for not disqualifying. They were correct to conclude that the appellant would have been advised by a sober, reasonable and responsible friend (see para 13.6.5) not to drive himself, but rather to wake his wife who would no doubt have driven.

13.6.4 Outward and return journeys; the duration of the emergency

In *DPP v Waller* [1989] RTR 112, the Divisional Court found that there had been an emergency on the outward journey, but not on the return journey. The defendant had not planned to drive on the day in question, but drove to the rescue of his fiancée, who was at a restaurant, at her request. Her estranged husband, against whom she had been granted a decree *nisi* of divorce on the grounds of unreasonable behaviour, had telephoned and threatened to go to the restaurant. There was no time for the defendant to call a taxi. While driving his fiancée away from the restaurant, he lost control of the car and caused extensive damage. He was arrested and breath analysis showed excess alcohol. It was conceded that an emergency existed when the defendant drove to the restaurant, but in relation to the return journey, he should have considered whether there was any means of concealing his fiancée from the ex-husband other than taking her away in his car. The emergency did not continue after the defendant had collected her from the restaurant.

Likewise, in *DPP v Sendell*, unreported, 18 April 1988 (DC), where the defendant drove to see his infirm mother-in-law who was in difficulty, there was an emergency on the outward journey, but not on the return journey. And in *DPP v*

Feeney (1989) 89 Cr App R 173 (DC), driving a friend with a defective colostomy bag to her home was an emergency, but driving home afterwards was not.

In *DPP v Goddard* [1998] RTR 463 (DC), the respondent had driven to his sister's house to escape assailants, and then, thinking that one of the assailants might realise where he was, drove eight and a half miles to his own home. It was conceded that there was an emergency in respect of the journey to the sister's house, but the court ruled that, once there, there were various options open to him, including calling the police, and it was not reasonable to have driven home.

13.6.5 Alternative responses: the advice of a sober, reasonable and responsible friend

Where a sober, reasonable and responsible friend would have advised against driving, and there were other solutions to the emergency, special reasons are not made out. In *DPP v Bristow* [1998] RTR 100, the respondent had been at home, drinking. His daughters were at a nearby park, with others. One of the daughters returned home, telling the respondent that two of the others had been assaulted and were being held in a house against their will. The respondent drove 400 to 500 yards to the place where he understood the children to be. He was found to have excess alcohol. The Divisional Court ruled that the key question is whether a sober, reasonable and responsible friend, present at the time, but himself a non-driver and thus unable to help, would have advised for or against driving The justices could properly find special reasons only if they thought it a real possibility, rather than merely an off-chance, that such a person would have advised the respondent to drive. The factors which would influence such advice would include:

- the amount which had been drunk;
- having regard to that, the threat to others when driving in that condition, given the distance proposed to be driven, the likely state of the roads and the condition of the vehicle;
- the acuteness of the problem; and
- any alternative ways of solving the problem.

These four matters complement the seven listed in *Chatters v Burke* [1986] 1 WLR 1321 (see para 13.4). On the facts, the only sober advice would have been that the respondent had had far too much to drink and that there were other solutions to the problem readily available. The finding of special reasons was overturned.

See also *DPP v Ubhi* [2003] EWHC 619 (Admin) (para 13.6.3).

13.7 LACED DRINKS

Where a defendant can show, on a balance of probabilities, that the excess alcohol in the specimen was attributable to alcohol consumed unknowingly, it may be possible to establish special reasons. The typical situation is where drinks are 'laced' or 'spiked', but see also the case of *Ng v DPP* [2007] EWHC 36 (Admin), [2007] RTR 35 (para 13.3) and *Brewer v Commissioner of Police of the Metropolis* [1969] 1 WLR 267 (DC) where a special reason was made out by a driver who had inhaled fumes from an industrial process. Unknown to him, the fumes contained alcohol, and the driver later drank an amount of alcohol which would not alone have made him unfit to drive or put him over the limit.

In *Pugsley v Hunter* [1973] 1 WLR 578, the motorist had been at a public house where he drank two light ales and a shandy. Unknown to him, two double vodkas were added to his drinks. He later drove, and his blood alcohol reading was 161. No expert evidence was adduced as to whether the added drink accounted for the excess alcohol. The Divisional Court ruled that the onus of proving the facts to establish a special reason is on the defendant, who must show, on a balance of probabilities, that the offence was caused by the added drink, and nothing else. The onus is to be discharged by admissible and relevant evidence. In some cases it may be obvious to a layman that the added drink, given its nature and quality, was the cause of the commission of the offence, as where the blood alcohol is only marginally above the limit, and the drink taken without the knowledge of the defendant is substantial. But unless the case is a really obvious one, in which a layman can reliably and confidently say that the added liquor must explain the excess alcohol, then the only way in which a defendant can discharge the onus is by calling medical evidence.

DPP v Younas [1990] RTR 22 is an example of a case in which a laced drinks argument succeeded without expert evidence. The justices heard evidence from the motorist, and from a person who had laced one pint of lager with a double measure of spirits, and witnessed the like lacing of another. They found that it was obvious that the amount the motorist had drunk excluding the added spirits – one and three-quarter pints of lager – would not have put him over the limit. The Divisional Court found that each case depends on its own facts and it was not possible to say that the justices' conclusion was perverse.

For a case in which it was not obvious that the additional alcohol had taken the driver over the limit, see *Smith v DPP* [1990] RTR 17 (DC). The motorist said he had drunk one and a half pints of lager, then asked for a fruit drink, to which, unknown to him, a single measure of vodka had been added. He adduced no medical or scientific evidence. The Divisional Court upheld the Crown Court's decision that it could not say, or was not prepared to say, that it was obvious that the vodka had taken this driver above the limit.

The principles relating to laced drinks arguments were neatly summarised in *DPP v O'Connor* (1992) 95 Cr App R 135. By admissible and relevant evidence, the driver is required to show:

- that his drink has been laced;
- that he did not know or suspect his drink had been laced; and
- that, if he had not taken the laced drink, the level of alcohol in his body would not have exceeded the prescribed limit.

Expert evidence is usually highly relevant, first, to indicate whether or not the amount of drink which the driver admits that he knowingly consumed would have put him over the limit in any event, and, second, to indicate whether or not the account which is being put forward is credible.

13.7.1 Evidence of lacing

There must be relevant and admissible evidence that the driver's drinks were spiked. In *James v Morgan* [1988] RTR 85, the defendant gave evidence that he had been with workmates at a public house, and discovered, about two weeks later, that two of his workmates had put gin in his drinks. The Divisional Court found that the evidence of lacing depended solely on what the defendant must have been told by one or more of his workmates. It was hearsay. There was no relevant and admissible evidence in support of the submission of laced drinks.

13.7.2 The responsibility of the driver

A driver must pay attention to the quantity and quality of the drinks he or she is consuming, and ensure that they do not cause the driver to be unfit to drive or over the limit. In *Alexander v Latter* [1972] RTR 441, the Divisional Court held that special reasons do not normally exist if a defendant fails, even mistakenly, to supervise his own drinking so as to remain within the limit. There, a pub landlord offered the defendant diabetic lager which, unknown to the defendant and without any warning from the landlord, contained twice as much alcohol as ordinary lager. The Divisional Court reluctantly upheld a finding of special reasons, on the basis that the defendant had been misled, referring to the facts as borderline.

Alexander v Latter was distinguished in *Adams v Bradley* [1975] RTR 233, where the defendant was bought a drink by a colleague. Unknown to the defendant, his usual brand was not available and he was drinking a stronger brand. The Queen's

Bench Division found there was no special reason for not disqualifying. The defendant should have inquired about what he was drinking. For a laced drinks argument to succeed, there must be some element of intervention, or the driver must in some way be misled. Neither was present in this case.

In *R v Krebbs* [1977] RTR 406, there was some such intervention or misleading. The defendant accepted from a colleague a particular brand of lager, knowing its strength. He accepted offers of further drinks but, unknown to him, he was given another brand which was twice as strong. The Court of Appeal (Criminal Division) held that that amounted to a special reason. The defendant's mistake was induced or contributed to by the actions of his colleague. The court again alluded to the difficulty of deciding exactly which side of the borderline these cases fall.

In *R v Newton (David)* [1974] RTR 451, Widgery LJ reiterated the important duty on a driver to be extremely careful about how much he drinks.

A laced drinks argument does not succeed where the driver should have realised he was not fit to drive. In *Pridige v Gant* [1985] RTR 196, the Divisional Court ruled that the proper approach is to decide, first, whether or not a special reason existed, and, second, whether or not the defendant should have realised that he was not fit to drive. The first point, that the defendant's drinks had been spiked, was conceded, but the court below had not allowed the prosecutor to ask the defendant if he had realised, given the high level of alcohol in his body, that he was not in a fit state to drive. That suggested that the second stage had been omitted.

Where a motorist made no inquiry about what wine he was drinking, then claimed he was drinking stronger wine than usual, he did not have a special reason: *Beauchamp-Thompson v DPP* [1989] RTR 54. He should have known he was drinking Chardonnay rather than Riesling, which were distinctly different.

In *DPP v Anderson (Marilyn)* [1998] COD 363, a motorist drank two 175-millilitre glasses of 13.5 per cent proof wine in a public house, rather than the 11.5 per cent proof wine the pub usually served to her. She believed she would not be over the limit but did not inquire about the strength of the wine. She adduced expert evidence which appeared to show that even if she had drunk the lower strength wine she would still have been over the limit. On those facts, the Divisional Court found that the evidence did not support the justices' conclusion that there was a special reason. It was a very plain case of a person who both drank and drove, thinking she would not be over the limit, but taking no steps to check that that would be the case.

A motorist who had taken a large amount of mouthwash which, unknown to him, contained alcohol, should have realised he was not fit to drive, and did not have a special reason: *DPP v Jowle* (1999) 163 JP 85. The motorist had consumed 800 millilitres of mouthwash which contained 26.9 per cent by volume of alcohol, although the presence of alcohol was not indicated on the bottle. He was a member of Alcoholics Anonymous and had not knowingly drunk alcohol for 21 years, but was addicted to the mouthwash and was aware that it gave him a 'lift'. He drove erratically, and his breath alcohol reading was 94. The Divisional Court found it plain that anyone in his position should have realised that he was not in a fit state to drive.

Where a defendant was not aware that he had drunk alcohol, but had made no inquiries about what he was drinking, a special reason for not disqualifying could not be made out. In *Robinson v DPP* [2003] EWHC 2718 (Admin), (2004) 168 JP 522, the appellant drank what he thought was fruit juice but which was in fact alcoholic punch. The justices found that he had made no inquiries about the contents of the drink and rejected his submission of special reasons. On appeal, the Divisional Court found that a driver who is at a party where alcohol is being served, and assumes without enquiry that a drink is alcohol-free, takes a risk, and if he turns out to be mistaken he must pay the price. If there is to be any mitigation of penalty, the driver must show that he did all that could reasonably be expected to avoid the risk of committing the offence.

See also *DPP v Barker* [1990] RTR 1, *Donahue v DPP* [1993] RTR 156 and *Dixon-Watmough v Preston Justices*, unreported, 22 November 1996 (see para 13.11).

Form MG DD/D contains guidelines on police investigations where it is believed (among other possibilities) that the suspect may raise a laced drinks argument. Officers are advised to ascertain, in interview, in as much detail as possible, exactly what the suspect claims to have drunk, and when. The practicality of doing so is, however, limited by the fact that many suspects do not raise the possibility that their drinks were laced until long after they have left the police station.

13.7.3 Expert evidence

Smith v Geraghty [1986] RTR 222 concerned an attempt by the prosecutor to back-calculate the blood alcohol level to the time of the offence. The motorist adduced expert evidence to show that at the time of driving his blood alcohol had been below the limit, and that it was the laced drink which had taken him over the limit. The prosecutor made counter-submissions on back-calculating the level of alcohol to the time of driving. The justices decided it would be unjust to attempt a back-calculation, but that the alcohol unknowingly consumed had accounted for the excess over the limit. The prosecutor appealed, on the question whether the prosecutor was entitled to show that, at the time of the offence, the defendant's blood alcohol concentration was higher than shown in the blood analysis. The Divisional Court found that the court is concerned to ascertain the difference it would have made if the spiked drink had not been consumed. Justices should not be drawn into detailed calculations, even if they are before them by way of expert evidence. While going back to the level of alcohol in the blood at the time of driving is permissible, it is practicable only if there is reasonably clear, straightforward and relatively simple evidence. On the facts, the justices were entitled to find special reasons.

And in *Woodward v DPP*, unreported, 23 February 1995, justices were in error not to take into account the defence expert's back-calculations and forward-calculations to show that the defendant's breath alcohol level would have been below the limit but for the lacing of his drink. One method of calculating the breath alcohol at the time of driving indicated that it would have been 35; another method indicated that it would have been 39 – marginally below the level at which a prosecution normally follows. The justices found that special reasons did not exist. On the motorist's appeal, the Divisional Court ruled that the justices had been in error. Whichever method of calculation was adopted, special reasons could apply.

In *R v Cambridge Magistrates' Court ex parte Wong* [1992] RTR 382, the fact that a motorist had taken cough linctus which, unknown to him, contained alcohol, was capable of amounting to a special reason. The breath alcohol reading was 40. The motorist adduced expert evidence that, but for the cough linctus, the reading would have been less than 40. The Divisional Court held that these facts were capable in law of amounting to special reasons, although a finding of special reasons would not necessarily mean that the motorist would escape disqualification.

In the unreported case of *DPP v Vincent*, 16 July 1996, the Divisional Court found nothing to suggest that the justices had not considered the appropriate matters, and their decision to find special reasons, while surprising, was not perverse. The respondent had decided to drink an amount of alcohol which he believed would not put him over the limit. He drank Coca-Cola between three pints of beer. His breath alcohol reading was 71. His friend gave evidence that he had seen the respondent drink two and a half pints of beer, and that others had been pouring drinks from tumblers into pint glasses. There was expert evidence that if the defendant had drunk only three pints, that would have produced a breath alcohol reading of 20. And in *DPP v Winfield-Grant*, unreported, 8 June 2000, the justices found that the respondent had drunk only two glasses of wine. There was expert evidence that that would leave her below the limit. The prosecutor argued that she had knowingly drunk vodka as well as the wine. The justices accepted that the lacing of her drinks was the deciding factor as to the excess alcohol and found special reasons not to disqualify. The Divisional Court found that the justices had applied the correct standard and burden of proof and upheld their decision.

A motorist who said she had drunk two half-pints of lager and eaten three slices of cake containing whiskey, failed to establish a special reason: *DPP v Wynne* [2001] EWHC 21 (Admin). Up to half a bottle of whiskey had gone into the cake and she had eaten about a quarter of it. Her expert witness said the lager would not have taken her over the limit. He had not tested the cake but said that if she had drunk an eighth of a bottle of whiskey, she would have been over the limit. The Divisional Court found it improbable that the respondent could have drunk an eighth of a bottle of whiskey through eating the cake, without realising it. The expert's evidence was speculative. The suggestion that two halves of lager and three slices of cake, consumed over a five-hour period, could have accounted for the reading taken two hours later must have been flawed. The justices' finding of special reasons was overturned.

In *Griffiths v DPP* [2002] EWHC 792 (Admin), (2002) 166 JP 629 (see para 8.9.2), the motorist adduced expert evidence that the breath alcohol was still rising when the specimen was taken, and so must have been lower at the time of driving. The Administrative Court had no hesitation in ruling that the motorist's hope of completing his journey before reaching the limit was special to the offender and was not a special reason.

In *DPP v Sharma* [2005] EWHC 879 (Admin), [2005] RTR 361, the Administrative Court found that although the justices' decision to find special reasons was surprising, it was not perverse. A friend of the respondent had bought her two 250-millilitre bottles of 'Smirnoff Ice', which contained vodka. Without her knowledge, he added 100 millilitres of vodka to each bottle. The respondent did not experience any effects of intoxication or display any signs of impairment, and the police who stopped her noticed nothing unusual. She adduced expert evidence that if she had drunk only the two Smirnoff Ice drinks, she would not have been over the limit. The magistrates accepted her submission of special reasons. The Administrative Court found it impossible to say that the justices were not entitled to find that the respondent was unaware of the additional alcohol. They found all the necessary facts, and reached a conclusion which was not perverse or wrong in law.

See also the cases on the 'post-incident consumption' defence (Chapter 8), concerning expert evidence that the driver would not have been over the limit but for the alcohol consumed after driving.

13.8 OTHER SPECIAL REASONS

In addition to emergencies and laced drinks, a number of other issues have been put forward as the basis for finding a special reason, most of them unsuccessfully. The following have been held not to amount to special reasons for not disqualifying:

- that the driver stopped driving as soon as he realised he was under the influence of drink: *Duck v Peacock* [1949] 1 All ER 318;
- that the defendant was tired and hungry, had drunk only a small amount, had been behaving soberly during the day and was fit to drive when he started his journey: *Archer v Woodward* [1959] Crim LR 461;
- that the defendant's ability to drive was not impaired. This may well be a mitigating circumstance, but is not sufficient to amount to a special reason: *Taylor v Austin* [1969] 1 WLR 264. Nor was the fact that the defendant was without fault in the accident which occurred. Nor was the financial hardship which would follow from disqualification;
- being only just over the limit: *Delaroy-Hall v Tadman* [1969] 2 QB 208, where the Queen's Bench Division ruled that drivers with blood alcohol concentrations of 82, 96 and 108 should have been disqualified. A special reason must be something other than the commission of the offence itself. See also *Jane v DPP*, unreported, 26 October 1987, where the Divisional Court again rejected this argument even though the breath alcohol reading was less than 40, below which prosecutions are not usually brought;
- that the driver was taking two types of prescribed medication and knew that one of them, combined with alcohol, would affect her ability to drive, but did not know that the other would have the same effect: *R v Scott* [1970] 1 QB 661 (CA). Compare the earlier case of *Chapman v O'Hagan* [1949] 2 All ER 690, where the King's Bench Division reluctantly declined to interfere with the justices' finding of a special reason where a motorist was taking drugs but did not know they would render him more susceptible to the effects of alcohol;
- the fact that the defendant was a general medical practitioner who would, if disqualified, feel compelled to resign: *Holroyd v Berry* [1973] RTR 145. This was so even though he practised in an area having insufficient general practitioners and it would be difficult, if not impossible, to replace him. The Queen's Bench Division rejected his argument that disqualifying him would prejudice the public interest;
- the fact that the driver drove at the request of a police officer: *De Munthe v Stewart* [1982] RTR 27 (DC), where a police officer saw the defendant park his car and walk away. The car was causing an obstruction, and the officer asked the defendant to move it. He drove it a short distance and

re-parked it. The officer then had reason to suspect he had been drinking, and the defendant was in due course convicted of driving with excess alcohol. His special reasons argument failed, the court taking into account that he had been driving voluntarily before the officer asked him to move the car;

- the fact that the driver was a police officer on a special assignment: *Vaughan v Dunn* [1984] RTR 376. With other officers, the defendant was visiting public houses and ingratiating himself with patrons, buying them drinks, with a view to gathering information. The Divisional Court took into account the manner of driving (he had driven straight into a lamp post), the high reading (nearly three times the limit), and the absence of any emergency;
- offering a urine specimen in response to a requirement for a blood specimen: *Grix v Chief Constable of Kent* [1987] RTR 193 (DC);
- the fact that a roadside screening test was negative, and a later roadside screening test was positive, the defendant having drunk nothing in between: *DPP v White* [1988] RTR 267. The motorist had stopped at a railway station to drop off passengers, where police asked him to take a roadside screening test, which was negative. He continued his journey and was stopped by different officers, and this time a screening test was positive. Breath analysis showed he was over the limit. The Divisional Court found that he must have consumed alcohol to such an extent that he was at risk of driving while over the limit. Alcohol is absorbed gradually and the motorist was at risk of being over the limit when he drove both to and from the station. His decision to drive was not made by reason of the clear breath test;
- having erroneously been advised by a solicitor not to provide breath specimens for analysis: *Dickinson v DPP* [1989] Crim LR 741 (see para 10.7.3), where the motorist submitted that this had deprived him of the opportunity to argue that it was alcohol he consumed after the offence which caused him to be over the limit. He gave evidence that he had consumed a quantity of drink between the time of driving and his arrest. The Divisional Court rejected this submission on the basis that the justices had made a finding that the appellant had not adduced sufficient evidence to show that he had been deprived of a defence;
- a 'feeling of justified resentment' about the manner and circumstances in which specimens were required: *DPP v Rose* (1988) 156 JP 733. Exceptionally, this case concerned a defendant convicted of failing to provide specimens. He had driven an extremely short distance (2 feet), and was seized extremely roughly by a police officer, marched to a transit van, and thrown in. At the police station, he asked for someone else to be present when he provided specimens, but his request was ignored. It was

agreed that these facts could not amount to a reasonable excuse for failing to provide, and the court remarked that although reasonable excuse and special reasons are separate expressions with different parts to play in the legislation, it might in practice be difficult to draw the line between them;

- the fact that the defendant drank knowing that she would drive afterwards: *DPP v Doyle* [1993] RTR 369, where the defendant had successfully sought injunctions against her former boyfriend by reason of his behaviour towards her, both violent and otherwise. Two and a half weeks before the incident in question, he had taken her car without permission. On the day in question, she went to his address to retrieve the car and certain goods he had taken. While there, he assaulted her and damaged the car. The defendant then drove to a friend's home, where she called the police and arranged to meet them at the former boyfriend's address. While waiting for a telephone call to say the police had arrived, she consumed sufficient brandy to take her over the limit. The Divisional Court held that where a driver has deliberately taken a decision to drink knowing that she will, or probably will, drive, it is not open to justices to find a special reason;
- not knowing that a 'Go-ped' motorised foot scooter is a motor vehicle: *DPP v Murray* [2001] EWHC 848 (Admin). The Divisional Court found no mitigating or extenuating circumstance directly connected with the commission of the offence. Ignorance of the law was peculiar to the appellant, and not to the facts of the offence. This was so even though it was not until some five months after the offence that the Queen's Bench Division ruled that the type of scooter in question is a motor vehicle (see *DPP v Saddington* [2001] RTR 15 (para 8.4.2)).

On the other hand, the following arguments have succeeded in establishing special reasons:

- that the defendant genuinely but mistakenly believed that a police officer had asked him to drive his car, when, in fact, the officer had advised the defendant not to drive: *R v McIntyre* [1976] RTR 330 (CA);
- that police told the defendant that he would not be prosecuted, and he threw away his part of the blood specimen. He was then prosecuted on the basis of the analysis of the prosecution's part of the specimen, which showed 81 milligrammes of alcohol in 100 millilitres of blood: *R v Anderson* [1972] RTR 113 (CA). The court found that the circumstances were special to the offence. The defendant had been deprived of the opportunity to challenge the accuracy of the prosecution's analysis.

13.9 FAILING TO PROVIDE SPECIMENS

In cases of failing without reasonable excuse to provide specimens, circumstances which have unsuccessfully been argued as amounting to a reasonable excuse (see para 10.6) have sometimes then been advanced as a special reason for not disqualifying. In *Daniels v DPP* [1992] RTR 140, officers suspected the defendant both of having stolen a motor cycle and of having ridden it with alcohol in his body. They then realised he had not stolen the cycle but did not tell him so. They asked for specimens of breath, but the defendant refused, being distracted from the request by his concern about being charged with theft, which he regarded as more serious. The Divisional Court ruled that, while he did not have a reasonable excuse, the circumstances could amount to a special reason. See also para 11.9.

Where a suspect was told by a police officer that failure to provide a specimen would not mean 'definite disqualification', and that affected the suspect's decision not to provide, this was capable of amounting to a special reason: *Bobin v DPP* [1999] RTR 375 (DC).

In *McCormick v Hitchins* [1988] RTR 182, the Divisional Court held that having no intention to drive was a special reason for not disqualifying and for not endorsing, since it related directly to the offence of failing to provide. This was, however, in the context that the defendant was in charge of the vehicle, rather than driving it.

On the facts in *DPP v Kinnersley* [1993] RTR 105, a fear of contracting AIDS was capable of amounting to a special reason, even though it did not amount to a reasonable excuse. The defendant had knowledge of the condition and how it may be contracted, and the sealed mouthpieces of the testing devices had not been shown or explained to him. The Divisional Court found that to a man with the defendant's knowledge there were mitigating circumstances not amounting to a defence, yet directly connected with the commission of the offence, and properly taken into consideration when imposing punishment. The fact that the defendant had not been given an explanation at the time did not as a matter of law exclude the possibility of finding special reasons, although it would usually be an important factor.

In *DPP v Daley (No 2)* [1994] RTR 107 (DC), it was again accepted that facts which do not amount to a reasonable excuse may amount to a special reason, albeit such a situation is unusual. But the facts must be established. The defendant had argued that he had tried his best to provide breath specimens but had been unable to do so. On an earlier appeal, the court had found no evidence to support that argument. It could not therefore be put forward in support of a submission of special reasons.

13.10 ARGUMENT AVAILABLE ONCE ONLY

Special reasons for not disqualifying for an earlier offence do not apply to a second offence. In *Bolliston v Gibbons* (1984) 6 Cr App R (S) 134, the defendant had been convicted in November 1971 of driving with excess alcohol, but the court found special reasons for not disqualifying, in that he had been taking a tonic which, unknown to him, contained alcohol. On pleading guilty to a second offence of driving with excess alcohol on 16 March 1983, he became liable to disqualification for a minimum three years rather than one, under what is now Road Traffic Offenders Act 1988, s 34(3) – second offence within 10 years (see para 12.4.1). He argued that the special reasons for not disqualifying for the earlier offence equally amounted to special reasons in respect of the later offence, and that an offender who had knowingly committed the offence once only should not be punished in the same way as a person who had knowingly committed the same offence twice. The court roundly rejected that argument, finding that it could have regard only to special reasons relating to the second offence.

13.11 THE DISCRETION NOT TO DISQUALIFY

The fact that a special reason has been made out does not mean that a driver escapes disqualification as a matter of course (*Taylor v Rajan* [1974] QB 424). In *DPP v O'Connor* (1992) 95 Cr App R 135 (para 13.7), the court again emphasised the two-stage process of determining, first, whether there is a special reason, and, second, whether, in its discretion, having regard to the special reason, the court should not disqualify, or disqualify for a shorter period than the normal 12 months. See also *R v Cambridge Magistrates' Court ex parte Wong* [1992] RTR 382 (para 13.7.3).

In *Vaughan v Dunn* [1984] RTR 376 (para 13.8), the Divisional Court emphasised that the discretion not to disqualify is to be exercised only in 'clear and compelling circumstances'.

Where special reasons are found but the breath alcohol level is high, the offender is unlikely to escape disqualification: *Mayhew v DPP*, unreported, 13 October 1987, where the lower breath reading was 119. The Divisional Court drew on the judgment in *Taylor v Rajan*, to the effect that if the alcohol content in the defendant's body is very high, that is a powerful reason against exercising the discretion in favour of the defendant.

On the facts in *DPP v Barker* [1990] RTR 1, the justices, having found a special reason, were correct not to disqualify. The motorist was unused to alcohol. She had drunk wine and had been given orange juice which, unknown to her, had been laced with vodka. She had no reason to drive on the evening in question, and remembered nothing after the first laced drink. On the basis of expert evidence, the justices concluded that the alcohol consumed would have had an immediate effect. The prosecutor challenged the exercise of the justices' discretion in favour of the motorist, arguing that they had failed to ask whether the defendant should have realised she was unfit to drive. The Divisional Court upheld the justices' decision on the basis that the defendant suffered a total loss of knowledge of her actions and was not aware that her condition was influenced by the consumption of alcohol. She could not therefore have appreciated that she was unfit to drive through drink.

By contrast, in *Donahue v DPP* [1993] RTR 156, the justices again found special reasons, but also found that the motorist must have realised he was not fit to drive and so disqualified him. He was a sales representative and had been entertaining customers in a hospitality tent. He was not young or inexperienced. He had asked to be served only alcohol-free wine, but that request had not been observed. He did not mention to the police that he believed he had been drinking alcohol-free wine, but asked the officer to overlook the matter because he needed his driving licence for his work. He adduced medical evidence that the effects of the alcohol could have been confused with excessive tiredness. The justices found that there were special reasons, but that the motorist must have realised he was not fit to drive. His conduct and answers to the police supported that, as did the high reading (99 microgrammes in breath). The Divisional Court upheld their decision to disqualify him.

Having found special reasons, a court should not then invite further evidence before exercising the discretion whether or not to disqualify. It should take into account only the factors in *R v Wickins* (1958) 42 Cr App R 236: *Lane v DPP*, unreported, 10 March 1995 (DC). Nor should the justices revisit the circumstances giving rise to the finding of special reasons in deciding how to exercise their discretion.

In *Dixon-Watmough v Preston Justices*, unreported, 22 November 1996, a stranger offered to buy the appellant a drink and she asked for Coke. He twice gave her a drink. On neither occasion did she see the drink poured. She suffered from multiple sclerosis and as a result was unable to detect the taste of alcohol. Her laced drinks argument was successful, but she was nevertheless disqualified.

The Divisional Court found that the justices rightly took into account that the driver should be responsible for what she drinks, and had taken a risk in accepting drinks from a stranger. But the justices had exercised their discretion against the appellant on the basis that, because the identity of the person who bought the drinks was unknown, the appellant was unable to adduce evidence to support her contention that her drinks had been tampered with. That might have been relevant to the special reasons argument in the first place, but was not relevant to their discretion whether or not to order disqualification once special reasons had been established. Although the Divisional Court considered the case borderline, it allowed the appeal against disqualification.

Where a special reason was made out, but the justices went on to disqualify the offender for longer than the obligatory minimum of 12 months, that would not necessarily be inappropriate, but on the facts in *R v St Albans Crown Court ex parte O'Donovan* [2000] 1 Cr App R (S) 344, it was not appropriate to do so. The offender had been convicted of driving with excess alcohol. He had been moving his car a few yards to clear the access to a car park. The justices accepted there was a special reason for not disqualifying, but, referring to the *Magistrates' Court Sentencing Guidelines*, disqualified him for 20 months. The Divisional Court found that there was no suggestion of any appreciable risk of danger to anyone, and it was difficult to justify disqualifying for more than 12 months. The courts below had paid more attention to the guidelines than was warranted on the facts. The guidelines were of little assistance where special reasons were made out. The disqualification was reduced to 12 months.

13.12 SUMMARY

The following principles concerning special reasons emerge from the cases.

- The burden of proof is on the defendant, on the balance of probabilities.
- The factor said to amount to a special reason must be special to the offence in that:
  - it amounts to a mitigating or extenuating circumstance, but not to a defence;
  - it is directly connected with the commission of the offence; and
  - it is a matter which the court ought properly to take into consideration when sentencing (*Whittall v Kirby* [1947] KB 194 (DC)).
- The defendant's medical condition, known or unknown, is unlikely to amount to a special reason.

- The seven points listed in *Chatters v Burke* [1986] 1 WLR 1321 are to be taken into account:
  - distance driven (not of itself a sufficient determinant);
  - the manner of driving;
  - the state of the vehicle;
  - whether the driver intended to drive further;
  - the road and traffic conditions;
  - any possibility of danger by contact with other road users (the most important); and
  - the reason the vehicle was being driven.

- Where it is argued that there was a special reason based on an emergency:
  - the emergency must have been sufficiently acute to justify driving, taking into account all the circumstances, including:
    - the nature and degree of the emergency,
    - alternative means of transport or methods of dealing with the crisis,
    - the manner of driving, and
    - whether the defendant acted responsibly or otherwise;
  - the matter is to be considered objectively;
  - a high alcohol level is a powerful reason against exercising the discretion in favour of the defendant;
  - the outward and return journeys are treated differently;
  - justices should be alert not to be taken in by hard luck stories;
  - where a sober, reasonable and responsible friend would have advised against driving, special reasons are not made out.

- To succeed in a laced drinks argument:
  - it must be shown, by admissible and relevant evidence, on a balance of probabilities, that:
    - the defendant's drink(s) had been laced,
    - the defendant did not know or suspect that the drink(s) had been laced, and
    - the defendant would not otherwise have been over the limit;

- expert evidence is almost always necessary;
- if the defendant should have realised he was unfit to drive, a special reason cannot be made out;
- if the defendant made no inquiry about the drinks being consumed, a special reason argument is less likely to succeed.

• The fact that a special reason is made out does not necessarily mean that the usual disqualification or endorsement is avoided, or imposed for a reduced period.

Index

References are to page numbers